Women and Monastic Buddhism in Early South Asia

This book uses gender as a framework to offer unique insights into the sociocultural foundations of Buddhism. Moving away from dominant discourses that discuss women as a single monolithic, homogenous category – thus rendering them invisible within the broader religious discourse – this monograph examines their sustained role in the larger context of South Asian Buddhism and reaffirms their agency. It highlights the multiple roles played by women as patrons, practitioners, lay and monastic members and the like within Buddhism. The volume also investigates the individual experiences of the members, and their equations and relationships at different levels – with the *Samgha* at large with their own respective *Bhikşu* or *Bhikşunī Samgha*, with the laity, and with members of the same gender (both lay and monastic). It rereads, reconfigures and reassesses historical data in order to arrive at a new understanding of Buddhism and the social matrix within which it developed and flourished.

Bringing together archaeological, epigraphic, art historical, literary as well as ethnographic data, this volume will be of interest to researchers and scholars of Buddhism, gender studies, ancient Indian history, religion and South Asian studies.

Garima Kaushik is assistant archaeologist in the Chandigarh Circle of the Archaeological Survey of India. She has excavated at a number of important historic and protohistoric archaeological sites in the country including Sravasti, Dholavira, Govishana and Adi Badri. She has been actively involved in academic as well as field research on early Buddhist historical sites for over 15 years.

Archaeology and Religion in South Asia

A RECOGNISED INDEPENDENT CENTRE OF THE UNIVERSITY OF OXFORD

Series Editor: HIMANSHU PRABHA RAY, **Chairperson, National Monuments Authority**

Editorial Board: GAVIN FLOOD, Academic Director, Oxford Centre for Hindu Studies; JESSICA FRAZIER, Academic Administrator, Oxford Centre for Hindu Studies; JULIA SHAW, Institute of Archaeology, University College, London; SHAILENDRA BHANDARE, Ashmolean Museum, Oxford; DEVANGANA DESAI, Asiatic Society, Mumbai; VIDULA JAISWAL, Jnana Pravaha, Varanasi, former professor, Banaras Hindu University.

This Series, in association with the Oxford Centre for Hindu Studies, reflects on the complex relationship between religion and society through new perspectives and advances in archaeology. It looks at this critical interface to provide alternative understandings of communities, beliefs, cultural systems, sacred sites, ritual practices, food habits, dietary modifications, power and agents of political legitimisation. The books in the Series underline the importance of archaeological evidence in the production of knowledge of the past. They also emphasise that a systematic study of religion requires engagement with a diverse range of sources such as inscriptions, iconography, numismatics and architectural remains.

Also in this Series

Negotiating Cultural Identity: Landscapes in Early Medieval South Asian History
Editor: Himanshu Prabha Ray

Women and Monastic Buddhism in Early South Asia
Garima Kaushik

Women and Monastic Buddhism in Early South Asia

Rediscovering the invisible believers

Garima Kaushik

Routledge
Taylor & Francis Group
LONDON AND NEW YORK

First South Asia edition 2016

First published 2016
by Routledge
2 Park Square, Milton Park, Abingdon, Oxon OX14 4RN

and by Routledge
711 Third Avenue, New York, NY 10017

Routledge is an imprint of the Taylor & Francis Group, an informa business

British Library Cataloguing in Publication Data
A catalogue record for this book is available from the British Library

Library of Congress Cataloguing in Publication Data
A catalogue record has been requested for this book

ISBN: 978-1-138-66751-8
ISBN: 978-1-315-65788-2 (ebk)

Typeset in Berling
by Apex CoVantage, LLC

Digitally Printed at Replika Press Pvt. Ltd.

For sale in India, Pakistan, Nepal, Bhutan, Bangladesh and Sri Lanka only.

For Sensei

Contents

List of illustrations viii
Preface x
Acknowledgements xi
Abbreviations xii
Diacritical marks xiii

Introduction 1

1 Sacred spaces and the feminine in Buddhism 19

2 Locating the *bhikṣunī*: identifying nunneries 42

3 Exploring women's space: conflict between the social and the asocial worlds 93

4 Women as patrons 148

Conclusion 221

Tables, site plans and plates 233
Bibliography 259
Index 279

Illustrations

Map of Buddhist sites in South Asia xiv

Figures

4.1 Distribution of laywomen donor or *upāsikās* at different sites 174

4.2 Distribution of *bhikṣunīs* as donors at different sites 175

4.3 Comparative visibility figure, showing *upāsikās* and *bhikṣunīs* at various sites of donation 179

4.4 Comparative figure showing percentage of men donors versus women donors 180

Tables

1 (Sites) native place and the place of residence of *upāsikās* and *bhikṣunīs* 233

2 Social identification categories used by *bhikṣunīs* and *upāsikās* in the donor records 235

3 Spread of donors from various sites in relation to the sites of donations, as known from the epigraphic records 236

4 Buddhist *stūpa* sites in India, with *āyaka* projections 239

5 Present-day identifiable geographical location of Buddhist sites mentioned in the epigraphic records 241

6 List of probable monastic sites 243

7 Buddhist sites with different types of structures, compiled on the basis on archaeological, epigraphic and literary sources 244

Site plans

1 Kasia, site plan showing excavated structures along with monastery E 246

2 Nāgarjunakonda, site no. 6, plan of *stūpa, chaitya* and *maṇḍapa* 247

3 Sravasti 248
4 *Sahēth*, Jetavana, ground plan of monasteries F and G 249
5 Sannathi, site plan 250
6 Ratnagiri Hill: contour map, showing excavated sites 251
7 Nalanda, site plan 252
8 Sanghol site plan showing excavated structures 253
9 Plan of circular *chaitya* (after Mitra 1980) 254

Plates

1 Birth of Siddhartha; *c.* second century A.D., Chandigarh Museum 255
2 Adoration of the Buddha by Viśākhā and her associates, Sikrai, *c.* second century A.D., Chandigarh Museum 255
3 Gift of Āmrapāli, Gandhara, *c.* third century A.D., Chandigarh Museum 256
4 Donor figures on the pedestal, *c.* second century A.D., from the erstwhile North-West Frontier Province, Chandigarh Museum 256
5 Khujjuttara, Sanghol, *c.* second century A.D., Archaeological Museum, Sanghol 257
6 *Stūpa* dedicated to Sujātā, Bakraur, Bodh Gaya, *c.* eighth to tenth centuries A.D. 257
7 Circular structure, SGL 5, *c.* second century A.D., Sanghol 257
8 Nāgarjunakonda (site VIII B): circular structure with inscribed pillar lying within it *in situ*. *Indian Archaeology: A Review*, 1955–6, p. 24, pl. XXXVI. 258
9 *Stūpa* with *āyaka* platform, Chaneti, *c.* third century B.C. 258

Source: All figures and photographs unless otherwise mentioned are by the author.

Preface

As a student of Archaeology and History I have always been fascinated by the countless number of Buddhist sites, spread across the Indian subcontinent. These archaeological sites are brought alive by the evidence and narratives about the monasteries and the monks who inhabited them. However, I have always been intrigued by the almost complete absence of evidence that marks the presence of women or more accurately the presence of female Buddhist renunciants or *bhikṣunīs* at these sites. Hundreds of Buddhist sites with no clue about the other half of the Buddhist population at these sites seemed illogical. It was this fact that led to the start of this work as a PhD thesis. With time I realised there is more than just the evidence of Buddhist nunneries that indicate the presence of female patrons within a sacred Buddhist landscape; and this work came to identify and analyse the different types of architecture that have been found to have association with the feminine in varied contexts. In my opinion, it is time we moved on from the simplistic classification of Buddhist sites simply as *stūpa* and *vihāra* sites to a more comprehensive examination of the sites.

Acknowledgements

I would like to express my gratitude to many people who saw me through this book; to all those who provided support, talked things over, read, offered suggestions, allowed me to quote their remarks and assisted in the editing, proofreading and design. Special thanks to Dr H.P. Ray, my editor, mentor and supervisor. Thank you, Ma'am, for your constant support through the years. Your encouragement and guidance at every step helped to make this book a reality.

I would like to thank Mily for encouraging me time and again to publish my work and for her timely advice, both professional and personal, and my family for their support and encouragement. Above all, I want to thank my husband Akshat for managing both home and work so that I could work on the book and my babies Rig and Anooshna for putting up with my erratic schedules, for all those lost weekends and for all the time it took me away from them. It has been a long and difficult journey for them.

Thanks are due to Kapil Kaushik for helping with the photographs and R.K. Dalal for helping with the drawings. Thanks to Aakash Chakrabarty and the Routledge India team for their support.

Last but not the least, my thanks and apologies to all those who have been with me over the course of the years and whose names I have failed to mention.

Abbreviations

There are references to Buddhist scriptures, specifically to the Pāli Text Society edition of the early Buddhist canon. The initial letter refers to one of the divisions (*nikāyas*) into which the Buddha's discourses (*suttas*) are collated. For example:

A – *Añguttara Nikāya*
D – *Digha Nikāya*
M – *Majjhima Nikāya*
S – *Samyutta Nikāya*
Vn – *Vinaya*

The Roman numeral (e.g. ii) denotes the volume number and the Arabic numeral (e.g. 95) denotes the page number. The prefix 'Vn.' refers to the *Vinaya* or monastic rules, which pertain to monastic life, for example (Vn. iv.95).

ASI	Archaeological Survey of India
ASSI	Archaeological Survey of South India
ASWI	Archaeological Survey of Western India
CII	*Corpus Inscriptionum Indicrum*
LL	Luder's List of Brahmi Inscriptions, published as appendix of *Epigraphia Indica*, Vol. X
MASI	Memoir of the Archaeological Survey of India
PTS	Pāli Text Society

Diacritical marks

अ	A	च	cha	भ	bha
आ	Ā	छ	chha	म	ma
इ	I	ज	ja	य	ya
ई	Ī	झ	jha	र	ra
उ	U	ञ	na	ल	la
ऊ	ṻ	ट	ṭa	व	va
ऋ	R	ठ	ṭha	श	śa
ए	E	ड	ḍa	ष	sa
ऐ	ai	ढ	ḍha	स	sha
ओ	O	ण	ṇa	ह	ha
औ	au	त	ta	क्ष	kṣa
अं	ṁ	थ	tha	त्र	ṭra
अः	N	द	da	ज्ञ	jna
क	ka	ध	dha		
ख	kha	न	na		
ग	ga	प	pa		
घ	gha	फ	pha		
ङ	ṅa	ब	ba		

Map of Buddhist sites in South Asia

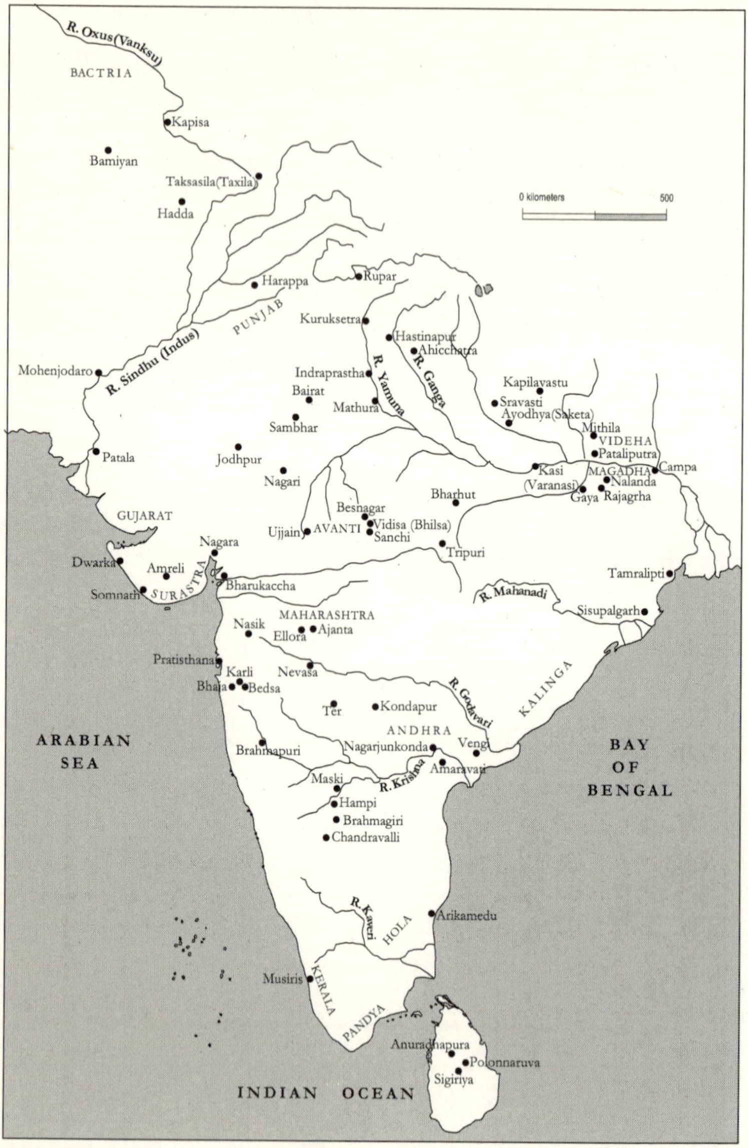

This is a historical map, used for reference only. For present-day borders, refer to Survey of India maps.

Source: Courtesy of Himanshu Prabha Ray

Introduction

It took a lot of insistence on Ānanda's part as also the unfailing persistence of Mahāpajāpati Gautamī and the 500 strong entourage following her, which finally led to the Buddha grudgingly allowing women as an institutionalised category within monastic Buddhism. On doing so he is believed to have said:

> If Ānanda, women had not received permission to go out from the household life and enter the homeless states, under the doctrine and discipline proclaimed by the Tathāgatha, then would the pure religion, Ānanda, have lasted long, the good law would have stood fast for a thousand years. But, since Ānanda, women have now received that permission the pure religion Ānanda, will now last so long, the good law will now stand fast for only five hundred years.
>
> (*Cūllavagga*, X.1,6)

This statement has been literally taken at face value by many,[1] and in spite of the generally accepted belief that the admittance of women as nuns into the order was for Buddhism the beginning of the end, there have been numerous women who have been linked to Buddhism in different ways, and in different contexts, as *upāsikās*, *thēris*, teachers and so on. They have all occupied significant, reverential positions within Buddhism and have become immortal, due to their association with the Buddha. Thus, there is an evident dichotomy within the fabric of its doctrine.

Monastic Buddhism exalts celibacy and has always been malecentric. This is reflected in the biographies and other texts that portray the female in the negative, while the male is relegated to some 'not female/not sexual hinterland'. Years of scholarship on the subject has brought out two major contrasting views on women as perceived in Buddhism. The more prominent of the two images is the negative portrayal of women as 'secular, powerless, profane and imperfect'! She is also 'mysterious, sensual, destructive, elusive and closer to nature'. While on the other hand, with her sexuality reined and controlled, a more positive view projects her as 'creative and sacred'. Women, in the capacity of wives and courtesans made frequent and meaningful appearances in the biographies of Buddha (566–486 B.C.E.). Buddhist iconography is prolific in its depiction of positive images of women and female deities that emphasise their beauty and their auspicious powers of fertility. Simply put, the iconography seemed to be expressively exalting women while the texts often condemned them. Many religions are rich in female imagery and symbolism, none perhaps more than Hinduism, but the symbolic ascendancy of the feminine often goes with a social denigration and the low status of women in everyday life. These two often stand in an inverse relationship to each other and remain poles apart. The variants of this conclusion range from hostility towards and fear of women, to pity for the misfortune of female birth (Gross 1993:63–4).

The nuns' order was founded on the premise (as affirmed in the Buddha's own teachings) that women were capable as men of reaching *arhatship* but for women, this would require the shedding of the sexual baggage first, because the state of Buddhahood is neither masculine nor feminine. The most positive images of women tend to be legendary, in the *Therigāthā* and in other records such as the poem attributed to the *upāsikā* Viśākhā, as daughters, mothers or religious women (Dharmasēna and Obeyesekere 2001). Discussing the significance of the portrayal of woman as 'the mother', Falk (1989:205) states that 'marriage and motherhood represent the proper and effective means of channeling a woman's generative drive, and her subordination to men further ensures its control'.

Early scholarship on the subject has tried to identify the 'status of the woman' in Buddhism, as most of the early works and even some contemporary works still try to study major historical processes and their corresponding impact on women. Certain socially enforced norms and rules such as marriage, divorce, sati, education and the like are taken as markers to arrive at an index to study civilisations. Thus, depending on the data retrieved from these markers, a woman's place in history is taken to be good, bad or worse.

A gendered study of Buddhism has drawn its primary data solely on the analysis of classical Buddhist texts. In studies pertaining to the history of Buddhism, the 'women's question is almost, always addressed in an androcentric manner. The issue is always, what to do about women, what special rules they would have to observe, whether they can become enlightened, whether they could progress as far as men on the Buddhist path. . . . In characteristic androcentric fashion, women are experienced and discussed as the other, as objects, as 'they' rather than 'we', as exceptions to the norms that need to be regulated, explained, and placed in the world' (Falk 1989:23). A few, more recent works have tried to 'envisage' a degree of agency for women *vis-à-vis* the historical process. The authors of this latter category have repeatedly attempted to study women and their contribution (to the religion). Though this is not a recent phenomenon, with authors like Horner taking up this issue in the 1930s, the emphasis has largely been on Buddhism's perception of women.

Scholarship on the subject of 'Buddhism and Women' is not new and has been in existence now for almost over seven to eight decades.

The first women scholars of Buddhist studies in the West C.R. Davids (1948) and I.B. Horner (1930/1975) were the proponents of the Orientalist school that lay emphasis on the translation of Buddhist texts such as the *Vinayas* and the *Therigāthā* and the like. These earliest attempts were aimed at identifying, locating and highlighting the female element within Buddhism.

The discourse of the second-generation feminist historians (Chakravarti 1987; Roy 1999) is essentially located in a Marxist framework, where the thrust has been on exploring the links between sexuality, reproduction and the production processes. This phase saw the shift in focus to the subject of women's subordination and the structure that make for their subordination. The focus shifted from the issue of high or low status of women, of the Altekarian model to the specific nature and basis of their subordination in the Indian society.

The works of the radical feminists (Gross 1993; Paul 1985) discuss multi-layered androcentricism in the previous secondary works as well as in the classical texts of the Buddhists that had monks as their editors. This genre encompassing aspects of both Buddhism and 'Women's issue' tended to be narrower in terms of space and time as well as categories of analysis. Women's spirituality and nuns' ordination have been the two main preoccupations of this group.

Falk's (1989) perspective offers a more socialist angle to the debate. She suggests that the Buddhist texts in relation to women are essentially misogynist in character. She looks at the lives of these women from outside the pail of the conventional feminist critique. The conservative notions of feminism and equality and the inevitable ethnocentric baggage of which it is a part has been successfully set aside as she tries to gauge the position and the problems of these women by trying to go back and think according to their notions of subjugation and/or equality.

Recent scholarship on Buddhism has detected an underlying tension within the Buddhist texts; while some reflect a positive attitude in their assessment of women and the feminine, others are blatantly negative. At times, this tension is evident within the reading of a single text also. This ambivalent Buddhist attitude has been the subject of study and debate in recent years.

Studies (Blackstone 2000; Zelliot 1992) that attempt to highlight gender differences in terms of experiences, articulation and the like have shown that gender can play an important role in both the experiences and the modes of expression typical of woman and man in a given social system. Issues of men's distinctive mode of textual interpretation and philosophical discourse or women's understanding of the doctrine or their typical use of ritual has been discussed in studies that have documented how women and men tend to tell different types of stories, emphasise different component of the stories and respond differently to stories.

Recent feminist scholarship (Bartholomeusz 1994; Blackstone 2000) has shifted the debate from inequality and subordination of womankind to emphasising the inherent as also the sociocultural and biological differences between man and woman. Their approach attempts to narrate the experience of the Buddhist women from their own perspectives. Bartholomeusz discusses the relationship between gender stereotypes of women in Sri Lankan society and Buddhist scriptures, on the one hand, and the actual roles of the lay renunciant women she studies, on the other. Focussing on issues faced by contemporary Buddhist women, Bartholomeusz situates those women firmly within their social, political and religious contexts.

In examining the role of religion in the construction of gender, Skilling (2001) examines the structural features of Buddhist social organisation and literature. He looks for the terminological gender equivalent for the male and, in doing so, studies 'the feminine' in various offbeat contexts.

Bernard Faure's (2003) work is also based on the premise that religion impacts the construction of gender. Faure challenges the conventional view that 'the history of women in Buddhism is a linear narrative of progress from oppression to liberation'. Examining Buddhist discourse on gender in traditions such as that of Japan, he shows that patriarchy/misogyny has long been central to Buddhism. However, women were not always silent, passive victims.

Ursula King (1995) discusses issues concerning women's experience of the sacred and female symbols associated with the sacred, or what some others prefer to call 'the human constructs of reality'. Another issue that figures in this debate is the subject of feminist spirituality. The issues voiced by Malmgreen (1986) and King (1995) that have been discussed above have a further bearing on this research and the same have been included in the analysis of gender against the religious backdrop of Buddhism.

In the context of South Asian Archaeology, gender has received little attention from scholars. Archaeological researches are restricted to stray, isolated pockets, and studying singular subjects or rather objects, from a gendered perspective, like the ceramic studies, which tend to focus on feminine involvement in the process of pottery production in pro-historic, Harappan context (Wright1991:198) or the study of terracotta and art objects, the latter being more in the nature of art historical works (Dehejia 1997). The analysis of the hero stones and the underlying gendered contexts has been attempted by Zagarell (2002). These studies have been few and far between; they have failed to take multiple archaeological data collectively into account to arrive at answers to larger issues concerning socio-economic and religious aspects.

Buddhism and archaeology

Traditional knowledge and the history of Buddhism have come from a combination of two sources: ancient texts and study of contemporary devotional practices. Archaeology has seldom been utilised in this process, save for identification of a large number of sites designated as 'Buddhist' on the basis of the finds of *stūpas*, *chaitya* and/ or *vihāra* at these sites.

The bedrock of present-day works on Buddhism in South Asia is based on the sites explored and identified by Cunningham during the 19th century. Cunningham's contribution to Indian archaeology is his initiative of using text-based archaeology.[2] His focus lay in the discovery and identification of Buddhist sites, especially in North India (across modern Uttar Pradesh and Bihar), though his search for Pundravardhana led him to Bengal, and led to the discovery of Mahāsthāngarh. Cunningham identified 'Buddhist sites' by correlating the data from the travelogues of the Chinese pilgrims, Faxian and Xuanzang, who visited the subcontinent during the early centuries of the Christian era. The present-day archaeological concerns with regard to Buddhism is limited to excavation of Buddhist sites identified by Cunningham, with the objective of 'discovering' structures such as *stūpas, chaityas, vihāras* and the like of distinctly 'Buddhist affiliation'. This documentation of Buddhist sites was neither comprehensive nor analytical, but paved the way for future researches on the subject.

Art has been one of the earliest and most deliberated upon themes within Buddhism. The works of the colonial period (Fergusson 1971) tended to overplay the element of foreign influence in art and architecture. This was set against those (Coomaraswamy 2001; Kramricsh 1985) that discussed the nuanced spiritualism and symbolic underpinnings that was reflected in these works of art. The latter argued that Buddhist art showed a high degree of borrowing from earlier pre-Buddhist religions in terms of symbolism and the like.

Works on gender in Buddhism have been relegated to the identification and classification of Buddhist female deities (Miranda Shaw 2006). Recent works like that of Kirit Shah explore the gender-based, social as well individual dimensions of the epigraphic records. Shah revises the existing historiography that presents women as silent voices in historical writings, laying bare the dichotomy between textual prescriptions and epigraphical records. The present-day archaeologists base their identification of the sites on the works of Cunningham. The dating of the site is based on broad generalisations and periodisation on grounds of dynastic timelines and the corresponding ceramic typologies, as proposed by Wheeler. Like their colonial predecessors, they mainly concern themselves with the identification and designation of the archaeological site as Buddhist, Jaina or Brahmanical. The identification, in case of a Buddhist site, being on the basis of structural finds that are broadly grouped as *vihāras, chaityas* and *stūpas*; the objective in most cases being the discovery of sculptures and in the case of *stūpas*, the discovery of relics.

The role of archaeology, especially in South Asia, has been relegated to the status of a supplementing tool, to further lend support to the conclusions provided by literature. Literary sources, inscriptions and travellers reports have been seen as providing the essential tools for the study of history of Buddhism in South Asia. The material sources – mainly numismatic and iconographic data along with architectural data – have simply served to provide visual illustration and corroboration to what is already known from literary documents.

The use of Buddhist canonical texts, which were both monastically created and oriented, projected the Buddhist *vihāra* as 'isolated retreats, where the monks underwent meditational practices'. The early Buddhologists, depending on the literal translations of these texts, echoed this monastic view.

By the latter half of the 20th century, with an emphasis on materialism, a new interpretation of Buddhist monasticism began to emerge which emphasised the economic role of monasteries. Romila Thapar (1996) discussed the involvement of Buddhism in fostering trade. This economic approach was further extended in the works of Ray (1986) and Lahiri (1992) that employed archaeological data in addition to textual sources to demonstrate that Buddhist monasteries played an active role in organising and promoting trade, both as consumers and direct facilitators. Hietzman (1984) went on further to stress that Buddhist monasteries were actively engaged in promoting agricultural production, 'serving as the nuclei of agrarian communities in the peripheries of developing states'.

Recent scholarship has seen a distinct shift in the methodologies pertaining to the study of Buddhism in South Asia. Ray's work (1995; 2006) draws the connection between trade, Buddhism and maritime linkages in South Asia, using ethnographic parallels along with archaeological and literary data, thus pushing the boundaries of existing scholarship on the subject. Contrary to earlier theories that suggested the agency of the state (court to court) in the expansion of Buddhism, Gombrich (1988) attempts to study the possibility of 'an autonomous religious network that cut across political boundaries' as instrumental in the propagation of the Buddhist religion, basing her study on archaeological and ethnographic data from across Asia and South East Asia. Most of these works tend to focus on single sites and draw generalisation on Buddhist monasticism, based on their analysis.

From his reading of the epigraphic sources, Schopen concluded that archaeology provides us with answers which are very often at odds with the textual records. The shift of focus from canonical records to other fields such as archaeology has made it possible to move beyond conventional research and analyse newer subjects. Julia Shaw's (2002) investigations around Sāñci were aimed at understanding the socio-religious mechanisms, which enabled early Buddhist monks to establish themselves in new areas. These data provide empirical basis for assessing the link between Buddhism and agrarian system of production in ancient India, a subject that received little attention largely because of the prohibitive attitude expressed in early Buddhist texts.

Lars Fogelin's work (2006), based on similar lines, employs data derived from survey of the sacred landscape and sacred architecture for his investigations. He demonstrated how religious architectural design and the use of landscape helped in shaping the relationship between the monastic centres and their immediate lay environs. His work explores issues of much wider concerns, like how the monastery functioned within the natural and social contexts, with regard to time and space, and other interpretive issues such as how monks adapted their surroundings to Buddhism and adapted Buddhism to suit their surroundings. His work analyses the multiple economic and social roles in addition to the ritual aspect of the monasteries.

One of the related issues with regard to the emergence and spread of Buddhism has been the question of the degree of lay engagement in Buddhist ritual practices. The lay character, of this essentially monastic religion, is amply demonstrated by Fogelin, who employs archaeological data and methods to demonstrate the differences in rituals and rites concerning lay adherents and the Buddhist clergy at sacred Buddhist sites. These conclusions, and also the issues discussed, stand in marked contrast to traditional discussions on early Buddhism derived from textual sources, which date from later periods.

Recent scholars on the subject (Ray 1986; Schopen 1988; Fogelin 2006; Shaw 2007) have argued for a communal identity for Buddhism with increasing lay involvement. This view has stemmed from an archaeological reading of Buddhism more than a simple literal interpretation of the classical Buddhist texts. They have continuously argued against the older, more conservative interpretation of Buddhism as an ascetic religion, which was the sole preserve of the monastics. This study also follows the same course and to a degree supports the argument by demonstrating the vital presence of laity in the actual practice and ritualism within Buddhism.

Time period of the study

This book covers an extensive time span, ranging from the sixth century B.C. to the 12th century A.D. The need to study 'the women' in the different evolutionary forms of Buddhism as changing and/or constant has prompted such a study. Moreover, by quoting only part of the record, one may run the risk of painting a portrait of Buddhism as hopelessly negative to women or as very egalitarian in its treatment of men and women.

The history of Buddhism and its women can be divided into three phases. The first period extends from the Buddha's first conversion (sixth century B.C.) till the time of Asoka (third century B.C.). The second period of Buddhist history extends from the time of Asoka (third century B.C.) to that of the Sātavāhanas and Kuṣāṇas (third century A.D.) and the last period starting from third century A.D. onwards till about 12th century A.D. While for the first period the sources are the *Thērīgāthā* as well as the *Thēragāthā* and oral traditions which comprise of such documented literature as the *Jātakas*, the second period provides rich inscriptional evidence in the form of 'donor records'. The third period, which is also known as 'the best recorded period in Buddhist history', has a dearth of data pertaining to nuns, but the archaeological data in the form of monastic plans and the like are abundant for this period. As the data are varied and uneven for different periods, it is crucial that the study adopt a wide time span.

Issues to be discussed

We have time and again seen in recent works on Buddhism, how and in what ways Buddhism shaped and looked at women. Studies on gender and religion discuss women as a single monolithic, homogenous category, thus undermining the agency of many of its members and rendering them invisible within the broader religious discourse.

This work examines multiple issues concerning gender, specifically women's issues. It attempts to envisage a reasonable amount of agency for women within Buddhism. It seeks to examine their nuanced, multiple roles as patrons, practitioners, lay and monastic members and so on.

Working on the premise that religion is an integral component in the analysis and the construction of social history for any given period, this work attempts to reread, reconfigure and reassess the historical data, in order to better understand Buddhism, and the social matrix within which it developed and flourished.

Taking gender as a crucial component for understanding hitherto little explored fields within Buddhism, the study aims to better understand the sociocultural foundation on which Buddhism rested. It attempts to look at women as a social category and to analyse the contribution of these women to the Buddhist *Samgha* in social, spiritual and economic terms, within the then prevailing setup, on the one hand, and, on the other, the impact of Buddhism on these women. It seeks to investigate the individual experiences of the members, and their equations and relationships at different levels: with the *Samgha* at large, their own respective *Bhikṣu* or *Bhikṣunī Samgha*, with the laity, members of the same gender (both lay and monastic) and the like.

The case is made for treating these women as social agents with relative autonomy and space of their own, within the patriarchal parameters of Buddhism and in doing so, it also tries to critique the feminist discourse portraying the women merely as 'victims of patriarchal oppression'. Responsibility involves not projecting the values and question of the present onto the past, which for feminist history means avoiding the temptation to see the historical record as either black or white in terms of that tradition's attitude towards women. Many of the issues taken up require exhaustive analysis of archaeological data, in the event of scarcity of literary data on the subject. The methodology employed questions the inadequacy of the existing archaeological methods applied to researches on Buddhism, and at the same time it also attempts to provide a more viable archaeological methodology for researching gender issues within Buddhism. It attempts to bring together art historical as well as archaeological and epigraphic data spanning a large number of Buddhist sites, and analyse the patterns that emerge to arrive at a consensus on ancient Indian monasticism in South Asia.

Sacred spaces and the feminine in Buddhism

This chapter discusses the concept of religious/spiritual space. It seeks to investigate the material proofs of the spiritual attainments of female Buddhists, both lay and monastic, and bring them to the fore, by making them more visible in the archaeological records. The issues that have been taken up for investigation are as follows: Were *stūpas* erected for women? If so, was there a subtle difference in *stūpa* architecture or in the manner of enshrining of the relics that set those dedicated to women apart from those for the men? Has this practice survived among the later-day Buddhists? Which particular group of women (laywomen or almswomen) enjoyed this privilege? These specific individual questions need to be evaluated and answered in order to arrive at a larger conclusion about the quantitative and qualitative contributions of women to Buddhism, and conversely the recognition of their spiritual attainments, in the archaeological records.

Locating the *bhikṣunī*: identifying nunneries

In broad terms, Chapter 2 addresses the issue of the invisibility of the Buddhist monastic women, that is, *bhikṣuṇīs* or nuns in the archaeological records, and in its course also attempts to devise an archaeological method for the same. Along with the exercise of trying to identify and locate the documentary and literary evidence and corroborating it with actual archaeological evidence on the ground, the concept of space in architectural plans of *vihāras* will be explored. The concept of public and private space and its manifestation in architecture need to be studied. Going by the premise that nuns in their living quarters feel a greater need for privacy and security and would hence restrict direct access to their inner quarters, the entrance to *bhikṣuṇis* residences would be so designed as to provide restricted access to the residents. Further, it seeks to highlight the essential structural differences between *Vihāra* and *vihārikā* for nuns.

Conflict between the social and the asocial worlds: attributing mental agency to women

Chapter 3 deals with the interaction between the *bhikṣuṇīs* and the lay community, and how this interaction defines the social space for *bhikṣuṇīs.* This interaction was dealt with at the level of rules and guidelines laid out for the community of nuns to be followed in the social and/or monastic sphere. It seeks to explore their epistemological space. Space is the medium through which social relationships are negotiated. 'It becomes a map in which personal identity and boundaries between social groups are expressed . . . It is a useful starting point in considering the gendered nature of power which, through control over the built environment, determines personal mobility and access to social and economic resources' (Gilchrist 1993, 1994, 1997, 2013).

Literary references abound with instances that record the fear and insecurities of the lay people, which prompted them to keep the girls and women away from the nuns, who they felt, posed a threat and had a corruptible influence on the vulnerable minds of their women. Blackstone (2000:37–51) attributes this to the fact that when nuns took to renunciation, they still managed to keep in touch with the society, which they had left behind. They did not sever all kinds of bonds, but instead there was a transformation in their attitude towards the society as against the *Thēras* who opted for complete severing of the social bonds.

This statement makes it clear that there was interaction at multiple levels between the two groups of women and also that a subtle tension existed between the laypeople and the community of the nuns. What were the agencies that the former employed to control and regulate the latter group of institutionalised women? Why were such measures needed? In addition, what were the different influences that these nuns wielded over their womenfolk, which led the men to undertake such extreme steps. It is an attempt to bring out the tension between the social and the spiritual roles of a woman, experienced by virtue of being a women and how they negotiated this dichotomy, between the private and the public sphere.

This in turn will help in analysing whether social relations and relationships forged between these two particular categories of women were governed by the dictates of the normative texts or whether personal ties operated beyond the parameters of the essentially patriarchal, normative texts.

Women as patrons

Literary as well as inscriptional sources mention numerous categories of women in either lay capacity or as nuns who subscribed to Buddhism. This chapter attempts to look at the various types of women, and how they contributed to the growth of Buddhism in social, cultural, economic and spiritual terms. It seeks to consider women not as a homogenous, monolithic category; rather, it seeks to analyse 'the woman' in various hierarchical capacities within the socio-religious sphere. It attempts to explore their lay and monastic identities, as *upāsikās* and *bhikṣuṇīs*, on the one hand, and as donors and patrons, on the other. It also dwells on the courtesans, who dwelled at the fringes of the social groups, and their agency within Buddhism.

The objective is to attempt a better understanding of the dynamics between the varied categories of Buddhist women, on the one hand, and the relationship between these different groups of women with the *Samgha* at large and the laity. The idea is to assess and evaluate the achievements of these women and see how and in what ways the admission of these members helped the cause of Buddhism.

These women based on their socially assigned roles have been identified as housewives, daughters, widows, spinsters, matrons and women workers such as farmhands, basket weavers, garland-makers, prostitutes, courtesans and many others. Of these, some have distinctly survived well in spite of the androcentric biases and the brutal editing by the monks, later commentators and historians. The objective is to identify the visible as well as the relatively invisible categories of women and to assess the reason behind their survival and/or their disappearance. This chapter also seeks to assess why and how, as Buddhists (patrons), some were distinctly more visible or more popular over others. It also attempts their identification in the sculptural records. Further it seeks to assess the social, economic and stereological attainments of these women, as individual donors as well as a part of communal donors.

The geographical and spatial limits of the study

In this study, the geographical north–south nomenclature has been avoided, as the same attempts to divide the study on neutral geographical terms. Here the case of the representations[3] on a stele from Amarāvati[4] is cited (Ghosh and Sarkar, *Ancient India* Vol. 20–21). This representation, even though depicted on a Buddhist monument in Andhra, sees itself seeking legitimisation with the North Indian Buddhist sites of Vaishali and Sravasti, by taking recourse to the depiction of Chapala Chaitya, Jetavana and the like. Therefore a linguistic division, instead of a geographical division, for the purpose of unity and homogeneity has been considered. The 'linguistic division of Buddhism'[5] into Gandhari Prakrit-Sanskrit and Pāli-Sinhala-Sanskrit Buddhism has seen a spurt in recent times and has been advocated over the more conventional approach which follows a geographical north–south division for the study of Buddhism. The Pāli texts were initially set against a North Indian backdrop, but since the Pāli texts have been worked and reworked several times, it is difficult to precisely locate them within a fixed geographical location, which also required taking recourse to a wider database (inscriptions and archaeological data) from a pan-Indian context. The sites that were Pāli-Sanskrit dominated have been considered for this study. The inscriptional and the literary textual sources for this study also belong to this category.

In this study, the comparing and contrasting of different types of sources has been undertaken. The data from these sources is diverse in content and has an extensive spread. While the concentration of inscriptional data is mostly from sites like Sāñci, Bhārhūt, Amarāvati, Nāgarjunakonda and the like, the archaeological data for nunneries and for the religious structures is diverse and has an extensive spread; starting from sites like Harwan in Kashmir, to Paharpur in the East, to as far south as the cluster of Buddhist sites in Andhra and Karnataka.

Hence, the quantum of data pertaining to this study is enormous and is spread rather unevenly throughout South Asia, taking in its ambit, a broad spectrum of Buddhist sites.

Scope and methodology of the present work

Previous works on Buddhism and Archaeology have seen an institutional neglect with regard to researches on issues and implications of gender. It is precisely for this reason that in studies pertaining to Buddhism, the presence of women has been minimal. This work is an attempt to bring together the two disciplines of gender and archaeology for the study of Buddhism. It is an attempt at analysing the Buddhist society at large and the agency of women in particular in the Buddhist society by employing archaeological, ethnographic and literary data.

The literary records are at times silent on the issue of the actual presence and participation of the female agents, and this absence cannot always be explained by archaeological data alone, as the physical presence of 'the feminine' in archaeological records may or may not be available. On the other hand, the presence of archaeological data that does not support literary data is significant, as it is suggestive of the material evidence pertaining to the actions of both men and women, beyond canonical prescriptions.

The analysis of donor records has been done on the basis of the examination of inscriptional sources while the review of the social context has required the study of the textual sources. The identification of nunneries has necessitated the survey of both textual and archaeological sources while the last section, which assesses the different types of structures found at the various sacred Buddhist sites, employs the examination of structural as well as epigraphic data.

The archaeological methodology will employ (i) an examination of the sacred landscape together with the study of the structural remains of the sacred sites and (ii) the study of epigraphic data from the Buddhist sites, and also specimens of art in the sculptures and paintings from Buddhist sites. In the absence of comprehensive, large-scale excavations at many of the Buddhist sites, the examination of the structural remains will focus on two kinds of structures:

(i) residential monastic structures/*vihāras* and
(ii) non-residential structures at sacred sites.

It will involve the reinterpretation of archaeological data from Buddhist sites. In order to distinguish between a conventional Buddhist *vihāra* and a *vihārikā* (monastic residential complex for *bhikṣuṇīs*), a comprehensive survey of the architectural layout and plans will be made, with a view to locate any possible difference between the broad general layout of a Buddhist *vihāra*, a common feature at most of the Buddhist sites. This will then be followed by an examination of the variant architectural features, its probable significance and its contextual correlation with artefacts/antiquities that reflect direct/indirect female presence and to see if at all any coherent patterns emerge from the documentation of these structural/architectural remains.

The study of ethnographic parallels is necessary to fill in the existing gaps, while interpreting archaeological and literary data. Epigraphic data that has been put to use are of the nature of individual donor records of Buddhist women donating at various Buddhist sites. These records offer valuable insights into the thought processes of the Buddhist women (both monastic and laywomen). It also helps in the evaluation of issues such as their patterns of patronage, their geographical location and the preferred modes of identification used by these women and so on. The epigraphic data pertaining to this study has been derived from a range of published inscriptions like those of Buhler and Luder. These epigraphic data have been analysed and are presented in the form of charts and tables. The charts and graphs are representative of relative statistical data from the different types of Buddhist sites, obtained from the analysis of inscriptional records, and offer an insight into various aspects such as the *upāsikās'* and *bhikṣunīs'* relative preference for a particular attribute for identifying themselves. On the other hand, the tables provide similar data that are based on absolute statistics. For the analysis of *stūpas* with *āyakas*, the data have been derived from published excavation records.

This study provides an insight in to the institutional character of monastic women, the *bhikṣunīs* and the *upāsikās*, and the practices they participated in. It seeks to carry forward the discussion by Fogelin, which suggests 'the sacred space around the *stūpas* etc. to be extended mortuary landscape, where the lay and the monastics interacted' by exploring this space to verify lay/monastic female presence and its implications. Gender has now become a critical category for the analysis of all data, including those of religion. This is a modest attempt at initiating an identification and documentation of the physical presence of Buddhist women in the archaeological records, which will help in determining and locating women within the larger social and religious framework of Buddhism. The terms *vihārā/vihārikā* have been used for a Buddhist nunnery, while the term *bhikkhuni/bhikṣunī* has been used for a Buddhist nun.

The issues discussed in this book have necessitated the survey of various kinds of sources: literary, archaeological and epigraphic sources pertaining to the period of study. For the data on female patrons, the data have been largely derived from epigraphic and literary sources while the conflict between social and the asocial worlds has been examined through the exhaustive survey of literary textual data. On the other hand, the investigation of secular spaces and identification of nunneries or *vihārikās* has been undertaken based on archaeological data.

Literary sources include Buddhist canonical and non-canonical texts like the *Vinaya* texts, the *Jātakas*, *Ittivuttaka*, *Vimānavatthu* and also the travelogues of the Chinese travellers like Faxian, Xuanzang, Itsing and the like. The *Prajañapāramita Sutras*, the *Mūlasaravastivādin* literature, the *Lotus Sutra* or the *Saddharmapundārikā Sutra*, the *Simhala Sutra*, the *Mahāparinirvāna Sutra*, the *Mahāsudassana Sutra*,[6] the *Thērīgāthā* among others, which were either authored by women and even those which were authored by men but were 'concerning women' have been look at anew. In addition, a cursory study of Brahmanical texts and commentaries that are contemporary to the period under study, like the *Dharmaśāstrā* literature is required to make a comparative analysis and to bring out the essential divergences and conflicts in the contents of the varied literary traditions of the period.

While *Dharmaśāstrās* provide the Brahmanical Canonical position on women, the *Cūllavagga* offers the formal Buddhist position on the subject. An analysis of the two (Brahmanical vis-à-vis Buddhist) approaches will bring out the broad points of similarities and divergences between the two, and this in turn will be useful in understanding the lay Buddhist as well as the larger social stance on the subject of 'the feminine' in the society.

The social milieu was a heterogeneous mix of many different religions and their adherents (which included the Buddhists as well as a larger non-Buddhist populace, comprising of Shaivas, Vaishnavas and Jains). As members of all these religious communities coexisted, it was but obvious that each would have some influence over the other. As Brahmanism was one of the most popular and dominant ideologies of the period with a large following, its impact on Buddhism and vice versa cannot be overlooked and therefore the need to look at sources that reflect the social temper and attitudes towards women from an extra Buddhist perspective is mandatory in order to understand the wider social implication of being a woman.

Archaeological sources include the review of published and unpublished archaeological reports and the *Memoirs of the Archaeological Survey of India*. These give an idea of the site plans and help in a comparative study of monasteries with those of the convents. Inscriptions have helped in providing the much-required donor records of these religious women, as also allied data pertaining to the subject of study.

Ethnographical data have been taken up in order to support as well as to understand many of the gaps caused by the paucity of literary data on the subject. It seeks to understand many of the rituals and practices of the present-day Buddhist women, both nuns and lay Buddhists. The inquiry involves both objective and subjective evaluation of the lives and communities of Buddhist nuns, their residences, their modes of worship, the prevailing hierarchies within the Buddhist nunneries, their interaction with the lay groups, issues of patronage and finance of monasteries and the like.

Notes

1 A school of thought believes that this statement was attributed to the Buddha at a later date, it is therefore a comparatively recent interpolation.

2 A. Cunningham, *Archaeological Reports*, 1871–2, 1961, 1962.

3 The top and one of the faces of the stele are missing. On the three extant faces scenes from the life of Buddha have been depicted. The first face represents episodes from the life of Buddha while he was at Vaishali; face two represents scenes from Sravasti and Jetavana while the third and last face represents Dhanyakataka itself.

4 A. Ghosh and H. Sarkar, 'Beginnings of Sculptural Art in South East India: A Stele from Amaravati', *Ancient India*, Vol. 20–21, pp. 168–77.

5 Kōgen Mizuno and Gaynor Sekimori, *Essentials of Buddhism: Basic Terminology and Concepts of Buddhist Philosophy and Practice*, Tokyo, Japan: Kōsei Publication, 1996; Richard Salomon, *Indian Epigraphy: A Guide to the Study of Inscriptions in Sanskrit, Prakrit, and the Other Indo-Aryan Languages*, New York and Oxford: Oxford University Press, 1998 and Jason Emmanuel Neelis, "Historical and Geographical Contexts for Avadānas in Kharoṣṭhī Manuscripts", in *Buddhist Studies*, Richard F. Gombrich (ed.), Delhi: Motilal Banarsidas, 2008, pp. 151–72.
6 T. W. Rhys Davids (trans.), "The Mahāsudassana Sutta", The Buddhist Suttas, *S.B.E.*, Vol. XI (rep.), Delhi, 1965.

One

Sacred spaces and the feminine in Buddhism

This chapter discusses the concept of sacred spaces for Buddhist women. It seeks to investigate the material evidence for the spiritual attainments of female Buddhists, both lay and monastic, and bring them to the fore, by making them more visible in the archaeological records. The chapter also discusses issues concerned with women's experience of the sacred and female symbols associated with the sacred. What religious authority and power have women held, and how has the spiritually empowering authority of their experience been experienced and transmitted to others? These questions relate to women's actual participation in religious life. Issues such as what religious roles and rituals women participate in, from which ones are they excluded and the expression of their participation in Buddhist religious architecture have been explored in this chapter.

The Buddhist position on the subject of association of the feminine and spirituality has throughout its history been cloaked in ambiguity. The constantly wavering attitude on the issue and the resulting contradictions are quite loud and cannot be glossed over. While, on the one hand, we have the Buddha's reluctance to admit women into the order, as attested in the Buddhist Canons, on the other, we have a plethora of female divinities, who occupy various positions as consorts and subsidiary deities within the pantheon. Contrary to the popularly projected view that the inclusion of these deities was very much a Mahayānist phenomenon, recent researches on the subject have brought to light literary as well as archaeological data which compel us to admit that the existence of these female forms as an integral part of the pantheon was a much earlier development and has been present throughout a considerable part of the Buddhist history.

Despite the exhaustive works on female deities, *dākinis, Siddhās* and the like in the field of archaeological research, there is very little that can be taken to identify the spiritual presence of these female Buddhists at the countless Buddhist sites that dot the South Asian landscape. The simplistic categorisation of structures into *stūpas, vihāras* and *chaityas* leaves little scope for the analysis and identification of other types of structures (like circular, apsidal structures) that are found coexisting with the widely known types, at the Buddhist sites (Ray 2009).

Stūpa, chaitya and *vihāra* are the three types of structures which are commonly used to designate an archaeological site as Buddhist. While some scholars (Bandaranayake 1974:27–8) have identified as many as twenty Buddhist structural sub-units, most accept Mitra's (Allchin 1995; Chakrabarti 1995; Mitra 1972; Nagaraju 1981) tripartite division of stupa, *chaitya-griha* or 'stupa sanctuary' and *vihāra* notwithstanding an expansion of the second category to include the bodhi griha or 'Bodhi-tree sanctuary' and Buddha image sanctuary'. Although the individual elements of this simple typology have altered through time and space, their presence or absence represents the major techniques for identifying Buddhist sites it should be acknowledged that whilst such monuments are frequently identified during excavation, they represent only a fragment of Buddhist practice. Second, overlap between categories, for example, *stūpas* within *vihāras* should be taken into account.

In this chapter, an attempt has been initiated to study the archaeological (structural) proofs that are testimony to the spiritual attainments of the female Buddhist practitioners. It pertains to the deification and worship of the 'female element' within Buddhism and the study of the religious architecture at the numerous Buddhist sites. This is an attempt to study and analyse whether the enshrinement of relics and their veneration was limited to male monastics and male Buddhist saints or whether female monastics also at times qualified for this distinction. It further seeks to study whether *stūpas* were erected for women? If so, was there a subtle difference in *stūpa* architecture or in the manner of enshrining of the relics that set those dedicated to women apart from those for the men? Which particular group of women (laywomen or almswomen) enjoyed this privilege? On the other hand, was this an isolated case where only the kinsmen of the Buddha were venerated in this manner? Has this practice survived among the later-day Buddhists?

There are numerous *stūpa* sites that have during the course of archaeological investigation yielded relics of the Buddha, and also those of some of his venerable disciples and venerated Buddhist saints. There is no precedence, however, of the enshrinement and worship of relics of any female Buddhist saint, while, on the other hand, we have a long list of Buddhist *Thēris* and their spiritual attainments.[1] There is a conspicuous absence of literary as well as archaeological data in the form of *stūpas*/temples or shrines dedicated to the Buddhist female masters.

The only available reference in this context is that of a modern flat-roofed temple with a spacious paved platform around it in Lumbini, Nepal. Inside the temple is enshrined a fragmentary image variously known as Rupādēi (Rupādēvi) and Rummindēi (Rummindēvi), the tutelary goddess of Lumbini. It presents in high relief the scene of nativity of the Buddha. A life-sized image of Māyā Devi, stands under a tree, grasping its branch with her right hand, her left hand resting on her hip. On her right side and supporting her, is a woman, presumably her sister Māhāprajāpati. Beyond the latter is the slightly bent figure of Śakra, with a high crown, who is in the attitude of receiving the newborn child as the latter emerges from his mother's right side. The small figure of Gautama with a halo round his head stands below. Just behind Śakra is a male figure. Stylistically ascribable to the early Gupta period, the sculpture is badly damaged (Mitra 1980:232–3).

Review of literary data

Often spaced out and far between, one comes across references to *stūpas* commemorating events that have women as their central character. Xuanzang mentions a number of *stūpas* commemorating important events and spots connected with the *mahāparinirvāṇa of Ŝākyamuṇi Buddha*. Among these is a *stūpa* that marks the spot where the men rested for seven days to commemorate the weeping of Mahāmāyā, mortal remains of the Buddha rested following his *mahāparinirvāṇa* (Mitra 1980). Another was the *stūpa* dedicated to Haritī, which was approximately 50 *li* from Puśkkalāvati (to the North West). It was here that the Tathāgata converted the 'Mother of the demons', and kept her from hurting men. It is for this reason the common folk of this country offer sacrifices to obtain children from her (Beal 1906). Yet another refers to a *stūpa* which was located at the site, where the house of Āmrapāli[2] (daughter of the Āmra-Āmradārikā) existed. According to

Xuanzang, it was at this very place where the aunt of Buddha and other *bhikṣūṇīs* also obtained *Nirvāṇa* (Hardy 1995:309).

The above-mentioned textual references have paved the way for a more serious enquiry of the architectural remains from Buddhist sites (especially *stūpa* architecture) and their association (if any) with gender.

An archaeological assessment

Certain structures, on the basis of the contextual finds and associated antiquities, have been found to be associated with the feminine, at a number of Buddhist sites. These structures are of two broad types:

(i) circular structures/ circular shrines and
(ii) *āyaka*-type *stūpas* (with cruciform ground plan)

Circular structures and their association with the feminine

Three main types of *chaitya-grihas* are known to exist at Buddhist sites: (i) circular, (ii) apsidal and (iii) quadrilateral. Sanctuaries with apsidal ground plans are fairly widespread, being found as far North as Harwan and as far south as Brahmagiri (District of Chitaldurg, Mysore). The quadrilateral *chaitya-grihas* are usually astylar. Their largest concentration is in western India at places like Junnar, Kūda, Karādh, Silawādi, Mahād and the like, though the type is also encountered at places in northern India like Dhamṇār and Taxila. *Chatiya-grihas* can broadly be divided into two main types: hall type and cell type. Within these two categories there are three further subtypes. They are (i) apsidal variety; (ii) oblong variety and (iii) circular variety, in the rock-cut series of Buddhist Architecture in western India (Nagaraju 1981).

The circular (hall variety) *chaitya* in western India comprises the *stūpa* in the centre, surrounded by a circle of pillars. The roof is domed, for example, Junnar-Tuljalēna 3. While the circular (cell variety) comprises a cell with domical or flat roof, for example, Bēdsa 3, Bhaja 26, Kānhēri 4 (Variants-Bhaja 24, Kanheri 36),[3] Salihundam, Guntapalli, Sāñci, Sravasti, Nāgarjunakonda and the like.

Circular structures have been represented in early reliefs of Sāñchī, Bharhūt and Amrāvati. One of the earliest of such structures known was excavated on top of a hill known as Bijak-kī-Pahādi, at Bairāt (200 B.C.). On the basis of associated finds, it has been ascribed to

Asoka (Sahni 1937:28). The site comprised of twin terraces and the circular structure was situated on the lower terrace. A gold casket was also stated to have been found in the course of the diggings at the site. It is circular in plan, 27 feet in diameter, and surrounded by a circumambulatory passage. The inner wall of the temple consisted of sections of brick walls alternating with 26 octagonal pillars, the charred bases of which alone had survived. The ceiling also consisted of wooden beams covered with well-baked pottery tiles and finished off with a tall terracotta finial in the fashion of the shrines represented in the Bharhūt reliefs (Sahni 1935–6:85). The temple was entered from the East. At a later date, the temple was surrounded by a rectangular enclosure wall.

This is probably the oldest known structural temple in Northern India and one of those which supplied models for the numerous rock-cut cave temples of western and eastern India. The nearest approach, both in plan and design, to this temple is the *chaitya* cave of about the first century B.C., in the rock-cut series; the earliest among such structures are known from the Tuljalēna 3 at Junnar and Guntupalli. This former is about the same size as the temple at Bairāt and has the same internal arrangement with the only difference being that the sanctum in the cave temple at Junnar is surrounded by a circular row of 12 rock-hewn pillars, with the temple at Bairāt consisting partly of bricks and partly of wooden columns. Though not very large in numbers, these structures can be traced to as far as Anuradhapura in Sri Lanka.

The structure reported from Guntupalli in Andhra Pradesh has been described as a circular brick *chaitya-griha*. Datable to *c.* third to second centuries B.C., it is at the eastern extreme of the hill over an elevated terrace, approached by a long flight of stone steps. A record of an *upāsikā*, datable to second to first centuries B.C., refers to the setting up of these stone steps at the entrance platform. Its external diameter is 11 m and has an imposing adhistana. The wall of *chaitya-griha* rises to 80 cm height and measures 2.14 m wide. It houses a *stūpa* at the centre. The circumambulatory path around the *stūpa* is 1.38 m wide.

Similar evidence comes from *Sāñci, Stūpa no.* 5, which was erected probably in the sixth century A.D. Unlike all the above-mentioned structures this structure is considerably late and is dated to the medieval period. Like all the *stūpas* of the medieval period its core is composed mainly of small rubble and earth, and its face masonry is laid in neat narrow courses with footings at the base, which is circular instead of square, having a diameter of 39 inches. Projecting from its south side is a statue plinth of Udaygiri stone, the design and construction of which indicates that it was set up about the seventh century A.D. (Marshall 1913–14).

Srāvasti (Sahēth): A similar structure is also reported from Sahēth (Marshall 1910–11), marked X on plan, in the northern part of the mound, in alignment with monastic units G and F. These two monastic units have been dealt with in the next chapter (Chapter 3) and have been taken to be probable convents or *bhikṣūṇī vihāras*.

Sanghol: At the south-eastern corner of the complex was exposed a structure which has been described as 'circular structure with a rectangular cistern sunk into it' (pl. 7).

Lauriya Nandangarh: In trench L about 4 feet 5 inches below the surface, a circular brick structure, 3 feet 5 inches high, was brought to light.[4] The diameter of this circular wall, when complete, would have been about 208 inches. It is possible that it did not form a regular circle but an apse with opening on one side for approach, as in the apsidal temples.

During the course of excavation of this structure, a large collection of terracotta figurines from trench L include different type of female figurines.

(a) A woman standing with her hands placed on the hips.[5]
(b) The one with bulged-out gown and disc-shaped ornaments for the head, and the arms hanging down.
(c) A woman with two wings. Similar winged male figures (*dēvaputras*/angels) appear on Bharhūt railing.
(d) The lower portion of a female figurine standing with crossed legs.

Stylistically, these terracottas are related to those of the Sunga period (second to first centuries B.C.) discovered elsewhere. Two points need to be noted here.

(I) First, all the mentioned sites that have such circular structures incidentally have a considerable number of female patrons and a distinctive female presence at the sites.[6]
(II) Second, if the circular types are taken to be the prototype of the apsidal *chaitya*, the former has to precede the latter but the date of both the architectural types is generally believed to be close to the Mauryan period. Both the types seem to have coexisted around the same period, though the circular types

are, as has already been discussed, quite rare as compared to the more popular apsidal variety.

As is evident from Chart 4, which is a comparative chart showing the percentage of men donors vs women donors (as given in Chapter 5), the relatively smaller percentage of female patrons as compared to male patrons could have been the reason for the small number of such architectural specimens, which are found to be widely spaced out throughout the subcontinent.

Contemporary to the circular shrines are the apsidal structures and rock-cut shrines. The exact significance of these structures has so far only been conjectured. They are placed within a broad category of religious Buddhist shrines, a structural variation of the apsidal variety.

At Nāgarjunakonda (site VIII of Longhurst) there are two such circular structures. On plan these structures were like a *stūpa*, with a single *āyaka*. Within one of these (Nāgarjunakonda (Site VIII B)) lay a long rectangular inscribed slab (pl. 8), which reads:

> *Chhaya khamba raised in memory of Vammabhata mother of Rudra-purushadatta & daughter of a Mahasatrapa.*[7]

Here it needs to be noted that this *chhāyā khamba* was raised in front of the apsidal hall, between the monastery and the *stūpa*. The positioning/location of a memorial dedicated to a lay Buddhist woman, within the sacred complex, in between the monastery and the *stūpa* needs to be noted. The location of the *Chāyā khamba* suggests that the lady commanded excessive influence within the *Samgha*, so as to get a memorial raised in her honour at such a place, which was probably out of bounds even for the monastics. It also further proves the significant and dominant position of the laity and more specifically its lay female members) with respect to the *Samgha*.

According to Dr Farzand Masih (2012), the recent excavation revealed a circular platform at Sui Vihāra, 16 miles southwest of Bahawalpur, built with sundried bricks and supporting walls to hold the platform and the cylindrical structure.[8] An earlier find from this very place is an inscription dating back to the 11th reignal year of Kanishka.

The text of this inscription is as follows:

> *(during the reign) of the Mahārāja Rājātirāja Devaputra Kaṇiṣka, in the eleventh year . . . on this day, when the friar (bhikṣu) Nāgadatta, the*

preacher of the Law (dharmakaṭhi) the disciple of the acarya Damatrata (ācārya Damatrāta śisya) the disciple's disciple of the teacher Bhava (ācārya Bhavapraśiṣya) raised the staff (yaṭhi) here in Damana,[for??] *the mistress of the Vihāra (vihārasvāminī), the lay votary (upāsika) Balanandi, and her mother, the matron, the wife of Bala (Balanandi kutumbinī Balajayamātā) in addition to this foundation of the staff, subsequently given this enclosure. May it be conducive to welfare and happiness of all beings.*

This inscription, as per my reading, records the raising of the staff/*yasthi* (a term used for a memorial pillar), along with the foundation of the staff and the enclosure that holds the staff, in Damana, by the *(bhikṣu)* Nāgadatta himself, for the *Viharaswamini* (who was a) lay *upāsikā* (named) Balanandi and her mother, the wife of Bala. The erection of memorial column (Yyastśṭhi or staff) by the monk Nāgadatta for the lay *upāsika* Balanandi, the *Vihāraswāmini* of Damana Vihāra, points to the active participation of the monk's fraternity in honouring and encouraging distinguished lay patrons, who probably formed the main support base for the *Samgha* within the local communities. This fact is attested by the Sui Vihāra inscription of the Kushana period. In my opinion these two inscriptions put to rest all previous ambiguities related to the nature and significance of circular structures found at Buddhist sites.

Similar specimens have also been recovered from Jēwārgi (Rao 1985) and Sannathi (Howell 1995). A pit in the south-west corner of the site, at Sannathi, has yielded a memorial pillar broken into two pieces. One of these contains sculptures depicted in two registers, with an inscription engraved in between, in early characters of the second century A.D.

The majority of the sculptures found from the site are memorial slabs (Howell 1995). These slabs are of varying height (approximately 3 m) as no complete piece has been recovered. These slabs are divided into a series of panels. The top panel is arched and decorated with a series of tired roofs with *chaitya* arched windows. The second panel carries a portrait of an individual or couple, presumably the persons commemorated. The central figures are usually flanked by attendants. A labelled inscription is usually found above or below this panel. The third panel usually has two depictions. The most common is of a unyoked bullock cart, with the bulls at rest in front of it. The driver of the cart is also sometimes portrayed. Alternatively, the scene can be of a horse, without a rider, usually being led by a groom and occasionally preceded by an attendant carrying an umbrella. Howell (1995:69) has questioned the purpose of these sculptures. From an analysis of the evidence from

Nāgarjunakonda and Sannathi in the South and the Sui Vihāra in the North West, it can be inferred that these were memorials which were either interred within circular *stūpa*-like dedicatory structures or set up upright in the memory of the departed souls. These were put up to commemorate the lay-Buddhist female patrons. So far no such references related to *bhikşunī* have been found. On these slabs, some of the more commonly depicted themes, are those of the rider-less horse, unyoked bullock cart and the mother–child motif. The first of these themes can be interpreted as 'the Great Renunciation' or the scene of *Mahābhiniṣkramaṇa*; on another level it can also be taken to denote the end of a journey, in this case the journey through life of the figure commemorated. The same interpretation also holds good for the second depiction. As for the third depiction it was a favoured motif and can be seen at both the sites. It was probably used to honour female lay Buddhist patrons. This highlighting of the maternal aspect of the donors further corroborates the high position accorded to motherhood within Buddhism. It needs to be added that the majority of the memorial slabs have female representations on them, while a good number also have representations of couples. The choice of themes depicted varied and depended upon their individual preferences and also to a degree on the social context in which the donors sought to situate themselves.

On the basis of circumstantial evidence (in this case the finding of the inscribed memorial slab found *in situ* from the circular structure at Nāgarjunakonda), it can be suggested that such structures could well have been shrines/sanctuaries meant for the female lay members of the *Samgha*. This undermines and underscores the dominant position and participation accorded to monks in all matters concerning the *stūpa* cult as suggested by Schopen (1997).

The next structural type that needs to be discussed while on the subject of the association of the feminine and sacred at Buddhist sites are *stūpas* for women.

The *stūpas*, both at Piparhawa (Lat. 27° 26′ N.; Long. 83° 7′ 50″ E.; District of Basti (Uttar Pradesh) and Lauria Nandangarh (Lat. 26° 59′ N.; Long. 84° 24′ E.; District Of Champaran, Bihar), which distinctly exhibit a cruciform ground plan during the process of archaeological excavations, have yielded relics. At both of these sites, along with many other antiquities, gold leaves with impressions of female figures,[9] (two at *Piparhawa* and one at *Lauria Nandangarh*), in repoussé were found.

Similar evidence comes from Nāgarjunakonda *stūpa* no. 6 on plan; it is a spoked wheel, divided into eight chambers. A gold reliquary containing a number of small, round gold lotus flowers, a broken jade, coral and pearl beads, a tiny piece of bone and two coin-like medallions made of thin gold and measuring 5/8th of an inch in diameter. One is embossed with the head of a Greek-like male figure and the other with the head of an Indian lady. 'They were portraits of two important personages probably a king and queen. Both are of the same size and the same foreign style and have holes drilled at the top showing that they were worn as pendants on a necklace. They seem to have been struck to commemorate some special event, perhaps the building of the great *stūpa* by the Lady Chamtisri, who was a sister of King Siri Chamtamula. She was a generous donor as is evident from the donor records at Nāgarjunakonda and perhaps the male figure represent a portrait of a ruling King of the Andhra country in the third century A.D.' (Longhurst 1929–30:144).

At Piprahawa, the relic casket carried an inscription, which provided epigraphic evidence, which further reinforces the notion of feminine presence at sacred Buddhist sites. The inscription reads:

Sukiti_bhatinām sa-bhagīnikānām
Sā_putta-dālānam iyam salila-nidhāne
Buddhasa bhagavate Sākiyānam

Three translations have been put forward for this inscription, which are as follows:

> *This relic shrine of divine Buddha (is the donation) of the Sakya-Sukiti brothers (i.e. either 'of Sukiti's brothers' or 'of Sukiti and his brothers'), associated with their sisters, sons and wives.*[10] Or, *This shrine for the relics of the Buddha, the August one, is that of the Sākyas, the brethren of the distinguished one, in association with their sisters and with their children and their wives.*[11]Or, *Of the brethren of the well-famed one, together with (their) little sisters (and) together with (their) children and wives, this (is) a deposit of relics; (namely), of the kinsmen of Buddha, the blessed one.*

According to the first two interpretations, the relics are those of the Buddha himself, while the third would mean that they were of Buddha's kinsmen and their sisters, wives and children (who had been slaughtered by Vidudabha).[12] Going by the third interpretation, it would mean that the precedent of enshrinement of relics of women as well as children also existed along with that of men.

This inscription along with the female impressed gold foil needs to be studied in the light of the notions of purity and pollution, as expressed in the Buddhist context. Early Buddhist texts contain references to the concept of pollution associated with womanhood. For example, the *Lalitavistāra Sutras* states that the Buddha remained untouched by the filth (of the womb), ensconced in a jewelled casket (Bays 1983). This statement is suggestive of the fact that the Buddha remained untouched by the filth of womb and pain of birth.

On the other hand, we have an instance from the present-day Thailand, seen particularly often in the north, where women are forbidden from circumambulating around the *stūpas*. The monks usually explain that the relics of the Buddha are placed in the centre of the *stūpas* at the time they built it. If women are allowed to circumambulate the *stūpa*, they would be walking at the level higher than the relics and hence might desacralise them.[13]

From the inception, Buddhism has always been wary of 'the feminine'[14]; this is evident from the textual perception for the feminine in the Buddhist Canons. In the light of the above-mentioned literary references, the finding of a gold leaf, etched with a female figure, in repoussé, obtained as a part of the reliquary from the *Dhātugarbha* (relic chamber) of *stūpas* (both from Piprahawa and Lauria Nandangarh), needs special mention. Given the above-mentioned notions of pollution and purity, the symbolic presence of 'the feminine' within the *Dhātugarbha* is a paradox. These symbols are significant, as Bynum (1992) explains, how gender-related symbols can act in many other ways in addition to simply mirroring or instilling the acceptance of the order of the society (Bynum 1992). The greatest threat to a practicing monk (according to many a *Jātakas*) was the snare of 'the woman' (Cowell 1885/1973). The symbolic presence therefore of a female, in the *Dhātugarbha*, dedicated to the Tathāgata or that of a male Buddhist monk, seems to be highly improbable. In the given circumstance though, the following version seems more appropriate.

> Of the brethren of the well-famed one, together with (their) little sisters (and) together with (their) children and wives, this (is) a deposit of relics; (namely), of the kinsmen of Buddha, the blessed one.

This would mean that the interred relics were those of Buddha's kinsmen and their sisters, wives and children (who had been slaughtered by Vidudabha). This would mean the prevalence of a custom for the dedication of *stūpas* to women also, at some early stage of Buddhism, which in due course of time came to be discarded, with the further crystallisation of notions of pollution and purity that came to be associated with women.

As Bynum (1986:2) states 'symbols can be seen as not merely reflecting and shaping but also inverting, questioning, rejecting and transcending gender as it is constructed in the individual's psychological development and sociological setting. . . . Gender related symbols, in their full complexity, may refer to gender in ways that affirm or reverse it, support or question it; or they may, in their basic meaning, have little at all to do with male or female roles. Thus, our analysis that gender-related symbols are sometimes about values "other" than gender'.

The case of Piprahawa and Lauria Nandangarh cannot be ignored as an aberration. There are a number of archaeological instances from a number of Buddhist *stūpa* sites that provide further support to this hypothesis. Sh. K.M. Srivastava undertook excavation at the ancient site of Bakraur, located on the right bank of the Niranjana (I.A.R. 1973–4:9–10). The site situated just north of the village is traditionally known by various names like Sujāta Kūti, Sujātāgarh and Sujāta Quilā, named after the maiden Sujāta, daughter of the village chief, who offered milk rice to the Buddha, after he had undergone severe austerities for six years to gain enlightenment. Archaeological investigation at the site yielded remains of a *stūpa* (pl. 6), with an extant height of 11 m. The legend of Sujāta was immortalised by King Devapala (*c.* ninth century A.D.). He erected a *stūpa* in Bakraur, embellished with terracotta plaques, which showed the Buddha in a meditative posture. The king record's in the plaques found at the *stūpa* that he had undertaken the work especially to commemorate the young woman, Sujāta, who had fed Gautama (Lahiri 2001). Though, in this case, the dedication of the *stūpa* was done at a much later date.

A gender-based analysis of *āyaka*-type *stūpas*

Moving on from the finds of circular variety with a single *āyaka*-like projection to the more symmetrical type with four *āyaka* projections, it needs to be stressed that the occurrence of the latter should not be dismissed as a regional variant. These squarish, platform-like projections, jutting out in the four cardinal directions from the circular plan of the *stūpa*, are, according to the generally accepted view, a regional peculiarity of the southern, more specifically the Andhra *stūpas.*[15] Their concentration at some of the sites like Nāgarjunakonda and Amarāvati is quite high where incidentally the presence of female Buddhist patrons is also quite large. Paradoxically, this feature is also to be found at many other Buddhist sites spread across the subcontinent, as has already been shown in Table 4.

A study of Figure 4.4 showing total number of men donors versus women donors brings out the relative proportion of female donors to male donors, wherein it is clearly visible that the number of records pertaining to women is much less as compared to men donors.

The one reason that calls for an analysis of these structures on the lines of gender is the conclusive evidence for the association of such a structure with the feminine at Lauriya Nandangarh. As has already been discussed, the feminine presence at the *stūpa* site proper in the form of an engraved gold foil is undisputable. The reliquary of which it formed a part was interned within a huge *stūpa*, also with the above-mentioned *āyaka* projections, which incidentally happen to be one of the earliest dated specimens of *stūpa* architecture. It was a huge, terraced *stūpa*, the basement and the lower two terraces above the basement having a polygonal plan and the upper being circular, with a basal circumference of 1,500 feet. The cruciform basement has 14 re-entrant angles and 13 corners in each of the four quadrants made by four arms, each arm, facing a cardinal direction, being 104 feet wide. At the four arms of the cruciform are projections, which do not seem to be very different from the *āyaka* projections of the Andhra *stūpas.* Second, one cannot overlook the remarkable similarity in the nature of the relics found from this site with the rest of the Andhra *stūpa* sites. Besides Lauriya Nandangarh, which happens to be one of the earliest of such structures (third century B.C.E. to seventh century C.E.), there are other sites extending from Shah-ji-ki-Deri in the extreme North-West, to Paraspora, Ushkura, Pandrethan in Kashmir in the North, Antichak (Vikramshila Mahavihara) in Bihar and sites like Paharpur (Somapura) and Mainamati in the East. All these sites have cardinal projections which betray their cruciform ground plan. This projection is visible in plan as well as in the elevations of these structures. The projections from the four arms in all probability were the precursor of the structural appendage known as *āyakas* that came to be seen in the *stūpas* of Andhra.

In these *āyaka stūpas*, shafts or columns of clay and earth have been found, encased in brick work, just as in the case of the circular structures. These have been reported from sites like Lauriya Nandangarh, Piprahawa and also from a number of sites in the south like Bhattiprolu. Marshall draws a parallel with the Vedic practice of erecting a wooden post in the centre of a mound, which has been found at Lauriya Nandangarh. Instead, at Lauriya, in the centre of the *stūpas* A and B is a column or shaft haphazardly made of brick, earth and concrete. A more regular shaft, filled with clay and encased by brick work, was discovered in the centre of the Piprahawa *stūpa* and this feature has been noticed also in the *stūpas* of Bhattiprolu and elsewhere in the South. Marshall further states, 'there is every reason to assume that this masonry column served the same purpose as the wooden post, namely to mark the centre of the *stūpa* where the relics were deposited' (Marshall 1935–6).

Chronology-based architectural analysis of these *stūpa* sites

One limiting factor in the study of these *āyaka*s has been the limitations imposed upon the dating of these structural appendages. At most of the *stūpa* sites, more than one structural phase is evident. The construction of the original tumulus, its subsequent enlargement and alterations need to be documented in a period-wise manner in order to arrive at a logical assessment. At most of the sites the *āyaka*s are a later addition to the original structure. Since at many of the sites the dating is done for the original structure only, the subsequent alterations/changes can at best only be conjectured. At some of these sites the *stūpa* dates back from the early centuries of the Christian era down to the eighth to tenth centuries. But the reports rarely mention the later additions and the periods to which they belong. From Table 4 it is evident that the *stūpas* from sites like Chaneti (pl. 9), Nāgarjunakonda, Amarāvati, Panagoria,[16] Gyaraspur and so forth belong to an earlier period. The *āyaka*s at these sites are the prototypes of the much more elaborate structures seen at sites like Paharpur and Antichak. At the former sites what we see are simple platform-like structures (*āyakas*) with pillars, popularly known as the *āyaka-stambhas*. These gave way to the elaborate structures that include a chamber, an antechamber and a pillared *maṇḍapa* in front. This evolutionary trend in Buddhist religious architecture is parallel to the architectural development that can be witnessed in the evolution of temple architecture in Brahmanical temples in the region, especially in the temples of the Nagara style, where the convention of incorporating an *ardha-maṇḍapa* and a *mukha-maṇḍapa* came into being during the eighth to tenth centuries C.E. The transitional phase is evident in the specimens from Orissa like Udayagiri and Lalitgiri (sixth century A.D.). The more elaborate structures later came to carry niches which held exquisite artistic sculptural specimens. These were monumental structures with large dimensions. The later *stūpas* of Paraspora, Mainamati, Paharpur, Shah-ji-ki-Deri dated eighth century and later belong to this category.

That these *āyaka stūpas* came to exist side by side along with the more popular simple *stūpas* (those without the *āyakas*) suggests that the two served two different purposes. These were probably dedications made to two different groups, most probably for men and women. This is evident when one looks at the location of the site clusters.

The first (i.e. those from the North comprise of sites like Lauriya Nandangarh, Piprahawa and Chaneti) in Bihar, Uttar Pradesh and Haryana, areas directly associated with the life of the Buddha. Piparahawa being associated with Vaishali was testimony to the formation of the *Bhikṣunī Samgha,* with 500-odd Sākya women resolving to take up monastic vows women under the leadership of Mahāpajāpati Gautamī. The region is also known for its association with the famous courtesan-turned–lay-Buddhist patron, Ambapālli and Viśākhā, the lay Buddhist ideal.

The next group of sites includes the sites from Madhyadēśa located in the centre of the subcontinent, which again shows high concentration of both lay and monastic female donors. Their contributions are recorded in the donor records found at Sāñcī and other nearby sites.

The third cluster consists of sites in the North, in Kashmir. Here again the association of women with Buddhism is exemplary. Just as in the case of the royal patrons from Nāgarjunakonda, here also we have a comprehensive chronicle of royal Buddhist votaries like Diddā,[17] Amritprabhā and Yukādevi,[18] Indradevi, Khadana and Sāmmā,[19] which document the munificence and visibility of these female Buddhist patrons (both lay and monastic). In Bengal, the site of Mainamati is named after the queen of that name (Madnāvati – consort of Mānikchandra of the Buddhist Chandra dynasty, which attests to the influence and popularity of this queen within the limits of the religion and also outside it).

Last but not the least is the cluster of sites in the Andhra region, which includes Nāgarjunakonda and Amrāvati as its more popular

Buddhist representative sites, which had the women of the Ikshavāku dynasty as its most staunch supporters and patrons. Thus, we see that the one point of similarity between the women of the three regions is their distinctive presence and contribution (both religious and economic) at these sites.

An overview of the tabulated sites has brought out the following points of consideration: Bakraur has definitive evidence of the presence of a *stūpa* dedicated to a celebrated lay Buddhist female patron, Sujāta. This is attested by epigraphic evidence testifying the construction and dedication of the *stūpa* by a Pala King. This piece of evidence derives further credence from the finds of the female figure, engraved on gold foil, found as part of the relics from Piprahawa and Lauriya Nandangarh. The epigraphic evidence from Piprahawa provides additional proof of the symbolic involvement of women at direct or indirect levels with the *stūpa*. There is a significantly large feminine presence at all the rest of the sites mentioned in Table 4. And the one point of commonality among these sites is the presence of a distinctive type of *stūpa* architecture found at all of them. This distinctive structural appendage has been termed *āyakas*.

Apart from the large number of donor inscriptions from these sites, which happen to be the direct evidence of female participation at these sites, another indirect indication of non-monastic, lay (female) presence at the site can be the profusion of sculptural data with depictions of women, *mithuna* couples, *jātakas* with lay themes and the like at all of these sites.

It needs to be mentioned that at many of the sites shown in Table 7 the circular structures are seen to coexist with the *āyaka*-type *stūpas* like in the sites of Nāgarjunakonda, Guntupali and Salihundam. On the basis of the *in situ* find of a memorial slab dedicated to a female votary (found lying within one of these circular structures reported from Nāgarjunakonda), the significance of such structures can be determined. Since these structures are known to be contemporary to the more common apsidal variety, it will not be correct to categorise the circular ones as the prototype of the apsidal variety. The two coexisted, side by side and were probably memorial shrines dedicated to women, especially the lay female votaries, as in the absence of any direct reference (in the form of epigraphic data) to female monastics/nuns and the profusion of sculptural data with depictions of *mithuna* couples among other types it can be presumed that it was the lay female votaries who were the honoured recipients of this tribute. At another level it is also possible that the construction of these shrines was patronised also by the generous and munificent, female lay patrons. This will also explain the comparatively fewer number of circular *chaityas* as compared to the more common apsidal type. The inscription from Sui Vihāra is testimony to the active involvement of the monk fraternity in the internment of such *yashthi* dedicated to distinguished lay female Buddhist practitioners.

The spread of circular structures is very extensive. While the earliest architectural specimen is known from Bijak-kī-Pahādi, Bairāt in Rajasthan, in the extreme North it is seen at Harwan, in Kashmir. The structures appear again in the cluster of Buddhist sites in the west coast in Maharashtra (Junnar, Bedsa, Bhaja, Kanheri and Kondivte) and in Guntupalli and Salihundam on the west coast.

From a cursory review of the placement of the sites on the map it becomes evident that the densest cluster of *āyaka*-type *stūpa* sites is in the Andhra region, mostly centred on either side of the Krishna River. But contrary to the widely accepted view it cannot be taken to be exclusive to the region. It was a regional phenomenon, which in due course spread to other areas, as it is evident from Table 7. The spread of the *āyaka stūpa* sites was very extensive, spreading as far east as Lalitagiri in Orissa and Paharpur in East Bengal; in the north they are seen in the Buddhist cluster around Kashmir.

The spread of this structural type can be attributed to the movement of ideas along with the mobility of patrons. As can be seen in Table 3, there are instances of female patrons from Rajgir donating in Amarāvati and one instance also records a donation by a resident of Ujjeni, donating in Nāgarjunakonda.[20]

This extraneous influence is also visible at Ratnagiri (Mitra 1981:110–11), in two monolithic *stūpas* (group II) at the south-west corner of *stūpa* 1. One of these preserves a square platform comprising a recessed part with a set of three projecting facets at its base and top, the two sets being connected by a central dome with its diameter slightly smaller than that of the drum. Each of the four sides of the drum is relieved with the likeness of seven pillars, reminiscent of the *āyaka* pillars of the Krishna Valley; these pillars rise from the top of the platform and reaches to the height of the drum, which again does not present any projection. This would indicate that the craftsman was totally unfamiliar with such *stūpas* of the Krishna Valley and merely made an attempt to reproduce *āyaka* pillars at the instructions of a pilgrim from the region. The other *stūpa* has a *tri-ratha* platform with a square portion below to be buried inside the ground and a drum with two mouldings at its base; the major part of the drum along with the dome and crowning members is missing. Against the four sides of the drum are four sets of seven pillars, the bottom of each set resting on the central projection of the platform. The pillars of one of the sides of the drum of this *stūpa* have moulded bases somewhat resembling a *ghata* resting on a stand. The most common type of monolithic *stūpa* (group VII) found at the site consists of plain or decorated *stupas* relieved with an image inside a niche, in one specimen two images within separate niches, the total number being two hundred and seventy.

The most interesting aspect of these *stūpas* is that, among the divinities represented in this group, Tara outnumbers others. The second group of divinities in the descending numerical order are Buddha, Avalokitēsvara, Manjuśri, Marīchi and Vajrasattva. The representation of the other deities is very limited. Mitra has explained the preponderance of the figures of Tara in these votive *stūpas* due to her popularity as goddess of protection, warding off all kinds of perils, for her devotees. But the predominance of Tara figures in this particular type of monolithic *stūpas*, and lesser representation in other types of sacred architecture, like temples and *chaitya*s need to explained.

Thus we can say that the subject of the existence of specialised funerary customs for women within Buddhism is something that cannot be discarded perfunctorily and needs to be further explored. Another issue that needs to be explored in conjunction with this subject is the social structures and organisation at all the above-mentioned sites with respect to women. This has not been taken up for want of space, in order to limit the discussion. It is a vast subject and will make up the subject matter of another investigation.

All acts of commission and omission, rules and procedures pertaining to the daily lives of the *bhikṣuṇīs*, their conduct within the *Samgha* and outside it and also rules concerning rituals and worship are all to be found in the *Vinayas*, which govern all aspects of the lives of the monastics. The canons even prescribe the worship of the *stūpa*, which has been accorded religious sanction, by attributing it to the Buddha himself. In the given circumstances it is strange that the *bhikṣuṇīs* conduct the worship of Ānanda, which finds no mention and spiritual sanction in the canonical texts. It denotes to some extent a contravention of the prescriptions of the *Vinaya*. The conduct of specialised rituals and worship by women within Buddhism suggests a separate and parallel growth on spiritual and religious lines within

Buddhism. The fact that they looked up to Mahāpajāpati Gautamī as their institutional head, that they came to occupy imminent organisational positions (just as the monks did in the *bhikṣu Samgha*) within the *bhikṣuṇī Samgha*, that the *bhikṣuṇī Samgha* in due course came to host a number of prominent spiritual guides and masters, and that the *bhikṣuṇī Samgha* came to possess its very own customised set of the *Vinaya* and other canonical texts, further attests this point.

Overview

Thus, it is evident that just as in the literary records, multiple attitudes towards the feminine can be seen in the archaeological contexts as well. These attitudes are an extension of the views put forth by Sponberg (1992), as judged from his reading of the Buddhist texts.

In order to sum up, one can say that one cannot be totally objective while estimating 'the association of sacred and the feminine in Buddhism'. One cannot brand the Buddhist attitude towards women in relation to religion and associated issues as totally positive or totally negative, as hopeless and bad or as absolutely good and encouraging. The essentials of Buddhism as structured by the Gotama were complex and an amalgamation of the multiple societal reflections of the age. The essence of his teachings were largely conditioned by the social matrix from which he came, and these can largely be seen as being positive to women.

Thus, it can be concluded that the practice of enshrining of relics of women cannot be dismissed as fiction; secondly as seen in the case of Piprahawa, the remains in all probability consisted of the kinsmen of the Buddha with their sisters, wives and children. This would suggest that the practice was extended to the whole clan. But in the light of very limited data on the subject at present, it can only be said that this could be the privilege of a distinguished few, in this case being the members of the Sākya clan. But the association of *stūpas* dedicated to/by women appears to be very probable. All the *stūpa* sites associated with women are distinctive on plan. They are circular with projections in the cardinal directions. Contrary to the popularly accepted view that such *stūpas* with *āyaka* projections are a typical Andhra phenomenon, similar *stūpas*, having cruciform ground plan, have been reported from the north, west and east as well.[21] An analysis of the relics present at these *āyaka* sites comes up with unmistakable association with the feminine in some form or the other.[22] There is a similarity in the contents of the relics from most of these sites.

In the context of the above discussion, mention needs to be made of the cruciform temple of Mala Devi at Gyraspur, a small town 30 miles north of Sāñci, Madhya Pradesh.[23] It houses a beautiful image of Mala Devi or Lakshmi.[24] It belongs to a complex of structures – fort, temples and tanks – erected by the Pratihara Kings of Western India.[25] Early studies like those of Marshall's at Sāñci (Marshall and Foucher 1940) have described some of the feminine depictions at Sāñci as Māyā Devi, which were later identified with Lakshmi. In this case also the connection between Māyā Devi-Mala Devi and Lakshmi cannot be ruled out and needs to be further examined. Also a matter of further investigation is the correlation of this Jain temple, dedicated to a female deity with a cruciform ground plan. Whether this architectural arrangement in due course came to be adopted by religions other than Buddhism is also a matter to be further explored.

Coming to the depiction of themes on the *āyaka* panels, the sculptural depictions are mostly those of Buddhist themes, *Jātakas*, mythical beings and also *mithuna* couples. Of these, the *mithuna* couple appears as the most popular motif occurring with consistent frequency. The themes are mostly mundane and hardly seem to have been executed keeping in mind spiritual and doctrinal issues, and more in keeping with the popular demand and viewer and patron responses during the period. The *āyaka*s bear a number of inscriptions of donors at most of the sites. Though this book does not provide an absolute statistical account of the inscriptions recorded on *āyaka*s only, it has been observed from a cursory survey of the published data that, of the total number of donor inscriptions on the *āyaka* platforms, a substantial number is that of female donors. This fact needs to be backed by further research on the subject.

Thus, going by the above argument it can be said that *stūpas* with *āyaka* projections and a cruciform ground plan could have certainly had some gender connotation, which in turn would suggest a difference in *stūpa* architecture dedicated to men from those of the women. This practice, though, does not seem to have survived among the latter-day Buddhists. In fact, present-day Buddhist countries seem to have well-entrenched notions of pollution and purity which cannot be easily shaken off. From the available data[26] it is evident that these structures were associated with laywomen. The find of *āyaka*-type *stūpas* from sites outside the Andhra region needs to be seen in a different context, and explained going beyond the simplistic explanation of being a regional peculiarity, and while doing so it must be borne in mind that they continued to exist alongside their more common counterpart, that is, the circular type, without the *āyaka* projections.

In course of time, as the Dharma spread across regions to areas far and wide, many changes and alterations had to be made into the original doctrinal fabric by the Buddha, contained in the *Vinaya*, in keeping with the prevailing social norms. These contradictions mainly sprang from the differences in the basic structuring of the societies,[27] and though most of the changes were made keeping in mind practical considerations, the social context that made these rules viable and relevant for the most part were patriarchal societies. This also probably explains the wide, unbridgeable chasm, between practicing Buddhist female patrons, on the one hand, and the great female divinities that invoke fear, subservience, devotion and the like, among their followers, on the other. Thus, on one hand, we have women followers who in their individual, lay or monastic capacities have been successful in attaining their ultimate spiritual goals and those who have successfully earned the reverence and devotion of fellow members; on the other hand, we have these divine forms or goddesses. The latter have been invested with extraordinary powers, spiritual, mental as well as physical. This conscious portrayal and rendering of the feminine as 'the ideal' by attributing to them superhuman qualities was done in order to create an unbridgeable divide between women and goddesses. This was a common phenomenon taking place at the time simultaneously within Brahmanism, Buddhism and Jainism, respectively.

Notes

1 The Tripitaka mentions 500 and more *bhikṣūṇīs*. There were 13 who were singled out and received praise from the Buddha for their different distinctions:
I. Maha Pajapati was praised for her long standing as the first *bhikṣūṇī*.
II. Khema Thēri, former queen of King Bimbisara, was praised for her wisdom.
III. Upalavanna Thēri was praised for her achievement in performing miracles.
IV Patacāra Thēri was praised for her good memory on the Vinaya.
V. Dhammadinnā Thēri was praised for being capable in teaching.
VI. Nandā Thēri was praised for meditation.
VII. Sonā Thēri was praised for her patience.
VIII. Sakula Thēri was praised for having divine sights.
IX. Kundalakēsi Thēri was praised for achieving sudden enlightenment.
X. Bhaddā Kapilani was praised for remembering past lives.
XI. Bhaddā Kaccana (Princess Yasodhara) was praised for her Great Abhinna.

XII. Kisā Gotami was praised for wearing coarse robes.
XIII. Sigalamātā was praised for holding fast to faith.

2 She is called the Mango girl (Āmra Girl) in the Southern records. (*Sacred Books of the East*, Vol. xi. p. 33). She was a courtesan, otherwise called Ambāpālī. For an account of her birth and history, see S. Hardy, *Manual of Buddhism*, p. 327.

3 Nagaraju, S. *Buddhist Architecture of Western India, c. 250* B.C.*-c.* A.D. *300*, New Delhi: Agam Kala Prakashan, 1981.

4 A.S.I., Annual Report, 1935–6, pp. 63–4.

5 A mould of the figure was recovered from the same trench, which suggests that it was made locally at the site.

6 Refer to comparative chart (Figure 4.4) showing total number of men donors versus women donors.

7 *M.A.S.I.*, No. 71, pl. XXXIX – a, p. 24.

8 Retrieved on October 20, 2014 from http://www.dawn.com/2012/02/07/rare-indus-seal-discovered-in-cholistan.html.

9 As a female deity has no place in the Buddhist pantheon of the early centuries before Christ, it may be concluded that she represents the survival of a pre-Buddhistic divinity and also that the custom of depositing her likeness along with cremated human remains is of pre-Buddhistic origins (Coomaraswamy 1928:68–9).

10 *Journal of the Royal Asiatic Society of Great Britain and Ireland*, 1898, p. 388.

11 *Ibid.*, p. 588, fn. 1.

12 *Ibid.*, 1906, p. 150.

13 Chatsumarn Kabilsingh, Buddhist Studies, Buddha Dharma Education Association and Buddhanet. www.buddhanet.net/e-learning/history/wbq21.htm.

14 In the Cūllavagga, Ānanda is believed to have enquired of the Buddha:
"How are we to conduct ourselves, Lord with regard to womankind?"
"Don't see them, Ānanda."
" But if we should see them, what are we to do?"
"Abstain from speech Ānanda."
"But if they should speak to us, Lord, what are we to do?"
"Keep wide awake, Ānanda."

(Cūllavagga; V.23)

15 Table showing Buddhist *stūpa* sites in India, with *āyaka* projections.

16 A Parasol Inscription from the site, dated on paleographical grounds to the third century B.C. (*E.I.*, Vol. XL, No. 21), further attests to female presence at the site. It records that the parasol was a gift of Samgharakshita, which was 'caused to be made' by three women – Pusa, Dharmarakshita and Araha, pupils (*antevasini*) of Koramika (probably a Buddhist nun).

17 Queen of Kshemagupta, who erected a *vihāra* in her name; also a bronze image of Lokeshwara (A.D. 950–1003) consecrated during her reign. (Debala Mitra, *Buddhist Monuments*, rep. 1980, p. 107.)

18 Queens of Meghavana.
19 *Ibid.*
20 Table showing spread of donors from various sites in relation to the sites of donations.
21 See Table 4. List showing details of all the *stūpa* sites with *āyaka* projections.
22 *Ibid.*
23 Retrieved on November 29, 2010 from http://www.pilgrimtrips.com/indiantemples/temple-of-india-where-it-all-began.
24 Retrieved on November 29, 2010 from http://www.tcindia.com/citifacts/jabalpur.
25 Constructed between the 10th and11th centuries A.D., Mala Devi is a precursor to the forts of Rajputana (as Rajasthan was formerly known), with its balconies and windows, elevated location and intricate carving of religious motifs across its exterior. Its curving *shikhara* is topped by a sculpted *amalaka* (dome or crown), and it possesses, in addition to its sanctum, a *pradakshina path*, vestibule and covered *maṇḍapa*.
26 Refer to the inscriptions from Piprahawa and Nāgarjunakonda.
27 We will, for convenience, term these as patriarchal and matriarchal societies.

Two

Locating the *bhikṣunī*

Identifying nunneries

In continuation of the theme from the previous chapter, which discusses the concept of sacred spaces for Buddhist women, this chapter attempts to identify *bhikṣunī vihārikās* or monastic convents for the Buddhist nuns. Primary as well as secondary works on Buddhism are either silent or skim through the subject of monastic residences for *bhikṣūṇīs* rather summarily. Though there are innumerable references to monasteries in the literary as well as the epigraphic records for monks, there are hardly any for the *bhikṣūṇīs*. At the few Indian sites where the archaeologically excavated structures have been identified with nunneries, the explanations are hardly convincing. At Sirpur, one of the monastic structures (SRP 1–2000) has been identified as a nunnery by the excavator (Sharma 2007) on the basis of a large number of glass bangle fragments from the site.

This view is hardly convincing, as one finds injunctions in the canons against the use of jewellery and cosmetics by the *bhikṣūṇīs*. The finding of a solitary bangle or similar possessions may be construed as objects preserved as souvenirs or memorabilia, kept by some nun from her premonastic days but the excessively large finds of bangle fragments from a nunnery cannot be accepted as a criterion by which to designate it a nunnery. Archaeological evidences for nunneries in South Asia are almost negligible. This chapter seeks to discuss the concept of residential quarters for the female monastics. Along with the exercise of identifying and locating the documentary and literary evidence on nunneries and corroborating it with actual archaeological evidence on the ground, the concept of individual and communal spaces for the *bhikṣūṇīs* in architectural plans of *vihāras* will be explored. With only a few stray literary references on the subject, this chapter is an attempt to correlate archaeological and literary data and formulate a model by which to identify nunneries or Buddhist *vihārikās* for the female monastics. Due to inadequate literary and epigraphic data on the subject and almost negligible archaeological data, ethnographic data from present-day nunneries and the lives of the *bhikşūṇīs* have also been incorporated in this study.

It involves examining the continuities and architectural patterns at the Buddhist monastic sites, taking into account the subtle architectural deviations. The emerging differences have been analysed from a gendered perspective, and these divergences are explained based on Buddhist architectural stipulations recorded in the canonical texts regarding the shape and form of nunneries.

The survey of literary data on the subject takes into account all the direct and indirect references to *bhikşūṇīs* and nunneries from various texts like the *Therigāthā* (that has references to the places the *bhikşūṇīs* hailed from), the *Mahasamghika Vinaya* and the like. The latter provides various regulations that governed the lives of monastic women. The first kind of evidence is in the form of direct reference to nunneries; for example, it mentions the various names of places visited by the Buddha, where he made additions/changes to the laws governing the lives of the *bhikşūṇīs*. Even if these events are taken to be later incorporations made into the original body of the *Vinaya*, there is little reason to doubt that these places may have housed *bhikşūṇīs*. Another reason that supports this point is that of the numerous places where Buddhism existed, only a handful of place names occur repeatedly. This repetition of place names in connection with the rules made by the Buddha, concerning *bhikşūṇīs*, points to the association of these places, in some form or the other with *bhikşūṇīs* and nunneries. The second kind of data is in the form of indirect references, such that the *Vinaya* rules provide an insight into the norms that governed the location of *bhikşūṇī vihāras*, their types and so forth.

In order to assess and identify nunneries, a comprehensive analysis of the monastic structures from the excavated Buddhist sites together with the associated finds has been undertaken. The choice of Buddhist sites has been done primarily on the basis of references to sites that find mention in the primary literary works in connection with *bhikşūṇīs*, such as Sravasti,[1] Sāñci, Vallabhi and so on followed by those sites that find mention in the donor records of the *bhikşūṇīs* and other related epigraphic data.

The epigraphic data (donor records) referring to sites associated with *bhikşūṇīs* have been discussed in the second chapter. An attempt to correlate the epigraphic records with archaeological finds has been attempted. One recurring problem encountered in this case is the identification of the archaeological sites from the donor records, and their archaeological correlation.

The determining of an archaeological model will, in the absence of adequate literary data, rely largely on borrowing from ethnographic data on the subject, compiled through field work and interviews with *bhikşūṇīs* based presently in Dharamsala and also other secondary, published, ethnographic researches on the subject.

Literary data on residential provision for the *bhiksūṇīs*

The *Pāli Vinaya* and the *Sutta Pitaka* consists of a mass of material which are overwhelmingly religious in nature and highly problematic in chronology. The historical material which can be extracted from this mass is mainly in the form of similes, stories, direct verbal statements and objective observation. Perhaps only a fraction is in the form of direct historical description and even that, in fact, is highly formalised. It is also very repetitive and full of contradictions. But the incidental nature of this material increases its value as a source of history. In the *Pāli Pitakas* most of the sayings and speeches are related circumstantially to where and on what occasion Gautama Buddha and/or various *theras* and *theris* voiced them.

The literary survey involves an analysis of texts such as the *Vinaya* literature, especially those pertaining to the *bhikşūṇīs*, like the *Bhikşūṇīs Vinaya*. There are incidental references in the *Vinaya* literature, for example, to certain places like Kapilavastu, where Mahāpajāpati Gautamī along with 500 others joined the order. These are casual references that occur in the context of rules being made at various places, visited by the Buddha during the course of his discourses. These rules pertained to various issues such as the day-to-day acts of the *bhikşūṇīs*, their interaction with the fraternity of monks and the laity and also rules related to their acts in faith and spiritual practice. Likewise in the *Therigāthā* (which are poems of a biographical character) one also finds references to place names that had their association, directly or indirectly with the *bhikşūṇīs*.

The other site names that find frequent mention in conjunction with *bhikşūṇīs* are Rajagaha, Vaishali, Kausambi, Sravasti and so on. Yet others are referred to in the memoirs and chronicles of the Chinese travellers; for example, the Chinese monk Sheng-chi, a contemporary of I-Tsing, who visited Samatata in the second half of the seventh century A.D., found 4,000 monks and *bhikṣūṇīs* there. I-Tsing himself stayed in the Bha-ra ha Monastery, where he learnt Sanskrit and Philosophy (Śabda Vidya) (Takakasu, Itsing, Ch. X: 62–5). Interestingly he also mentions also a monastery which was then 'inhabited by both monks and *bhikṣūṇīs*'. Clearly it needs to be noted that the *Bhikṣūṇī Samgha* was an extension of the *Bhikṣū Samgha* and therefore all the rules and procedure laid down for the latter applied to a large extent to the *Bhikṣūṇī Samgha* as well, even though the *bhikṣūṇīs* were governed with more stringent regulations than their male counterparts.

This is further attested by an examination of the *Bhikṣūṇī Vinaya* where all the norms governing the conduct and lives of the *bhikṣūṇīs* are the same as that for the *bhikṣū*, except for a few alterations.

A few of the terms from the *Bhikṣūṇī Vinaya* that elucidate the norms governing monastic living for both *bhikṣūṇīs* and *bhikṣūs* are cited below.

> Harmony (*samagga*) refers to cooperation in the life of the order (*samana-samvasaka*), to being within the same boundaries (*samana-simaya thito*). Cooperative life (*samana-samvasaka*) refers to both cooperation materially (*amisasam-bhoga*) and spiritually (*dhamma-sambhoga*).

Cooperation in material things refers to the equitable use of the monastery, its beds, bedding, implements and property. Also contributions from lay believers, such as food or clothing, are to be equally divided between both the groups. Cooperation in spiritual matters means that all members of the fraternity put their faith in the three jewels, observe the precepts and practice in the same way. Performing the *kamma* together is especially important since the *kamma* determines the will of the order. *Samana-simaya thito* refers to the fact that the order's communal life is established using the boundaries (*simā*)[2] to define the basic unit (Hirakawa 1999).

These terms applied significantly to members of both the orders and are a reflection of the close ties between them. The rules governing the *Samgha* were structured such so as to make interaction and cooperation between them in everyday matters a prerequisite for the smooth functioning of the *Samgha* and for the existence of the *Samgha* as one, unitary organisation.

The references to the order of the *bhikṣūṇīs*, in the literary texts, appear in various contexts. There are references to Mahāpajāpati Gautamī being made the superior of the order of the *bhikṣūṇīs* by the

Buddha. The following terms like *samhasthavira, Saṁghamahāttari* and *Saṁgha-thavirina* denote the term superior in the *Bhikṣūṇīs Vinaya.*[3]

There are references to a co-resident disciple (*antevasini sardhavi-harini*) which refers to some kind of organised residential facility for the *bhikṣūṇīs* that also had novices (*antevāsinis*) as its residents.[4] The same text employs the term *Sramanerikās* for female novices and *Shiksamana* for probationary *bhikṣūṇīs*. The difference between the various categories for the female monastics is further brought out by the use of such terms as 'visiting *bhikṣūṇīs*' (who have been referred to as being assigned rooms (in the nunnery) in accordance to their ages).[5] Reference to the *kappiya-kārika*, or the nunnery servant girl, indicates the provision for an organised, institutional residential set-up for the female monastic members with a structured and well-defined hierarchy of support personnel that included among others the *kappiya-kārika*[6] and the *kalpiya-karika* (temple servant girl).[7] There is also a rule on the delegation of duties to the *bhikṣūṇīs* within the nunnery.[8]

Relations between the *Bhikṣu Samgha* and *Bhikṣūṇī Samgha*, as reflected in the literary texts

The order of the monks and the order of the *bhikṣūṇīs* were basically independent of each other. They were self-governing institutions basing themselves on the *Pratimokśa*. However, the two orders could not remain entirely separate for various reasons enumerated below, and also for reasons of security; it was laid down in the canons that a *Bhikṣūṇī Vihāra* should preferably be located within the bounds of a city/village unlike a monastery, which should be neither far nor very near to the city. Literary evidences of nunneries in direct terms, though meagre, give sporadic insights to certain aspects of identifying the *Bhikṣūṇī Vihāras*. There are numerous rules pertaining to the location of retreats and/or monastic quarters for the *bhikṣūṇīs*. These rules give an indication to the precise location for the situation of *bhikṣūṇīs*' residences. This is further substantiated by archaeological evidence, as during the course of excavation at Sravasti, quite a few monasteries such as Jetavana and others were found close to the city walls. Also in literature (Vn. V., IV.264), the almswomen are incidentally portrayed as bringing raw wheat for their food from the fields, through the toll at the city entrance, into their *vihāra* at Sāvatthi.

The rules laid down concerning the relations between the two orders of the monks and the *bhikṣūṇīs* had a significant bearing on the location of monastic residences for the *bhikṣūṇīs*. Some such rules that had affected and determined the situation of monastic sanctuaries for the *bhikṣūṇīs* are discussed below.

Since the men and women of the two orders were to live lives of abstinence, strict rules concerning the relations between the two orders were necessary. These were called the *gurudhamme* or *gurudhammah*. There are eight of these. According to the *Bhikṣūṇī khandaka*, when the Buddha, in response to Mahāpajāpati Gautamī's request, allowed women to become *bhikṣuṇīs*, he also set forth the eight *gurudhammas* (Hirakawa 37–8).

Following is a concise list of the conditions regulating the relations between the two orders:

(1) The *Bhikṣūṇī Samgha* sits below the *Bhikṣu Samgha* indicating a formalised hierarchical composition within the *Samgha*.

(2) The *bhikṣuṇīs* are to report to the *Bhikṣu Samgha* every fortnight so as to ascertain correct observation of the *uposatha*. At the same time they ask for admonitions from the *Bhikṣu Samgha*. The *Bhikṣu Samgha*, using a *nattidutiya-kamma*, chooses one of its members to admonish the *bhikṣuṇī*. That monk then goes to admonish the *bhikṣūṇī*.

The second *gurudharma* stipulates the correct procedure for the ordination of the *bhikṣuṇī*. The full ordination of the *bhikṣuṇīs* should first be performed in the order of the *bhikṣuṇī* and then in the order of the *bhikṣus*. This is termed ordination in both orders (*ubhatosaṁgha*).[9]

(3) When the *bhikṣūṇīs* hold the rainy season retreat, they must choose a place in the same vicinity where monks are holding their rainy season retreat. *Bhikṣūṇīs* may not hold their retreat in a place where no monks reside.

(4) When a *bhikṣuṇī* commits a *Saṁghadisesa* offence, she must perform a fortnight's penance (*manatta*) in both orders. (A *bhikṣu* would only perform it for seven days in the *Bhikṣu Samgha*.)

(5) The *upasampada* ordination for a *bhikṣuṇī* is first performed in the *Bhikṣuṇī Samgha*, and then in the *Bhikṣu Samgha*. It cannot be performed only in the *Bhikṣuṇī Samgha*.

Living by the norms laid out in the *gurudhamma* would clearly necessitate the situation of the residences for the two orders reasonably close together, as most of the practices were to be performed jointly by members of both the orders. This point becomes clearer when we look at other similar practices that were laid down for the *bhikşūṇīs*, for instance when a *bhikṣu* has been appointed as instructor to the *bhikşūṇīs*. There were eight rules concerning the instruction of the *bhikşūṇīs* by the *bhikṣus*. Of these eight, the last pertains to 'greeting the instructor'. Hirakawa discusses the various acts that constituted infringements of *Vinaya* rules and the associated punishments for the different kinds of transgressions. From the above-mentioned rules, the following facts are borne out: nunneries were assumed to be located reasonably close to a monastery or monasteries for the observance of common rituals jointly. But this was not applicable at all times. Sometimes the location of nunneries could be at reasonable distance from the monasteries. This is clearly brought out in the last mentioned rule.

The *Vinaya* also mentions the various circumstances when the *bhikşūṇīs* could stay away from the boundaries of the convent. If a nun was invited to spend her period of retreat with her kins, she could do so, provided she had a senior monk to accompany her.

The seventh *gurudhamma*[10] stipulates that a *bhikşūṇīs* should not pass the rainy season by living alone without relying upon a *bhikṣu*. She must ensure before accepting the invitation that first the 'high and respected (Order of *bhikṣus*)' is invited. The arrangement of putting up with the lay relatives could not be a permanent dwelling for a nun, but only a temporary retreat, especially during *vassāvāsa*. It also elucidates that, 'If there is residence for members of the Order (*Saṁgharāma*) within three *yojanas*, her residence should be included within the same boundary (*simā*) and she ought to go each half-month and observe the *Upōsatha* (day). When the rainy season[11] has ended, the *bhikşūṇīs* ought to repent their offences in the two orders'. A related reference to this can be found in the *Mahasaṁghika Bhikşūṇī Vinaya* which states:

> The Buddha was staying in the Monastery of the Sākya clan in the Nyaggrodha (Forest) of Kapilavastu. At that time, the Blessed One set forth the precepts, and did not permit the *bhikşūṇīs* to stay in the *araṇya* (forest-dwellings). Now, as there were yet no nunneries within the villages, the *bhikşūṇī* Rastra stayed at the house of the Sākya clan and taught the sutras to the young people of the Sakya clan.[12]

Gradually in the absence of adequate provision for monastic residential accommodation for the *bhikşūṇīs*, this temporary arrangement that was restricted to the period of *vassāvāsa* came to acquire a permanent character, with many *bhikṣūṇīs* preferring to continue to live with their families. This system continues till the present day, and can be seen in the case of many of the *bhikṣūṇīs* hailing from Kinnaur, who live in the villages of Kanum and Kalpi with their relatives.[13]

It was also considered an offence to live in solitary confinement. The *Vinaya* mentions an instance wherein several *bhikṣūṇīs* took up separate lodgings, each living alone outside of the city. It was considered an act of transgression, to be repented; but an exception was to be made if there was a crisis or confusion due to war in the city (Hirakawa, *op. cit.* p. 148).

There was also an injunction against staying at one place for long. A *bhikṣu* or a *bhikṣūṇīs* is allowed to eat one meal at a public rest house. If a *bhikṣu* or *bhikṣūṇīs* stays for several days at a rest house when he or she is not sick, it constitutes a *pacattika* offence (*ibid.*, p. 234).

If a *bhikṣūṇī* took up lodging apart from the other *bhikṣūṇīs* during the period from sunset to dawn, her act constituted a *Saṁghatisesa* offense. This indicates a rule that made it mandatory for *bhikṣūṇīs* to stay in an organised group, and not outside it, in the absence of valid reasons (*ibid.*, p. 237). There was also an injunction against staying over three nights (with someone who is not a fully ordained nun).[14]

If a *bhikṣūṇīs* has taken the *upasampada* ordination, she ought to serve and attend to her preceptor (*upadhyāyini*) for at least two years. Unless she serves and attends to (her preceptor), her act constitutes a *pacattika* offense. This can be taken to mean that the two continued to dwell in the same place or monastic residence for a minimum of at least two years. This precept must have necessitated the provision for some sort of monastic residences, governed by *sima* regulations, for the newly ordained novices and their preceptors.

Another rule required that two monastic residences or nunneries be situated at a distance of at least five to six *yojanas* apart. The need to punish a novice *bhikṣūṇī* for transgression by her superior by sending her away, to a distance of at least five to six *yojanas* called for the making of this rule. (If she fails to do so, her act constitutes a *pacattika* offence.)

This can further be taken to suggest that, if a *bhikṣūṇī* lodges outside of the precincts during the rainy day assembly, her act constitutes a *pacattika* offence. A *bhikṣūṇī* should not ask for a *karma* from the order that she be allowed to leave in order to manage the *stūpa's* or monastery's affairs during the rainy season assembly. The boundaries used for the rainy season retreat were narrowly defined, often as the fences or walls surrounding the monastery. The term 'travel' in this precept referred to leaving the Order's boundaries and spending the night beyond them.

If a *bhikṣūṇī* does not go away at the end of the rainy season assembly, her act constitutes a *pacattika* offence. 'Going away' in this context denotes 'change of station'. This could also mean going out of the nunnery or village/town (in case she was putting up with her relatives) where the *bhikṣūṇīs* had spent her rain retreat, and spending a night beyond the limits of that nunnery or village/town.

'Not go away for pilgrimage' means: if she does not go out of the village at least, her act constitutes a *pacattika* offence. Unless a *bhikṣūṇīs* goes out of the boundaries and stays away at least one night, her act constitutes a *pacattika* offence (Hirakawa 1999).

Evolution of Buddhist monastic architecture

A discussion on the monastic residences/retreats for Buddhist *bhikṣūṇīs* would require a survey of the history, origin and subsequent development of different kinds of monastic accommodation as recorded in the literary works.

The early *Samgha* at its inception came into being as a small yet distinguished community of wanderers, and in due course transformed itself from a wandering community to a settled order. But even at this later date, quite a few monks preferred a life of seclusion, often keeping their retreat in the forests.

The *bhikṣūṇīs* order from the very beginning was an extension of the monks order, which meant that, from the very outset, all the rules and norms that applied to the monks was automatically applicable to the order of *bhikṣūṇīs* also. As a result there is reference to *bhikṣūṇīs* who lived lives of seclusion as wanderers, some even dwelling in the forests as mentioned in the *Mahāsamghika Bhikṣūṇī Vinaya* (Hirakawa 1999). In due course this order was revoked and female Buddhist mendicants were prohibited from leading solitary lives in the forests.

The rule that a wanderer must suspend wandering and remain in retreat during the season of rains, that is, *vassā*, in a congregation of fellow *bhikṣūs* or *bhikṣūṇīs*, led to the emergence of *vassa-vāsa*. For that purpose, the settlement needed sequestration within its own boundaries. The demarcation and fixing of boundaries (*simā*), therefore, became a matter of some significance in order to allow a body of *bhikṣūs/bhikṣūṇīs* to live together by themselves.

Though a class among them preferred to live in the forest clearings for which they earned the name of *Arannakās* (forest dwellers), the majority of *bhikṣūs* preferred to have their *vassā* retreats in localities where alms were available. Normally these settlements were located in both towns and villages where the *bhikṣūs* could live in congregation of their own and subsist on alms. The problem of accommodation for the rain retreat, however, would not be the same in the city as in the countryside.

In the latter, the boundary settlement would be the first task for the monks and the shelters would have to be built by them unlike in a town or city, where a wealthy lay patron would generously provide (as an act of piety), permanent dwellings or parks, for the use of the monks, during the *vassā* period, his or her own private park or pleasure garden. Thus two kinds of settlements for rain retreats or *vassā-vāsa* came into existence: (1) the *āvāsa* in the countryside, staked out, built and maintained by the monks themselves and (2) the *ārāma*, in or near a town or city, situated within its own private enclosure and looked after by the donor.

When first instituted, the *āvāsa* and the *ārāma* were in the nature of encampments strictly temporary in character: residence in them being limited to the three rainy months. If any residential house was temporarily left by the monks for repairs, it could be reserved for reoccupation, but never beyond the limited *vassa* period. There are indications of a growing practice among the monks of returning to and reoccupying the same *āvāsas* and *ārāmas*, on the termination of the wandering period. Thus, those who habitually lived together for the *vassā* in one *āvāsa* (*Samana-samvasaka*) were distinguished from those who habitually lived together in another (*Nana-samvasaka*). And thus gradually these annual sojourns of the monks, that is, *vassa-vāsa*, tended to increasingly turn into establishments of a semi-permanent character.[15]

The monk-built *avāsa* was after all a temporary set-up, liable to be deserted, robbed and dismantled after its evacuation by monks at the end of the *vassā* period. An *arāma*, on the contrary, was more durable and resilient. It stood within an enclosure, obviating the laborious necessity of *simā*-fixation. Perhaps there were also some readymade structures within it. Besides, its maintenance was the voluntary responsibility of the donor. Even a more important consideration perhaps was that an *arāma*, by its permanent situation, favoured the continuance from one *vassā* period to another, of those features of collective life that had already emerged in the *Samgha*. While in the legends we find many references by name to those *arāmas* which became famous *Samgha* centres, none of the a*vāsā* centres bear a name. The *arāmā* was thus apparently a superior kind of habitat for *vassa-vāsa*.

The name *arāma* denotes a pleasure ground (an orchard or a flower garden), usually the property within a town or city or in the suburb of an affluent patron. When the owner offered it permanently to the *Samgha*, it was named a *Saṁgharāma*. The term, meaning originally an *arāma* owned by the *Samgha*, later came to shed its implication of a donated pleasure ground and meant simply a campus, and eventually came to denote a large monastery, occupied by a company of monks. The donor of an *arāma* would willingly continue to maintain the property and for the purpose employ a special staff of servants (*arāmika*) and superintendents (*arāmika-pesaka*) to look after the *arāma*.

An *avāsa* was by no means an organised monastery, but only a colony of monks which constituted the seat of the *Samgha*. It was also circumscribed by its *simā*[16](limits) as to be completely independent and unitary. There are many textual references to the broad features of Buddhist monastic sites. Within its boundaries or *simā*, an a*vāsa* or an *arāma* had huts for the monks' dwelling, and *vihāra* was the name originally given to such a hutment, although the term in its later usage came to mean something different. A *vihāra* might be occupied by a single monk or by a small group of monks, and in the latter case, the allotted portion for each monk was called a *pariveṇā*. In the earliest cave monasteries (second century A.D.) of Western India, the arrangement is to have in each cave a living room comparatively large, entered through a narrow porch in front, and dormitory cells around the living room, opening into it. But in the *vihāras* of the North which were originally of wood and thatch, the *pariveṇās* were probably just partitioned apartments. A common storage room or area for such articles as were allowable to monks was called *Kāppiya-kuti*, which was a necessary adjunct in Buddhist monastic structures.

Among the structural needs that arose from the institution of congregational rites and activities was the need for a permanent meeting Hall, especially for the *uposatha* observance.[17] The constant need for a specified congregational venue culminated in the creation of the *upatthana-śāla*, which came to be a permanent architectural appendage of Buddhist monastic architecture.

Though *simā* regulations governed the situation of Buddhist monastic residences for *bhikṣūṇīs*, the stipulations pertaining to monastic residences for the *bhikṣūṇīs* were slightly more flexible than those for their male counterparts. A synoptic account of the rules enumerated above leads us to conclude that

> A *Bhikṣūṇī vihāra* should be located close to a *vihāra* for various reasons like
> (i) security,
> (ii) observance of common rituals like *uposatha* and the like, in the company of monks and so on,
> (iii) economic considerations, like the sharing of the proceeds of *dāna*, made to the *Samgha* also necessitated that the *bhikṣūṇīs*' residences be set up close to that of the monks. As has been discussed earlier, it was the monks' community that was more inclined to receive the donations from the lay community, as compared to that of the *bhikṣūṇīs*.

As the community of the *bhikṣūṇīs* was not as economically prosperous as the community of the monks nor was it likely to receive large donations (for various reasons) like its counterpart, the *Bhikṣūṇīs Samgha* was a loosely constituted body, as far as rules pertaining to residential norms were concerned. In the absence of large donations, the number of convents for the *bhikṣūṇīs* must have been severely limited, and could not have accommodated all its members. Therefore as has been pointed out earlier, it was not uncommon for *bhikṣūṇīs* to continue to stay with their kin, in their houses, although they continued to strictly observe the rules with regard to celibacy, that is, the *silās* or the moral precepts. Though in the case of the monks there are no references to monks putting up permanent residences with their kin, once they had taken up the renunciant's robes. The *bhikṣūṇīs*' residences were to be located in the close vicinity of a monks' *vihāra* so as to make the routine and periodic observance of rituals possible. Considerations of security were instrumental in the formation of rules that prohibited a practicing nun from

(a) leading the life of a wanderer,[18]
(b) living alone in the forest[19] or
(c) travelling alone.[20]

Even 'going away' at the end of the stipulated three-month '*vassā*-retreat' was circumscribed by 'going out of the village' or probably to the next village, 'on pilgrimage' and staying away from her 'place of residence' for at least one night.

In the absence of adequate literary references to *vihāra/vihārikas* for *bhikṣūṇīs*, it can be inferred that most of the *bhikṣūṇīs* found sanctuary in *avāsas*, which were located in the villages or in their close vicinity. These were temporary, short-term settlements that fail to make their presence felt in the historical records of the period. Moreover the erection of *vihāras* and *arāmas* would also require the mobilisation of large resources, which was a daunting task for the *bhikṣūṇīs*, as most of the *dāna* that came to the *Samgha* was made to the community of the monks. Therefore, it can be presumed that the residential provision for the *bhikṣūṇīs* was most likely of the nature of makeshift encampments to which additions and alterations were made as and when resources were made available to them. (Most of these were situated in the villages. These improvised, makeshift nunneries came up in most cases, at places that happened to house a group of *bhikṣūṇīs*.)

Epigraphic data pertaining to institutionalised residential accommodation for the *bhikṣūṇīs*

The term *Vihārasvāmini* which occurs in two inscriptions – the Sui Vihāra copper plate inscription of the year 11 of Kanishka's reign (Konow C.*I.I.*, Pt 1:140ff) and the Mathura Stone Image inscription of the year 135(Fleet C.*I.I.*, III:263) – has been variously interpreted. Hornele, who edited the Sui Vihāra inscription in 1881, rendered the term as 'the owner of the *Vihāra*'. Similarly Fleet (C.*I.I.*, III:263) and Sten Konow (cf. C.*I.I.*, II. Pt 1:141) explained the term mentioned in the Mathura Stone Image inscription of the year 135, as 'mistress' (lady-superintendent) of a *vihāra*. D.C. Sircar, reading of the term, also explains it as the female owner of a *vihāra*.[21] Hence we have a definite linguistic terminology for a superior or in-charge of a Buddhist convent for *bhikṣunīs*, that is, the *Vihārasvāmini*.

It is also supported by the Pāli tradition, where a clear distinction is drawn between the two types of *vihāras* called *sāmika* (*svāmika*) and *asāmika* (*asvāmika*). The most senior monk or nun of *asāmika vihāra* was called an *achārya*, *nāyaka* and so on but never a *Vihārasvamin* or *Vihārasvamini*. On the other hand, in a *sāmika-vihārahe* monk in charge or the most senior nun alone was known as *Vihārasvāmin* or *Vihārasvaminī*.[22] Taken in this light, both the terms can be understood as 'monk-in-charge' of a *sāmika-vihāra* for *vihārasvāmin* and 'nun-in-charge' for *vihārasvāmini*, respectively.[23] A copper plate of unknown provenance (now in the possession of the Asiatic Society) records the grant of lands to the ratna-treya of the *Vendamati Vihārika*[24] by the Buddhist king Bhavadeva (*c.* eighth century A.D.). This charter was issued from Devaparvata (Mainamati–Lalmai range) (Mitra 1980:245). Another reference from this region was that of the Jayasrama vihāra, situated in Northern Tosala in the mid-ninth century A.D. It was in this monastery that Sivakaradeva III at the request of the Ranaka Sri Vinitatunga executed a copper plate grant in the year 149 Bhauma Year or A.D. 885 , donating the revenue of the village Kallani, according to the rules of Nividharma, for Buddha Bhattaraka.[25] The said plate was discovered in a small village named Jagati near Talcher. The only Buddhist Buddhist remains so far discovered are probably associated with the Jayaśrama Vihāra, and Pt B. Misra (Misra, B. *Orissa Under the Bhauma Kings*, Calcutta, 1934, p. 34) suggests this might be the location of the Vihara. The sanctuary of Buddha Bhattaraka was built by Amubhattarakara probably within the precincts of the Jayasrama Vihāra, where both monks and *bhikṣūṇīs* were residing together, and it is known from the plate that 10 attendants had been appointed to look after the comforts of the *bhikṣūṇīs* only.

A few donations reveal a small cluster of convents near the famous Buddhist 'University' at Valabhi (last on record, A.D. 629) (Virji 1995:263, 287). A *maṇḍala* (group of monasteries/nunneries), founded by one Yaksasri, was intended for the *bhikṣūṇīs*. The names of these nunneries too appear from the grants: (i) Yaksasura Vihāra built by Yaksasura (ii) Purnabhatta Vihāra built by Purnabhatta and (iii) Ajita Vihāra built by a merchant named Ajita. Both Siladitya I and Dhruvasena II made grants to some of these nunneries, in Vallabhi under the patronage of the Maitrakas (Dutt 1962/1988). One of the important monasteries of Valabhi was the one built by the *upāsikās*, the sister's daughter of the Maitraka ruler Dhruvasena I, the latter granting to it two villages in Gupta – Vallabhi years 216 (A.D. 535–36) and 217 (A.D. 536–37). This *vihāra* flourished for nearly a century and a half, due to lavish patronage it recieved for its maintenance, from the successors of Dhruvasena I. It became the head of *Vihāra Mandala* into which were included the monasteries built by Āchārya Bhikṣu Sthiramatī, Ācharya Bikśu Vimalagupta, Gohaka and the merchant Kakka. Besides these, there were others of which Buddhadasa Vihāra, Abhayantrika Vihāra built by Mimma, Bhatarkka Vihāra, Bappadiya Vihāra built by Acharya Bhadanta Stiramati, the nunneries built by Yakshasura, Puranabhatta and the merchant Ajita and a *Vihāra* made by the Divirapati Skandabhata, the last constructed by Yodhavaka deserve special mention. The Yakshasura Vihāra in course of time became the head of the Vihāra Mandala and the Purnabhatta Vihāra was included within its precincts. Hiuen-Tsang refers to the large monastery near the capital in which the P'usas Gunamati and Sthiramati had lodged and composed treatise which had great vogue (Watters 1905:246). According to Chau-ju-kua (*c.* A.D. 1250) Hu-Ch'-la (Gujarat) had at this time '4000 Buddhist temple buildings, in which lived over 20,000 dancing girls who twice daily offered food to the Buddha (i.e. the idols) and while offering flowers'.[26]

This reference to the existence of dancing girls or Devadasis as part of Buddhist establishments is not the only one of its kind Rani Karpurasri who finds mention in the copper plate of 12th century A.D. of the Somavanshi King Karna. She is described in the inscription as the 'daughter of' and as the 'grand daughter of' suggests that she was born of a promiscuous woman. This idea is also supported by the fact that her mother's name Mahari means 'devadasi'. Sircar is of the opinion that Karpurassri and also probably her mother had been Devadasi attached to the Mahavihara at Salonapura as dancing girls or Devadasis before she went to the king's harem (Ep. Ind., Vol. XXXV; No. 12, p. 97–98).

Inscriptions record that Kumāradevī, the Buddhist queen of Govindachandra (*c.* A.D. 1114–54) of the Gahadawala dynasty of Kannauj, built at Sarnath a monastery, which was the last great monastery at the site.

The Mathura Lion capital inscriptions of about the beginning of the first century A.D. records the establishment of a *stūpa* and monastery by the chief queen of Mahakshatrapa Ranjuvula, a Saka.

Yet another record of a nun is recorded around A.D. 550, while the rare instance of a nunnery being constructed in 888 C.E. by a king is that of the Bhaumakāra king, Sivakaradeva, who, at the request of a local chieftain Ranaka Sri Vinitatyunga, built a *vihārikā*. A 10th-century image of Tara from Kurkihar, Bihar,[27] clearly identifies the donor as 'bhikṣuṇī Guṇamātā' (nun Guṇamātā). The text of the inscription reads, *deya dharmoyaṃ śākyabhikṣuṇī guṇamāteh*. Though not as frequent as in the early period, it is evident that donors and their donation seemed to be marked in the historical annals for posterity. Kim (2012) discusses a 12th-century donation of an illustrated Aṣṭasāhasrikā

Prajñāpāramitā sūtra palm leaf manuscript, by a nun, dated to the 17th regnal year of the Pāla king Madanapāla (*c.* 1160 C.E.). The donor of the manuscript was a nun (*bhikṣuṇī*) named Mahāśrībhadrā, who is identified as a disciple (*śiṣyā*) of a śākya elder (śākyastharā [*sic*]), Vijayaśrībhadrā. The inscription reads, 'This is the meritorious [gift] of the elderly Buddhist nun Vijayaśrībhadrā, belonging to the branch (?) (viṭapī) of Mallikādevī' (mallikā-devī-vitovī-sthitā-śākyasthavirā/ vijayaśrībhadrāyā deyadharmmo yam. //). As per Gouriswar Bhattacharya's reading, the inscription seems to suggest that Mallikādevī was a patron of a nunnery, of which Vijayaśrībhadrā was an elder. This Mallikādevī can be identified with the patron of 'Mallikarama of Sravasti',[28] Queen Mallika, and the two nuns could have been residents of the convent at Sravasti. As is known from epigraphic records the practice of travelling long distances (on pilgrimage) and making donations was not unknown to these religious women.

Analysis of archaeological data pertaining to *bhikṣūṇī vihārikās*

The concept of public and private space as discussed in the literary texts and its reflection in architecture needs to be re-examined. However, it is difficult to derive relevant information for the reconstruction of Buddhist settlements solely on the basis of archaeological evidence. In the absence of well-planned horizontal excavations and the precise lateral context of various archaeological antiquities, the problem of interpreting the evidence becomes all the more complex. In these circumstances, it is desirable to seek the help of textual tradition, discussed earlier alongside the archaeological and surface data.

This chapter seeks to verify the viability of the corroboration between archaeological and textual evidence, as well as attempts to discover a methodology by which the usefulness, consistency and reliability of chosen sections of the *Pāli Vinaya* for the study of the Buddhist settlements may be tested against the evidence provided by archaeology. One of the foremost problems arising in attempting to correlate the textual and archaeological evidence in Ancient Indian History is the nature of the texts involved. Literature fails to give a realistic picture of urban settlements, descriptions being repetitive and conventional to the extreme. For example, references to cities with 'sky touching mansions with banners, wide streets and large portals' has to be treated with utmost caution. For the most part such description tends to be no more than a verbal formula produced to accompany a reference to a *Vinaya* rule. But such verbose descriptions tend to provide at times references pertaining to our subject of study like for example names of monastic centres, references to patrons, *bhikşūṇīs* and nunneries, monks and their *vihāras* and so on.

Many of the places mentioned in the texts have been taken up for study, especially in the 18th–20th centuries, but the work of scholars such as Cunningham in identifying the places mentioned in the texts, in most cases, cannot be disputed, even though they had their own limitations.

One of the major areas where the correlation between the textual and archaeological data may be considered reasonably satisfactory is the identification of the ancient sites mentioned in literature. This aspect of ancient Indian Historical Geography received attention as early as the mid-18th century. The geographical bearing of important Indian sites, as given both in Indian textual tradition and the classical writings on India, formed the core of this type of study.

This approach matured in Cunningham's *Ancient Geography of India*, first published in 1871. He depended for this, in addition to the sources used by the earlier scholars and his own extensive field investigations, on the then newly published records of travels of Faxian (fifth century A.D.) and Xuanzang (seventh century A.D.). Xuanzang's records were the more important of the two, because he was more specific about the directions and distances between the various places that he went to. The identifications proposed by Cunningham were not all undisputed, though disputes or uncertainties occurred because of the discrepancy and incompleteness in the Chinese accounts themselves. It is in these areas of uncertainty that there has been a steadily increasing volume of satisfactory correlation between the textual tradition and archaeological evidence.

According to the Buddhist textual tradition, Ghosita, a rich merchant, built for the Buddha a monastery at Kosambi.[29] The Allahabad University excavations at Kosam revealed a Buddhist monastery complex along with an inscribed terracotta sealing and some inscriptions. The inscriptions (the earliest perhaps date from *c.* first century A.D.) clearly refer to the organisation of monks in the great monastery founded by Ghosita. Their discovery thus not only helped in the identification of Kosambi but also substantiated the validity of Buddhist tradition of the foundation of a monastery at Kosambi for the Buddha (Sharma 1980).

Similarly, the Sujāta legend has also been substantially supported by the excavations at Bakraur near the famous temple at Bodh Gaya.

The excavations here brought to light three constructional phases of a *stūpa*, the last having been constructed in the ninth century A.D. An inscribed legend found on a number of terracotta plaques, showing the Buddha in a meditative posture, clearly suggests that this last phase was constructed to commemorate the place where Sujāta lived. The *stūpa* though was constructed much after the lifetime of Sujāta, in her honour, by a Pāla King.

In the *Pali Vinaya* and *Sutta Pitaka*, there are numerous references to various capitals, cities, towns, marketplaces, ports and villages, which the Buddha and/or his disciples are stated to have visited from time to time. Most of the records of these journeys are based upon a precise and detailed tradition and most of them can be substantially corroborated from present-day topographical and historical knowledge. As Jennings (1947) mentioned, 'though there is doubtless a superstructure of fictitious localities, claims and incidents among the *Sutta*, the conviction of the general truth of the itineraries, however, remains . . .'.

Thus, the primary focus of this study has been on those sites that had a direct bearing on the lives of the female Buddhist patrons (especially on the lives of the *bhikṣūṇīs*) that is reflected in the literary sources and second those sites that find mention in the donor records of the female monastics.

To start with, a tabulated chart[30] of the sites that have a mention of those places that were associated with *bhikṣūṇīs* in the donor records has been compiled and their identification attempted, based on the premise that these sites must have had some provision for housing *bhikṣūṇīs* and/or nunneries.

Correlation of archaeological and literary data

The prerequisites of monastic architecture discussed earlier in this chapter will be kept in mind while attempting to identify *bhikṣūṇī vihāras*. This will involve a survey and analysis of the points discussed earlier in the section on literary sources followed by their archaeological correlation. This investigation of the aspects of monastic architecture, pertaining to *bhikṣūṇīs*, will further seek to examine its implication on their everyday lives and also on the doctrinal aspects of Buddhism. And this in turn will require a comprehensive analysis of the site plans of the Buddhist sites.

'The underlying principle of any organized architectural tradition is the concept of 'plan'. A plan in its formal sense is not just the basic layout of an individual structural unit but the character and location of buildings and their relationship to the site as a whole' (Bhandaranayeke 1974). The concept of plan is dependent upon a number of factors such as climate, terrain, demography distribution and circulation, social function and purpose, density circulation, building materials and techniques and the like. It takes into account the logical interaction and interplay of the various factors of the formal aspects of building with regard to social needs, including architectural purpose and aesthetic character and material factors such as the existing technical potential and limitations, the natural location and other environmental conditions.

Any monastic unit would have two distinctive parts. The first will be the outer, more accessible section, which in most cases also houses the *stūpas*, and *chaityas* that were also frequented by the laity, and a more private part that would be comparatively less easily accessible, and this area would have the cells for the inmates.

Assuming that *bhikşūṇīs* in their living quarters would have probably felt a greater need for privacy and security as compared to their male counterparts and that this requirement would manifest itself in the architectural designing and planning of the monastic apartments, the issue of privacy and its reflection in architectural compositions has been taken as the first step towards identification of *bhikşūṇīs* quarters.

This would require a nuanced study of the architectural peculiarities at each of the sites undertaken. One of the main characteristic features that need to be looked for is that the convents be so designed as to restrict direct access to the inner quarters. Thus the entrance to women's residences would be so designed so as to provide controlled access into the inner quarters. Aspects of privacy can also be seen in the architectural arrangements made for the personal hygiene of the *bhikşūṇīs*, in the form of washing and bathing places, as mentioned in the *Vinaya* literature, and the *Cūllavagga*. Excavations at some Buddhist monastic sites such as Ratnagiri, Mohen-jo-Daro, Sirpur and Nāgarjunakonda have evidence for the same. But these cannot be taken as the identifying criteria for the classification of nunneries, as a reference pertaining to the same in the *Mahasanghika Vinaya* states that

> It is not permissible for you to enter bathrooms. If a *bhikşūṇīs* is ill in bed, she will be permitted to make fire in the cell and rub oil on her

body. If a *bhikṣūṇīs* takes bath in a bath room, her act constitutes a light infringement of the rule concerning bath rooms.

(Hirakawa 1999:408)

While on an archaeological investigation for the identification of nunneries, certain elements and facts need to be kept in mind. These are as follows:

(i) location of the site;
(ii) shape/architectural plan of the monastic site and
(iii) associated antiquarian remains from the site.

Based on the above-mentioned factors an analysis of some Buddhist monastic sites has been attempted. These sites are, starting from the East, Ratnagiri, Kiching and Udayagiri in Orissa, Nalanda in Bihar, Kasia, Sravasti, Sarnath and Kapilavastu in the Tarai region of Uttar Pradesh and Nepal, Sāñci, Nadner and Tumain in Madhya Pradesh and Nāgarjunakonda and Sannathi in Andhra Pradesh.

From a survey of the probable monastic sites one of the chief determining character is the situation of a *bhikṣunī vihārikā* was the issue of privacy and security, which manifested in a number of different ways.

For instance at Udayagiri, which is situated 102 km north-east from Bhubaneswar (Lat. 200 38′ 45″ N. and Long. 860 16′ 25″ E.), excavations brought to light the remains of a huge Buddhist monastic complex, protected by a large enclosure wall and a 7 m high *stūpa*, having four Dhyani Buddhas in all four cardinal directions. The site was identified as *Mādhavapura Mahāvihāra* on the basis of epigraphical findings. The excavations partially revealed a double-storey monastic complex datable to eighth century A.D. and important antiquity images of Buddha, Tara, Manjusri, Avalokitesvara, Jatamukuta Lokesvara and terracotta sealings. The main structures that were encountered during excavation are a massive double-storey, quadrangular monastery, a tank, a *stūpa* and a rectangular shrine. Altogether 14 *stūpas* (datable to first century A.D. to *c.* 12th century A.D.) built of different sizes of bricks with mud mortar were discovered.

A good number of stone inscriptions datable from fifth to 13th centuries A.D. were also recovered. A long stone-paved pathway, votives *stūpa* made of stone and a brick-built residential complex comprising six rooms and a courtyard were also discovered to the east of the *chaitya-griha* along with household appliances.

One of the monasteries at Udayagiri, in Orissa,[31] has an L-shaped entrance that leads inside where the *stūpas* were located; this was the sacred space that was shared by the lay as well as the monastic members of the *Samgha*. In order to demarcate this section from the more private, *bhikṣūṇīs*' quarters, there was a provision for a small wicket gate in the north-east corner while the main entrance was from the east and it led directly to the inner chambers and cells of the residents. Even the less-private or rather public domain within such complexes which include the *chaityas* and *stūpas* had a private entrance leading through an alley, directly into the *bhikṣūṇīs* quarters. According to the excavator, the site dates back to the seventh century A.D. or the early part of the eighth century A.D. and continued to exist up to the 12th–13th centuries A.D. He is of the opinion that, unlike the monasteries of Lalitgiri and Ratnagiri (the three are located at the distance of less than 10 km on the Cuttack–Jajpur Road), the monastery at Udayagiri is enclosed within an enclosure wall, which has evidence of being repaired and rebuilt at least thrice. He believes that this was because the monastery was either a seat of *Vajrayana* Sect or probably a *bhikṣūṇī vihāra* which necessitated privacy.

Nalanda (Lat. 25° 8′ N.; Long. 85° 27′ E.) District Of Patna, Bihar. The Buddhist remains lie 7 miles to the north of Rajgir. According to Buddhist literature, the place was visited several times by the Buddha. The mango grove of Pavārika was his favourite halting place. It also acquired the sanctity of being the birthplace of Sariputra, which is also mentioned in the records of Faxian.

Most of the structures at Nalanda are from the Pāla period, though a number of them have an earlier nucleus. Unlike the structures at some of the other sites like Sravasti, at Nālanda the structures were constructed on a predetermined plan, and even after centuries of rebuilding there seems to be very little deviation from the original plan.

The monasteries, of which 11 have been uncovered – nine on one row facing west and two joining them at right angles on the southern side – follow the usual *chatusāla* pattern (with rows of cells on the four sides and a courtyard in the centre), and show evidence of having been rebuilt again and again.

Excavations at this Buddhist site exposed a row of monastic units, all of which had a familiar *Chatushala* ground plan. Of these, a few of monastic units showed slight deviations from the conventional architectural scheme that can be witnessed at the other monasteries in Nalanda as well as the other Buddhist sites in the subcontinent. The ones that are especially relevant in this context are monasteries nos 9–12. All these monasteries are located in the western wing, contiguous with other monasteries

Monasteries 1, 4, 6, 7 and 8 stand apart as they are all interconnected, and are separated from monasteries 7 and 8, as there is no interconnecting passage that connects monasteries 9–12 with monasteries 1, 4, 6, 7 and 8.

Excavations conducted between 1932 and 1933 was concentrated in and around monastery no. 9, situated at the northern end of the row of monasteries, all facing west. While the earlier monastic units (nos 1,4, 6, 7 and 8) are interconnected, there is no connecting passageway between units 8 and 9. On the other hand, monasteries 9–12 are again interconnected. These structures stand apart from the earlier structures in another respect. They have been found to have evidence of bathing platforms. This structure, seen in monastery no. 9, consists of an oblong stone platform (12′ by 7′) bounded by a stone curbing 9 feet high and provided with a small drain. This construction is probably a bathing platform; it occurs at the south end of the east front of the monastery and on the immediate south of the steps referred to. No such bathing platforms had been discovered in any other monastery exposed in the previous years (I.A.R. 1930–4:138).

This cannot be taken to be a general architectural feature of monastic buildings in this region, as even in this region there is a relative low incidence of this particular structural appendage in Buddhist architectural scheme. This can only be explained as a measure adopted to provide privacy and convenience to the female monks residing in the monastery. There was strict injunction against the use of bathrooms by the *bhikṣūṇīs*; but the use of an open, paved area, without doors, within the monastic enclosure could have served the same purpose. Thus, the construction of such open spaces by a slight circumvention of the *Vinaya* injunction served to provide additional security and privacy to the inmates.

Monastery no. 11 is identical in ground plan with the other monasteries mentioned above, with similar paving and arrangement for drainage and is flanked by monasteries 9 and 10 to its left and no. 12 on its right. Of these, only monastery no. 9 has provision for storage of water and it needs to be noted that all these monasteries (i.e. 9–12) are connected to each other by passages. 'No traces of concrete or brick floor were found in any of the passages, but at the west end of the passages, was found a wall not exactly in alignment with the west verandah of the buildings. These walls may have served to connect the inner verandahs of the two monasteries' (Chandra 1934–5:39).

The evidence that further strengthens the notion of feminine presence in these monastic units is the associated antiquities from these sites. The significant finds include a number of remarkable bronzes. These are as follows:

(i) One image of Māyā Devi standing under an Asoka tree in the Lumbini Garden with the newly born Gautam Buddha.
(ii) An image of Nun Soma standing on a pedestal bedecked with *Vajras* and reclining elephants at the four corners and holding with both hands a long branch of a tree.
(iii) An image of Padmapani seated in *varada mudra* on a pedestal with attendants including Hariti holding a child.
(iv) Another interesting find was a miniature bronze *stūpa* provided with a flight of steps on all four sides of the platform which contains holes perhaps indicating the existence of four subsidiary *stūpas* at the corners.[32]

Hariti image is a common feature in the early historical period, especially encountered in the Kushana levels and, as has been discussed earlier, the image of Māyā has been seen to be associated with sites with distinctive female presence. But it is the image of the nun which needs special mention. The image of Māyā and Hariti can be in rare cases be found in monasteries, but the image of a nun would have no place in monks' residences.

The site of *Kasia/Kushinagara* was first identified by Cunningham and after much debate was acknowledged as Kushinagara, near Gorakhpur (Lat. 26° 44′ N.; Long. 83° 55′ E.; District of Deoria, Uttar Pradesh). The site is associated with the *parinirvāṇa* of the Buddha. One of the earliest references to the site is in the travelogue of Hiuen-Tsang, who refers to three *stūpas* built by Asoka at Kushinagara, and in front of one of these *stūpas* was a stone pillar with an inscription recording the event of the *mahāparinirvāṇa*. In spite of the record of the activities of Asoka at Kushinagara, nothing that is definitely earlier than the Kushana period has been found in the excavations.

The focus of the ruins at the main site is a *stūpa* (*nirvāṇa chaitya*) with a shrine in front (west), both standing on a platform 9 feet high. The other remains at the site consist of votive *stūpas*, monasteries and miscellaneous buildings. The votive *stūpas* are clustered to the south of the main *stūpa*, but small groups occur elsewhere as well. Some of them, to the east of the *stūpa*-platform, are to be seen partially buried under it, indicating their earlier date.

The excavated monasteries, including the partially exposed ones, are eight in number. They follow the usual *chatusālā* plan – the earliest datable to the Kushana period and the latest in the 10th–11th centuries A.D. The earliest evidence for the occupation of the site goes back to the Kushana period, and comprises coins of Kadphises II and Kanishka and a fragmentary inscription.

The site plan (Site Plan 1) shows a number of excavated monastic structures, all of which lie within a distinctly marked area on plan. This is probably the best representation of *simā* fixation prescribed for Buddhist monasteries. Lying within this extended *simā*, yet distinctly away from the rest of the monastic structures is monastery E, which has been described as 'slightly varied specimen of the ordinary type of Buddhist convent, its existence outside the boundaries of the mound and beneath the even surface of the fields opened a wide prospect of further discoveries' (Vogel 1905–6:73). Here the distance of this particular monastic unit with the rest of the structures needs to be noted.

Detailing the architectural peculiarities of the monastery known as monastery E, Vogel mentions that on both sides of the main entrance (which faces east unlike all the other monastic units at the site whose entrances face the Nirvāṇa Temple) are the same rectangular projections which are also found in monastery D of the same site. In the present case, however, these projections (13′ wide) do not consist of solid masonry, but each of them contains a narrow room (15′ 6″ × 5′ 5″), which communicates through a doorway with the cell (9′ 4″ × 7′ 7″) adjoining the entrance chamber. The entrance chamber itself (18′ × 12′ 8″) is, as usual, larger in size than other cells. It will be seen from the plan that it is entirely open towards the courtyard, but there is reason to assume that originally there existed here a partition of wood-work. This I believe may be inferred from the existence of a kind of threshold provided with four grooves probably used as mortises. In the outer doorway giving access to this room, we notice similar grooves which are evidently meant to receive the tenons of a wooden threshold or door frame. It is of much interest that at both ends of the doorway two iron sockets were found *in situ*, which evidently were once let into a wooden threshold and served the same purpose as our hinges.

The plan shows that here again we find the ranges of cells alternating with closets such as we have noticed in the monasteries D and L. In the present case, however, the arrangement is somewhat different, as the north-west and south-west corner rooms have such a closet on each side and consequently are isolated from the other cells. The rationale behind this peculiar arrangement is not apparent.

In this context it may be added here that, if one assumes that the establishment was intended to house the *bhikṣūṇīs* (who were certainly much lesser in number as compared to the monks), such an arrangement would provide more privacy to the inmates; further as mentioned earlier, as the *bhikṣūṇīs* were much fewer as compared to the monks, there was no constraint of space and so the dwelling units could be spaced apart.

The most striking feature of building E is that the space between the cells (43′ by 42′ 6″) is not left open, but contains a detached chamber of considerable size (approximately 30′ square) provided with a doorway in the centre of its north wall and with two windows (2′ 11″ wide) on each side. From the existence of these windows it may be concluded that the passages between the central hall and the cells was not covered over. In the middle of this chamber we find a kind of masonry platform, 12′ square, having on each side two grooves 2′ 9″ long, 5′ wide and 4′ 6″ deep, and in its centre a brick square 3′ 5″ by 4″, which is built of large-sized bricks (16″ × 10″ × 21/2″). The grooves seem to be meant as mortises for woodwork. Vogel assumes it to be a *posathagārā*, on the basis of the accounts of the Chinese traveller Xuanzang.

The presence of a covered space/hall instead of the usual roofless courtyard normally seen in monastic plans can be further explained when we assume that this space was used for periodic congregations, when all the *bhikṣūṇīs* gathered for *uposatha*, ordination and the like, in the presence of one or more monks. Such an architectural arrangement would offer additional privacy to the residents of the convent, especially in the event of periodic religious gatherings. This would further explain the curious circumstance of the situation of the entrance of monastery E away from the central group of monuments.

The associated antiquities found in the monastery are almost negligible and include a solitary carnelian bead discovered in the central hall and a clay tablet inscribed with the Buddhist creed, which was found on top of the outer wall of the southern projection on the south side. But the feminine presence at the site is attested by interesting sculptural finds.

The iconographic finds from the site include the following among other things:

(i) Certain earthenware vessels roughly shaped as human (female) figures, the head serving the purpose of a stopper. One of these is described as a 'clumsy' female figure seated with her arms resting on her knees. She wears a necklace and two bracelets round her left arm. The right arm and the legs beneath the knees are broken. The head is missing. This was found during debris clearance in the area between shrines K and G.

(ii) During the removal of debris deposited to the west of monastery E, near building V, a large image, which perhaps represents some female deity, was found. It was evidently not lying *in situ* near the north-western corner of A, opposite the two small cells which stood by the wall. Its upper portion was missing. It was a seated figure, with left leg extended downwards as in *lalitāsana* and having an anklet on one foot. Vogel describes the depictions of the two worshippers on the pedestal. One of them with a curious and gleesome air clings to the left knee of the principal figure, his right arm passing under the left leg of the deity to take some object probably sweets or fruit held in a wide-mouthed vessel by the attendant on the opposite side. The figure to the left, except one arm, is entire and its drapery is somewhat similar to that found in Kushana sculpture. The head of the other is missing. The whole figure is one block of hollow terracotta and measures 2′ 1″ high and 2′ 8″ long.

Sravasti (Site plan 3) was situated on the banks of the River Achirāvati and was the kingdom of Kosala. In the *Mahaparinibbana Sutra*, Sravasti is mentioned as one of the six important cities (others being Champa, Rajagriha, Saketa, Kausambi and Varanasi) where Buddha had a large following. Some of the well-known *bhikṣūṇīs* hailed from this place. The sacred structures at the site have been discussed in the previous chapter. The main monastic structures that need to be discussed in this chapter are monasteries F and G (Site plan 4). The monasteries F and G are placed side by side on the north side of the road leading to the eastern gate and face naturally towards it (Marshall 1910–11:7–9). The smaller monastery F is nearly square plan, measuring about 75 feet each way, and is built in the usual *chatusāla* plan, with an open courtyard surrounded by a verandah and rows of cells on each of the four sides. The entrance which faces towards the road on the south consists of a flight of steps, 9′ 10″

wide, flanked at each side by a small oblong chamber. This is the same type of entrance that is found in the earlier monasteries at Kasia, and it is noteworthy that in their case the chambers communicate only with the cells at the back of them. At Sahēth, unfortunately, the ruinous condition of the walls makes it impossible to determine whether this arrangement was followed or not. The floors of the cells and the courtyard were neither paved nor plastered, but their level was clearly indicated by the hardness of the earth and by a drain which carried off water from the courtyard. This drain starts near the north-west corner of the courtyard, crosses the verandah and cell no. 16 and empties itself into the space between this monastery and monastery G. On the basis of the finds of a coin hoard from one of the cells of this monastery, it has been dated to the Kushana period.

Monastery G is considerably larger than its neighbour and oblong in plan, an extra strip being added for some purpose on the north side of the monastery proper. The courtyard measures 40′ square, the verandah passage 8′ wide and the wall between them about 3′ 6″ in thickness. It is monastery F that needs to be taken into account here, and since the two, that is, monasteries F and G, are situated together, side by side, the latter also needs to be mentioned. What is most noteworthy is the situation of the two with respect to each other and with respect to the site as a whole. A look at the site plan brings to the fore various issues that need to be discussed in detail.

(1) The two are situated very close together with only a thick wall separating the two. It is under this wall that the underground drain flows, carrying the water from the courtyard of monastery F to the outside.

(2) They are the only two monastic structures that were constructed one against the other; all the rest of the structures are separate, independent units.

(3) If the two units were supposed to house monks of one particular sect also, there was no need for two separate entrances. The existence of two separate entrances shows that the two buildings were intended for two separate group of residents, and were independent of each other. Most probably these two units accommodated the *bhikṣūs* and *bhikṣūṇīs* of one particular sect. Interestingly I-Tsing mentions a monastery which was then 'inhabited by both monks and *bhikṣūṇīs*' (Takakasu 1896:62–5).

The references of Fa-Hien mention that the Jetavana had two gates, one towards the east and the other towards the north. Cunningham located the north gate a little to the west of temple no. 1, and the east gate immediately to the east of temple no. 2. Marshall excavated this eastern gate and the road that led to it. The construction of this road is contemporary to buildings marked F and G, and assigned the same to the early Kushana period. This date was later reaffirmed by the discovery of a number of copper coins of the Kushana kings, in a cell of monastery F. Among the smaller antiquities which turned up in the debris above this road were some terracotta figurines and two inscribed sealings of the Gupta period. Another significant find from this area was the lower portion of a red sandstone statuette of a Bodhisattva of the Kushana period with a short dedication inscribed on its pedestal:

Bhikśuniyē Raj[i]yē dānam – 'the gift of nun Raji'

The Purvārāma of Viśakha was identified by Cunningham as being located on a large mound, known by the name of Orajhar, then about 70′ in height, to the southeast of Jetavana, where he traced partial remains of a Buddhist temple over which stood the tombs of two Muslim fakirs. However, as no proper horizontal excavation at the site was undertaken, the exact ground plan of the structural remains at the site is not known. Site 6 on plan would correspond with the locations of the Purvārāma, as mentioned by the Chinese pilgrims. He also traced the remains of a *stūpa*, that he identified with the *stūpa* of Viśākha, to the north-east corner of Orajhar, which was 40′ in diameter. It was the *stūpa* constructed by Viśākha to commemorate the spot where the Buddha had overcome the Brāhamanas in argument. Whereas the spot marked Y on plan was identified by Cunningham as the spot where a *stūpa* was constructed to mark the spot where 500 Sākya maidens were massacred by Virudhaka for refusing to enter his harem. However, no structural remains were to be found at the spot.

However, a re-examination of the site leads us to infer that Orajhar (which is situated on the left bank of Khajua, a tributary of Rapti in district and tehsil Balrampur, Uttar Pradesh). It may be identified with the celebrated 'Purvārāma' or eastern monastery, built by Viśākha as seen by Fa-Hien. Here, excavation has revealed a threefold cultural sequence, starting from Kushan period (first century A.D.) followed by Gupta and medieval periods *c.* 11th–12th centuries A.D.). The Kushana period has revealed remains of a monastic complex with the usual plan. The Gupta period is witnessed in the form of a plinth of a temple which is enclosed by a wall. The medieval period revealed a star-like structure at the top of the Gupta temple.

Sarnath: (Lat. 25° 22′ N.; Long. 83° 1′ E.; District of Varanasi, Uttar Pradesh) 4 miles to the north of Varanasi, Sarnath represents the site (Figure 5) of the ancient Rishipattana or Mrigdāva (variantly Mrigdāya) or deer forest in the vicinity of the ancient city of Kāśi.[33] An inscription recovered by Sir John Marshall in 1907–8, found to the north of Dhamek *stūpa*, states that Kumāradevī, the Buddhist queen of Govindachandra (*c.* A.D. 1114–54) of the Gahadawala dynasty of Kannauj, built a monastery at Sarnath, which was the last great monastery at the site (Mitra 1980:66–7). It is written in 26 verses in Nagari characters and mentions the renovation of the *Dharmachakrajina Vihāra* with creation of the *navakahnda maṇḍala* dedicated to Vasudhara as part of the *vihāra*. V.S. Agarwala (1956) identified monastery 1 at Sarnath, located in the northern area as the *Dharmachakrajīna Vihāra*, the impressive gift of Kumāradevī. This structure measures 232 m in length, from east to west with two eastern courtyards with gates and structures having neatly chiselled brickwork, decorated with elegant mouldings on both the faces. This structure was constructed over the remains of earlier monasteries, II, III and IV, belonging to the Kushana period. Interestingly, the location of monastery I is quite away from the find spot of the inscription of Kumāradevī.

It is generally believed that the northern area of the site represented Buddhist monastic establishment and the southern area represented the religious worshipping one (*stūpa* area), the two divided by a massive wall. However, this argument does not appear to be very convincing since the monasteries are found in both north and south of the *Mūlagandhkuti* (main shrine) as *stūpas*, votive *stūpas*, *chaityas* and such other shrines appeared all around the main shrine which was approached from east. Towards the west there was a stream which was connected with River Varana, which terminated in the *puśhkarni* (lake) in the north. Therefore the residential area could develop only in north and south of the main hub, which itself symbolised their turning of the wheel of law with the Dharmarajika *stūpa* in the south, apsidal *chaitya* in the west and circular/apsidal shrine in north, almost equidistant from the main shrine in the centre.

The massive wall dividing the two areas was definitely a late addition much after the Gupta period as is evidenced by the monastery IV of Gupta period which lies below it.

Nonetheless, the finds of several (Brahmanical and Jaina) sculptures in the northern area suggest that the particular sacred space could have had a shared multi-religious identity with shrines of more than one religious affiliation coexisting or could even have been a workshop for the manufacture of stone sculptures. The two courtyards of some (until then unknown) shrine connected with a subterranean passage to its west was generally identified with *Dharmachakrajīna Vihāra* of Kumāradevī. However on the basis of relative dates and stylistic dating of its architectural features, this monastery appears to be a construction of the 11th century C.E. and not of the 12th century C.E., as also believed by its excavator John Marshall and Sten Konow (Mani 2005–6) who proposed that the location of Kumāradevī's monastery approximately must be 20 m south of the massive wall. Alexander Cunningham had much earlier proposed in 1835–6 that a monastery must have existed at that spot. This monastic structure must have comprised two parts: first having a pillared courtyard in the centre, surrounded by an open verandah, which gave access to ranges of five small rooms on all sides. It was supposed to have been a 68-foot square, chapel monastery with entrance from south as suggested by its 4.5-foot-thick outer walls, three or four stories in height. Close to its west was exposed the second part of the building, 34-foot square, with a small porch on each of the four sides. The edifice had 3-foot-thick walls and was divided into three parts from east to west and the central part was further subdivided into three parts making the entire structure including the four porches into a building consisting of nine segments. Interestingly, Kumāradevī's inscription refers to the structure as *nava khaṇda maṇḍala mahavihārah* which was in the shape of a *maṇḍala*.[34]

During the course of the excavation, Cunningham noticed that the plaster was still adhering to the inner walls of the verandahs at the time of excavation during 1835–6, 'with borders of painted flowers, quite fresh and vivid'. This description tallies with the mention in Kumāradevī's inscription where the building is described as 'accomplished with the highest skill in the applying of wonderfull [*sic*] arts and looking handsome with the figures of the Gods- "*Yam drishtvā pravvichitra- silparachanāchāturyyasimāśrayam girvānaih sudrishañcha*"'. Kumāradevī's inscription on the stone slab was discovered near this building excavated by Cunningham, quite far away from the monastery I.

On the basis of the above evidence, Dr Mani had proposed that Kumāradevī's *Dharmachakrajīna Vihāra* should be identified with the twin buildings excavated by Cunningham in 1835–6. These buildings, however, disappeared soon afterwards, as reported by Cunningham himself in his report on Sarnath for the year 1861–2 (Sahni 1914).

Kumāradevī's inscription which dedicates the monastic shrine to Vasudhara was found nearer to the building exposed by Cunningham in 1835–6 and from the same area the famous 12th-century sculptures of Jambhala and Vasudhara were also found which might have been installed in her monastery, which further adds to the evidence for the identification of the monastery. Three remarkable sculptures of Vasudhara, datable to about the 12th century A.D., two seated and one standing, have been found from the area east of the main shrine and north of Dhamek *stūpa*, which also point to the location of Kumāradevī's monastery in that area.

Kapilavastu[35] According to Hiuen-Tsang, there existed a royal monastery near the royal precincts. There is a reference to the ruined foundations of Suddhodana-raja's palace at Kapilavastu (Beal 1958:268–9). Above it a statue of the king was erected, not far from this ruined foundation, which represented the sleeping palace of the queen, Mahamaya. Above this they have erected a *vihāra*, which had a figure of the queen. By the side of this is a *vihāra*[36] where the Bodhisattva descended spiritually into the womb of his mother. There was a representation of this scene drawn in the *vihāra*.[37] This *vihāra* site has till date not been identified, for want of proper excavation at both the sites. Thus, the archaeological correlation of this significant textual reference is still awaited.

Sāñci: There are a number of monastic structures at Sāñci (Figure 9). None of the extant monasteries can be dated earlier than the sixth century A.D., though some of them seem to have been raised over earlier structures. The most imposing among these is monastery 51, designed on the familiar monastic plan – an open brick-paved courtyard with an enclosing verandah and beyond the latter a range of cells, 22 in number excluding the entrance passage and the spacious chamber outside. The entrance is flanked by pylons. Monasteries 36, 37 and 38 are nearly of the same plan, but on a smaller scale, datable to the seventh century A.D. Monasteries 36 and 37 have central platforms, while 36 and 38 had an upper storey originally. Monasteries 46 and 47, of the 11th century A.D. built on the ruins of earlier monasteries, belong to one complex. Monastery 47 is a court flanked by a pillared verandah with a small cell and a long room behind it on the south, a covered colonnade on the west and on the north a pillared verandah leading to an antechamber and shrine at the western end and at the back to a corridor with five cells. Monastery 46 had entrance through 47, and had a courtyard with cells on three sides. Monastery 45, with remains of two periods of the seventh and eighth centuries respectively, is remarkable for its temple. The cells of the first period are arranged in the usual quadrangular plan. The remains of the shrine, which evidently occupied the central portion of the back flank, are now invisible except for a small section of the platform in the front which projected considerably into the courtyard. Over the ruins of this temple was built the temple of the second period which is still extant along with the lower portion of its spire.

A *vihāra* was exposed during the excavations conducted in the year 1936–7 (Hamid 1936–7). It was dated to the Mauryan period on the basis of a number of facts:

(i) Owing to its architectural/ constructional style it was dated to the Mauryan period.
(ii) From the size and fabric of the bricks, it may be concluded that it was erected during the Mauryan epoch, on the basis of the find of a seal bearing the name of Basali (which incidentally also occurs on a pillar of *stūpa* no. 2, which dates from about 200 B.C.).
(iii) Lastly, it is the only structure with brick facing at Sāñci.

The excavator has tried to identify this excavated structure with the *vihāra* of Devi (the queen of Asoka,[38] whose literary references are to be found in the Mahavaṁsa) on the basis of its architectural features and the associated finds from the site. The significant finds include 'various kinds of precious and semi-precious cut and uncut stones, fragments bangles of ivory and crystal, copper and brass toe-rings, ankle and toe ornaments etc. along with other artifacts, which tends to prove that it was once inhabited by a royal personage/nun' (Hamid 1936–7).

Monastery 44 at Sāñci, located in the eastern area of the complex, has been dated to the eighth to ninth centuries. Marshall has described it as one 'which appears from the disposition of its foundations to have been a small monastery of a somewhat unusual type' (Marshall 1913–14:37). It consists of an antechamber covering the whole width of the building and of a rectangular hall behind it containing the remnants of a pavement with what appears to have been a *stūpa* in the centre. On plan this *stūpa* is cruciform in shape. On either side of the hall were foundations, which seemed to indicate that a row of small chambers had been built above them; 'but such chambers are manifestly too small for the habitation of monks . . .' (Marshall 1913–14:37). According to the excavator, such cells were intended for the reception of images as in some of the Gandhara chapels, and in many of the Jain temples. It stands on a stone plinth, 4 feet high and ascended by a flight of steps in the middle of its western side.

An analysis of the plan shows that the utility antechamber, mentioned by the excavator, must have been provided to act as a screen. It divided the monastery into two parts. As it extended through the breadth of the monastery, any religious gathering or congregation of the two orders would be contained within this rectangular hall, thus providing a measure of privacy to the inmates of the cells inside. Within the nunnery, contact between social groups (*bhikṣūṇīs*, novices, monks, laity, etc.) was regulated through the manipulation of spatial components according to their placement and routes of access. Studies of religious space have often focused on the interface between sacred and profane, locating symbiotic and physical progression to a ritual centre. Encounters between the various groups may be studied according to the boundaries and entrances through which social space was categorised (Fogelin 2003).

Moreover, it needs to be added that the cells were too small to accommodate the monks, the possibility of it accommodating the *bhikṣūṇīs* has not yet been explored fully. As for the assumption of it being a temple, the usual plan comprises a sanctum sanctorum that is confined to the inner-most recesses. While the outer space or the *maṇḍapa* is structured to accommodate the devotees and is so devised that maximum mobility of the visitors may be achieved. The plan in such cases does not serve to restrict entry in to the inside. In this case, the chambers, presumed to be housing the images, is located in the inner portion, where entry is somewhat structurally regulated.

Bairāt also known as *Bijak-kī-Pahādi* (Lat. 27° 27′ N.; Long. 76° 12′ E.; District Jaipur, Rajasthan) is the find spot of two inscriptions of Asoka. The Buddhist remains are located on two terraces with a brick monastery on the upper terrace and a rectangular structure and a circular temple on the lower one (Sahni 1935–36). M. Renaud identified Bairāt with *Po-le-ye-to-lo* of the Chinese pilgrim Hiuen-Tsang, who mentioned eight monasteries at the site, but the remains of only one monastery has been found during excavations.

It consists of two or three ranges of cells on each side of a central quadrangle. This building had been built at least twice, at short intervals of time. The dimensions of the bricks are the same as used in the circular structure discussed in Chapter 2 and the two structures seem to be contemporary. In the eastern wall was found a small earthen jar, containing 36 well-preserved silver coins: 8 punch-marked coins and the remaining 28 of the Greek and the Indo-Greek kings, the earliest being Heliokles (*c.* 140 B.C.) and the latest Hermaios (*c.* A.D. 20–45).[39] The punch-marked coins were found, wrapped in a piece of cotton cloth, in a hoard. As no object of a date later than the second century A.D. was found, the whole establishment must have been deserted by the second century A.D.

The finds from the monastic unit include terracotta figurines of *Yakshis* (executed in the same style as those in the Bhārhūt reliefs), numerous fragments of alms bowl of fine polished clay, which had evidence of being repaired with copper rivets and pottery fragments and the like. A noteworthy feature of the excavations is the total absence, among the finds, of Buddha images in any form, which suggests that the Buddha image had not appeared until about the second century A.D.

Nāgarjunakonda[40] (Lat. 16° 31′ N.; Long. 79° 14′ E.; District of Guntur, Andhra Pradesh). Dr Hirananda Sastri on the basis of inscriptional evidence identified the hill locally known as Naharallabodu with Sriparvata. In his summary of the inscriptional record he states that the Ceylonese monks and *bhikṣūṇīs* erected a *chaitya* and a *vihāra* on a hill named Sriparvata, and that they apparently also erected a group of similar monastic buildings on a hillock named Chuladhamagiri. This is somewhat confusing as there are several hillocks close to Naharallabodu and most of them show signs of having possessed a small *stūpa* on their summits. The likelihood of the existence of one or more nunneries at Nāgarjunakonda is quite probable, given the large female presence at the site, and this possibility is further strengthened by the finding of the above-mentioned inscriptional evidence of the Ceylonese Buddhists.

Naharallobodu is the only hill containing any remains of monasteries and temples. It is, indeed, the only hillock in the valley with sufficient space on its summit to accommodate a group of monastic buildings. Longhurst suggested the possibility of a *bhikṣūṇī vihāra* at the site. 'Possibly the Buddhists regarded the terminal hillock at the northern end of Naharallobodu[41] as a separate site and named it Chuladhamagiri to distinguish this small group of monastic buildings from the larger one on the main hill. Perhaps the larger monastery may have been for the monks and the smaller one at the end for the *bhikṣūṇīs*. A similar arrangement can be seen in the rock-cut Buddhist monasteries at Guntapalle in the adjoining Kistna District, described and illustrated in the Annual Report of the Archaeological Survey, Southern Circle for 1916–17' (Longhurst 1927).

The site to be discussed in this section is site no. VI. It is a complete unit comprising a monastery, a *stūpa* and a circular structure (which is discussed in detail in Chapter 2). This chapter is confined to a discussion of the monastery proper.

The monastery at site no. VI was enclosed within an enclosure wall, with a landing faced with Cuddapah slabs in the centre of this wall, that led into the inside of the monastery proper. The monastic plan shows a row of five cells on each wing, with a *manḍapa* 55-foot square in the centre. It holds rows of limestone pillars forming five bays and with an outer facing edged by vertical Cuddapah slabs over limestone mouldings, in turn placed on horizontal Cuddapah slab courses, the whole supported by brick courses. The southern wing of the cells held traces of plastering. There was also a paved verandah 52 feet long and 3.6 feet wide in this wing only. The passage between the verandah and the *manḍapa* is 5.5 feet wide.

To the east of cell 5 is a room, probably a bathroom (8′ 8″ × 5′) with an opening 2 feet wide leading to it. In this room was found a stone trough (1′8″ × 81/2″) in the shape of a rectangular socket with Cuddapah slabs placed vertically on the four sides. There was a provision for underground drainage that drained the waste to the south of the monastery into a soakpit.

To the east of the drain is an open area (17′ 6″ × 7′ 10″) in which no traces of cells were found. This might have served as a convenient place for washing and bathing for the monks and/or *bhikṣūṇīs*. But no drains apart from the drain in the bathroom were noticed. A similar arrangement of five cells is found on the eastern wing of the monastery. An opening on the back wall by the side of the fifth cell appears to have served as an exit on this side. To the west of the shrine again a row of five cells was encountered.

Site no. VIII[42] is yet another monastic structure at Nāgarjunakonda, which adheres exactly to the plan of site no. VI. Its plan revealed the four wings of a *vihāra*, with a pillared hall in the quadrangle, besides a *stūpa chaitya*, a votive circular-shaped chamber with a *chhaya khamba* in it.[43]

Sannathi (Lat. 16° 49′ 30″ N.; Long. 76° 54′ 20″ E.; District of Gulbarga, Andhra Pradesh), also known as Sonti or Sannati, is located on the eastern bank of the River Bhima about 60 km due south of Gulbarga. It is a fortified site with various religious as well as secular structures. The secular structures consist of a tile-manufacturing site, bathing *ghats* and so on. The main religious structures at the site consist of a Buddhist shrine, identified with the Chandralabha Temple, two *stūpas*, two Brahmanical Devi shrines and a monastic complex.

The excavated remains from the site have revealed the association of women. Based on those assumptions, an enquiry was made into the structural remains of the monastic site. The report (Howell 1995) mentions a monastic complex at Benagutti. This is located on the river bank, upstream from the city on a low mound. The *vihāra* complex comprises eight cells (7 × 3.4 m, 5.7 × 3.1 m, 4.6 × 2.6 m) and a large assembly hall of 10 × 8.6 m at the centre connected by a corridor of 18 × 1 m, running north to south. All the cells evidently have entrances connected to the corridor. The floors of the chambers are paved with longitudinal schist pebbles, which were subsequently plastered with lime mortar. The floors of the corridor and the main assembly hall were further covered with schist slabs. At a later date schist slabs were also used for veneering the western corridor.

The most noteworthy aspect of this monastic structure at Sannathi is the double boundary wall. The one on the northern side is in a better state of preservation, measuring 24.6 m long with a maximum width of 1.55 m. It has an entrance in the form of a small chamber 2.7 × 9 m with provision for a door. The southern boundary wall is damaged and the available portion measuring 21 × 1.40 m with a height of 20 cm. The burnt bricks of the walls measure 46 × 24 × 7 cm and were laid over a bed of longitudinal schist pebbles. They were also used for paving pathways.

The provision for a chamber-like, curtain wall at the entrance of the gate is not a usual feature that is to be found in the Buddhist monasteries. The utility of employing such a structural device is to provide additional security and regulate entry to the inside.

The antiquarian remains encountered here consist of a good number of sculptural fragments, some of them bearing inscriptions in *Brahmi* characters of the third century B.C. Moulded terracotta figurines including those of kaolin, a variety of semi-precious beads of chalcedony, agate, carnelian, crystal, faience and paste; objects of ivory and bone which include stylus, crochet needles, dice, glass bangles, terracotta plaques and copper objects including hair-pins, antimony rods and necklace were found. More than 60 coins of copper and lead datable to late Satavahana period were also found.

Two ancient bathing *ghats* have been found during explorations round Sannathi. The first lies on the left bank of the Bhima, close to the *stūpa* 1 and the tile-manufacturing site, while the second is located on the far bank of the river, opposite Ramamandal Mound. First of these lies close to *stūpa* 1 and the associated complex. There is little need and justification for the construction of a bathing *ghat* exclusively for the community of monks. This brings to mind the injunction[44] that *bhikṣūṇīs* were not to make use of the bathing *ghats* that were frequented by men. This would also explain the existence of two *ghats* in the same area. Here it needs to be stressed that there was a marked female presence at the site, which has been discussed in the subsequent chapter.

Sanghol. A monastery is located to the northeast of the main *stūpa*. A close inspection of the monastic plan (Figure 10) shows that there was a distinct demarcation between the areas of public activity that is the *stūpa* and the monastery. Also noticeable is the fact that there are remnants of a walled enclosure around the assembly area. The presence of a covered space/hall instead of the usual roofless courtyard normally seen on monastic plans can be explained when we assume that this space was used for periodic congregations, when all the *bhikṣūṇīs* gathered for *uposatha*, ordination and the like in the presence of one or more monks. Such an architectural arrangement would offer additional privacy to the residents of the convent, especially in the event of periodic religious gatherings. The *stūpa* is located outside the monastery, unlike other monasteries at the same site (like SGL 11) where the *stūpa* is accommodated in the courtyard of the monastery. This phenomenon has also been observed at other probable sites with *bhikṣūṇīs vihārikās* like the Monastery-E in Kasia/Kushinagara in District of Deoria in Uttar Pradesh. From the contextual finds, this monastic structure has been dated to the second to sixth centuries A.D.

Ratnagiri (Lat. 20° 38′ N.; Long. 86° 20′ E.; District of Cuttack, Orissa). Owing to textual as well as epigraphic references one cannot entirely rule out the presence of *bhikśūṇī vihārikās* in Orissa, but so far this survey has only yielded the remnants of a unique *three-roomed structure* (Figure 7) that has provided evidence for its association with women. It is not a singular specimen as other similar structures with three rooms have been reported from sites like Kiching and Sanghol also.

In the area south of monastery 2 and temple 1, as well as at an inconspicuous and isolated mound to the north–north-east of monastery 1, a plan of the single-winged monastery was exposed. The structure was fronted by a running verandah and consists of a row of three brick cells. The central cell possibly served as a private chapel and the flanking cells were used for habitational purposes. The ceilings are spanned, as in the cells of monastery 2, period III and passages of cells 4 and 11 of monastery 1 of period II, by semicircular arches. This monastery was built on the ruined walls of an earlier monastery, also of three brick cells, opening into a common verandah.

The significance of this structure lies in its association with an inscription. The mound, long before its excavation, yielded a charter of three copper plates of the Somvamsi king Karna (end of 11th and beginning of 12th centuries A.D.), which records the grant of a village to Rani Karpurasri who hailed from the Salonapura Mahavihara, the site of which is probably represented by Solampur, near Jajpur, 13 miles from Ratnagiri. 'Presumably, Karpurasri settled in Ratnagiri, either as a lay devotee or a nun, and the village was granted to meet her personal expenses and to provide her to make contributions to the Buddhist establishment of Ratnagiri. . . . The find of the Copper plates at this mound may suggest that Karpurasri passed her retired life at Ratnagiri, possibly in this very structure, a secluded one farthest one from the establishment' (Mitra 1958–61).

The associated finds from this site include bronze objects including images of Buddha, both standing and seated, Lokesvar, Maitreya, Manjusri, Yamari, Tara, Jambhala, Vasudhara, Arya-Saraswati Aparajita, the Dhyani Buddhas along with the *stūpas*, *chatthris*, a female devotee and decorative pieces inlaid with stones and so forth.

Similar structures have also been reported from other Buddhist sites like Kiching (Lat. 21° 56′ N.; Long. 85° 52′ E.) District of Mayurbhanj; ancient Khijjinja was the capital of the Bhanjas of Mayurbhanj, which was once a flourishing settlement. The excavations at this site has been a small scale, haphazard dig, due to which it has not been possible to determine the exact plan of the site or the structures present there. Excavations at the site revealed a Buddhist monastery along with several isolated sanctuaries of varied plans. Of these, one is similar to the structure at Ratnagiri, described above (Mitra 1958–61:232).

The brick structure called Itamundia consists of three brick cells in one alignment preceded by a common verandah. The central cell is longer than the side ones. Evidently it served as a shrine. It has a stone door frame, some of the stones of which were collected from older structures.

Yet another evidence of a similar structure comes from the site of Sanghol, locally known as Uchha Pind, on the banks of the ancient Sutluj, which is situated 40 km from Chandigarh in Punjab. Immediately to the east of the main *stūpa* was a brick pathway along which were three small votive *stūpas* and a small three-roomed building. A single-winged monastery was reported in the north-east corner of the mound. The site has exhibited a strong female lay presence (Kaushik 2014).

The available evidence thus can be indicative of the fact that such structures were meant for lay female Buddhist women, who wielded considerable social power and influence but had overtime taken up renunciation and preferred to spend the rest of their lives in such solitary retreats that were parts of monastic complexes.

The complete absence of any literary reference to such structures associated with women can be explained according to Eichler's (1987:12) model as 'gynopia', which entails women's invisibility. The repeated references to 'monasteries' in Buddhist literature and the absence of any specific reference to *bhikṣuṇī vihāras* can be explained as the phenomenon of 'overgeneralization', which tends to occur when a study presents itself as if it were applicable to both (or all) sexes, but in fact deals with only one sex (most often male) and 'familism' is a term denoting a type of gender insensitivity: where the *Samgha*, or community of nuns/monks is treated as the smallest unit of analysis, when it is actually the individual members of the *Samgha* (the monks and the nuns) who are the smallest units of analysis. Familism also occurs when the family (*Samgha*) is assumed to be uniformly affected by an event or condition, when the same event or condition may have different effects on different members of the family (*Samgha*).

Conclusion

As has already been seen, the data on the subject are scanty and unevenly spaced. There are large gaps in the data derived from literary, archaeological and epigraphic sources. It is for this reason that sometimes interpreting the data and deriving a reasonable conclusion becomes a daunting task. This gap between the different kinds of data can be lessened to some degree by incorporating ethnographic data on the subject. The ethnographic inputs for this study have been collected from personal interviews with *bhikṣūṇīs*, based on the various nunneries in Dharamsala, Himachal Pradesh. In addition, the inputs from ethnographic studies as discussed in the various secondary works on the subject have also been used.

What is most obvious from the data discussed in this chapter is the uneven distribution and spread of nunneries. This can be attributed to a number of factors. Though women have constituted almost half of the population at any given period of time, their presence, especially in the context of Buddhism, in the various types of archival records at our disposal has shown considerable fluctuation and variation over time. The data derived from epigraphic sources are also at variance with the available archaeological evidence. A quantitative survey of donor records of the early historical and historical period, for some sites like Sāñci, Bhārhūt, Nāgarjunakonda and so on, leads us to conclude that women were almost equal to men, if not more, so far as patronage issue within Buddhism was concerned. Sāñci, Amarāvati, Bhārhūt, Taxila, Gandhara, Sarnath and Nāgarjunakonda are sites that point to flourishing *bhikṣūṇīs*' communities. These are sites where *bhikṣūṇīs* commanded sufficient resources to have erected railings and monuments and have their names inscribed in the donor records. Bühler's list of epigraphs at Sāñci lists the names of 141 monks, 104 *bhikṣūṇīs*, 250 men who were not designated as ordained and 150 women who are not designated as ordained. (This tabulation has some degree of uncertainty as there is possibility of repetition of names.) It is significant that the ratio of *bhikṣūṇīs* to monks exceeds the ratio of undesignated women to men. The former is 104:141 or 3:4 and the latter 150:250 or 3:5. Thus in Madhya Pradesh, early Buddhist institutions apparently enjoyed a great vitality of women's participation – they represented 43 per cent of the total clerics in inscriptions and 38 per cent of the laity. 'Even though Indian *bhikṣūṇīs* and laywomen at this time (as at other times) were relegated to a secondary status, they actively involved themselves at both householder and monastic levels to an extraordinary degree' (Davidson 2003:94).

A review of the epigraphic materials shows a decline in the presence of women in epigraphic records.

The medieval period however does not indicate the enthusiastic participation of women at this level. Davidson reinforces this argument by the data from Kurkihar bronze hoard, a group of specific Buddhist statutory; of the 93 inscriptions listed, 42 provide the names of donors, 9 are clearly donated by women, wherein the *bhikṣūṇīs* are conspicuously absent, while 33 are by men of which 10 are monks. These data are further supplemented by the data obtained from the numerous personal sealings found at Nalanda. As many as 173 personal sealings were listed by Hirananda Sastri as the complete excavated inscriptions up to 1942 for the Nalanda Mahavihāra. Of these only three could be identified as women. There are hardly any epigraphic data demonstrating early medieval benefaction by a Buddhist queen or a Buddhist lay *upāsikā* to a Buddhist nunnery, despite their sometimes extensive, even excessive, donations to monks. The very few nunneries recorded during the period seem to have been constructed by kings, rather than by queens, such as the institution established by the Bhaumkara king Sivakaradeva in 888 C.E.

The number of convents that appear in the literary texts is also few and most of these were the munificence of the royalty and are associated with the likes of the Ikshavaku queens, the royal women from Kashmir and their consorts, Vallabhi, Kumāradevī and Rani Karpurasri. During the medieval period, however, as has already been substantiated by epigraphic data, this royal patronage declined substantially. Throughout the history of Buddhism, and more so during its latter phase, the inflow of *dāna* meant specifically for the *Bhikṣūṇīs Samgha* was declined considerably less as compared to the *Bhikṣū Samgha*. This fact is further substantiated by the archaeological records. The nunneries are few and far between and do not stand in comparison with the grand edifices that were constructed for the monks.

In the absence of the much-needed lay patronage, the requirements for the accommodation of the *bhikṣūṇīs* could hardly be met. In the prevailing circumstances, the *bhikṣūṇīs* must have taken recourse to the economical, frugal alternative of residing in *āvāsas*, as these *āvāsas* were makeshift, crude structures, which required much less resources as compared to the *vihāras* and *pasādas*, and were also much easier to raise. These structures were of a semi-permanent character, hence it would be next to impossible to find any tangible remains of archaeological importance. Beside the *bhikṣūṇīs* also preferred to take sanctuary in solitary hermitages, which in most cases came up in and around the large monasteries. As has already been seen in the textual tradition there are references to *bhikṣūṇīs* putting up with their kin also, even after ordination, especially during *vassāvāsa* and sometimes even afterwards. This trend though was not so popular for the monks and nor was it encouraged. As can be adjudged from the available ethnographic data[45] on the subject, most of these 'nunneries' were 'village level'[46] entities, which had its members from the villages themselves. These modest structures would require little resources for their maintenance, and hence could be supported by the local lay population, even in the absence of large or royal patronage.[47] These structures were much more numerous in number than the regular *vihāra* for the *bhikṣūṇīs*, at all times. Thus it can be presumed that during its lean phases, the latter-day Buddhism did not lose its female *bhikṣūṇī* population altogether, as is generally believed on the basis of the almost negligible epigraphic records, but they only tended to become less visible. With the desertion and disappearance of the large *vihāras*, fuelled by the socio-religious exigencies, the *bhikṣūṇīs* merely shifted base to the more inconspicuous and unobtrusive, village-level *āvāsas* and hermitages.

According to recent survey of Tibetan Buddhist nuns and their order, it has been observed that in many areas there were no nunneries and the singular option for the *bhikṣūṇīs* living there was to attach themselves to a monastery. According to Garje Khamtrul Rinpoche, a monk/lama of the Nyingmapa sect:

> In the lower part of Derge there were mostly monasteries and only a few small nunneries. However there were many *bhikṣūṇīs* who did not stay in nunneries. In the case of Amdzom Gar Monastery for instance there were 300–500 affiliated *bhikṣūṇīs*. Many of the *bhikṣūṇīs* did retreats and when there were big gatherings or rituals in the monasteries they would come there. Most of these *bhikṣūṇīs* belonged to the Kagyupa School. Mostly in Central Tibet one would find separate nunneries.
>
> (Havnevik 1998)

Ngawng Dondup Narkyid, a layman originally from Lhasa, claimed:

> In the Tsang area there were many big nunneries. There were more nunneries in this part of Tibet than in others. These were mostly Nyingmapa and Kagyupa nunneries. I believe that the Kagyupa School had the largest number of *bhikṣūṇīs* in Tibet, while there were few *bhikṣūṇīs* belonging to the Sakya School. Probably the number of *bhikṣūṇīs* is affected by the local influence of lamas.
>
> (Havnevik 1998)

Bhikṣūṇī presence is noticeable in small clusters or colonies at specific sites. The largest known concentration of sites with epigraphic and archaeological data supporting the presence of *bhikşūṇīs* during the historical period in the Indian subcontinent comes from the region in and around Madhya Pradesh, with Sāñci as its focal point. This clusterisation can also be attributed to certain factors like the attitude of the different sects towards the *bhikşūṇī* order, the stance and position of the officiating clergy and most importantly the local lay support[48] towards the nuns' order.

Nunneries were often affiliated to monasteries, and the initiative to start a nunnery could come from the founder of the mother monastery, as in the case of the Nyingmapa nunnery Gonlung Champa Ling, affiliated to Charu Monastery. The monk who visited Dharamsala in 1984 maintained that both were founded by Charu Nyima Dragpa (1647–1710). The nun Khacho stated that Gechak Thekchen Ling was founded by gechag Tsangyang Gyatso. About the monastic establishment of Gechag Tsangyang Gyatso, Karma Thinley writes:

> I have heard that there were thirteen sub-monasteries (to the main one) and these included monasteries, nunneries and hermitages. Also, there are many other non-sectarian nunneries there (in Nangchen Kham).[49]

Some nunneries were started as a result of the initiative and joint effort of the *bhikşūṇīs*. Disciples of a great lama often settled near his monastery or hermitage. If there were a sufficient number of *bhikşūṇīs*, they sometimes started their own monastic establishment.

The focal point of all religious communities was usually the monks or the lamas. We have, however, information about one nunnery that was established by a famous female teacher, Shugsep Lochen Rinpoche, and her disciples. Yutog Dorje Yudon's (an aristocratic lady from Lhasa) account of the Lochen Rinpoche's nunnery: 'It was not exactly a nunnery. The *bhikşūṇīs* had a three-storied house and on the second floor there was an assembly hall where they performed offering rituals. The *bhikşūṇīs* stayed in twenty or more retreat huts that were spread out on the hill-side, not too close to each other. The site was beautiful with many juniper trees and small springs'.[50] Thus, as can be gathered from ethnographic data, the order of nuns was loosely structured, as compared to a monastery and it was not unusual to have houses turned into makeshift *vihārikās* for the *bhikşūṇīs*.

The modern-day Buddhist nunneries that I visited in Dharamsala did not adhere to any fixed structural monastic plan based on textual records. Most of them were fairly large establishments, multi-storeyed, with rooms for the inmates, often two in one room. They have a reception/office for the lay visitors, in addition to one or more large halls for their ritual functions, communal worship and the like. Other than these broad features, and the strings of prayer flags on their roof, it was difficult to tell these convents from the other large secular structures in their vicinity.

There were some monastic institutions where both monks and *bhikṣūṇīs* lived. This arrangement probably stemmed from the need to perform communal rituals together and receive religious teachings from the same lama, while their housing remained separate. One informant, *Bhikṣūṇī* Tendzin Palmo, a British national, who has been a nun in the Tibetan tradition for 25 years, mentioned that there is a monastery in Lahoul, Tayu Gonpa, housing both monks and *bhikṣūṇīs*. The monks and *bhikṣūṇīs* participate in the same rituals and are given the same religious instructions. However, the monks have a higher status than the *bhikṣūṇīs*; the *bhikṣūṇīs* have the responsibility of serving tea and food for the monks. This would probably help in better understanding the reference to the monastery in Kashmir which was founded by Queen Yukadevi, in her Nandanavana *vihāra*, which accommodated, curiously enough, not only the *bhikṣū* but also those Buddhists who were in possession of wives, children, cattle and property (Hazra 1996:377). Archaeological parallels for this phenomenon can be seen in the monasteries F and G at Sravasti. When we see the site plan of Sravasti, the situation as also the structural layout of monasteries F and G can be better understood, when viewed from this perspective.

Ethnographic analogy to this phenomenon is to be found in Tibetan Buddhist sects, belonging to the Kagyupa School, where there were some types of nunneries with a very loose organisation. These *bhikṣūṇīs* had long hair and they were married. Their husbands were called *onpo*. They lived in the monasteries which were called Serkhyim gonpas.

Tibetan *bhikṣūṇīs* pursued three main careers. A large number of *bhikṣūṇīs* stayed in nunneries. Some of these *bhikṣūṇīs* were advanced religious practitioners. However, the level of religious practice and education in Tibetan nunneries varied, and the informants maintained that the majority of *bhikṣūṇīs* staying in nunneries mainly performed rituals and were not engaged in advanced religious practices.

A second class of *bhikṣūṇīs* concentrated all their efforts on meditation and yoga. These *bhikṣūṇīs* wandered about on pilgrimage searching for gurus who could give them further teachings, or they stayed in solitary hermitages, pursuing meditation. The number of *bhikṣūṇīs* following this solitary career was nevertheless relatively small.

The third category consisted of a large number of *bhikṣūṇīs*, who neither stayed in nunneries nor engaged in yoga and meditation. Most were uneducated, and many of them had only taken formal ordination when they became old. Some might have stayed in nunneries for a part of their life, but found it difficult to adjust to monastic life. Others were itinerants, constantly on the move. Their main religious practice consisted of performing prayers, reciting mantras, turning prayer wheels, performing circumambulations and going on pilgrimage.

Though there was no structured plan for the construction of a *Bhikṣūṇīs Vihāra*, the *Vinaya* has definitive, hierarchical inventory of support staff meant for the smooth functioning of the nunnery. This scheme seems to have been followed till the present day, with some additions. The duties found in nunneries were those of chanting master (*umtse*), disciplinarian (*chotrimpa* or *geko*), caretaker of the shrine room (*chopon*), her assistant (*choyok*) and the kitchen duty (*nyerpa*). The task of playing instruments during recitation in the temple rotated among *bhikṣūṇīs* qualified for the task.

When nunneries were affiliated to monasteries, the leader of the monastery, the abbot (*khenpo*), could also be the abbot of the nunnery, or a monk from the monastery could be appointed to teach or to function as the abbot of the nunnery.

> The ordinary nunneries, with twenty to thirty *bhikṣūṇīs*, were generally insignificant institutions compared to monasteries, and often under the supervision of the male abbots, Tibetan nunneries seem to have a large degree of self-rule. Often the nunnery was established some distance away from the mother monastery, as this was considered the best solution to apostasy. Even though the *bhikṣūṇīs* had a monk abbot, he did not always live in the nunnery, but visited it now and again.
>
> (Havenik 1995:48)

Here it needs to be noted that even in case of the ancient monastic structures that one comes across in the excavations, most of them are large structures planned and executed in such a manner as to accommodate a large number of monks, generally 50 or more. At times one also comes across multi-storeyed structures with a number of monastic cells. Small structures that were originally intended to house 25 or less inmates is hard to find, and ironically all the structures discussed in this chapter seem to have been originally constructed with a small residential population in mind.

Since there was no clear-cut prescription in the *Vinaya* literature enumerating the exact structural plan of a *Bhikṣūṇī Vihāra*, the same was modelled on the lines of a *Bhikṣū Vihāra*. As there are no direct epigraphic evidence from any of the excavated sites for the identification of a nunnery, it can only be presumed that of the hundreds of Buddhist monastic sites laid bare during excavations, some of them must have been *vihārikās* for the Buddhist *bhikṣūṇīs*. A number of small, outwardly imperceptible modifications in the plan of the usual Buddhist monasteries at some of the sites have shown that in spite of having all the structural appendages to meet the canonical and ritual needs of a Buddhist monastic unit, these structures show slight divergences. From Table 6, it is evident that of the total number of studied Buddhist sites, more than 80 per cent of the monasteries are located on the eastern extremity of the site. This could be as a result of a conscious decision (based on canonical prescriptions or contemporary conventions) to locate such structures in a predetermined location. However, it needs to be further evaluated whether this space was negotiated and was a conventional practice. In either case a strong, influential group of dedicated Buddhist practitioners is evident whose presence could not be ignored by the *Samgha*. These structural manifestations therefore take on a gendered connotation.

Sometimes nunneries came up in close proximity to the important pilgrimage sites. For example, the Nyingmapa nunnery Gonlung Champa Ling was situated behind the mountain Gonlung Gyabri, an important pilgrimage site. These nunneries were sustained by the lay patrons on pilgrimage.

An overview of the sites discussed in this chapter shows that most of discussed sites like Sravasti, Kasia and Sarnath were primary sites that were associated with the life of the Buddha while the rest were secondary sites like Nāgarjunakonda, Sāñci and the like, which were no less important, in terms of their significance as Buddhist pilgrim centres. This is evident from the numerous magnificent edifices, which stand there till date, with a multiplicity of donor records of the visiting pilgrims, the vestiges of the glorious phase of Buddhism in the subcontinent.

Notes

1 The other important monasteries which were patronised by the female Buddhist patrons being the *Purvārāma* (situated in the North-East) of the city, erected by an *upāsikā* the celebrated *Vishakha*, the *Mallikārāma*, built by Queen Mallika. Sravasti is known by its ancient name of *Sahet-Maheth*.

2 However, it should be noted that there are many types of *simā*, and that the *simā* defining the *Samgha* that is present is only one particular type.

This is shown in a passage explaining the eight types of donation. Of the eight, the first, fourth, fifth and sixth are directed towards the *Samgha*.

(1) If the donation is made to the *simā*, it should be distributed to all the *bhikṣus* within the boundaries (*simāya deti: yavatika bhikkhu antosimagata tehi bhajetabbam*).
(4) If the donation is made to *Sangha*, it should be distributed in the *Sangha* that is present (*Sanghassa deti: sammukhibhutena samghena bhajetabbam*).
(5) If the donation is made to the two *Sanghas*, it should be divided into half and given (to the two orders), even if there are many *bhikṣus* and only one *bhikṣuṇi*. Or, if conversely, there are many *bhikṣuṇis* and only one *bhikṣu*, it should still be divided in half and distributed to the two orders. (*UbhatoSanghassa deti: bahukapi bhikkhu honti eka bhikkhuni hoti, upaddham databbam bahukapi bhikkhuniyo honti eko bhikkhu hoti, upaddham databbam*).

If it is donated to the *Sangha* observing the rainy season retreat, it should be distributed to all the *bhikṣus* residing there and observing the rainy season retreat (*vassam vutthaSanghassa deti: yavatika bhikkhu tasmim avase vassam vuttha, tehi bhajetabbam*). Hirakawa (1999:22).

3 *Ibid.*, p. 48.
4 *Ibid.*, p. 124.
5 *Ibid.*, pp. 204–5.
6 *Ibid.*, pp. 250 & 333.
7 *Ibid.*, p. 270.
8 *Ibid.*, p. 339.
9 *Ibid.*, p. 50.
10 *Maha*, no. 7; *Pali*, no. 2; *Mahi*, no. 2; *Dharma*, no. 7; *Sarva*, no. 4; *Mula* Chinese, no. 3; *Mula* Tibetan, no. 3; T. 1461, no. 7; T. 26, no. 3; T. 60, no. 3.
11 *Ibid.*, p. 94. There are two rainy season retreats. The former rainy season retreat starts with the beginning of the rainy season and continues for three months. The latter rainy season retreat begins one month later and continues for three months.
12 *Ibid.*, p. 111.
13 This information has been received through personal communication from Dr O.C. Handa, who made this observation during his field study of the region, pertaining to Buddhist monasteries of the Himachal (July 2003).
14 *Ibid.*, p. 237.
15 A whole long section of the *Mahāvagga* (III on *Vassā*) is given to *avāsas*, probably because they represented the unaided enterprise of the monks themselves, involved in the setting up of an entire monks' settlement from scratch. It deals with the demarcation of an *avāsa*, its construction, maintenance, regulations for communal living within it and also manners and points of etiquette to be observed.

16 As per the *Mahāvagga* (II,6; II,7,1–2; II,12.7 and II,13,1–2), the rules for the settlement of the *simā* are that 'the limits should generally coincide with natural boundaries such as a mountain, a rock, a wood, a tree, a path, an ant-hill, a river or a sheet of water, but they must not extend beyond three *yojanās*, nor to the opposite bank of a river unless facilities existed for crossing over. Where no such limits could be fixed, the boundaries of the village or of the market town (*gāma-simā* or *nigama-simā*) could serve the purpose. In a forest, the community of residence would extend to a distance of seven *abbhantaras*. It is further laid down that the boundaries of the two *avāsa*s must not overlap: an interstice must be left between'.

17 At first the service used to be held in the monks' *pariveṇā* in succession, but the exigency of space made it impossible to accommodate all the monks. The next alternative arrangement called for the use of an entire *vihāra* instead of a *pariveṇā*, but when even this failed to serve the purpose, an artificial limit called *uposatha-pamukha* was set, making the service valid up to a certain distance. The *vihāra* temporarily arranged for the service was called *uposatha-gāra* and it was swept and cleansed, appointed and provided with lights for the occasion.

18 During the ordination procedure, the *trayo nisrayah* are explained to the candidate. These are three for a *bhikṣūṇī* but four for a *bhikṣū*, namely: (1) using robes made from rags, (2) begging for food, (3) lodging under trees and (4) using cow's urine as medicine (cf. Pali *Mahāvagga*, I,77,1, Vol. I, pp. 95–6); the second dharma, lodging under a tree is omitted for the *bhikṣūṇī*, thus making it three *dharmas* for them. These *dharmas* are the minimum requirements for the life of a *bhikṣū* or *bhikṣūṇī*. Hirakawa (1999, *op. cit.*, Patna; p. 65).

19 *Ibid.*

20 Travelling alone was also forbidden. If a *bhikṣūṇī* goes anywhere, she must not leave the confines of the village without being accompanied by other *bhikṣūṇīs*, except under special circumstances. (Special circumstances refer to times when she is passionless and to times when she is ill.) Otherwise, at that instant, her act is to be considered a *Sanghatisesa* offense (Hirakawa 1999).

21 *Ibid.*, p. 371.

22 J. F. Fleet, *op. cit.*

23 For titles of administrative significances, see Ajay Mitra Shastri, *An Outline of Early Buddhism*, Varanasi, 1965, pp. 131–2.

24 It has however not been possible to identify this *vihāra* yet.

25 See Thalcher Plate of Sivakara Deva III, Pt B. Misra, *Orissa under the Bhaumakara Kings*, p. 40ff.

26 Bhatta Somadeva, Charles Henry Tawney, Norman Mosley Penzer, *The Ocean of Story: Being C.H. Tawney's Translation of Somadeva Katha Sarit Sagara*; Or, *Ocean of Streams of Story*, Vol. 1, Motilal Banarsidass, New Delhi, 1968.

27 Now in the Indian Museum, Kolkata (I.M. 5862/A25133); see Huntington (1984: Figure 113).

28 'A pleasuance in Savatthi belonging to Queen Mallika'. It is described as *Samayappavādekatindukācirā-* (v.l. *tindukakhira*)*-ekasalaka*; the commentary says it was called the *Samayappavādeka* because of teachers holding various discourse on their doctrines. G.P. Malasekera, *Dictionary of Pali Proper Names*, 2003, p. 458.

29 *Digha Nikaya*, London: P.T.S., i.157, 159; *Samyutta Nikaya*, London: P.T.S., ii. 115, iii.125, iv.110; *Anguttara Nikaya*, iii.132, iv.110; iv.37; *Majjhima Nikaya*, London: P.T.S. i. 320, 513, iii. 152.

30 See Table 5: Table of the location of the Buddhist sites mentioned in the epigraphic records, in chapter III.

31 Personal communication by the Late Dr G.C. Chauley, ex-director, Archaeological Survey of India (July 2004).

32 See the discussion on *stūpas* in Chapter 1.

33 The first name owes its origin to the fall (*patana*) of the bodies of 500 Prateyeka Buddha (*rishis*) at this spot after their attainment of nirvana. Sarnath is also one of the four most important places associated with the life of the Buddha. Rishipattana, Mrigdāva (Mrigdāya) or deer forest is known as the place where the Buddha set the wheel of law in motion and thenceforth the place became famous as *Saddharmachakra* or *Saddharmachakraprava rttanamāhavihāra*.

34 *Maṇḍala* is a mystic circle in Buddhist pantheon with the main deity in the centre, surrounded by subsidiary deities and geometric diagrams representing the textual prescription for the situation of the deities, which can be transcribed into a building form. In Tantric Buddhism, the shape of the *maṇḍala* or enclosed *yantra* as depicted in paintings and relief looks quite similar to the shape of the building illustrated in the plan drawings by Cunningham.

35 The location of the capital of the Sākyas and the birthplace of the Buddha, which finds frequent mention in the Buddhist texts, is shrouded in controversy. One of the primary reasons for this is the difference between Faxian and Xuanzang on the location of Kapilavastu, with reference to Lumbini. The identifications put forward by Lassen, Cunningham and Carlyle, of some sites in Gorakhpur and Basti (which were proposed on the basis of the distance and bearing of Kapilavastu from Sravasti) were held untenable since the discovery of two fragments of inscribed pillars by the side of a tank called Nigali-Sagar along with an inscribed Aśokan pillar and *stūpa* in the Nepalese Tarai region. In 1899, P.C. Mukherji, after an excavation, declared Tilaurakot, in Nepal as Kapilavastu, while T.W. Rhys Davids took Tilaura Kot and Piprahawa to be the old and the new cities of Kapilavastu respectively, the latter being built after the destruction of the old city by Vidudhabha.

36 Carlyle places this *vihāra* about 50 feet WNW from the bed chamber ruins, the *stūpa* of Asita being situated to the north-east of it.

37 This representative scene is one of the best known of the Buddhist sculptures. See *Tree and Serpent Worship*, pl.XXXIII; *Stupa of Bharhut*, pl. XXVIII; *Lalitavistara* (Foucaux), pl.v.

38 The queen of Asoka was a devotee of Buddha and is stated in the Ceylonese chronicles to have constructed a monastery on the Vidisagiri (variantly Chetiyagiri), generally identified with the hill of Sāñci.

39 On the basis of this find, Sahni states that punched-marked coins must have continued in circulation down to the first century A.D. and, second, the monastery was still in occupation in the mid-first century A.D.

40 Nāgarjunakonda means 'the hill of Nagarjuna'. It is identified on the basis of the Tibetan tradition, with the famous Buddhist teacher Nāgarjunakonda, who is said to have spent his last days in a monastery on the Śriparvata, the latter identified with a chain of hills (offshoots of the Nallamalai range) around Nāgarjunakonda on the evidence of the inscription of Bodhisiri.

41 Naharallobodu happens to be the most favourable building site as it is centrally situated in the most fertile portion, and is close to the main *stūpa* and is only 1½ miles from the river. The inscription also mentions that Sriparvata was conveniently situated with regard to the adjacent town of Vijayapuri.

42 I. A. R., 1955–6, p. 24.

43 The circular structures have been discussed in Chapter 2.

44 Friedrich Max Muller, *The Sacred Books of The East*, Vol. 20, Vinaya Texts, Part III, 'Cullavagga', X, 27, 4. p. 369.

45 A survey of Tibetan monasteries and nunneries was made by the Council for Religious and Cultural Affairs of H.H. the Dalai Lama, based on government records and on the recorded statements of the exiled Tibetans, concerning the number and geographical distribution of monastic institutions, based on findings up to May 1984. These data were compiled by Hanna Havnevik, in her book *Nunneries and Bhikṣūṇīs in Tibet*, Norwegian University Press, 1989.

46 Per Kvaerne classifies Tibetan monasteries into three main types: the national monasteries, the village monasteries and the hermitages. National monasteries were large institutions, offering advanced religious studies and recruiting monks from all over Tibet. The function and organisation of these monasteries resembled medieval European universities. The village monasteries were smaller, and recruited their members from the surrounding district. The monastic education offered was aimed at meeting the needs of the local population. There was extended contact between the village monastery and the local inhabitants. The hermitages were inhabited by a limited number of monastics or *yogins*, who devoted their life to meditation. We have no information of any nunnery in Tibet that resembled a monastic university and the majority of nunneries belonged to the village and hermitage type. While the largest 'monastic universities' could have several thousand monks, we have no information about nunneries with

more than a few hundred *bhikṣūṇīs*. There is little evidence that nunneries ever resembled or functioned as Buddhist Universities. Nunneries rarely had the economic resources, the organisational structure or able teachers to impart higher education.

47 In Tibetan monasteries and nunneries there were two parallel economies, that of the individual monks and *bhikṣūṇīs* and that of the monastic institution. A family who sent a son or daughter to a monastery was expected to continue to support them. Marlam Nyenlag maintained: *bhikṣūṇīs* came from both rich and poor families. Usually their families built houses for them and they received a fair share of the food. Even poor families built houses for their nun daughters. In the case of farmers, they divided the farm and one share was for the nun. Generally the villagers would support the nunnery with firewood. If their parents were poor, the *bhikṣūṇīs* could also form a group of four or five, and go begging during the autumn.

48 A monk who lives in Kham, but visited Dharamsala in 1984, stated, 'In the area of Nagsho Driru (upper Kham) I do not know of other nunneries than the Nyingmapa Gonlung Champa Ling. However, there were individual *bhikṣūṇīs*, most of them Gelugpa. They stayed in their homes or in retreat. Many of these *bhikṣūṇīs* were serious and wanted to study, and some of them practiced high-level meditation. Some of the independent *bhikṣūṇīs* were better religious practitioners than those staying in the nunneries. These independent *bhikṣūṇīs* didn't have to work. They were supported by their relatives or by others'.

49 *Ibid.*, 1965, p. 69

50 *Ibid.*, p. 41.

Three

Exploring women's space

Conflict between the social and the asocial worlds

I

This chapter attempts to examine the multi-layered pluralism in the roles of a Buddhist *bhikṣūṇī* and to bring out the tension between the social and spiritual roles of a Buddhist practitioner, experienced by virtue of being a woman. It deals with the interactions between *bhikṣūṇīs* and the lay community and examines how this interaction defines the social space for *bhikṣūṇīs*. The interface between *bhikṣūṇīs* and the social world led to the formation of rules and guidelines for the *bhikṣūṇīs*, and the implementation of these rules had a significant bearing on the lives of these monastic women in the social as well as the monastic sphere. This study seeks to inquire how they defined their domestic as well as religious space, and how they negotiated the dichotomy, between the public and the private spheres.

In the process, the concept of their personal as well as stereological and epistemological space will also be explored. This study seeks to examine what circumscribed and/or enlarged this space? It seeks to look at the perceptions of female renunciants who engaged in alternate lifestyles and their understanding of the term 'liberation'. The study is divided into two parts; the first part discusses the conflict between the social and the asocial worlds; the concept of mental and psychosomatic space of the *bhikśūṇīs* and the differentiation between domestic, public and private space, which reflected in their behaviour, in relation to the immediate social sphere in which they existed. Thus, in the following pages an attempt has been made to examine if the above-mentioned statement holds true. It seeks to assess whether there was a perceptible social divide between lay and monastic women? What was the degree of interaction between them? Did men really employ varying degrees of control over their womenfolk? If so, it further seeks to assess and analyse the various agencies that the patriarchal society employed to control and regulate the latter group of institutionalised women. Why were such measures needed? What were the different kinds influence that these *bhikśūṇīs* wielded over their lay counterparts and to what extent? What measures did the society employ to keep their womenfolk in harness? The second part of the chapter deals with an analysis of their epistemological space and epistemic capabilities.

Unlike the other chapters, this chapter focuses on a re-evaluation of Buddhist texts – both canonical and non-canonical. The issues dealt with in this chapter require the analysis of intangible data, which provide insights into the thought processes of the Buddhist women, their male counterparts and so on. Such a study falls beyond the scope of archaeological analysis, as archaeological researches are based on the examination of tangible, material remains from the past. The texts that mainly occur in the discussion that follows include Pāli texts of the *Theravāda* as well as the *Mahāyāna* Buddhism. The reason which merits their inclusion in this present study is that all of these texts, in either direct or indirect terms, discuss the feminine and their associated social, religious and spiritual roles.

The texts that have primarily been used for analysis in this chapter include the *Cūllavagga*[1] from the *Vinaya Pitaka*, some discourses of the *Añguttara Nikāya*, the narratives from the *Khuddaka Nikāya* which include the *Jātakas,*[2] the *Therigāthā,*[3] the *Ittivuttaka*[4] and the *Vimānavatthu,*[5] the *Mahāyāna* Sutras – *The Lotus Sutra*[6] and the *Vimalakirti Sutra*[7] and the Tamil epic *Manimekalāi.*[8]

Examining similarities and divergences: the *Jātaka* versus the *Therigāthā*

All the above-mentioned works belong to different genres and discuss women in different contexts and capacities. The fundamental differences in the composition, content and reading of the texts are illustrated by bringing out the differences in the two texts that are crucial to this study. The *Therigāthā* is, as stated, a composition about women, composed by women. It articulates various personal and spiritual experiences of the *thēris*, their joy, sadness, happiness 'at going forth' their assessment of their past life experiences and so on, while the rest of the texts under discussion have been composed by male authors, and therefore embody an essentially male perspective. Even within the texts of the latter group, that is, those of male authorship, there are certain essential differences, which will be discussed in due course. The *Jātakas* were early oral compositions, composed by common men in the common dialect, Pāli. These tales were a reflection of the social sentiments of the general masses and also a projection of the official Buddhist position on the subject of women. The subject of the narratives incorporated incidents and anecdotes from the contemporary, localised social milieu. It was because of their mass appeal, and a highly flexible and resilient narrative structure, that in due course they came to be incorporated as a part of Buddhist literature. The canonisation of the folk *Jātaka* tradition and its absorption into the larger body of Buddhist textual tradition was made possible by inserting short introductory sub-narratives with Buddhist themes, in which the Buddha appeared as the narrator of the underlining moral tale, within the main narrative framework. These tales explore various roles of women – as mother, daughter, lover, courtesan, *bhikśūṇī*, queen and the like. Sometimes animals have also been discussed as subjects, with the depiction of their nature as analogous to female character. These tales provide direct or indirect insight into the male gaze and how they perceived women in their midst. Contrary to general opinion that the *Jātakas* are always negative and distrustful in their portrayal of women, there are both positive and negative references to the feminine, sometimes accompanying analogies from the animal world. 'Like women, who lure unsuspecting men, the female deer lures the stag away and leads him to his doom; the male fish when caught in a net worries, that his wife-fish will think that he has abandoned her for another female fish' (Cowell 1885/1973:42).

In the last instance, the female fish is shown as possessing qualities of vulnerability and insecurity, traits that are stereotypically linked with the feminine. The two major perspectives that can be obtained from a cursory reading of the *Jātakas* are as follows:

(1) The perception of the common man, which was brought forth in the form of the narratives.
(2) The perception of the Buddhist clergy that identified with the given perspective and incorporated the same to drive home the basic tenets of Buddhism to the common man.

Buddhist acceptance of the *Jātakas* and the incorporation of the latter into the larger body of Buddhist didactic literature leads us to infer that the Buddhist clergy not only accepted the ideas and perspectives of the *Jātakas*, but also took back the same to the masses, to illustrate the finer doctrinal and moral positions of Buddhism, with the *Jātakas* as an effective tool which was familiar to the Buddhist as well as to the uninitiated lay population.

As against the above-discussed literary works, the *Cūllavagga* offered the official, doctrinal position on the subject of women. Its textual content was normative and authoritative in character. It lays down that the interaction of the monk's community with women should be restricted to a bare minimum as 'women are the embodiment of lust and evil, which keep them from attaining their ultimate goal, "nirvana"'. The *Jātakas* reverberate with the same sentiments with regard to women, in most cases, the stories carrying numerous examples of scheming, adulterous women, with an insatiable sexual appetite. Thus, a common, dominant undercurrent of mistrust and negativity runs through most of the Buddhist texts, with regard to women.

Against this backdrop one needs to analyse the incidents of transgressions, enumerated in the *Jātakas*, together with the rules to prohibit and forestall these transgressions in the *Vinayas* which only go to show that women during this period exercised considerable discretion in taking decisions that had a significant bearing on their lives, as individuals.

Buddhist perception of the feminine: a textual overview

Nancy Falk (1989) believed that the Buddhist attitude towards women declined in the years following the appearance of written Buddhist literature. However it needs to be noted that it is during the later phases of Buddhism that the doctrine of *sunyata* and the ungendered self becomes articulated.

Although woman's status might have improved with Buddhism, this is not to say that Buddhism was without its own forms of patriarchy and even perhaps misogyny. However, when further examining some of the textual foundation and principles of these religions, it becomes clear that a number of their fundamental teachings are neither sexist nor patriarchal. Indeed, they possess concepts and principles that are exactly contrary to patriarchy and sexism (Gurholt 2004–5).

A survey of Pāli Buddhist texts (mentioned above) helps us in tracing the various levels of interaction and conflict between the monastic women vis-à-vis the society. The textual position does not favour a single monolithic position with regard to the subject of women. In these texts, one can discern many differing levels and layers of gendered perceptions.

Margrit Eichler (1987) discusses seven common 'sexist problems' in research methodology. Many of the phenomena discussed by her can be seen reflected in the classical Buddhist texts, like androcentricism.[9] Two acute forms of androcentricism include gynopia (women's invisibility), and misogyny (hatred of women). Overgeneralisation/overspecificity results when a study presents itself applicable to both (or all) sexes, but in fact deals with only one sex (most often male). This phenomenon could also at times lead to gender insensitivity that would cause ignoring sex/gender as a socially (or historically, in this case) important variable. 'Sex appropriateness', the fifth problem in gender-based research, which occurs when the so-called appropriate sex roles/appropriate gender identity are deemed as the only appropriate role for a given sex/gender. This occurs when human traits or attributes are assigned to only one sex/gender. While double standard entails the use of varying yardsticks for evaluating, treating or measuring identical behaviour, traits or situations for different gendered groups, 'familism' (a type of gender insensitivity) entails treating the family/*Samgha* as the smallest unit of analysis, when it is actually the individual members (monks and nuns) of the *Samgha* that is the smallest unit of analysis. Familism also occurs when the family (*Samgha*) is assumed to be uniformly affected by an event or condition, when the same event or condition may have different effects on different members of the family. The seventh has been identified by Eichler as 'sexual dichotomism', which is the treatment of sexes, as two distinct social, psychological and biological groups, when, in actuality, much overlapping does occur among men and women.

Though applicable to modern gender-based researches, even in the classical texts one can identify many of these biases; for example, many of the monastic rules in the *Vinaya* often start with a general address to the monks, without any mention to the order of the *bhikśūṇīs*, indicating the condition of gynopia as well as overgeneralisation. On other occasion one can trace misogyny in the records.

There are multiple contradictions in the textual records, with regard to the subject of women. Different texts engage themselves differently, in the discussion on the subject of the feminine. These contradictions can be viewed from two levels. At one level, there are conflicts between the representations of women in the different texts and on another level there are inherent conflicting ideas within the contents of individual texts. These contradictions need to be seen in the context of the genre of text, the contents of the text and their purported message, the targeted audience and last who authored these texts.

The *Añguttara Nikāya, Buddhacharita* of Asvaghosa and the *Jātakas* all belong to different literary genres and are entirely different in content and composition. While the first of these is a canonical text, which contains the discourses of the Buddha, the second is a full-length biography of the Buddha and the third is a narrative text, compiled into the third book of the *Khuddaka Nikāya*, which, like the *Añguttara Nikāya*, is another text within the larger *Sutta Pitaka*. However these three texts have some fundamental similarities between them. All three present a strong anti-woman rhetoric. They were authored by men and were largely intended to be for a male audience (Falk 1972–3:105). Even the *Añguttara Nikāya* was probably composed keeping in mind the male monastics; as it states:

> *Monks, a woman even when going along, will stop to ensnare the heart of a man;*
> *Whether standing, sitting or lying down, laughing, talking or singing,*
> *weeping, stricken or dying, a woman will stop to ensnare the heart of a man*

and

> *Womenfolk are uncontrolled Ānanda,*
> *Womenfolk are envious, Ānanda,*
> *Womenfolk are greedy, Ānanda.*
>
> (*Añguttara Nikāya*)

These were compositions composed by men primarily for male (monastic and lay) audience. These texts vastly differ in content to compositions by women like the *Therigāthā* or a composition like the *Ittivuttaka* that was intended for mixed audience wherein the content has a considerably neutral and even positive female representation.

Contradictions in the contents of the different texts

The different perception of the feminine, as has been discussed earlier, is evident, for example, in the *Therigāthā* and the *Jātakas*. In the *Jātakas*, we find that in most cases, while for the monk, the woman was represented as a hindrance, a temptation or snare that would keep him away from the ultimate goal of salvation, for the common man, the wife was projected more often than not as a scheming adulteress, highlighting the women's transgressions. The narratives represent women as being prone to laziness, slovenly, scheming and adulterous. Even the stories about animals exclusively reflect the same anxieties and mode of conduct, reflecting the norms and values, which prevail in the world of men. Thus, even the animal kingdom has been depicted as having thoroughly internalised the psycho-social value systems of the humans. The fear of women's sexuality (which was widely shared by all categories of men) is put to effective use while indoctrinating the *bhikṣus*, about the innate threat that women represent.

The *Thērigāthā* brings out various facets of the women's nature, at times contradicting the *Jātakas*, but they cannot be overlooked, as these were composed by women authors and therefore provide us with one of the most accurate, factual and interpretive data on the subject. They provide us with a sum total of the pre- and post-renunciation experiences of the women, with crucial insight into their own perception of the family and society at large. In these tales the feminist element in a selection of the *gāthās* is amply evident. This distinctive gender consciousness is projected through a complex range of images, perceptions and thoughts. It can be seen in the articulations of Subhā (Davids 1909:142), for instance, which begins with a poignantly invoked reference to her existence as a female:

A maiden, I, all clad in white, once heard
The Norm, and hearkened eager, earnestly,
So in me rose discernment of the Truths.

(PsS: 142)

As against the negative estimations of women in the *Jātakas*, there is a sensitive awareness as well as acceptance of the feminine as seen in the *Therigāthā*, where in the introspection of self, none of the flaws of character and negativities attributed to women's intrinsic nature by (mostly male) critics were either perceived or acknowledged. On the contrary, there is a conscious acceptance of the female physical form at one level of understanding, while on another level is the belief that the limitations caused by the female form can be overcome and need not be a hindrance in one's spiritual quest.

In the *Therigāthā*, reliance on the feminine models of experience and reflection, backed by images and symbols that can likewise be linked to them, is particularly noteworthy. One of the *theris* recounts her experience of recognising the universality of impermanence (*aniccā*) as taught in Buddhism initially amidst domestic chores, actually in the course of what emerges as a cooking mishap.[10] Ambapālī arrives at a similar recognition in an even more strikingly feminine fashion: contemplating on the faded charms of her youth.[11] The sensitive portrayal, juxtaposing expression of the youthful female figure and the unlovely changes wrought upon it through the passage of time are evident in her articulations (Davids 1909:121–6). These are examples of Buddhist doctrinal reflection, rooted in feminine self-perceptions.

Then again, it is on the basis of a portrayal of a characteristic set of unhappy feminine experiences, emphasising on the pervasiveness of suffering (*dukkhā*) is highlighted in Kisaa Gotamī's *gāthās*; sharing home with hostile wives, giving birth in bitter pain, attempting suicide and the sad fate of still others when mother and child 'both alike find death'[12] have been well articulated in their verses as the 'woes of womanhood' (*dukkkho itthibhāvo*).[13]

In these compositions, one can discern an inversion of male paradigms. In many Buddhist writings, women are cast in roles of seductresses, bent on weaning away men from their spiritual quests.[14] However, in the *Therigāthā* (as in the verses of *therīs* Śubhā and Sumedhā[15]), there are evidences of an absolute role-reversal: far from fostering passion, in its verses, women proclaim piety and dispassion to worldly and passionate *men*. Accosted by a potential male stalker in her jungle retreat, Śubhā replied in the following manner:

> *Me pure, thou of impure heart; me passionless, thou of vile passions;*
> *Me who as to the whole of me freed am in spirit and blameless.*
> *Me whence comes it that Thou does hinder. . . .*[16]

It is thus evident that it is women's accomplishment in overcoming the carnal temptations of men and their attempts to divert women from spiritual endeavours that the verses of both the above *theris* most strikingly record.

'Liberty', 'liberation' and 'free womanhood' are ideas that are frequently dealt with in different contexts within the *Therigāthā*. The joyful expression of successfully overcoming the limitations imposed on them by culture and social structures on account of their gender are highlighted by quite a few of the *thērīs*. The use of the terms 'liberty', 'free womanhood' and the like are quite subjective and wide-ranging in the *Therigāthā*, and take into account freedom from household/domestic chores, and looking after ailing relatives, to more abstract, spiritual and philosophical interpretations of '*nibbānna*' and the like.

There are two different versions of the episodes of Bhaddā Kundlakesa joining the *Samgha*. The *thērī* who was well known as the foremost in debating and oratory skills was, according to the Dhammapada Commentary, humbled by Śāriputra, in a debate. She admitted defeat and wanted to know the answer to a particular query to which she had no answer. Shariputra agreed to oblige her on the condition that she join the order of the *Bhikśūṇīs*, to which the *thērī* Bhaddā readily consented. The Elder sent *Bhikśūṇīs* and had her ordained. Nevertheless, the verses of Bhaddā Kundalakesa,[17] in the *Therigāthā*, present quite a different picture of the same event.

In the Dhammapada version, the episode is located in Sāvatthi, while in the version of the *Therigāthā*, this incident is said to have taken place in the Vulture's Peak near Rājagaha (Paul 2005:270–1). Moreover in the version of the *Therigāthā* there is no mention of the verbal contestation that is mentioned in the Dhammapada. Instead it dwells on her own struggle to overcome the inner delusion and dilemmas that plagued her.

Contradictions within individual texts

Different texts reflecting different gendered perceptions have been traced to the fundamental gendered sensitivity of the authors of the ancient texts. At another level one can identify conflicting ideas within the contents of an individual text as well.

This is better explained by discussing a single text, for example, the *Añguttara Nikāya*. As has been seen above, the contents of the *Añguttara Nikāya* have a clearly misogynist perception. The following verse from the *Añguttara Nikāya* better explains this position:

> *Monks, it is impossible that a woman can be an arahant, a fully enlightened one; this status cannot be found. But, monks, it is possible that a man can be an arahant, a fully enlightened one. Monks, it is impossible that a woman can be a wheel turning King; this status cannot be found. But monks, it is possible that a man can be a wheel turning King. Monks, it is impossible that a woman can be a Sakka, a Mara, a Brahma.*[18]

However given the contents of the Doctrine of Incapability, the *Muluposattha Sutta*[19] of the *Añguttara Nikāya* is a paradox. The ideas expressed in it are in direct conflict with the excerpts discussed above. In this *Sutta*, the Buddha describes to Viśākha, the laywoman, the right and wrong ways of observing the *uposatha* days. Those who observe the *uposatha* correctly are destined to reap heavenly rewards, irrespective of one's gender. It states:

So whoever – man or woman —
is endowed with the virtues
of the eight-factored Uposatha,
having done meritorious deeds,
productive of bliss,
beyond reproach, goes
to the heavenly state.[20]

It is imperative to examine the issue of 'women's status' within its particular historical and cultural context, rather than analysing women's status in ancient Buddhism from contemporary feminist standards. It needs to be recognised that there was an ongoing discussion about sex/gender roles in the ancient Indian religious society which is reflected in the contemporary Buddhist textual tradition. The *Therigāthā* contains excerpts that do reflect that a female birth is difficult and regrettable, highlighting the travails and tribulations of a woman like 'sharing home with hostile wives' or 'giving birth in bitter pain', but nowhere do these texts delimit or question women's spiritual capabilities, unlike the above-mentioned texts like the *Añguttara Nikāya*. Even in spite of the Eight Chief Rules (*Gārudhamma*) and the Doctrine of Women's Incapability, apparently women were not deterred from entering the ascetic community, or *samgha*. In fact, when considering the other options available to women at the time, joining the monastic order might have been preferable, even with the Eight Special Rules and the Doctrine of Women's Incapability in place (Gurholt 2004). In fact, in the *Therigāthā*, we find a Buddhist woman's record of delight to be free of her house and husband:

O woman well set free! How free am I
How thoroughly free of kitchen drudgery!
Me stained and squalid 'mong my cooking pots
My brutal husband ranked as even less

Than the sunshades he sits weaving always.
Purged now of all my former lust and hate,
I dwell, musing at ease beneath the shade
Of spreading boughs – Oh but 'tis well with me!

Ancient Buddhist texts are replete with instances that reveal discussion on gender. This is better explained through an episode from the *Samyutta Nikāya,* which refers to the exchange between *bhikṣūṇīs* Soma and Mara, the latter derisively telling the nun that 'no woman can ever hope to achieve arhatship, "with her two finger wit"'[21] challenging while returning from her alms round was sitting under a tree in the forest, meditating.

Another episode on similar lines is found in the *Samyutta Nikāya,* where there is the mention of Queen Mallikā giving birth to a daughter (Paul 2005:257). The king, Pasenādi of Kośala, was distressed at hearing this news. The Buddha, on this occasion, is said to have told the king:

> *If a woman is clever, virtuous, well behaved and faithful, she is superior to a man. Then she might become the wife of a great King and give birth to a mighty ruler.*

In fact the inherent contradictions and conflicts within the contents of an individual text are indicative of the fact that there was an ongoing debate and, as stated by Ruth Vanita (2003), 'the often seemingly self-contradictory pronouncements about women found in accretive ancient texts may reflect that debate'.

Although Buddhism might have been a step forward for women in some regards, such as the start of organised female asceticism, ancient Buddhism certainly had a patriarchal and androcentric record of its own. However a religion that is patriarchal need not necessarily be fundamentally misogynistic or inequitable (Derris 2008). In fact a number of Buddhist literary compositions are contrary to patriarchy and sexism. Another excerpt from the *Therigāthā,* the *Isidāsi Sutra,*[22] better explains this point. *Bhikṣūṇī* Isidāsi, through her mystic powers, recounts her past life experiences to another inquiring female ascetic.

Learning of her past seven births, Isidāsi remembers that she has borne the consequences of her karma of having committed adultery in a past life by being reborn as afflicted animals, a slave girl and finally as a wife who could not satisfy her husband. This individual went from manhood to a life in hell, from hell to animal life and from animal life to that of a hermaphrodite and was finally reborn as a female. This journey through many lifetimes completed the sex change. Although it is certainly of interest that Isidāsi was reborn in the human form, only as a female after committing adultery (perhaps indicating female rebirth as penalty for the earlier misdeeds), what is more significant (at least with regard to this analysis) is that the offender was male, and after undergoing karmic retribution was born as a female, and it was only in this feminine state that Isidāsi realised awakening, and the causes of her failed relationships, and it was through the agency of this feminine form that she was eventually free of her karmic actions and attained arhantship. In fact, Isidāsi was not only reborn as a female after her male incarnation but also an androgynous human being.

> *Then I was born of a household slave in the street, neither as a woman or a man, because of having seduced another's wife.*

The introduction of the concept of androgyny in this narrative is significant. This narrative is also noteworthy for the fact that that the perpetrator was a male and not a female. Additionally, it was Isidāsi, a woman who ultimately achieved Enlightenment. What is most remarkable, however, is that the *Isidāsi Sutra* almost introduces us with the notion of the ungendered self. The concept of androgyny that is introduced in the narrative at this juncture is in its nascent stage. It is represented in the context of past life of Isidāsi. This concept gained ground over time and space, and in the later texts one can discern a distinctive undercurrent of androgyny in the compositions which, unlike the *Isidāsi Sutra* of the *Therigāthā*, is projected in the present as well as the future contexts.

In due course of time, as different sects of Buddhism like the *Mahāyāna* advocated for a more gender-inclusive approach, the representations concerning women became all the more unambiguously positive, which is reflected in a number of *Mahāyāna Sutra* like the Yogachāya literature, *Srimālā-Devī-Simha-nāda-Sutra*, which states: '*even a woman can obtain awakening*'.[23] Some of the much bolder projections of the androgynous theme can be seen in the *Vimalakirti Sutra*, the *Aśṭaśaṣrika* and the *Lotus Sutra* of *Mahāyāna*.

In the narrative, "the appearance of the Stupa" in the *Lotus Sutra*, is a similar conversation between the monk Śāriputra and a young princess who wishes to become a fully enlightened being (Bodhisattva). This *sutra* differs from the previous example in that, ultimately, the princess chooses to transform herself into a male in order to demonstrate to Śāriputra her enlightenment and spiritual ability, showing Śāriputra that he should not regard a woman as incapable of receiving the law. Different readings of the text brings out different meanings and different readings are brought about by differences in the perception of the readers. As Lisa Owen (1997) points out, 'One reading of this Sutra, the androcentric one, relies on the implicit assumption that a woman cannot overcome the limitations inherent in her female sex, and that there is something incompatible between the female form and enlightenment'. However, another reading of these *sutras* is that one should not depend on transient characteristics, such as gender, to determine one's true identity. Additionally, the women in these *sutras* did not necessarily change their sex because they *had to* in order become enlightened, but because they were *capable* of doing so in order to demonstrate their spiritual competence in a patriarchal religious society. This would also justify the performing of various miracles by Mahāpajāpati Gautamī and Yaśodharā (which is mentioned in the later Sinhalese Theravada texts) (Hardy 2003) immediately preceding their *nirvāṇa*, in spite of the fact that the Buddha clearly forbade his followers from performing miracles.[24] The popularity and resilience of this narrative is attested by its incorporation in numerous later Buddhist compositions like the *Princess Jātaka* (popular in South East Asia, composed during the 16th century) which eventually came to be incorporated within the biographical narrative of the Buddha, as his third lifetime.

The concept of female birth as a consequence of transgressions made and bad Karmic consequences can be detected in many of the Buddhist texts. However equally common are the narratives that negate this view. In the *Itthivimāna*, in answer to the verse questions put by senior *thēras* like Mahamoggallana, the goddesses explain in verse the meritorious deeds that have led to their rebirth in fabulously beautiful conditions. It is noteworthy that the stories present without comment or condemnation, female continuities across rebirths: in their past lives the goddesses were also female. Another instance can be seen in the verses of Patachāra in the *Therigāthā*. Patachāra was able to effect the change from a frivolous young girl to a *Samgha* elder quickly because in her previous births she had already developed the requisite spiritual facilities under previous Buddhas; it is said she was a nun many times in her past lives. Also nun Khēmā, whose experiences are also recorded in the *Therigāthā*, due to her superior deeds was always born in the proximity of the Bodhisattva. In one of her past lives she was born as the wife of the Boddhisatta, once as the daughter-in-law of the Bodhisattva and many a times as a queen, but she never took on a male birth (Cowell 2003).

These narratives stress on the equality among the sexes. Rather, Buddhism expounds that sexual differences belong to the phenomenal sphere, which is transient and illusory. In reality, beyond all appearances, sexuality is transcended. A similar story in *Surañgama Sutra*,[25] where the Bodhisattva Dridamati asks Gopaka-deva as to what kind of merit enables a woman to transform her female body? The male god replied that the issue is irrelevant because for the aspirant of the *Mahāyāna*; the discrimination does not exist in the mind of the enlightened being.

Given the multivocal and multivalent character of the Buddhist texts, it needs to be recognised that this textual tradition evolved over many centuries, accommodating within it the sociocultural milieu and religious requirements of the different periods. The texts cannot be treated as a single entity, professing a singular idea. The survey shows that the Buddhist texts exhibit different shades, where in the earlier texts one cannot overlook the strong misogynist overtones, with time, an all-inclusive gender approach led to the composition of texts with androgynous undertones. This was also at times visible in the early texts of the *Theravāda* like the *Therigāthā*; with the theme gaining ground, it found bolder expressions in many of the later texts of the *Mahāyāna* and other Buddhist sects. This phenomenon spread to other women-related subjects within Buddhism. One of these was the gradual social acceptance of the institution of the *Bhikśūṇīs* and this is effectively brought out in the narrative of the Tamil epic *Manimekalāi*. Thus one can observe the Buddhist textual tradition engaging itself with the issue of gender in various ways and in varied contexts. The difference in the treatment of the subject in different texts and also within a single text reflects an ongoing debate on the subject. Ironically, this debate is more overtly expressed in the texts composed by male authors as compared to the works of the female authors. This is better understood when we look at the episode of Bhaddā Kundalakesi in the Dhammapada Commentary and in the *Therigāthā*, respectively.

Buddhism was the first religion to officially establish organised, female asceticism (Ruth 2003). But even though women were officially permitted to join the *Samgha*, the social acceptance for this class of women happened gradually. Acceptance of the order of *bhikśūṇīs* was a gradual process and its slow acceptance is reflected in the subsequent Buddhist texts as well. Here it needs to be pointed out that some significant Buddhist texts that have survived like the *Manimekalāi* of Chathanar tried to mediate in favour of the concept of female renunciation and asceticism. He combats prevailing criticism of female renunciation by comparing the protagonist of his play – *Manimekalāi*, to a mother par excellence; her inexhaustible begging bowl enabling her to provide thousands of hungry people with nourishment. In order to address some of the anti-religious sentiments that Chathanar's sixth-century audience might have felt, he introduces the character of Cittirapati, Manimekalāi's grandmother, who advocates the futility of renunciation. In addition to discrediting the activities of the courtesan community, Chathanar makes an even stronger case by claiming that a female renouncer is worthy of the respect and acclaim accorded to a chaste wife. He develops this argument through the structure of the ascetic's speech to King Mavān Killi. The ascetic carefully draws parallels between the chaste wife and the woman who gives up marriage in order to undertake ascetic discipline. In this way, Chathanar likens the unfamiliar status of a Buddhist nun to that of an ancient Tamil cultural ideal – the woman who practices absolute conjugal fidelity. He identifies two types of women that one should not approach with lustful attentions. These two are the chaste woman and the ascetic women (renouncers).

With the insertion of these two subplots within the main narrative framework, Chathanar has tried to drive home the point that it is the responsibility of the king to protect female renouncers. Thus, the author employs this narrative to communicate with Royalty, interceding on behalf of the community of nuns to ask for support, protection and patronage. Chathanar adds another variable to his dialogue on the powers of women because he deals with both a female renouncer and a laywoman. Although, he believes, the two deserve the same status and respect, they practice self-control and discipline in different ways. The female renunciant gives up sexual union, while the chaste housewife circumscribes her behaviour and worships none but her husband. In each case, self-control yields rich consequences. Complimentary to the notion of female self-control is Chathanar's idea that the king must support and protect such disciplined women, especially members of the monastic community. In arguing that point, Chathanar encourages his audience to accept the Buddhist view of kingship rather than the Hindu one. Classical Hindu texts depict the righteous king as one who maintains the social order. But *Manimekalāi* argues that a righteous king's real duty is to support and protect members of the monastic community.[26] Thus, through the complex weaving and interweaving of plots and subplots with the primary narrative framework, the author tries to restructure the society's perception and its attitude towards chaste women, both ascetics and laywomen.

Buddha and his disciples did not and could not fail to come into contact with women. The seclusion of women from the outer world (which later customs has enjoined) was unheard of in ancient India, with women actively participating in various capacities in the social and religious activities, as is also attested by the female donor records. And it was all the more difficult to procure the isolation of these women from the *bhikśūṇīs*.

Conflict between the social and the asocial worlds

There was a perceptible distinction between the lay and the monastic world, which is amply brought out in the canonical texts, in the form of prescriptions and injunctions which sought to distinguish and differentiate the lay patrons from the members of the *Samgha*. However, interaction between the *Samgha* and the laity was inevitable – *dāna*, being the umbilical cord that bound the two groups in a bond of interdependence and called for their interaction at various levels. The second half of this chapter analyses the social dynamics and level of interaction and conflicts between each of these numerous groups, namely:

1. Interaction between *bhikśūṇīs* and *Bhikṣu Samgha*
2. Interaction among the *bhikśūṇīs*
3. Interaction amidst *bhikśūṇīs* and *upāsikās*
4. Interaction between *bhikśūṇīs* and the lay society (both laymen and women)

Historians studying this sociopolitical system of the early centuries of the Christian era generally believe it to be a period of large-scale sociopolitical instability and decline, in which the position of the woman was believed to be particularly abysmal. During this period the social opposition to female ascetics was particularly strong. The contemporary Buddhist tradition entailed that for a woman, the most important duties to be fulfilled were those of a wife and mother. In spite of all odds, the woman of this day and age, in various capacities and in multiple roles of daughter, wife and mother, managed to walk against the tide, successfully exercising her option of not always opting for a lay life like the decision to forgo the much celebrated and most important role of a mother and/or a wife for most part. At other times she succumbed to familial and social pressures and gave in to conventionally accepted roles. This must have been the cause of considerable social conflict and resistance. It would also account for the deep-seated antagonism and distrust against those who decided to tread the less-travelled path of a *bhikśūṇī*, as against the conventionalised and traditional roles of wife and mother.

There are various references to instances of interaction between the *bhikśūṇīs* and the '*upāsikās* or women of the world' that we come across in literature (e.g. in the *Thērigāthā*, the *Jātakas*, etc.) and along with it also instances of resistance to this interaction by the society at large. When *Bhikśūṇīs* took to renunciation, they still managed to keep in touch with the society, which they had left behind. They are sometimes mentioned to have gladly given up 'the toils and drudgery of a life of crisis', but at times the need for the assertion of their epistemological space tore their minds into two halves. This is evident in the case of nun *Samgha*[27] who felt an intense and urgent need for spiritual fulfilment but once in the *Samgha*, she could not stop herself from thinking about her lay existence, prior to her renunciation, of her children and the like.

The *bhikśūnīs* did not sever all kinds of bonds, but instead there was a transformation in their attitude towards the society as against the *thēras* who opted for complete severing of social bonds (Blackstone 2000). The literary records reflect various shades of interaction between *bhikśūnīs* and the society, which reveal both positive and negative implications. The lay Buddhist community which was, on the one hand, patronising the *Bhikśūnī Samgha* also bore a deep-seated mistrust and prejudice against the same. The fear and insecurities of the lay people prompted them to keep their girls and women away from the *bhikśūnīs*, who they felt posed a threat and had a corruptible influence on the vulnerable minds of their womenfolk (Davids 1930).

This reflects a subtle tension that existed between the lay people and the community of *bhikśūṇīs*.

Relationship between *bhikśūṇīs*

Bhikśūṇīs were members of the *Bhikśūṇī Samgha* that required its members to coexist amicably in a communal set-up. The organisation of the *Bhikkhunī Samgha* comprised of a structured hierarchy of monastic/ascetic women and rules were formulated which would help maintain order and decorum within the community of the nuns. However, in their everyday interactions, differences were bound to surface among the members. These differences also find mention in the *Bhikśūṇī Vinaya*, often with accompanying examples of the instances when the altercations took place and rules that were eventually made in order to resolve those differences. The *Bhikśūṇī Pāṭimokkha* contains 311 rules. Most of these rules are similar to those of the *bhikṣūs* in the *Bhikṣū Vinaya*. But there are 85 such rules that do not find corresponding mention in the *Bhikṣū Vinaya*. More than one-third of these extra rules were formulated to protect *bhikśūṇīs* from being the direct recipients of the abusive or careless behaviour of other *bhikśūṇīs*. According to the stories that often precede the formation of the rules, all but three of the extra rules[28] (*Pācittiyas* 59, 94 and 95) were formulated only after *bhikśūṇīs* complained to the *Bhikṣūs* about an aberrant *bhikṣūṇī's* behaviour.

Relationship between *bhikṣūṇīs* and *bhikṣūs*

The relationship between *bhikṣūs* and *bhikśūṇīs* was a matter of some concern for the Buddha, right from the time of the formation of the nuns' order. He is said to have forewarned that the entry of women into the order would have a negative impact on the existence of the *Bhikṣū Samgha*, which led to the creation of the eight *gārudhammas* that were to be practiced by the Buddhist nuns in their interactions with the monks' community. These rules are the earliest references to differences between the order of monks and the *Bhikṣūṇīs*, as Mahāpajāpati Gautamī felt the need to speak against the rule which stated that a senior *bhikṣūṇī* would stand up in reverence on seeing a much junior monk was not fair to the *bhikśūṇīs*. Subsequently the *gārudhammas* became the framework on which the monk–nun interactions came to rest.

Sponberg views the discussion between Mahāpajāpati Ānanda and the Buddha, on the subject of women's renunciation within Buddhism, as a 'document of reconciliation, as a symbolic, mythologised expression of a compromise between several factions of the order, including the nuns and their male supporters. The issue was resolved only over a period of time . . . and the document is a still later attempt to rationalize and legitimize post facto what had already become status quo' (Sponberg 1992:16).

There were other rules besides those mentioned above, which were also aimed at maintaining cordial relations between the two communities; for example two of the extra rules pertaining to *bhikśūṇīs in* the *Bhikkhunī Vinaya* (*Pācittiyas* 6 and 44) prevent *bhikśūṇīs* from putting themselves in a position of servitude to *bhikṣus* or the lay community.

'The focus of concern for the monks is public opinion. The issue is not stereological theory as much as preserving the social acceptability necessary to financial support. The problem faced by the community at this stage of development in fact was a true dilemma, one born of the shift towards coenobitic monasticism, an institutional structure that had no precedent in the history of Indian religions. On the one hand the two sub-communities of monks and nuns had to maintain sufficient distance from each other to avoid questions of impropriety, and on the other hand they had to deal with the social unacceptability of an autonomous group of women not under the direct regulation and control of some male authority'.[29]

Interaction between *bhikśūṇīs* and laywomen

Interaction between *bhikśūṇīs* and laywomen is clearly reflected in some of the literary sources like the *Thērigāthā*. As discussed earlier, even post renunciation, the *theris* find it difficult to break free from the social matrix they originally were a part of, while for the *theras* the most outstanding aspect of their spiritual struggle as seen in most cases deals with overcoming of sexual desire and lust which for them is personified in the feminine form, and not disengaging themselves from their family ties.

This explains one of the reasons why severing of ties with the lay community was more difficult for the nuns as compared to the monks. This fact is better understood when we look at the epigraphic records of the period. Even in the donor records pertaining to the *bhikśūṇīs*, there is the merging of their social as well as their asocial or monastic identities. A woman entering the Buddhist *Samgha* was required to take oath, 'I go forth to a homeless life, following the Lord Sākyamunī . . . I abandon the superficial characteristics of a householder'.[30] The oath clearly implies breaking off of all familial ties, and yet, in some form the family ties continued. Various donor records prove this point. For example:

> *The gift of a vēdikā by the nun Kodī, mother of Ghunika, made by Nādika.*[31], and, *Pious gift of a lion pedestal of the Thēra, Bhayata Budhi the enlarger of the* Chaitya *and of his sister (bhaginī) the nun (bhikhunī) Budhā.*[32]

It was also far easier for *bhikśūṇīs* to interact with laywomen, who they once shared their lives with. Furthermore the laywomen, given the sociocultural condition of the period of study, found in these nuns ready listeners along with the opportunity to share the woes of their lives of toil and drudgery. For most of these *bhikśūṇīs*, once having lived these very experiences themselves, they could easily identify, bond with and relate to these women and their experiences. Second, some of the rules of the *Samgha* made interaction between the two female groups inevitable, for example, one of which prescribed that *bhikṣūṇīs* should bathe at a bathing place used by women.[33]

The *bhikṣūṇīs* talking about their new-found 'freedom' and happiness, more often than not, found in these 'women of the world', 'enthusiastic listeners' and ready followers. This probably explains the large number of conversions that were brought about by the *bhikṣūṇīs*. One finds numerous instances where a number of *bhikṣūṇīs* became models to be emulated by their ardent women followers like Patachāra,[34] who was revered by many women, to whom she had shown the way. Another instance is that of Sundarī[35] who appears to have made a great many converts including all her kinsfolk, beginning with her mother, and their attendants. There are numerous instances of nuns making religious grants with members of their families. The coming together of (family) laywomen along with nuns on a common religious platform is better elucidated by the following example of the Amarāvatī Votive Inscription:

> *The gift of the female lay-worshipper (upāsikā) Kāmā, with daughter (duhitā) of the householder (gahapati) Idā, daughter (duhitā) of the housewife (gharani) Kānha, with her sons, brothers, sisters and nun (Bhikśūṇī kā) Nāgamitā. . . .*[36]

Chathanar, the author of *Manimekalāi*, also dwells on the 'donor–donee' relationship and focuses on the positive aspect of the relationship between laywomen and *bhikṣūṇīs*. He does this by describing how Atirāi, who is known throughout the city (of Pukār) as a chaste and virtuous housewife, places the first alms in Manimekalāi's begging bowl. From this point onward, it never again becomes empty. Wandering through the streets of the city with her miraculous vessel, Manimekalāi distributes food to the needy. Chathanar compares her generous acts to 'rains nourishing the land and to a cow nurturing its calf'. Because of her dedication she convinces the king to transform the city prison into a complex of religious buildings – including rooms where virtuous people can reside and halls for cooking and dining.

Social antagonism towards the *bhikṣunīs*: the lay society versus *bhikṣunīs*

Women during this period exercised their individual discretion to a large extent, in matters that shaped the quality of their lives. This is evident in the varied alternate preferences that women opted for during this period, for example, giving up the most common and popularly accepted role of a 'wife and mother' and instead embracing 'spinsterhood'. There are numerous examples of women who chose to remain spinsters throughout their lives, for example, *bhikṣūṇī* Abhirūpa Nandā,[37] daughter of the Sākiyas of Kapilavatthu, and *bhikṣūṇī* Somā of Rājagaha.[38] Renunciation was not the only option available to this particular segment that chose not to marry. There are more than just a few examples of women who went on to become celebrated courtesans of their day and age, for example, Ambapāli[39] of Vaiśāli, Vimalā[40] (herself an ex-courtesan as also the daughter of a courtesan of Vaiśāli).

Drawing a clear line between personal space and domestic space, these women identified the latter by the home and the hearth. Their acknowledgement of a private individual space vis-à-vis public and/or domestic space is well documented. When we look at the *Thērigāthā*, a number of women, from all kinds of socio-economic backgrounds for different reasons found their present status as a wife, daughter, queen or maid and so forth inadequate and unfulfilling. It was this sense of inadequacy that, in many cases, led them to renunciation.

These women were worldly-wise, capable of assimilating true knowledge derived from the lessons from their life as well as those of others, as also of imparting it. Patachāra's[41] eloquent statement, 'Sons are no shelter, nor father, nor kins folk, overtaken by death, for these blood bond is no refuge . . .' is in direct contradiction and confrontation to the popular quote by Asvaghosa in which he states that '[d]ependence on others is great suffering, self dependence the highest bliss; yet when born in the race of Manu, all women are dependent on others'.[42]

Manu, the famous author of the ancient Hindu law in his Manusmriti (200 B.C.E.–100 C.E.), also states in the same vein that 'in childhood a female must be subject to her father, in youth to her husband, when her lord is dead to her sons; a woman must never be independent. . . . By a girl, by a young woman or even by an aged one, nothing must be done independently, even in her own house' (Manu 3.56-8, *Laws of Manu*, trans. George Buhler, New York: Dover Publication, 1969).

Patachara's statement, other than being a blatant refutation and inversion of the contemporary social norms, also shows the need as well as the capability for independent thought and action, which was hardly ever credited to women. The need and the will to speak the mind clearly becomes evident in this case.

It will not be an exaggeration to state that the awareness and acknowledgement of the concept of personal space was deeply ingrained in the minds of these women. A strong sense of individuality and the desire to assert their need for personal space manifested itself in a number of ways, in different situations. Nevertheless, the expression of personal space was done in subtle ways and one needs to read between the lines of their personal chronicles (e.g. the *Thērigāthā*) to understand and appreciate how, in that day and age, they managed to cling on to and celebrate their individuality.

Even though in most of these cases the decision to remain unmarried and also the decision to renounce the world were individual decisions, there were a few exceptions. 'It was largely the socio-political climate, that opened up the renunciation alternative for women. The despondency prevailing in the society at about the beginning of the Christian era began to wear down the opposition to the *saniyāsa* ideal' (Altekar 1956). This probably explains the rather flexible attitude of parents towards their offsprings who wished to take up the monastic vows. The insecurity that was rampant in the society, following incessant foreign aggressions, also helped them to decide in favour of monastic living for their daughters, instead of having unmarried daughters in their houses. For example, Abhirupā Nandā, the daughter of a wealthy and distinguished Sākiyan of Kapilavastu (*Thērīgātha*, 19), was made to leave the world, against her will, by her parents, when Cārabhuta, her young

Sākiyan kinsman and suitor, died. In another instance, Uppalāvanna of Sāvatthi, daughter of a treasurer (*Thērīgātha*, 64), was sent to the convent by her father, as he was not able to choose one from the many suitors who came for her, and not willing to displease any one of them asked her opinion. When she willingly consented, he honoured her and then took her to the order of the *bhikśūṇīs*. In a slightly different case, Sundari Nandā of Hansāvati (*Thērīgātha*, 41), who belonged to the family of the Sākyas of Kapilavastu, decided upon renunciation as all the members of her family had taken up the resolve to renounce the world. Thus, we have women who joined the order of their own volition, others were forced to join the *Samgha* while yet others succumbed to familial pressures.

This individual freedom to lead their lives on their own terms, as 'renunciants', was not available to all. In many cases this freedom was circumscribed and curtailed to a large extent, and in most of the cases it was the overburdening responsibility of the house and the family, which kept them from doing so.

There are examples of extraordinary resilience and perseverance of women who had set their minds on to the spiritual path. This is better understood when we look at the instance of Sumana, the sister of the king of Kośala, who delayed her decision to join the order, so that she could take care of her ailing grandmother (*Thērīgātha*, 16), while Dhammā of Sāvatthi (*Thērīgātha*, 17) waited till her husband was no more, as during his lifetime he would not permit her to join the *Samgha*. In the first two instances, it was the male kin facilitating the process – the husband in the first case, the brother (king of Kośala), who took the respective women to the *Samgha* while the third is an instance of discouraging and unsupportive opposition by the family.

Widowed as well as unmarried girls and women formed a considerable part of the *Bhikṣūṇī Samgha*. The general mistrust and hostility towards women, who for whatever reasons, failed to comply with their traditionally laid down role of motherhood and as wife, is well documented. Their decision to forgo this much-celebrated role in the society and opt for this less-accepted role of a renunciant shows them as having mind, character and will of their own, which they ascertained in their own way, at different times. This was bound to raise the antagonism and hostility towards them, in the society. Certain incidents like the relationship between a *bhikṣūṇī* and a woman, who bore a child, wherein the *bhikṣūṇī*, acting as her confidant, carried away the foetus in her alms-bowl (*Cūllavagga*, X, 13.1) further eroded their credibility in the society, as by such negative acts they further earned the mistrust of the society. These renunciants, it was generally believed, with their self-centred, independent existence, had a negative and corruptible influence on the vulnerable and easily influenced the minds of their lay sisters. Men sought to control and regulate the interaction between their womenfolk and the community of *bhikśūṇīs* and keep it at a barest minimum. This they did by exercising their influence (as lay supporters and as donors to the *Samgha*) directly and indirectly over the *Bhikṣu Samgha*, where the Buddha and the community of monks acted as intermediaries, between the lay community and the order of *bhikśūnis*.

In most of the laws pertaining to the order of *bhikśūṇīs*, it can be seen that they start with a frequently repeated quote: 'the people murmured, were indignant and complained, saying; "as the women who are still enjoying the pleasures of the world do!' in the *Cūllavagga*. This was always followed by enumeration of an incident where the nun or group of *bhikśūṇīs*' actions or behaviour was identical to that of the women of the world. These complaints were almost always immediately addressed, followed by immediate redressal of wrongdoing, which involved formulation of the rules by the Buddha, for the Order of *bhikśūṇīs*.

The Buddhist *Samgha* was also in a way responsible for lesser number of women joining the *Samgha*. Compared to the order of the monks, the chapter of the *bhikśūṇīs* was always in need of resources, with very few patrons that the order of the *bhikśūṇīs* attracted.[43] This also restricted the avenues open to women who chose to renounce lay living.

Their individuality is reflected in a variety of situations, most frequently in the way they choose to identify themselves, as discussed in the previous chapter. The *thēris* in their autobiographical compositions have more often than not identified themselves by their clan groups, as also by their caste names and occupational group (e.g. daughter of a Brāhman, daughter of a *sēthi*, daughter of a burgess). Occasionally, they refer to themselves as the 'wife of . . .'. The husband's name is mentioned rarely and in case of their being prominent personalities, for example, Khēmā, daughter of the king's family at Sagala[44] in Magadha, wife of King Bimbisara, Rājagaha, foremost of the sisters who were distinguished for insight ranked by the Buddha as a model sister.[45] Here it is important to note that in most cases (see Table 2) the biological family gains precedence (in direct contravention of social conventions) over the family into which they were married, that is, being 'wife of . . .', was a secondary criterion. They asserted their individuality by identifying themselves by their native place in most cases. In this particular case,[46] referring to her intellectual and spiritual attainments was also her way of proclaiming and alluding to the individuality. This though does not necessarily mean that marital relations were strained. In fact in most cases the references pertaining to marital relations are cordial and in a number of cases it is the husbands who not only permitted their wives to join the *Samgha* but also understood their need to do so and even actively supported them. This is in direct contrast to the image of marital discord and dissatisfaction as reflected in the *Jātakas*.

Defying the conventional mode of identification (i.e. by referring to their patriarchal affiliations), some even chose to identify themselves through the names of their mothers. Though for courtesans and their daughters, this was an accepted practice (Davids 1989).[47]

The acknowledgement and assertion of personal space by these ladies is reflected in the number of decisions that they took and in their actions pertaining to their everyday lives. Though the classical commentators enjoined time and again that women due to their inherent nature were creatures not to be trusted and rather to be controlled and safeguarded, these women surfaced very often as individuals with sound individual judgement, as rational, opinionated beings.

Very often within Buddhism, we come across these women patrons and lay devotees who choose to follow the religion, independent of their families, with or without the support of the latter. A suitable example here is that of Śubhā,[48] the goldsmith's daughter, who comprehended and acknowledged her spiritual call, and devoted herself to the 'higher paths'. Though there are numerous instances of this kind, the most famous is that of Mahāpajāpati Gautamī, who decided to take refuge in the *Samgha*, followed the Buddha relentlessly, forced him to give in and ultimately allow women into the order.

Though renunciation was an extreme step in one's exercise of individual choice in religious matters, there were others who even in the capacity of the lay-*upāsikās* strove to keep the precepts (*silās*) and strictly adhere to them. Some such strong-willed women were Yashodhara (wife of Gautama Buddha) who after the *Mahābhīniṣkramaṇa* of the Buddha lived the life of an ascetic, while still residing in the palace, even before she had taken up the monastic vows (Davids 1989). There is also the case of an anonymous *thēri*, popularly known as 'Sturdykin', who was the wife of a nobleman of Vaiśāli. As her husband would not consent to her wish of joining the order, she as a lay-follower went on practicing the precepts laid down in the doctrine and observing the precepts, till he finally agreed and gave in, allowing her to join the order. These acts of subtle yet determined assertion of their personal spaces need to be closely looked at.

The demarcation between the personal and public as well as domestic space comes out distinctly in the works of the *thēris*. The desire and also the reasons which finally brought about renunciation were varied and individual-specific in each case. While for some, death of a close member of the family (children, husband) was the moving force (*Thērigāthā*, Canto III, XXIX, XXXIII, XXXV; Canto VI, LI, Canto IX, LXIII, Canto XII, LXIX), in other cases, it was the chain of the circumstances that impelled women to break out of the traditional social groove. Escape, deliverance, and freedom (from suffering, mental, moral, domestic, social) from circumstances that had become unendurable are reflected in the verses and explained as the varied reasons for renunciation. 'The bereaved mother, the childless widow are emancipated from grief' (*Thērigāthā*, Cantos V, XLVII, XLVIII, VI, LI.); the courtesans get deliverance from remorse and social ostracism (*Thērigāthā*,Cantos II, XXII, XXVII, Cantos V, XXXIX, Cantos XIII, LXVI) and the like, a wealthy lady from the satiety and emptiness of an idle life of luxury (*Thērigāthā*, Cantos XIII, LXX, XVI, LXXIII), the poor man's wife's escape from care and drudgery (*Thērigāthā*, Cantos XI, XXI, LXIII), and the young girl, from the humiliation of being handed over to the suitor who bid the highest (*Thērigāthā*, Cantos IX,LXIV).

Apart from the above-mentioned negative reasons which became the immediate cause of their leaving the world, there are more positive (rather spiritual) causes that led them towards renunciation. One common reason being 'the drawing power of the *Dhamma*' that led them to give up lay life. The mental upheaval or commotion (*samvēga*) produced in the hearer is occasioned, not so much by a 'sense of sin' as by the flash of insight into the universal impermanence in all things human and divine, and by the prospect of being reborn in the world, without and in the infinite chain of life, even renewing itself in the resultants of its own acts (*Thērigāthā*, Cantos I, II, III, Cantos II, XXV, XXXIII, XXXIV). In one instance, Candā (*Thērigāthā*, Cantos V, XLIX), the daughter of a poor Brahman (poverty-stricken and lonely), was begging for food. The *bhikśūṇīs* fed her. But it was not the immediate redressal of her material needs, but an understanding of the doctrine, as it was only after being convinced by the philosophy and hearing their discourse that she decided to join the order.

Thus, in opting for a particular religious sect and/or becoming its member, these women exercised their sole prerogative and discretion. Though the crisis in their personal lives did at times have a catalytic effect on their decisions to join the *Samgha*, this one aspect has been rather overplayed by scholars.

It is evident that the right to opt for a particular religious group, the decisions to provide alms/*dāna* and the like was very much the prerogative of 'the women of the house'.

In personal lives also, the decision to remain a spinster and forgo marriage were very much personal and though the societal conditions of the period are believed to have been very constricting and 'anti-women', it was quite often that such transgressions on the part of women did occur. Even within the *Thērigāthā* there are a number of instances where a girl chooses the convent over an eligible bridegroom of her own free will (*Thērigāthā* Cantos XVI, LXXIII). Some of these woman even settled for less-respectful options. Addhakāśi, the daughter of a *sētthi* of Kāśi, who came from an affluent family, opted for the life of a courtesan (*Thērigāthā*, Cantos II, XXII). Among them the famous were Vimalā, Śirimā, Ambapāli, Bindūmati, Salāvati, Sulāsā and others (*Jātaka* no. 419).

One often comes across references to self-supporting women who were engaged in various trades and professions. For instance, a certain woman was the custodian of a paddy field, another watched the cotton fields (*Jātakas*, Cowell, 546). Women like 'Kāli' are also referred to as keepers of the burning grounds (*Thērīgāthā* Commentary on CXXXVI; *Dhammapada* Commentary on verses 7–8), though no mention is made of any wage she might have received. But she had at heart the welfare of those who came to mediate in the charnel field and so provided them with objects suitable for the contemplation of impermanence. An interesting description of a women acrobat is also obtained (*Dhammapada* Commentary on verse 348). Probably some of the 500 tumblers with whom she was were also women, who used to visit Rājagaha (annually or twice a year) and give performances for seven days, before the king. But more numerous were domestic female slaves. They formed part of the property of the most wealthy householders. But the references are inadequate with regard to data pertaining to the financial security and independence enjoyed by the women.

Be it in the actions of *thēris*, or be it in the actions of that of the laywomen, subtle as well as indiscrete actions which reflect the often-discussed 'transgression' in secondary literature on the subject surface time and again. Contrary to the essentially feminine virtues attributed to these women in the classical texts like gentleness, tenderness and a certain patient resignature, one comes across attitudes reflecting defiance, spirit of determined resistance, desire for revenge and retribution, in their acts.

There are instances where young women unhesitatingly professed their love and preferences for the man of their choice. For example, Patacāra, a beautiful girl, being reborn in the treasurer's house, when grown up, grew intimate with one of the serving men of her house and on the day of her marriage eloped with her paramour.[49] In another instance, Bhaddā, the daughter of the king's treasurer, fell in love with Sātthuka, the chaplain's son, who was being led to execution by the city guard. Later, on realising that she had been exploited and fooled by Sātthuka, she became intent on revenge and pushed him over the precipice. Her wit, presence of mind and cleverness are praised by the mountain deity as follows:

Not in every case is man the wiser ever;
Woman, too, when swift to see, may prove as clever.
Not in every case man the wiser reckoned
Woman, too, is clever, as she think but a second.[50]

A similar tale of revenge and murder at being duped is seen in the case of a courtesan Sāmā, who lived in Banaras (*Jātakas*, nos 318 and 419).There are also instances when girls on attaining the proper age, which generally ranged between 20 and 30, went of their own accord in search of husbands. The *Bidāla Kukkuta Jātaka* lays special stress on the requirement of the girls' declaration of chastity by beat of drums in such a '*swayamvara*' marriage.

Divorce was permissible if either party was found guilty of adultery or unfaithfulness. These were the only grounds on which a woman was allowed to divorce her husband, who, on the other hand, might put away his wife if she was barren, and if he found her uncongenial as is shown in Isidāsi's case. Isidāsi was given in marriage thrice and deserted each time. Uppalavama's husband left her after the birth of a daughter. The practice of remarriage was not an aberration but very much a social practice, and Isidāsi was in all probability acting in conformity with contemporary public opinion rather than in opposition to it (*Thērīgāthā*, LXXII).[51] Queen Mallikā followed the teachings of *ahimsa*. She decried animal sacrifice by King Prasenjit (*Dhammapada* Commentary, verse 60). King Udāna was converted through his Queen Samāvati (*Dhammapada* Commentary, verses 21–23). Another queen influential in the spread of Buddhism was Dhananjani; her husband became a *bhikşu* and attained *arhatship* (*Samyukta Nikāya*, 7).

Women in various roles, even as matrons of the house at times, did command their own space. They were instrumental in most of the decision-making process in the family. Just as the father, mother's permission was also required by those novices the *Samgha*. There is also a reference of a mother dedicating her unborn child to the *Samgha*.[52] Mothers are known to have encouraged their sons and daughters to enter the order.

With the coming of Buddhism, the options open to the women increased considerably. They had the luxury of varied options rather than living out their doomed existence. They now had a refuge that would give them the much-desired space that they yearned for. They were free to join the *Samgha* with the prior permission of their parents and spouses. This was made mandatory so as to ensure that they amicably bid farewell to their worldly existence and did not carry any emotional baggage to the world of the *Samgha*. It also ensured that they fairly handed over their responsibilities and charges over to their kin. There are references to some mothers entrusting their children to the care of their own people and the children being well looked after, in the absence of the mother. It is stated that after being ordained, *Samgha* experienced tranquility. For that, she left her home, children and domesticated beasts, 'along with their attachment, repulsion and ignorance and extracted craving (*tanha*) completely' (*Therīgāthā*, 64.). The *Samgha* imposed no limitation on these women. Though prior to their being ordained they were asked a number of questions, so as to make sure they were not joining the *Samgha* under duress, were of the right age and mature enough to decide upon their future course of life. As *bhikśūṇīs* also, there were no restrictions or limitations on these women, which would keep them tied to the *Samgha*. They were free to leave the *Samgha*, if they wished to. Thus, these women on becoming a part of the *Samgha* were liberated both spiritually and physically. Another factor which provided them the much-needed mobility and freedom was the delegation of property rights (which were not recognised in the Vedic age when women were better-educated and enjoyed greater freedom).

Relationship between the laity and the Samgha

Without a laity, which professed a faith in Buddha and Buddha's teachings, and evinced its faith in pious offices, above all in works of helpful beneficence, an order of mendicants could not be thought of, and the religious movement of Buddhism would have been unable to command the immensely popular social base which it did. Tradition represents, as part of this religious organisation, not merely the *bhikṣūs* and *bhikṣūṇīs*, but also (*upāsakas*) and (*upāsikās*), the last two forming the vital support and resource base for the *Sangha*.

The growing needs of the *Bhikṣūs Samgha* naturally resulted in the establishment of permanent ties between the *Samgha* and the laity. So long as *bhikṣūs* toured incessantly, no continuing relationship between the *Samgha* and the people was likely to emerge. The original relationship had existed in the basic gift of alms in exchange for which the *bhikṣūs* taught *dharma* to the giver and then moved on. With the concept of permanent residences or *vihāras* emerging for the monks, a constant relationship was built up between the *Samgha* and some sections of the people, who became *upāsakās* and *upāsikās*, supporting the *Samgha* for its minimum needs and accepting the Buddha's basic teachings at the same time.

The transformation of the *Samgha* from a loose group of wandering *bhikṣūs* to a settled monastic organisation was made possible only due to lay support. *Dāna* was the link between the laity and the *Samgha*. While, on the one hand, it was the support base of the *Samgha* for the laity it was the most important means available to the layman for accumulating merit (A. 11.69).

The relationship between the Buddhist *Samgha* and the laity, through the medium of *dāna*, brought the laity more sharply into focus in the Buddhist world. Since the laity provided for the *Samgha*, they were an important constituent of the Buddhist society and often exercised their influence on the *Samgha*. The conduct of the *bhikṣūs* was ultimately shaped and moulded by the very society that they had opted out of. This is clear from the many rules laid down for *bhikṣūs* that were criticised by the laity.

The association between the society and the *Samgha* was based on certain fundamental rules. Rules were laid out for the monks as well as for the laity, which clearly sought to establish the code of conduct for both the groups, also with respect to women. In the *Cūllavagga*, Ānanda is believed to have enquired of the Buddha: 'How are we to conduct ourselves, Lord with regard to womankind?'

> *Don't see them, Ānanda.*
> *But if we should see them, what are we to do?*
> *Abstain from speech Ānanda.*
> *But if they should speak to us, Lord, what are we to do?*
> *Keep wide awake, Ānanda.*
>
> (*Cūllavagga*, V.23)

Even if these were not necessarily the words of the Buddha, it still certainly stands till today as the widely accepted Buddhist attitude on the subject. In the 'Legend of Angulimāla', as is mentioned in the Singhalese source *Amawaturā*, there are four things that are not to be trusted – a robber, a branch, the king and a woman (Hardy 1995). This social sensitivity which looked down upon women was decisive in largely shaping the lay and monastic perceptions, including those of the *bhikṣūṇīs*. The numerous rules, around which the superstructure of the *Bhikṣūnī Samgha* came to support itself, were initially formulated in keeping with this perspective.

It is against this backdrop that we need to study and assess the actual position of women and more so of the *bhikṣūṇīs*, within Buddhism and to analyse whether there actually did exist a situation of conflict between the social world and its asocial counterpart.

Buddha's disciples (monks) kept themselves aloof from the female sex, as was expected of them and as were also laid down in the rules pertaining to the conduct of *bhikṣūs* with regard to women.[53] Admission into the order was conceded to women only with reluctance and under conditions, which involved their absolute subjection to the monks.[54] The eight chief rules that were specially made for the *bhikṣūṇīs* were never to be transgressed and were made mandatory, primarily in order to conform to the laid norms of the period. Mahāpajāpati Gautamī's request that salutations and reverencing of a novice *bhikṣū* by a superior *bhikṣūnī* be disallowed was turned down by the Buddha, who told Ānanda, 'this is impossible, Ānanda, and unallowable that I should so order. Even those others Ānanda, teachers of ill doctrine, allow not such conduct towards women; how much less, then, can, the Tathāgatha allow it?' (*Cūllavagga*, X, 3,1).[55] This statement from the *Cūllavagga* is suggestive of the fact that even the Buddha was not entirely unresponsive to the pressures and perceptions that governed the society.

Thus, we see that these words of the Buddha reflect the contemporary social as well as Buddhist attitudes towards the female sex. The Buddhists had a dialectical relationship with the new system of production and the new society emerging in the sixth century B.C., demonstrating simultaneously both an opposition and unity with it (Kosambi 1994).

Controls and sanctions imposed by the laity on the Samgha

A notable feature of the relationship between the *Samgha* and the laity was the *bhikşūs*' limited control over their lay followers. According to the *Cūllavagga* on occasion of discord between the two, the only available option for the *bhikşūs* to express disapproval was to turn their alms-bowl upside down in a symbolic refusal of the proffered alms, thereby depriving the alleged lay follower of merit.[56] More often than not, the *Samgha* gave in to the demands of its lay patrons, thus ensuring for the *Samgha* its sustenance.

The *Samgha* was, for the common man, an ideal to be emulated in their everyday lives. It was the embodiment of all perfections, which men strove to achieve all through their lives. Thus the motive behind the numerous complaints by the laity was to get rules enforced that would keep the *Samgha* tied to all the ideals and perfections that it stood for. So, by their self-appointed moral policing and censure, they tried to control and circumscribe the activities of the *Samgha* more so of the *bhikśūṇīs.* This is evident from the specific issues on which they thought fit to comment and object. Rules for the *Bhikśūṇī Samgha* can broadly be divided, on the basis of the subjects they relate to, into five categories.

(1) Rules pertaining to *Vinaya* and *Dhamma.*
(2) Rules pertaining to conduct towards *bhikśūs.*
(3) Rules pertaining to conduct between *bhikśūṇīs.*
(4) On dress and physical appearance of *bhikśūṇīs.*
(5) On their relationship with the laity.

Rules pertaining to the practice of the *Vinaya* and *Dhamma* were for both the orders (of *bhikśūs* and *bhikśūṇīs*) almost identical. Rules pertaining to conduct towards *bhikśūs* prescribed unquestioned subservience and subjugation of *bhikśūnis*. Rules pertaining to relations among the *bhikśūṇīs*, within the order of *bhikśūṇīs*, were such as to facilitate amicable and cordial relationship between the members of the *Bhikśūṇī Samgha*.

The Buddha and his monks formulated these rules with little or no interference by the lay community, as these laws were not likely to have any telling effect on lay lives. The rules that came under these broad categories were as follows:

(i) Rules related to conferring of *upasampada* initiation to the *bhikśūṇīs*, on the conduct of *bhikśūṇīs* towards *bhikśūs*, within the order,
(ii) (ii) on inheritance of property (monk's, nun's garments, bedding, etc.) and
(iii) (iii) rules pertaining to giving up of renunciants life and rejoining the Order and so on.

But the last two category of rules (nos 4–5) (which involve prescriptions on dressing,[57] rules related to travel[58] and any other aspect) that involved *bhikśūṇīs'* (direct/indirect) interaction with the laity were largely dictated by the laity. The constant interaction between the lay community and the *bhikśūṇīs* led to cropping up of differences and confrontation between the two. This conflict was more so in the case of the *bhikśūṇīs* as compared to the monks for two reasons. First, as compared to the *bhikśūṇīs*, the interface between the monks and the lay community was minimal and limited to certain planes only, like the giving and the receiving of *dāna*, as compared to the nuns, who interacted with the lay community at numerous levels. The second reason was the inherent distrust of the female, which prescribed that the monks maintain a bare minimum contact with women (both lay and monastic) and more so of women who opted for the socially less-accepted role of a female ascetic. This conflict is reflected in the contemporary literature and was also acknowledged by the laity and the *Samgha* alike. The *Samgha*, in order to ease these differences, made rules that would help in resolving the differences to a large extent and avert further conflict.

Some rules were made with the purpose of marking a sharp distinction in the physical appearance as also habits of the *bhikşūṇīs* with those of the laywomen. A woman's love for decoration and ornaments was well known. The *Psalms of Nanduttarā* highlights a woman's deep attachment to ornaments. It reads:

I sought delight in decking out myself
With gems and ornaments and tricks of art.
By baths, unguents, massage, I ministered
Unto this body, spurred by lust of sense.[59]

As it was probably felt, sharper the differences, more difficult it would be for their womenfolk to identify with these monastic women. Hence interaction on certain levels at least would be kept at a bare minimum. Furthermore, these rules would indirectly also aid the *bhikṣūṇīs* in their spiritual quest, as these worldly trappings were generally considered (by the *Samgha* as well as the laity) to be encumbrances in the quest for the ultimate goal.

II

Exploring epistemological spaces

This section deals with the assessment of the epistemological space in the spiritual lives of the Buddhist women, and the same can best be illustrated by an examination of the distinctive philosophical undertones within the contents of the *Therigāthā*. A defining attribute necessarily associated with the *arahant* state is *aññā*. It can be regarded as the shared essence of the articulations of the different *therīs* drawn together in *Therigāthā*. 'Though Buddhism's archetypal religiosity has been identified loosely as "mystical" in certain modern interpretations, a careful reading of *Therigāthā* indicates that accession to spiritual perfection is depicted in its articulations as entailing an acquisition of "gnosis" (*aññā*), replete with higher epistemic capacities. The more striking elements in these capacities are often collectively referred to as the "triple knowledge" (*tisso vijjā, tevijjā*)'.[60] When a *therī* proclaims, 'the threefold wisdom have I gotten now', significantly, these higher capacities are traditionally taken to be: (i) knowledge of one's previous existences in *Samsāra* (*pubbenivāsānussati-ñā.na*); (ii) knowledge of the death and rebirth of beings under the influence of their *kamma* (*sattānam cutūpapāta-ñā. na*) and (iii) knowledge of the destruction of the cankers of attachment or 'influxes' (*āsavakkhaya-ñāna*).

The *therīs* regarded truth as a subjective and inward experience best approached through personal engagement and introspection. It is precisely for this reason that the description of 'engagement with truth' varies from individual to individual. In this connection, the distinctive terms in which some of them recognise and contrast their inner natures in early 'unconverted' and later 'converted' states are especially noteworthy. It should be noted, however, that viewed within the doctrinal frames of early Buddhism itself, the 'unconverted' mind can be said to reflect the proclivities and the psychological makeup of ordinary persons (*puthujjana*) and the 'converted' those of the spiritually awakened elite (*ariyā*).[61] The aspiration for deliverance is rooted in a soteriological concern, and accession to a truly authentic realm of being is highlighted by such expressions as 'cool', 'calm' and 'serene' condition of the *arahant*.

Nibbuta (from *nir* + *.r*) is often treated as the past participle of the verb *nibbāyati*, and *nibbāna* is the nominal form of that verb. It means happiness, contentment and peace. *Nibbāyati* also means to extinguish, to blow out as in the blowing out of a lamp (*Nibbantī dhiirā yathāyaí padīpo:*).[62] *Nibbāna* is so called because it is the blowing out of the fires of greed, hatred and delusion (*rāgaggi, dosaggi, mohaggi*).[63] When these fires are blown out, peace is attained, and one becomes completely cooled – *siitibhūta*.[64] Thus, the state of 'cool' is achieved when the negative emotions are completely eradicated. When such negative emotions are completely eradicated, never to arise again, the temperament is described as cool.

The *therīs* in their articulations show that they possess a veritable awareness of the varying degrees and stages of awakening and realisation of the spiritual state. The mention of 'second *jhāna*'[65] in Vimalā's verse points to this fact:

How was I once puff'd up, incens'd with the bloom of my beauty,
Vain of my perfect form, my fame and success 'midst the people,
Filled with the pride of my youth, unknowing the Truth and unheeding!. . .
Today with shaven head, wrapt in my robe,
I go forth on my daily round for food;
And 'neath the spreading boughs of forest tree
I sit, and Second-Jhaana's rapture win,
Where reas'nings cease, and joy and ease remain.[66]

The contents of this verse can be summed up as unified, coherent and focused; it also reflects a deep-seated satisfaction and contentment in the composer, which are all characteristic of a 'higher spiritual state'.

'Each one of the *therīs*' anthology displays a singular commitment to spiritual self-culture and the consummation of its admitted goals. Existentialist categories of freedom, choice, commitment and authentic existence in particular are indeed discernible underpinnings at many levels of the text'.[67] It is noteworthy, for example, that several *therīs* here embark on their religious careers after making agonising choices by and for themselves, highlighting in the process an acknowledgement of their essential freedom. Striking testimony to this is found in the verses of Sumedha,[68] who resisted both parental pressure and a king's love, spurned marriage and adopted the religious life of a nun. Each one of the *therīs* of the anthology displays a singular commitment to spiritual self-culture and the consummation of its admitted goals. *Therīs* project some of their basic emphases in philosophical terms, describing at length their own engagement with impermanence (*aniccā*), suffering (*dukkhā*) and insubstantiality (*anattā*), their verses highlighting *aniccā* and *dukkhā* as influences felt in their respective lives.

In Ambapālī's verses the main doctrinal point emphasised is of impermanence. It is depicted not as an abstract principle but rather as one that affects one's being intimately. It emerges from the series of poignant contrasts drawn between the body's youthful beauty and its later decline into a pitiful state which is 'weakly and unsightly' and a 'home to manifold ills'. It is an intimate knowledge of *aniccā* that is imbued with transformative, soteriological meaning.

Pain and adversity (*dukkhā*) often constitute a veritable backdrop against which a number of compositions are situated. In the articulations of Punnā and Isidāsī, for instance, the burdens of domestic labour (with which poor women in particular were commonly charged) are clearly related to *dukkhā*. Kisā Gotamī, while dwelling on confinement experiences, goes even further through her identification of suffering that touches womankind specifically, '*dukkhō ittībhāvo*'.

dukkhō ittībhāvo akkhāto purisadammasārathinā
sapattikā.m pi dukkhā.m appekaccā saki.m viātāyo
gale apakantanti sukhumāliniyo visāni khādanti
janamaarakamajjhagatā ubho pi bysanāni anubhonti.[69]

Aññā, which stands to denote the 'triple knowledge' (*tisso vijjā*, *tevijjā*), occurs frequently in the *Therigāthā*. The verses of Addhakāsī,

Mettikā, Cālā, Uttarā and Punnā offer notable evidences of their use.[70] But acquisition of *tisso vijjā, tevijjā* was not the only consequence of becoming an *arahant*. Many *therīs* refer pointedly to a distinct 'state of being' that accompanies the acquisition of knowledge. When they joyfully proclaim that they are 'free', or that their minds are 'liberated', it implies an accession to a realm of being that transcends the one experienced in ordinary life. Escape from the cycle of birth and death (*punabbhavo*) was one admitted attribute of the Buddhist saint (who has successfully rooted out all lust, *sabbo rāgo samuhato*).[71] The *Therigāthā* repeatedly depicts the *arahant* as one who has reached a condition that is 'cool' (*siitibhūta*) or 'calm and serene' (*upasanta*).

The awareness of this intrinsic, individual-specific and intensely personal space for Buddhist women can be traced to different categories of women. The acquisition of this space was not circumscribed by such extraneous factors like formal education, which the nuns were mostly devoid of. Even lay living did not inhibit women from yearning for and attaining liberation. Women in the *Thērigāthā* have been described as reaching various attainments in spiritual path such as *mettā, bhavitindiyāta, vipāssanā saddha* and the like. Dhammadīnā is regarded foremost among *dhammakathikā thēris*. Patacāra, well versed in the *Vinaya*, was honoured by women whom she showed the path to happiness as a saviour of no less persuasiveness than Gotama himself.[72] The Brahamāni Bhaddā of the Kapilās was learned, fluent, wise and famed for higher vision as *dibbācakkhuleā*.[73]

The *Vimānavatthu* describes the *vimāna* (a kind of personal heavenly mansion) which was inhabited by beings reborn as gods or goddesses (*devatā*) as a reward for meritorious deeds performed by them as human beings. The verses of *Vimānavatthu* with references of Śirimā,[74] a courtesan and Sesvati,[75] a laywoman, attest to the fact that even women followers from diverse social backgrounds were successful in attaining this much-desired spiritual state.

The Buddhist canons, especially the early *Theravāda* texts, are ambiguous on the subject of women's spiritual capacities. The presence of these two verses in the *Vimānavatthu* is symptomatic of the early monastic tradition acceding a level of spiritual emancipation to its female members, or rather its tacit acknowledgement of the gradually expanding, exclusively feminine spiritual domain.

Another text, the *Ittivuttaka*, like the *Vimānavatthu*, approaches this spiritual potential in a rather circuitous manner. In one of the verses[76] Buddha, addressing both the communities of monks and nuns, is said to have mentioned that complete deliverance is achieved only by abandonment of desire. This sermon was addressed to both the groups – monks and nuns.

> *This was said by the Blessed One, said by the Arahant, so I have heard:* 'Anyone – monk or nun – in whom passion is unabandoned, aversion is unabandoned, and delusion is unabandoned, is said not to have crossed the ocean with its waves, breakers, and whirlpools, its monsters and demons. Having crossed over, having reached the far shore, he/she stands on high ground, a brahman'.
>
> *One whose passion, aversion, and ignorance*
> *are washed away,*
> *has crossed over this ocean*
> *with its sharks, demons,*
> *dangerous waves,*
> *so hard to cross.*
> *Free from acquisitions*
> *– bonds surmounted,*
> *death abandoned —*
> *he has abandoned stress*
> *with no further becoming.*
> *Having gone to the goal*
> *He is undefined,*
> *has outwitted, I tell you,*
> *the King of Death.*[77]

The 'flow of the river' stands for craving, while 'lovely and alluring' stands for the six senses. The 'pool further down' represents the five lower fetters – they being self-identity, uncertainty, attachment to practices and precepts, sensual passion and resistance. The 'waves' stand for anger and distress. The 'whirlpools' is the simile for the five strings of sensuality. The 'monsters and demons' stand for the opposite sex. 'Against the flow' stands for renunciation. 'Making an effort with hands and feet' stands for the arousing of persistence. 'The man with good eyesight standing on the bank' stands for the Tathāgata, worthy and rightly self-awakened.

It is noteworthy that in this particular text the reference to 'monsters and demons' is not directed to members of any particular gendered group, and takes both men and women within its sphere. Unlike the representations in the other texts which more often than not equate temptation and lust with female nature, this text offers a contradictory stance, and desire here is not represented by any specific gender. This basic difference stems from the fact that unlike all the other texts that were intended for an exclusive monk audience, the *Ittivuttaka* was intended for a female-inclusive audience. According to the tradition, *Ittivuttaka* was first delivered to Khujjuttara by the Buddha, who then later delivered it to some 500 more women of the king's harem. It was at a point later in time also delivered by Ānanda, who is known to have been a champion of women's causes during the time of the Buddha. His association with such a text further attests the association of the feminine with the text. Thus it is evident that this text espouses and accepts the spiritual potential of women practitioners, albeit in a roundabout manner.

A more direct acknowledgement can be found in the narrative of the *Princess Jātaka*, which makes the dramatic point that *Theravāda* tradition in the past acknowledged the possibility of women as bodhisattvas, as striving for Buddhahood. This narrative is found in a variety of Pāli and vernacular texts[78] popular in the Theravādin world from the 14th to 16th centuries C.E., and has been exhaustively studied by Karen Derris[79] ('When the Buddha Was a Woman: Reimagining Tradition in the *Theravāda*'). The story is complex and contains contradictory representations of women on the surface: while the *Princess Jātaka* asserts that a woman can be a Bodhisattva, it attributes the Bodhisattva's flaws to her female sex. The *Princess Jātaka* is unique in two ways; first, as it is the only story to envision the Buddha Gotama as female in one of his previous lives. Remarkably for the *Theravāda*, which imagines a Buddha as exclusively male, the Bodhisattva is reborn in this narrative as a woman. Second, as in several medieval biographies of the Buddha, the *Princess Jātaka* is part of an extensive preamble to a canonical biography of the Buddha, the Buddhavamsa. The narrative framework of the Buddhavamsa begins with the *Jātakas* narrating the Buddha's previous lives and develops chronologically to the final lifetime when the Bodhisattva finally attained Buddhahood and became the Buddha Gotama. In the medieval biographies, the *Princess Jātaka* is third of all of the Buddha's previous lifetimes. This is an important point: by its placement as one of the very first *Jātakas*, the events in the Bodhisattva's lifetime as princess laid the foundation for the development of the Bodhisattva path and, ultimately, Buddhahood.

The category of a 'preliminary prediction' as seen in the case of the *Princess Jātaka* is a significant innovation in *Theravāda's* understanding of the Bodhisattva path, since neither canonical nor commentarial texts include such a device. 'This "predicted prediction"' creates a space for a woman to be acknowledged as progressing along the Bodhisattva path while clearly remaining mindful of the canonical and commentarial conditions obstructing that progress. The narrative pushes very hard against the gendered rule of the Bodhisattva path, thus paving the way for the advent of the '*Sunyata*' doctrine. It does not technically subvert the canonical structure limiting predictions to male Bodhisattvas, but instead it invents an entirely new category of prediction in order to establish firmly that this woman is indeed a Bodhisattva and capable of progress and attainment on that path (Derris 2008).

In this particular text, the scope for the representation of the epistemological space is vast, and the protagonist, the princess, moves unbridled, and without the trappings of convention. One of the versions of the story states that the princess is not inspired by the monk to make an aspiration for Buddhahood, as in the first narration, but rather, the monk is inspired by the woman. He had yet to progress on the Bodhisattva path. It was his encounter with the princess that allowed him to have his most significant exchange with the Buddha's former incarnation Dipankara. This raises the possibility that, if this elderly monk had not met the princess, he might not have received his own prediction of Buddhahood. Thus, this account emphasises the pivotal role of the princess not only in directing her own religious path but also in affecting the spiritual destiny of the monk. The story does not portray female gender as an obstacle to the cultivation of the ethical and soteriological virtues of a Buddha in that lifetime. While this formulation of the prediction event highlights the princess's success, rather than her limitations, the Buddha still emphasises that she must be reborn as a man in order to receive her/his prediction. According to the *Princess Jātaka*, some aspects of the princess's present identity result from previous immoral actions, while others represent rewards for previous ethical behaviour. In order for a Bodhisattva to fulfil her or his aspiration of Buddhahood, she or he must first attain a set of eight conditions, among them a male birth. The princess is depicted as charting her own future course through her (positive) karmic actions, with the aim of being born a male, in her journey towards Bodhisattvahood. In the second version of this story, the princess's virtues are displayed implicitly through a description of her physical beauty. This is a significant development that is also noticeable in the *Vimānavatthu*. Physical beauty of the feminine has been frequently used as reference to denote impermanence and, in extreme cases, equated with desire that should be forsaken and overcome, if one is to progress in the spiritual path. But in the case of the *Princess Jātaka* and also the *Vimānavatthu*, feminine beauty is dealt with positively. In Buddhist thought, morality is not only an internal quality but also manifests materially – the beauty of the princess's face, body and, most poetically, her voice as an outward sign of her inner qualities (Mrozik 2006).[80] The second version of the story places even greater emphasis on the princess and creates a more positive representation of this female Bodhisattva as a perceptive woman of virtue directing her own Bodhisattva career. The narrative in the Sotatthakhi incorporates a passage from this fifth- or sixth-century C.E. commentary[81] describing the beauty of the Buddha's voice, which has the power to stop beings in their tracks – in order to describe the beauty of the princess. This inter-textual reference makes a very strong implicit argument. Her beauty suggests not superficial desires but unseen spiritual moral qualities, just as the virtues of a Buddha. This would implicitly mean that the female Bodhisattva is progressing on the path to Buddhahood, to the extent that she is beginning to physically resemble a Buddha in her present lifetime. This statement makes the case for a woman to possess the moral and physical qualities, a Buddha manifests, albeit in a not-yet-perfect form.

The characters and episodes of the *Princess Jātaka* are woven skilfully into the Buddhavamsa, by repositioning the canonical biography into a new narrative structure. The *Jātaka* substantially reimagines the canonical biography while preserving the traditional narrative. The Bodhisattva's shift from female to male across these two lifetimes (from princess to the male ascetic Sumedha) is the key to the ongoing progress on the Bodhisattva path. Sumedha can receive a full prediction of Buddhahood because he is male, while as the princess, the Bodhisattva could not reach this crucial step in the Bodhisattva career. Yet this transformation from female to male, while prescribed by orthodox definitions of the Bodhisattva path, is not completely upheld. Even when forecasting the princess's rebirth as male, the Buddha's former incarnation Dipankara remarkably continues to use a feminine pronoun to describe the Bodhisattva's experiences. In this narrative the protagonist is accorded considerable liberty, as she does not just make her own aspiration for Buddhahood; she even defines her future identity as a Buddha. She announces that in her final lifetime, her name will be Siddhartha, the prince who goes on to become the Gautama Buddha. This particular event underscores her sublime awaked state, and her knowledge of the *tisso vijjā, tevijjā* which include knowledge of one's previous existence, knowledge of the destruction of the cankers of attachment or 'influxes' and knowledge of the death and rebirth of beings under the influence of their karma.

Diverging from the traditional biography in which the name Siddhāttha is given the meaning of an 'accomplished aim', in this medieval *Jātaka*, the princess explains that this will be her future name because of the gift of *siddhātthaka tēla* (mustard oil) that she gave as an act of generosity to the monk. It can also be taken to mean that the act of making the *dāna* of *siddhātthaka tēla* is an 'accomplished aim', by which she has made the right cause that would eventually lead her to Buddhahood. Here the princess can be seen as making her own future prediction, and directing the course of her imminent Buddhahood. Also, with this revised etymology, the princess's presence is again asserted into the traditional biography, insisting that the Bodhisattva's lifetime as the princess cannot be forgotten.

Buddhist traditions vary on the possibility of the existence of female Buddhas, with some believing that pursuing the Bodhisattva path is not barred to women because of their sexual identity. Texts such as these, while technically staying within the traditional rules, challenge the gendered idea of the Bodhisattva path. The limitations of a female birth determine the most important event in the story. The princess herself acknowledges this gender hierarchy and believes that it is because of some past karmic deeds that she has been born in a female form. In the second version of the story, the princess directs the merit of her gift of oil to the monk to the goal of overcoming female birth in her future lifetimes. In this story, this female Bodhisattva is highly valorised as a woman. The Bodhisattva's female birth is not merely a pause on the path to work off some negative karma. Rather, as the princess, the Bodhisattva actively constructs her own future Buddhahood. The *Princess Jātaka* shows a woman creating her own opportunities and directing her own future on the Bodhisattva path.

Though the text devotes considerable space to the subject of 'rebirth of a female into a male so as to achieve Buddhahood and therefore cannot be taken simply to mean that the narrative is aimed at valorising women; however, it is definitely an attempt to accede theoretical space to the issue of female bodhisattvahood within an otherwise austere and unyielding *Theravāda* doctrine.

The introduction of such a narrative with its innovative subject and structure at such a juncture when the presence of women in Buddhism was clearly at a decline is significant. In spite of an early period of spiritual and institutional achievements by Buddhist nuns, as described in literary representations and donative inscriptions, the position of *Theravāda* women in the *Samgha* (monastic community) was clearly in decline in the medieval times, when the nuns' order was universally going through a period of decline as is attested by archaeological records and the marginal availability of inscriptional sources. The nuns' lineage died out in Sri Lanka in the 11th century C.E., after a devastating period of natural disasters and warfare, and disappeared in Burma during the same historical period. *Theravāda* societies in Thailand, Cambodia and Laos never established full monastic ordination for women.

The entire narrative frame of the Buddha's biography, beginning with the first Bodhisattva lifetime as the ascetic Sumedha and the final lifetime as the prince Siddhartha, who attains enlightenment becoming Buddha Gotama, is moulded into new forms in the *Princess Jātaka*. The introduction of such a narrative in such a point in time when the participation of women was at an all-time low suggests theoretically acceding epistemological space to women within the Buddhist canonical texts.

Conclusion

Thus from the above discussion the following facts emerge. The awareness of 'the self' among the ancient Buddhist female patrons cannot be debated. It surfaced in numerous ways and its expression and assertion manifested itself in their decisions that had a significant bearing on their lives. They were opinionated individuals, whose need and yearning for epistemological space often led them to give in to their true calling. The reasons for their breaking away from the conventional mould and taking up less-charted course of a renunciant could be varied like the need for spiritual fulfilment, breaking free of the toils and drudgery of domesticity, grief over the loss of a close relative and the like. It cannot be debated that Buddhism did present these women with increased avenues, in which to express and fulfil their desires.

For *bhikśūṇīs*, the perpetual struggle was to emotionally break free from kinship and familial ties as against the monks, for whom freedom from sensual desires was the most decisive struggle. For women renunciants, even after giving up lay lives, it was very difficult to completely sever familial ties. One reason for this could have been the lack of institutional support that the *Bhikṣunī Samgha* received. This was one of the primary reasons due to which all *bhikśūṇīs* could not at all times be permanently accommodated in the *bhikśūṇī viharās*, and had to put up in the houses of their lay relatives. In addition, unlike the monasteries which had the support of the royalty and the trading groups, the *bhikṣunī vihārikas* were largely, small scattered units, which were largely self-supported, running within limited resources or were at the mercy of the patronage received from the local villagers and the families of the *bhikśūṇīs*.

Security was another practical concern, which made severing of all social bonds impractical. Since it was practically not feasible for the *bhikśūṇīs* to travel alone on pilgrimage, or undergo solitary retreat, the family again came into focus, providing them their necessary sanctuary. It was for this reason that the *Bhikśūṇī Vinaya* made a provision that the *bhikśūṇīs* under certain conditions could put up in the houses of their kin, especially during *vassa-vāsa*.

It is thus apparent that for various reasons, for the *bhikśūṇī*, there was no explicit demarcation of domestic and religious space. The rules relating to their security and other related practical, day-to-day concerns forced them in a way to exist in a kind of a liminal zone/an intermediary space, which was neither entirely lay nor entirely isolated, as that of the monks. This was a perpetual struggle that they strove to overcome.

This ongoing conflict between the social and the asocial worlds, and the inherent distrust towards the female ascetics in particular, must have also been one of the causes for the economically pathetic condition of *bhikśūṇī vihārikās* and the comparatively lesser patronage that it received as compared to the monks' order. In the Pāli Canon, *bhikśūṇīs* are known as those who receive things with difficulty (*Kicchalabhā, dullabha*). It was probably the lack of an established institutional structure, backed by a financially strong support system, that necessitated the practice of *bhikśūṇīs* living with their lay relatives. At another level it also reflects that the two conflicting groups seem to have come to a tacit compromise, or rather the laity's gradual acceptance of the concept of female asceticism that led to the development of the convention of *bhikśūṇīs* living in the villages and towns, in the houses of their kinsmen (families) more than the nunneries. This practice has continued and we have evidence for the same even during the later times, and is also prevalent in present-day Buddhist Sri Lanka and in parts of present-day Kinnaur, Himachal Pradesh. This phenomenon further gained momentum with the decline of formal Buddhism during the medieval period, when the Buddhist monasteries were being pulled down, the Buddhist temples being razed to the ground and the Buddhist scriptures being destroyed by the Muslim invaders. Even with the concept of a secluded convent gradually diminishing, the existence of *bhikśūṇīs* continued (albeit in small, scattered pockets) and their newly found sanctuaries were none other than within those very groups that had initially been wary, distrustful and antagonistic towards them.

Contemporary literature mirrors the social conditions and conventions of its age and is representative and indicative of a deep-seated antagonism towards the female Buddhist ascetics. Chathanar's *Manimekalāi* was aimed at rectifying this inherently negative social attitude by bringing about a definitive change in the society's perception of women renunciants. On the one hand, it forces us to acknowledge the fact that the social antagonism that we see so often reflected in the classical texts was not the only prevailing viewpoint. There did exist another school of thought also, albeit very weak, with only a handful of people who subscribed to it. Chathanar's *Manimekalāi* attempts to break away from the rigidly entrenched social prejudices of the age and at the same time it tries to remodel the attitude of the society and make it more favourable and supportive of the *bhikśūṇīs* and their order.

With certain concessions coming from the *Samgha* itself, which gave the *bhikśūṇīs* protection (from physical aggressions) like rules which forbade women renunciants from dwelling in forest hermitages alone, travelling alone and the like as also protecting their self-esteem and self-respect by regulating the behaviour of erring monks towards these *bhikśūnis*, the *bhikśūṇīs* managed to survive and struggle for their ultimate goal of *nibbāna*.

The endowments (however scanty) kept coming (a grant dated A.D. 885 records allocations for a large establishments of *bhikśūṇīs*, in a monastery of Eastern India, included 10 servants for the house of *bhikśūṇīs* that was housed within the monastery's precincts).[82] The *bhikśūṇīs*' diligently carried out their personal spiritual exercises along with the task of bringing through conversions, large sections of the lay society within the fold of the Buddhist *Samgha*.

Thus from the above discussion it is evident that women were successful in carving out their own individual spaces, and this found expression in their personal, socio-economic and religious spheres. The personal discretion used by these women in the choice and effecting of their desires led them at times to subvert the conventional social norms. An underlying gender debate that seems to pervade all Buddhist discourses and the resultant views that stem from the reading of these contradictory views can be summed up according to the four kinds of attitudes towards women and the feminine, as reflected in the Buddhist texts, proposed by Sponberg (1992). Sponberg categorised these canonical attitudes into the following four basic types:

1. *Soteriological inclusiveness* that professes that both sexes can attain their respective spiritual goals by following the same path. Thus, it implies that the texts do not overlook gender differences, but that such differences are ultimately insignificant in their stereological quest.
2. *Institutional androcentricism* that preserves and reinforces the conventionally accepted social standards of male authority, and female subordination is indicated in the eight preconditions thrust upon women desirous of joining the *Samgha*.
3. *Ascetic misogyny* that reflects in the negative portrayal of women and the feminine in Buddhist texts. The statement from the *Añguttara Nikāya* has been used to elucidate this stance:

   > Monks, I see no other single form so enticing, so desirable, so distracting such a hindrance to winning the unsurpassed peace from effort . . . as a woman's form. Monks, whosoever clings to a woman's form-infatuated, greedy, fettered, enslaved, enthralled- for many a long day shall grieve, snared by the charms of the woman's form. . . .
   >
   > (A.III. 67)

4. *Soteriological Androgyny*. Sponberg is of the view that this phenomenon did not become fully articulated, in the written literature at least, till the sixth to seventh centuries C.E., with the coming of the Vajrayāna and the like. But as has been discussed earlier in the chapter an early form of this phenomenon is visible even in the early texts like the *Therigāthā*. It entails that certain psychological characteristics are conventionally distinguished as feminine or masculine, but the emphasis is

> on the soteriological potential of those differences rather than on the social limitations they often reflect.

Thus this survey is largely an extension of Sponberg's model.

The privilege of taking on the robe of a renunciant came, albeit with preconditions, for women during the age of the Buddha. But in spite of the preconditions many of these women were able to carve out their own individual niches within Buddhism. A similar parallel development can be seen in the Buddhist literary tradition. A timeline survey of the textual sources reflects that gradually women did manage to create a space for themselves in the textual tradition which over time became increasingly positive in its acceptance and portrayal of the feminine.

Some of the earlier Mahayanic texts conceded that women could attain enlightenment but it required women to first change their sex. Later texts however built on the theory of *sūnyatā* (or voidness) like the *Prajañapāramita Sutra* which asserts that sexuality is irrelevant to spiritual pursuit. The even later *Vimalakirti – Nirdeśa Sutra*, which had the laity as its primary audience, stated that the female form is no hindrance to comprehending the ultimate reality. Last in this list is the *Srimala Sutra*, a comparatively later composition of third century A.D. in which *Dharma* is interestingly personified as 'mother'. The text is significant for a number of reasons. Just like the *Vimalakirti – Nirdeśa Sutra*, which also addressed the laity (as both sons and daughters), it has the female Bodhisattava Srimala as its chief protagonist. The narrative, as it unfolds, displaces the conventional order in which conversion of Srimala is followed by the conversion of all women above the age of seven. The conventional hierarchy of men preceding women in achieving enlightenment is inverted in this text, where the king and all men above the age of seven years are the last to get converted.

On both the levels, be it their physical presence as members of the *Samgha* or their presence in the Buddhist textual tradition, it must have been the increasingly active participation of the female members that was instrumental in the creation of this exclusive space.

In the following two chapters the aim will be to discuss the archaeological evidence for female presence at the Buddhist sites and see if this model holds true for the analysis of similar issues, studied from an archaeological perspective.

Notes

1 It is a continuation of *Mahavagga*, which deals with the disciplinary code and conduct with regard to minor matters, contained in the *Vinaya Pitaka*. It consists of 12 *khandas*. The first nine chapters deal with the disciplinary proceedings and settlement of disputes among the fraternity and other things such as the daily life of the monks, their residence, furniture and the duties towards one another. Chapter X describes the duties of the *bhikśūṇīs*, while chapters XI and XII are a kind of appendix to the *Cūlavagga* furnishing an account of Rajagaha and the Councils.

2 The period between 600 B.C. and 500 B.C. saw a major shift in the didactic literary tradition of India, which coincided with the major upheavals and changes in the social, economic, religious and political life of the country. Jainism and Buddhism whose complex principles had to be explained to an uneducated populace favoured the development of a didactic literature and collection of exempla such as the *Jātaka*. The *Jātakas* hardly ever make direct references to the central themes of Buddhist philosophy but they do take up Buddhist ethics and deal with them using a more popular idiom. The minimal presence of a philosophical content and the adoption of a narrative strategy make it possible for more of everyday life to be represented in the *Jātakas*. They were composed in the Madhyadēśa, before the time of Aśoka. The *Funk and Wagnalls Standard Dictionary of Folklore, Mythology and Legend* describe the *Jātakas* as a collection of *gāthās*. These *gāthās* are embedded in a prose commentary, which consists of a prose story of the present explaining why the Buddha is telling a tale of the past, a commentary of the *gāthās* and an integration of the two parts. They include fable, Märchen, moral tales, maxims and legends. More than half the stories are not of Buddhist origin. They have been immensely popular with the Buddhist audience and have served as the canonical readings of Buddhism. The *Cullaniddeśa* points to a canonical collection of 500 *Jātaka*s. That 500 was the original total of the *Jātaka*s is proved, on the one hand, by the 500 *Jātaka* representations witnessed by Fa-Hien round the Abhayagiri monastery of Ceylon and, on the other hand, by the mechanical multiplication of the stories in order to raise the total from 500 to 550 from the days of Buddhaghosa. It is widely accepted that they were collected before A.D. 400, mostly between 200 B.C. and 200 C.E.

3 In this discussion the most significant work that needs to be subjected to a detailed study is the *Therigāthā*. It happens to be the only known available text in which the experiences and thoughts of the *thēris* have been articulated; an ancient religious verse anthology of women's authorship, the *Therigāthā*, is the ninth book of the *Khuddaka Nikāya*, consists of 73 poems – 522 stanzas in all – in which the early *bhikśūṇīs* recount their struggles to attain supreme enlightenment. It is replete with articulations that record some characteristic viewpoints, experiences, attitudes and

thought patterns of women. The one underlying feature of all the narratives in the *Therigāthā* is to record the success of committed Buddhist soteriological endeavours of the Buddhist *thērīs*. The *Thērigāthā* was composed and pressed according to a strict form. The *gāthās* ('songs') were descriptive rather than lyrical or presentational and could sometimes be very technical. The songs were not spoken but chanted. However, some lines originally may have been sayings that were converted from prose to metric form to facilitate recollection. In other words, although *gāthās* do represent the earliest stratum of the Pāli canon, *gāthās* may not have been the form of the original utterances. The most accepted dates for the composition of the *Therigāthā* is 80 C.E. The significance of the *Therigāthā* can be assessed from the quote of John Stuart Mill, in *The Subjection of Women* (1869), where he expressed the view that the 'knowledge men can acquire of women' will indeed be 'wretchedly imperfect and superficial and always bound to remain so until women themselves have told all they have to tell'. John Stuart Mill, *Collected Works of John Stuart Mill 21*, Toronto, 1981, p. 271.

4 The *Ittivuttaka* is a book of questions of genuine sayings of the Buddha, not referring to any canonical work or to any historical event ascertaining its date, though it seems that it was the result of an afterthought, of a critical study of the authentic teachings of the Buddha in a certain light and for a specific purpose. The *Ittivuttaka* (Pāli for 'as it was said') is a Buddhist scripture, part of the Pāli Canon of *Theravāda* Buddhism and is attributed to Khujjutara's (she is mentioned with others as a lay disciple of the Buddha. The *Dhammapada* and other commentaries describe them as 'teachers of the laity') recollection of Buddha's discourses. She then repeated them to the 500 women of Udēna's palace, chief of whom was Sāmāvatī. It is included there in the *Sutta Pitaka's Khuddaka Nikāya*. It comprises 112 short teachings ascribed in the text to the Buddha, each consisting of a prose portion followed by a verse portion. Some scholars consider it one of the earliest of all Buddhist scriptures, while others consider it somewhat later. At the Rājagaha Council, Ānanda repeated the *suttas* to the Assembly and they were compiled into this collection.

5 The *Vimānavatthu* is a Buddhist scripture, the sixth book of the *Khuddaka Nikāya* in the Pāli Canon of *Theravāda* Buddhism. It is an anthology of 85 short stories written in verse, describing the *vimāna* (*vimāna*) – a kind of personal heavenly mansion – inhabited by beings reborn as gods or goddesses (*devatā*) as a reward for meritorious deeds performed by them as human beings. All the stories follow a similar pattern. They begin with an introductory verse (or verses) in which the god or goddess is asked about the cause for his or her rebirth within that particular mansion. The *dēva* thereupon relates his or her previous good deeds. Its name is Pāli for '*Vimāna* Stories'. The stories are similar to each other in that each of them describes the life and deeds of a character who has attained residence in

a heavenly mansion, the *Vimāna*, due to his/her meritorious deeds. It is dated shortly after Buddhaghosha's compilation (A.D. 412).

6 The *Lotus Sutra* was probably compiled in the first century B.C. in Kashmir, India, some 500 years after the *Parinirvāṇa* of Buddha. Therefore, it is not included in the more ancient *Āgamas* nor in the parallel *Sutta Pitaka* of the *Theravāda* Buddhists, both of which represent the older Buddhist scriptures which to a greater degree of certainty can be historically linked to the Buddha himself.

The *Lotus Sutra* purports to be a discourse delivered by the Buddha towards the end of his life. It was conventionally thought that the *Lotus Sutra* was originally translated from Sanskrit into Chinese by Dharmarakṣa around 209 C.E. However, the view that there is a high degree of probability that the base text for that translation was actually written in *Prākrit* has gained widespread acceptance. Jan Nattier has recently summarised this aspect of the early textual transmission of such Buddhist scriptures in China thus, bearing in mind that Dharmarakṣa's period of activity falls well within the period she defines: 'Studies to date indicate that Buddhist scriptures arriving in China in the early centuries of the Common Era were composed not just in one Indian dialect but in several. . . . [I]n sum, the information available to us suggests that, barring strong evidence of another kind, we should assume that any text translated in the second or third century CE was not based on Sanskrit, but one or other of the many Prākrit vernaculars'. This early translation by Dharmarakṣa was superseded by a translation in seven fascicles by Kumārajīva in 406 C.E., although it is known that Kumārajīva made extensive use of the earlier version to the extent of borrowing readings directly from Dharmarakṣa's version. This *sutra* is well known for its extensive instruction on the concept and usage of skillful means (Sanskrit: *upāya*; Jp: *hōben*), mostly in the form of parables. It is also one of the first *sutras* to use the term *Mahāyāna*, or 'Great Vehicle' Buddhism. Another concept introduced by the *Lotus Sutra* is the idea that the Buddha is an eternal entity, who achieved *nirvāṇa* eons ago, but willingly chose to remain in the cycle of rebirth to help teach beings the Dharma time and again. The *Lotus Sutra* also indicates that emptiness (*sūnyata*) is not the ultimate vision to be attained by the aspirant Bodhisattva: the attainment of Buddha Wisdom is indicated to be a bliss-bestowing treasure which transcends seeing all as merely empty.

7 *Vimalakirti Sūtra* or *Vimalakirti Nirdeśa* is a *Mahāyāna* Buddhist *Sutra*. It dates from no later than the third century C.E., based on its earliest Chinese translations, and most likely from the first or second century C.E. It is a polemical text, since it portrays highly revered Buddhist *arahant* saints as being foolish and having incorrect understanding of the Buddhist teachings. An important aspect of this scripture is that it contains a report of a teaching addressed to highly accomplished and revered Buddhist disciples, Śāriputra, Moggalana and Mahakassapa, by the lay man and

bodhisattva Vimalakirti. In the sūtra, Bodhisattva Vimalakirti, in the guise of a layman and householder significantly, instructs deities, learned Buddhist *arahants* and lay people in all matters concerning the nature of enlightenment and Buddhist truth. He does so while lying sick in bed, although this is just a ruse designed to draw an audience of visitors who have come to wish him well and inquire about his health. As crowds of well-wishers come to see him, Vimalakirti employs his superior understanding of 'skill in means' (upāya) to teach them about the nature of'emptiness' (sūnyatā), the *Mahāyāna* Buddhist doctrine that culminates in the counterintuitive claim that *nirvāṇa* and *saṃasāra,* at an ultimate level, are not different. Vimalakirti, prompted by his chief Mañjuśri to supply his own answer, responds with silence, indicating that true understanding of non-duality is ineffable. 'This particular teaching by Vimalakirti is thus used to portray the most accomplished disciples of the Buddha as deficient in understanding, in order to be able to present the ideal of Bodhisattvaship as higher than Arahantship'.

8 *Manimekalāi,* written by Seethalai Chathanar, is one of the masterpieces of Tamil literature and is considered as one of the five great epics of Tamil Literature. *Manimekalāi* is a sequel to *Silapathikaram* and tells the story of the daughter of Kovalan and Madhavi. The narrative is centred around the life of a courtesan-turned-Buddhist nun. This epic tale was composed between second and sixth centuries A.D. *Manimekalāi* points to the dramatist's attempt to initiate a social renaissance in the social image of a Buddhist nun. *Manimekalāi* presents in contrast to the negativity and mistrust against women (that is so frequently met with in Buddhist literature like the *Jātakas*), an unconventional and innovative approach in introducing the positive image of the protagonist, a courtesan-turned-Buddhist nun. Chattanar's position is in direct contrast to that prevailing in the contemporary society.

9 Viewing the world from a male perspective, wherein women are viewed and treated as passive objects, rather than active subjects of history.

10 *Therigatha,* verses 315–18.

11 *Ibid.,* verses 252–70.

12 *Ibid.,* verses 108–9.

13 *[D]ukkho itthibhaavo akkhaato purisadammasaarathinaa sapattika.m pi dukkha.m appekaccaa saki.m vijaataayo gale apakantanti sukhumaaliniyo visaani khaadanti janamaarakamajjhagataa ubho pi bysannaani anubhonti* (*Therigāthā,* verses 216–17).

14 The male articulations in *Therigāthā* offer striking evidences of this; cf. PsB, p. 59; also pp. 14, 15, 39, 72–3.

15 *Therigatha,* verses 448–522.

16 *Ibid.,* verses 366–99.

17 *Formerly I traveled in a single cloth*
With plucked hair, covered with mud,

Imagining flaws in the flawless
And seeing no flaws in what is flawed
Having come out from my daytime dwelling'
On the mountain Vulture's Peak
I saw the spotless Enlightened One
Accompanied by the Sangha
Then I humbly bowed down on my knees
And in his presence saluted him
'come Bhadda', he said to me-
And that way my ordination.

(*Therigāthā*, verses 107–9)

18 Anguttara *Nikāya*, "The Doctrine of Incapability", Pali *Nikāyas* (trans.) *Asian Journal of Women's Studies*, Vol. 8, No. 2–4, Ihwa Yoja Taehakkyo, *Asian Center for Women's Studies*, 2002, p. 15.
19 "*Muluposatha Sutta: The Roots of the Uposatha*" (AN 3.70), translated from the Pali by Thanissaro Bhikkhu. *Access to Insight*, July 3, 2010. Retrieved from http://www.accesstoinsight.org/tipitaka/an/an03/an03.070.than.html.
20 *Ibid.*
21 *S.* i.128, *Sutta of the Sisters.*
22 *Therigatha* verses 400–447.
23 Retrieved on October 29, 2009 from www.opensourcebuddhism.org/series7-*Mahāyāna*literarythemes.ppt.
24 The Buddha himself refused to spread his teachings by impressing his audience with miracles. According to the *Añguttara Nikāya*, on the collections of the Buddha's sayings, there are three kinds of miracles – the miracle of magic, the miracle of thought reading and the miracle of instruction – and of these the last is the most wonderful and excellent.
25 *S.*i.128.
26 'Asoka, the first great patron-king of Buddhism in India is credited with establishing the pattern of duties for such righteous kings. In addition to his generous support for Buddhist institutions, Asoka went out of his way to encourage their activities'. As Reynolds comments, '. . . there developed alongside the Buddhist Samgha, which was constituted by the order on monks and *bhikkhunīs* and the laymen and women who supported them, the ideal of a Buddhist state governed by a pious monarch who modeled his rule after the example of Asoka'. In Paula Richman, *Women, Branch Stories, and Religious Rhetoric in a Tamil Buddhist Text*, New York, 1988.
27 *Therigāthā*, Canto I, XVIII.
28 *The Buddhist Monastic Code*, Vol. II, Chapter 23.
29 A. Sponberg, *Buddhism, Sexuality and Gender*, p. 17.
30 Diana S. Paul, *Women in Buddhism*, p. 88.
31 The Karle Cave Inscription of a nun; *A.S.W.I.*, Vol. IV, No. VII (16).
32 James Fergusson, *Tree and Serpent Worship*, Appendix E, No. XVIII.

33 Akira Hirakawa, *Monastic Discipline for the Buddhist Nuns*, Patna, rep. 1999.
34 *Therigāthā*, XLVII.
35 *Ibid.*, LXIX.
36 *A.S.S.I.*, Vol. I, No. 13.
37 *Thērigāthā*, Canto.II, XIX.
38 *Ibid.*, Canto.III,XXXVI.
39 *Ibid.*, Canto XIII, LXVI.
40 *Ibid.*, Canto. V, XXXIX.
41 *Thērigāthā*, verse 47.
42 Edward Hamilton Johnston, *Asvaghosa's Buddhacharita or Acts of the Buddha*, 47, Delhi, 1992, p. 67.
43 Due to various reasons discussed in the previous chapter.
44 *A.* i.25
45 *S.* ii.236.
46 *Ibid.*
47 *Thērigāthā* (Cantos II, XXI, XXVI; Cantos VII, LIX).
48 *Thērigāthā*, LXX.
49 R. Davids, *Psalms of the Early Buddhists*, Vol. I, pp. 68–9.
50 *Ibid.*, pp. 64–5.
51 *Ibid.*, LXXII.
52 *M.* 2.97.
53 *Cūllavagga*, V, 23.
54 Eight chief rules to be accepted as initiation to nunhood. *Cūllavagga*, X.I, 4.
55 *Ibid.*, X, 3,1.
56 *Ibid.*, 214.
57 *Ibid.*, X, 6,1.
58 Their mode of travelling necessitated making rules, as they would control the degree of proximity and interaction between the monks and *bhikśūṇīs*, thereby minimising the chances of any moral transgression by the two groups especially by the *bhikśūṇīs*, who would only then be able to set a healthy and morally correct precedent for the society which patronised their institution.
59 R. Davids, *Psalms of the Early Buddhists*, Vol. 1, p. 58.
60 Vijitha Rajapakse, *The Therigāthā, a Revaluation*, Wheel No. 436/437, Copyright © Kandy, Buddhist Publication Society (2000), BPS Online Edition © (2007). Retrieved on September 8, 2008 from www.bps.lk/olib/wh/wh436.pdf.
61 Cf. *Compendium of Philosophy* (*Abhidhammatthasa.ngaha*), trans. Shwe Zan Aung and C.A.F. Rhys Davids (P.T.S. 1979), Introduction, p. 49.
62 *S.*235.
63 *S.*IV.19.
64 *Ibid.*, 542, 642.
65 The experience of non-sensuous physical bliss for limited periods is possible even before the attainment of *nibbāna* through the practice of *jhāna* or

meditative absorption. The *Saamattaphala Sutta* describes these physical experiences with the help of eloquent similes (DN 174). When bath powder is kneaded with water into a neat wet ball, the moisture touches every part of the ball but does not ooze out; similarly, the body of the adept in the first *jhāna* is drenched and suffused with joy and pleasure born of detachment from sense pleasures (*vivekaja.m piitisukha.m*). The experience in the second *jhāna* is elucidated with a different simile. A deep pool filled to the brim with clear cool water is fed by underground springs, yet the waters do not overflow and no part of the pool remains untouched by the cool waters. Similarly joy and pleasure born of concentration (*samādhija.m piitisukha.m*) pervade the body of the meditator in the second *jhāna*. The simile for the third *jhāna* is a lotus born in water, grown in water, fully submerged in water and drawing nourishment from water, with no part of the lotus remaining untouched by the cool water. Thus, happiness/pleasure suffuses, drenches, and permeates the entire body of the adept in the third *jhāna*. These are the experiences of non-sensuous pleasure before the attainment of *nibbāna*. On the attainment of *nibbāna* more refined non-sensuous pleasure is permanently established. The *Cankii Sutta* specifically states that when a monk realises the ultimate truth, he experiences that truth 'with the body'. Lily de Silva, "Nibbana as Living Experience"/"The Buddha and The Arahant; Two Studies from the Pali Canon", *Access to Insight*. Retrieved on June 7, 2010 from http://www.accesstoinsight.org/lib/authors/desilva/wheel407.html, originally published as "Nibbaana as Living Experience" the *Sri Lanka Journal of Buddhist Studies* (Vol. I, 1987).

66 R. Davids, *Psalms of the Sisters*, P.T.S., pp. 52–3.

67 Vijitha Rajapakse, *The Therīgāthā a Revaluation* (2008).

68 R. Davids, *Poems of Early Buddhist Nuns (Therīgāthā)*, verses 448–522, p. 142.

69 *Therigāthā*, pp. 216–17.

70 See R. Davids, *Therigāthā, Psalms of the Sisters* 26, 30, 180, 187, 251; cf. PsS, pp. 26, 28, 95, 98, 119.

71 *Therigāthā*, p. 34.

72 I. B. Horner (trans.) *The Book of the Discipline*, Vols IV and V, trans. 1951–2, P.T.S., Lancaster, p. 169.

73 *A*. I.25.

74 John D. Ireland, translated from the Pali, Vv 137–49; No. 16, "Sirima: Sirima's Mansion" (Vv 1.16), *Access to Insight*. Retrieved on June 7, 2009 from http://www.accesstoinsight.org/tipitaka/kn/vv/vv.1.16.irel.html.

75 "Sesavati: Sesavati's Mansion" (Vv 3.7), translated from the Pali by John D. Ireland. *Access to Insight*. Retrieved on June 7, 2009 from http://www.accesstoinsight.org/tipitaka/kn/vv/vv.3.07.irel.html.

76 {Iti 3.20; Iti 57} *The Itivuttaka: The Buddha's Sayings*, translated from the Pali by John D. Ireland (Kandy: Buddhist Publication Society, 1997). Copyright © 1997 Buddhist.

77 *Ibid.*

78 Five versions of the *Princess Jātaka* are found in Pali texts belonging to different genres. The story appears in two extended biographies of the Buddha, the *Sotatthakhimahanidana* and the *Mahasampindanidana*, and in a 16th-century chronicle, *the Jinakalamali*, from Lan Na, a kingdom in Northern Thailand.

79 Karen Derris, *Journal of Feminist Studies in Religion*, Vol. 24, No. 2, OUP, 2008, pp. 29–44.

80 *Ibid.*

81 This description is drawn from another text altogether, the *Madhuratthavilasini*, *Commentary* to the *Buddhavamsa*.

82 Nancy A. Falk, *Case of the Vanishing Nuns*, p. 164.

Four

Women as patrons

I

In the previous chapter, we had argued that existing secondary literature has generally used archaeological data as a tool to corroborate frameworks derived from other sources. This section involves the examination of two primary sources. The first involves the donor records of the female Buddhist patrons while the second are the literary texts, which were in most cases compiled by the monk editors. The first category of data refers to real women patrons who are almost invisible in the canonical records while the second deals with women who were celebrated figures, made legendary by the Buddhist canonical authors. In this chapter, the focus is on inscriptions recording donations to religious centres as a basis for understanding gender relations in society, especially the role of women as patrons. It re-examines the data taking gender as crucial component for analysis to arrive at conclusion on various social, religious, economic issues. The male authors of the classical Buddhist texts have continually downplayed the involvement and agency of the female Buddhist patrons. The use of epigraphic records, for analysis, composed and articulated by women themselves, therefore eliminates or marginalises the risk of androcentric bias in the reconstruction of history. It attempts to study women not as a homogenous, monolithic entity but as multiple categories, and analyse their multilevel dynamics within the *Samgha*. It investigates the contribution of women (as a social, demographic component) in the growth of Buddhism in social, cultural, economic and spiritual terms. The idea is to assess and evaluate the achievement of these women and to see how and in what ways the admission of these members helped the cause of Buddhism.

It also seeks to analyse 'the woman' in various capacities within the socio-religious sphere. It explores their lay and monastic identities, as *upāsikās* and *bhikṣunīs*, on the one hand, and as donors and patrons, on the other. It also dwells on the courtesans and their agency within Buddhism.

The objective is to arrive at a better understanding of the dynamics between the various categories of monastic and laywomen, on the one hand, and the relationship between these different groups of women with the *Samgha* and the society at large, on the other. Another issue that merits its inclusion in this chapter is the concept of identity. How did these women perceive themselves? How was this self-perception shaped or influenced by Buddhism? For an analysis of 'the perception of self' the donor records are an indispensable tool as 'the idea of identity' was articulated by these women themselves, without any external influence and the biases of the editors, often found in textual accounts. It also investigates whether this 'self perception' was in any way affected by affiliation to Buddhism.

A survey of the diverse records pertaining to women and their association with Buddhism brought to the fore two distinct categories of women. Of these, the first consisted of women who have recorded their presence in the numerous epigraphic (donor) records for posterity. These were real women, who were representatives of a wide sociopolitical spectrum. They included queens, commoners, wives and mothers of *Gahapatis*, traders and the like.

The next group comprises of those women whose presence can be seen in the various canonical and non-canonical literature, who acted as significant characters in the plots that were meant to convey the essence of the religion to the masses. These were women like Mahāpajāpati Gautamī, Viśākhā and Sujātā, who were contemporaries of the Buddha. In due course, these historical figures acquired a cultic status, with many plots and subplots woven around them in the main biographical narratives.

The former class of women was ironically less visible than the latter, and the main source for their study are the inscriptions, while the latter are more conspicuously the focus of literary records. Therefore, different kinds of sources have been employed for the study of the two groups.

The data for the first section have been derived primarily from inscriptions, as it addresses the issue of donors and patronage. The epigraphic sources show the greatest variation in women's position in Buddhism over time. These inscriptions range from fourth century B.C. to about fourth century A.D., after which there is a distinct paucity of epigraphic records pertaining to the subject of study. Since the earliest inscription makes its appearance not before the fourth century B.C., the same has been fixed as the upper time limit for this study.

Another reason in favour of this periodisation (fourth century B.C. to fourth century A.D.) is that the records of this period were composed in either Prakrit or Sanskrit. In order to delimit the scope of this study and to make the study more cohesive, the sites of the North-West with inscriptions in Kharoshti have been excluded from the scope of this study.[1] Use of a certain script is significant, as it represents on a macro-level a homogenous, unitary group, within a more or less similar sociocultural backdrop, within a distinct geophysical unit. Restricting the data to one script (Brahmi) also lends an air of uniformity to the treatment of the subject.

Thus, the parameters of periodisation are based on the content as well as form of the source material having a direct bearing on the subject of our study. These data can broadly be divided into two major groups based on the qualitative and quantitative nature of the data. Those that can be dated palaeographically before A.D. 400 have been placed in one category and those that come after A.D. 400 in the second category.

A recent survey (Kim 2012) demonstrates that although the presence of Buddhist women in epigraphic data on stone sculptures declines considerably during the medieval period, they continued to make their presence felt in other ways such as donor figures in the bases of pedestals of stone sculptures and as donors of palm leaf manuscripts in eastern India – the inscription of names giving way to the practice of representing donor figures. However, this method of representation dates back to much earlier times and the early finds from Gandhara, Mathura and Amarāvati among others. This last category of analysis, that is, manuscripts, has however not been included in this analysis. Even though Kim demonstrates the affluence and economic prosperity of these female Buddhist patrons, it needs to be noted that this group of Buddhist women were in terms of numbers very few. Thus, it can be concluded that, although there was a steady decline in the finds of epigraphic data that recorded the presence of these women at various monuments and sites, it is equally true that these women made their presence felt in other ways and through other mediums. Jinnah Kim, for example, demonstrates that during the latter period there was the convention of marking their presence through the depiction of donor couples at the bases of pedestals of sculptures, as donors of palm leaf manuscripts and the like as seen from the examination of sculptural data from eastern India for the medieval period (800–1200 C.E.). A cross-sectional analysis of epigraphic data across time and space brought out these facts. If we look at Buhler's list (1894) of epigraphs at Sāñci, it lists the names of 141 monks, 104 nuns and 250 men and 150 women who are not designated as ordained. This tabulation has some degree of uncertainty, as there is a possibility of repetition of names. It is significant that the ratio of nuns to monks exceeds the ratio of undesignated women to men. The former is 104:141 or 3:4 and latter is 150: 250 or 3:5. Thus, in Madhya Pradesh, early Buddhist institutions apparently enjoyed a great vitality of women's participation – they, respectively, represented 43 per cent of the total clerics in inscriptions and 38 per cent of the laity. The epigraphic data compiled from a number of Buddhist sites for this study, which include inscriptions, published after Buhler for the historical period, also show similar results. Records pertaining to women are not uniform and unevenly spaced apart and the data for some of the sites that reflect active participation of female Buddhists show similar results. (See Figure 4.4, showing total number of men donors versus female donors.)

In the second phase, the quantum of epigraphic data is significantly small as compared to the earlier period. The early medieval period (A.D. 600–1200) saw a marked decrease in data that directly reflect the presence of women in Buddhist activities at various levels, both lay and monastic (Davidson 2003; Falk 1980). Huntington's review (1981) of 77 inscribed and dated sculptures from the Pāla-Sēna schools – both Buddhist and Hindu – lists no nuns at all. The only inscription by women claiming religious affiliation as a committed laywomen (*upāsikā*) comes from a pre-Pāla fourth-century image. Of the other Buddhist images, inscriptions record donations by two queens, a princess, the wife of a chieftain, a vintner's daughter, the wife of a wealthy donor, a monk's mother and four otherwise undistinguished wife of gentlemen of means. All the women listed in these inscriptions identified themselves through their relation to men, probably following the conventional pattern of the age. The information is reinforced by the data from the Kurkihar bronze hoard, a group of specific Buddhist statuary of the Pala period (8th–12th centuries A.D.). Of the 93 inscriptions listed, 42 provide names of donors, 9 are clearly donated by women (no nuns), while 33 are by men (10 monks) yielding 22 per cent by women.

There is dearth of epigraphic data demonstrating early medieval benefaction by a Buddhist queen or a Buddhist laywoman to a Buddhist *vihārika* or nunnery, despite their sometimes extensive, even excessive donation to monks. The very few *vihārikas* recorded during the period seem to have been constructed by kings, rather than by queens, such as the institution established by the Bhaumkara king Sivakāradēva in 888 C.E. at the request of the local chieftain Rānula Sri Vinītātunga (Misra 1934:40–51). Under the Bhaumkara kings of Orissa, the Vajrayana cult reached the apex of its development in the East.

A number of *sites* have been taken up for this study.[2] The choice of these sites has been done depending upon the availability of data (in this case the sites with the maximum number of epigraphic records pertaining to women as also sites from which the data in the form of visual arts have been taken). The sites can broadly be divided into two broad categories: those from the North of the Vindhyas (North and Central India) and those South of the Vindhyas. The Vindhya and the Satpura ranges act as a physical and cultural divide between North India and the Deccan Plateau in the South. To the North are sites like *Sāñci, Bhārhūt, Sārnāth, Bodh Gayā, Srāvasti and Mathurā*. While the sites[3] that have been grouped under the second category are *Kanhēri, Amarāvati, Kārlē, Kūdā, Junnar, Nasik, Ajantā, Ghantaśāla, Banavāsi, Bhattiprolu, Pitalkhorā and Nāgarjunakonda*. Sāñci, located as it is in the Malwa Plateau, is drained by two rivers, Betwa and Bes, while the others like Mathura, Sravasti, Bodh Gaya, Sarnath and the like lie in the Ganga Yamuna plains. A few like Amarāvati and Nāgarjunakonda are located in the Krishna delta, one of the most fertile regions in the subcontinent and home to the Satavahana and the Ikshavaku dynasties. Most of the sites further south are Buddhist cave sites, located in the Western and Eastern Ghats. Excluding Bodh Gaya, all the other sites under discussion are secondary Buddhist sites that were never visited by the Buddha during his lifetime. The presence of Asokan pillars at/around Buddhist sites attests to a relationship between imperial expansion and religion. Even though state patronage was crucial in the introduction of Buddhism in most of the areas, its subsequent growth witnessed a change in its patronage base. As the concept of *dāna* and the religious and spiritual merit accruing from it gained popularity, the lay patrons increased manifold. Epigraphic records attest to a shift in patronage base from royalty to commoners during the latter phase, with more and more commoners taking on the task of construction and embellishment at the pilgrim sites. The most numbers of records of royal women making grants at the Buddhist sites come from Nasik and Nāgarjunakonda. At Nāgarjunakonda almost all the inscriptions are those of women, associated in one way or the other with royalty and mentioned as founding/establishing *chaityas*, monasteries and the like. Another point of commonality between the sites under discussion is that almost all of them were invariably located on the ancient trade routes (Uttarapatha and the Dakshinapatha). Trade and pilgrimage have always been interconnected. The Buddhist landscape very often overlapped with existing inland routes like the Dakshinapatha and the Uttarapatha. Even the riverine trade routes were not immune to the presence of Buddhism – as in the case of Amarāvati and Nāgarjunakonda, both located on the right bank of the river Krishna. On the opposite bank of the river is the site of Jagayapetta. Remnants of monumental edifices adorned with marble reliefs in the sites of Gummadiduru, similar to the finds from Amarāvati, attest to the wealth and prosperity of the Buddhist community in these parts; the decline of sea-borne trade in the West may have conversely contributed to the decline in the fortunes of the religion in the region.

Here it needs to be noted that certain specific sites exhibit distinct features which are exclusive to those sites, for example, Bhārhūt, where there is a predominance of inscriptions that serve as captions/labels, which identify the visuals depicted in the architectural scheme of the *stūpa,* instead of taking recourse to the more conventional form of engraving the name of the donor along with/without mentioning the object of donation. Mathurā is unique in the sense that the maximum number of free-standing images/sculptures has been known to have their provenance in Mathurā in the North and Amarāvati in the South. These are well documented, as they have detailed records of the donor, engraved usually on the base of the pedestal of the images. Here it needs to be emphasised that sites which show certain resemblances and similarities can broadly be grouped together for convenience of study but then the site-specific regional peculiarities cannot be overlooked. One such feature is the convention of representing the donor figure with/without their names at the base of the sculptures, mostly in the finds from eastern India.

These inscriptions have been found engraved on architectural members, bases of *stūpas,* pillars, railings and coping stones. Some have also been found inscribed in the caves as seen in the cave sites of the Western Deccan. A large number of inscriptions are also found inscribed on sculptures. This epigraphic data can largely be grouped under two heads. The first category includes those *in situ* finds which are found in their primary context, the location where they were intended to be placed, like the inscription on architectural fragments, bases of *stūpas*, cave walls and the like, which allow us to analyse the data in context to the site. The second kind of data is found moved out of its primary context. They do not provide us with any kind of contextual data pertaining to the object, the inscription and their provenance, unless the inscription itself mentions such information, for example, displaced/ loose sculptures, pillars, architectural fragments, manuscripts and the like. While at sites like Sāñci, Mathura, Bhārhūt and Bodh Gaya the inscriptions record donation of mostly individuals making donations towards the embellishment of the site by providing resources towards the making of railings and so on, at sites in the Deccan, where the resources were quite large owing to the communal nature of the grants, the donations were made mostly for primary works like excavation of tanks and cisterns at the cave sites and the like at sites like Kanheri, Kūdā and so on. From the inscriptions it also becomes evident that women (both nuns and laywomen) made donations mostly at pilgrim sites which were closer to their place of residence. The accessibility of the pilgrim centre was also a determining factor, as there is a greater incidence of women making donations at centres which were easily accessible like Sāñci. Sāñci occupies a unique position and remains unparalleled with the most number of donations, by both *upāsikās* and bhikhuṇis alike. The cave sites being relatively less accessible with their hilly terrain saw less of women donors. At Nasik, one mostly finds royal endowments or donations made by women associated with royal officials, like the daughter of the royal treasurer[4] or the wife of the Mahasenapati Bhavagopa,[5] who must have travelled with their spouses during the rule of Nahapana, during his sojourns to the Western Ghats. In contrast, one finds only a single mention of a female ascetic at the site.

The huge corpus of literary data derived from the *Theravāda* Pāli Canon also refers to these donor women and supplements our information on these women donors, though one cannot overlook the issue of interpolations and editing in these works over time. References to women in literature, being fully contextualised, may often contain a heavy dose of androcentric bias, whereas those in the inscriptions, being decontextualised, as these were caused to be executed by the women patrons themselves, reduce the measure of prejudice and, at times, allow women to articulate themselves. However, we should also admit that the content and purpose of textual records put serious limitations on the nature and number of questions one might pose to them. The data derived from these works are mostly in the form of legends and myths, stories and similes.

Another source that adds to the subject of our study is the largely spread data in the form of visuals. These include the various art forms like sculpture and paintings that often use these patrons as their subject.

The issue of identity in inscriptional records

Identity formation in an inscription is always with a particular purpose and in a particular context, whereas this is hardly the case with literary texts, whether secular or sacerdotal, written and used for a different purpose and in a different context. An analysis of the inscriptions showed that the donors tended to identify themselves using different kinds of attributes such as familial, professional, royal, religious and the like. These are applicable in the case of individual donors but then there are instances of communal/group donations as well. Group donations from Central India reflect a wide variety of such associations attested by the terms *kūla, gotthī, jnāt, gāma* and the like (Kumkum Roy 1988). We get only an indefinable association called *sah-ya* or *sahāyara* figuring in the North-West Indian records.

An analysis of the above-mentioned sources allows us to assess some hitherto unanswered issues that have been crucial in understanding women as a major component within the larger support group that patronised Buddhism.

The inscriptions unlike the normative texts provide us with in-depth views on the behavioural propensity of the donors. These donative inscriptions are short in content, donatory in character and often include references to categories in terms of which the donors tended to identify themselves, that is, by their native place, occupation, the kinds of economic resources at their disposal, the kind of donations they made, their position within the kinship structure and their relationship with the *Samgha* and the like. One of the primary issues that needs to be addressed is that of 'the donor's identity' and how this particular group of women patrons perceived/identified themselves within the Buddhist socio-religious framework.

We have women figuring by proper name alone: women figuring by attributes of familial framework or religious framework or familial and religious framework both; women mentioning their motherly status with reference to daughters only and daughters identifying themselves with reference to their mothers exclusively and we have women with wifely status forgetting to mention their husbands, and women renouncers constituting their identity in familial terms. What we get therefore is a self-perception of women with regard to their social self rather than a social construction of their individual identity. We have no reason to doubt that the people entrusted with the task of drafting the documents and executing them on stones, pillars, images and caves were guided by the details of identity offered by the women as also by their preferences with regard to the chronology of the attributes. However, there are exceptions to this rule as eulogies such as those of Queen Gautamī Balāśri and Mahātalvari Cāmtisirī which were certainly drafted by royal scribes and contain, therefore, social construction of their identity based on conventionally followed norms rather than self-perception.

It can be seen that these women donors employed different attributes for identification (such as that of mother, wife, daughter, nun, etc.) in order to introduce themselves in the inscriptions. What were the reasons/factors that were instrumental in determining the particular social categories that each of these donors employed in order to identify themselves?

For the purpose of recording their identity, these women donors have made use of one or more attributes or markers of identity, and based on these attributes the records can be categorised into different types: (i) royal attributes; (ii) familial attributes; (iii) religious attributes; (iv) professional attributes; (v) place of residence and so on. Through these inscriptions, these women donors sought to get for themselves a 'customised social address', which was not based on *kūla, gotra* and the like but one which they sought to create for themselves, often choosing such social or religious elements to identify and describe themselves, which were for these women the most crucial and significant.

In our epigraphic records, the representation of royal women in regional as well as religious terms is uneven; also, royal women have not found adequate space for themselves in the epigraphic records. There is hardly any data for the East and the North-West. The Deccan and the South dominate the scene, but here also the records from the former are evenly spread over the region while those of the South come from the single site of Nāgarjunakonda. Significantly, again, out of the 327 women figuring in the Sāñci votive inscriptions only one has royal credentials, whereas in contrast almost all women from the

Nāgarjunakonda records belong to the royal house of Ikśavāku or their feudatories. The number of royal women donors in the Nasik inscriptions is also quite large.

This regional imbalance in the visibility of royal women is evident on the religious plane as well. An overwhelming majority of queens from the sites under study are Buddhists. Interestingly, while queens were strong supporters of Buddhism, kings figuring in their inscriptions are eulogised for patronising Brahmanical sacrifices. If it can be interpreted in terms of state policy of supporting prominent religions, on the one hand, it can also be taken as a reflection of religious freedom enjoyed by the queens, on the other.

Almost all of our queens have figured in the familial framework. However, in the selection of attributes from the familial framework, almost all have been usually guided by considerations of power relationships. The cases of Nāgamulanikā[6] and Sivaskandanāga-śri,[7] in which husbands have been absolutely ignored in the construction of identity, clearly reflect it. Samadinikā[8] in the Bedsa inscription and Dhamasiri of the Kol inscription mention their husband and father both, while introducing themselves. As a matter of fact the cases of male identity covered by our inscriptions also reveal the role of power relationships in identity-formation. Mahābhoji Vijaya is the sole source of identity for her Mahābhoja son Khandapalita.[9] While in most of the inscriptions women derive their attributes of identity from men, this record is testimony to one case where the woman is the sole source of identity to her son. Since the consideration of power relationship was central to the construction of identity, adhering to the normative ideals was hardly possible not only in cases of self-perception but, at times, in those of social construction as well.

On a normative plane, the picture of an ideal wife in Buddhist lore is hardly different from the Brahmanical one. The 'women treasure', or *Itthi-ratnam* as mentioned in the *Mahāsudassana Sutta*[10] of the *Digha Nikāya*, has to be fully at the service of her husband for his pleasure[11] which is identical to the *Manusmriti*[12] ideal in which service to the husband is rewarded with entry into heaven.[13] Viewed from this perspective the instances of women donors discussed above represent deviations from the ideals as represented in the Buddhist classical texts rather than an approximation to it. The case of Gotamī Bālāśrī[14] is a case of social construction of identity in which she has been portrayed as an ideal widow, and yet nowhere do we have a reference to her husband in the context of making the benefaction or assigning to him the religious merit accruing out of it. Although most of the women in our records identified themselves as mothers (21.7 per cent) and wives (30.2 per cent), there were others who went beyond conventions and chose to identify themselves through more than one relation, for example, Kuramgi who has been found in six of the inscriptions at Bodh Gaya. While the first four have a bare mention of Aya Kuramgi,[15] the last two have her introducing herself through different relatives – 'as the sister-in-law of . . .' and as 'the daughter of . . .'. Thus, it is evident that there were no set parameters for expressing individual identity. The donors were driven by personal choice and priorities while recording their donations. However, the Buddhist ideal of a woman as mother and wife seemed to have been popular and scored over others.[16]

The high visibility of women in the Deccan and Nāgarjunakonda inscriptions may have something to do with the survival of matriarchal elements in the societies of these areas. The custom of cross-cousin marriage is well attested in the records of Camtisirī, Bapisirī and Chathsirī, but others are not that explicit. The profuse use of matronyms and the conscious absence of patronyms and patrilineage in the Satavahana records (230 B.C.E.–220 C.E.) for constructing identity point in the same direction. Finally, the group of women figuring in the Collective Memorial Inscription include only sisters, mothers and wives of the deceased king and the daughters and daughters-in-law have been absolutely excluded, unlike at Sāñci where there are many references that allude to the donors as 'the daughter-in-law of . . .'. Perhaps matriarchal traditions coexisted with patriarchal ones in the societies of the Deccan and the South. It, however, needs to be noted that almost all the women figuring in the Nāgarjunakonda records are related to royalty and are associated with the initial phase of structural development at the site. They occur in inscriptions that mention them as founders of temples and monasteries. The complete absence of records pertaining to women patrons during the latter phases at site is noteworthy.

Not all the titles that we come across in the inscriptions are royal; most are feminine forms of feudatory statuses enjoyed by their husbands, where the records refer to them with the modest title of *Dēvi* and *Mahādēvi*.[17] Feminine forms of masculine titles like *Mahārathinī* and *Mahābhojī* are available only from the Deccan from sites like Nasik and Nāgarjunakonda. Though it is difficult to assess the measure of power behind the titles, it is evident that their use was not altogether ornamental and spells a measure of autonomy for these women. At Nāgarjunakonda, the use of the honorific 'śri' as suffix also sets apart the royal from the non-royal women.

No generalisation is possible concerning the autonomy enjoyed by women in the epigraphic space they entered. The treatment in some of the records like those of *Dāmila* and *Samādinika* indicate complete autonomy in the construction of self-reference, as opposed to those of Gautamī Balāsri and Nāganika.

Kinship terminologies employed as social identification categories

Frequent use of kinship terminologies in order to identify themselves was employed by both monastic and the lay donors, though this phenomenon is more commonly seen in inscriptions referring to the *upāsikās*.[18] These women identify themselves as wife,[19] as mother,[20] as granddaughter[21] in one case as daughter-in-law,[22] as sister,[23] as *antevāsini*,[24] as *upāsikās*[25] occasionally also by caste[26] and at times only by their names also.[27] Such kinship-based identifications are generally more common for *upāsikās* than for the *bhikṣunīs* and are also varied for the former as has been mentioned.

Sometimes we also come across inscriptions of nuns who are recorded as making donations together with a close relative and other members. An inscription in *Prākrit* found on a Buddhist sculpture from Amarāvati mentions:

> Gift of the nun (*Bhikkhūnī*) Buddharakhitā (Buddharakshita) . . . female pupil (*atevāsi{nī}*) of the elder (*thēra*)*bhayata* (*bhadanta*) Buddharakhita (Buddharakshitā), the overseer of works (*navakarmikā*) of the Chetikās (Chaityakās) who lived at Rājagiri, together with her daughter, and of Dhamadinā (Dharmadatta) and of *Sangha*rakhitā[28]
>
> (*Sangharakshitā*)

This inscription recording communal patronage mentions a nun who introduces herself as an *antevāsini* (a pupil). The mention of her teacher is important, as he is probably well known as 'the *Navakamikā*' (a superintendent of building operations). The fact that she mentions as living together with her daughter is remarkable. It could mean that her daughter too had taken the monastic vows and the two lived together in the same convent in Rājgiri. Alternatively, it could also be taken to mean that in spite of having become a nun, she continued to live in her house with her daughter and not in a *vihārikā*.[29]

Another inscription[30] in *Prakrit* found on a copying-stone from Amarāvati mentions:

> *(Gift) of the lay-worshipper (upāsikā) Kāma (Kāmyā) daughter of a housewife Kānha (Krishna), daughter of the householder (gahapatī) Idā (Indra), together with her relatives, and of the nun (Bhikkhūnī) Nāgamitā (Nāgamitrā).*

But in this case, the exact relation of the nun with the other donors in not clearly brought out. Other than those cited above, there are many more such instances where these nuns are seen interacting closely (albeit in a religious context) with members of their family, with whom they were supposed to have severed all social and familial bonds. This is seen to be ubiquitous in the case of nuns as compared to monks. This further reinforces the view put forward by Blackstone (2000) that the perception of 'struggle' in their quest for liberation for the *thēris* is a struggle to break away from the social, kinship bond structure.

The *bhikṣunīs* continued to maintain their social ties under various circumstances. The *Mahavagga*[31] states that they were allowed to maintain contacts with members of their families, visiting them even in *vassā-vāsa*, if necessary, when travel was normally forbidden. The loss of kin is described as the greatest loss that could affect a man and therefore kinship was rated much higher than the wealth (*A*. II. 401). The cutting of ties with kinsmen was the greatest sorrow to be faced by a family, which was being renounced by the imminent *bhikṣu*. Even the Buddha recognised the importance of family life when he ruled that various categories of people had to obtain permission from their kinsmen before being ordained in the *Samgha*. The Buddhist society was kinship-based rather than caste-based. It is possible that the influence of kinship bonds on the Buddhist *Samghas* can be attributed to the stronger basis of kinship ties in the *gaṇa-Samgha*, of which the Buddha had been a member before he renounced the world (Wagle 1995).

Of the various familial and kin-based references that one comes across in the inscriptions, the most frequently alluded to is the *wife*.[32] The high incidence of women donors, identifying themselves as wives in the donor records, shows their keenness to be identified through their husbands. In many cases, even though the donor does not mention her own name, the name, occupation and sometimes the caste of the husband are also duly acknowledged. In most of the cases, wifely status has been indicated by the term *pajāvati*, and a few times one also comes across its synonyms, *jayā* and *grhinī*. 'The lexicons define the word *pajā* or *prajā* as offspring, progeny or children . . .'. Thus, the term *pajāvati* has the dictionary sense of a mother[33] and its usage to indicate the wifely status clearly shows that, conceptually, a wife was unthinkable without children in some section of the society in Central India.

Marital relationships as portrayed in the literary texts like the *Therigāthā*[34] are cordial. Though sometimes one does come across instances of wives being abandoned and of remarriages being solemnised, as in the case of Isidāsi (*Therigāthā*, 72). Conversely, the predominant themes that one encounters in the *Jātaka* are of infidelity, adultery committed by the women, and also the latter's complete disregard for the institution of marriage and its sanctity. While the *Jātakas* reflect the contemporary social attitude towards women, *Therigāthā* echoes the woman's own perception of her marital relationships, and how she chooses to visualise and assess the marital association during her lay existence.

The 'wives' have been variously referred to as *pajāvati* (*Prajāvati*), *jayā* and *bhāyā* in the inscriptions. Polygamy was also prevalent, which is attested to by the use of the term '*sapatna*' for the co-wife. Within the household group, a man's duty is to provide for his wife (*dārā*). Of the total, almost half of the women seem to refer to their marital status with indications of the social standing of the husband or his family. These include references to *setthis*, *gahapatī*, kings, *Mahābhojas*, *Mahārathis asavārika* (trooper) and the like. This phenomenon is seen to be more common in the southern inscriptions.

Among the various wifely attributes that a woman going to the husband's house must possess, the Buddha mentioned that among other things 'she should safeguard her husband's property, his money, grains, silver and gold, and she is not like a robber, wastrel or carouser'.[35]

In the *Añguttara Nikāya*, the Buddha mentions the duty of the husband towards the wife as vice versa. He also mentions in the same *sutra* the seven different kinds of wives, namely: the *wadhaka* (or the executioner), the *chorasama* or thief-like wife, the *ayyasama* (or the mistress-like wife), *Mātusama* (the mother), *Bhaginīsama* (the sister), *sakhīsama* (the faithful friend) and *dāsisama* (the slave).

In a discourse delivered by Yashodhara Dēvī, in the presence of men, *Dēwas* and *Brahmās*, immediately preceding her *nirvāṇa*, she is described as having delivered a *sutra*, describing the seven different kinds of wives (Wagle 1966:91).

There are incidentally no references to *widows* making donations. Sometimes these women are seen making donations together with their sons. The absence of any reference to the husband should be taken to be her expression of independent identity, social and self (Shah 2001). This trend has been differently explained as probably being a result of the control of economic resources earlier by the husband and later by the son or sons (Roy 1988). On another level it can also be understood as the urge/need to express one's comparatively greater closeness with the living relatives, whether they be sons, daughters, parents and the like rather than identify with a deceased kin.

The data derived from the analysis of the Buddhist textual tradition (the *Therigāthā*) are juxtaposed with the data derived from analysis of the archaeological records (see Table 2 showing social identification categories used by *Bhikṣunīs* and *upāsikās* in the donor records), which indicate that the preference for motherhood as a mode of identification is almost as common as that of a wife and one of the most favoured and frequently employed criteria for identification. There are about 54 (21.7 per cent) references to mothers, of which more than half (i.e. about 37 references) comes from Sāñci alone. It thus becomes clear that this mode of identifying oneself was more prevalent in the Central India, as compared to the South. Even royal women preferred to introduce themselves in the inscriptions, as mother.[36] It is thus evident that the value assigned to maternity and paternity was by no means similar, and while maternity was an important as well as popular means of identification for women donors, paternity was relatively less important for men. Second, while women are commonly identified through sons, identifications through daughters also occur.[37] The recording of donations at sacred sites appears to be a well-established custom. The act of recording the donations was however not limited to the site where the *dāna* was offered as there are instances of women making grants at one site and recording the grant at other sites, much later in time and space, for example, Junnar Buddhist Cave inscription[38] where the donor records the grant made at the site and also grants made elsewhere, in this context the grants made to one or more nunnery in the town also together with the excavation of a cave and cistern at the site where the inscription was recorded.

It mentions, '. . . Gift of a cave (*lena*) and a cistern (*podhi*) by Patibadhaka these establishments and the nunnery (*bhikhuni upasaya*) of the Dhammutaiyas (Dharmottariyas) in the town (*nakara*). The inscription also seems to mention a nunnery of Sivapal[i]tanika (Sivapalita), wife of Gribhuti, in the town (*nagara*)'.

This also indicates a certain degree of control over/access to economic resources along gender lines (Roy 1988:217–8). This indicates a conscious attempt to record the mother–daughter bond, which was probably as strong as that of mother–son or others, if not stronger. In purely numerical terms, mothers in relation to sons far outnumber those in relation to daughters, but the fact that incidence of women constituting their identities in reference to their daughters show that daughters were not as unwelcome in the society of Central India, as is generally assumed.

In inscriptions that record the donations of patrons who identify themselves as mothers, multiple patterns emerge. There are references to anonymous mothers as well as those mentioning their names at the beginning of the record. There are mothers who identify themselves singularly by their motherly status and others who added the attribute of native place or attributes of their various children. We have mothers in relation to sons as well as daughters. There are records of a mother each of a monk-son and a nun-daughter, as also a nun-mother of a lay daughter. On the other hand, a nun-mother like Rsidāsi was unable to sever her maternal bonding and is seen recording her benefaction with her lay daughter and, therefore, constituted her identity with reference to her.[39]

It would not be out of place to suggest here that there are instances[40] where sons are identified through matronymics such as Vachiputa, Gotiputa and the like. This would suggest that a patrilineal system of identification was by no means the only one in use, and for sons in particular, identification through the mother was certainly important.[41]

Daughters as donors are seen as another important category by which women donors identified themselves.[42] Almost 15.7 per cent of the total of *upāsikās* and about 2.24 per cent of the total number of *Bhikṣunī* donors identified themselves by this particular category.[43] Daughters were the responsibility of parents; like sons, daughters also needed to seek prior permission of their parents in order to become nuns.[44] There is a close tie of affection between a mother and her daughter. A girl Kana who returns on a visit to her parent's home is referred to as going to her mother's house (*mātughara*) and not her father's.[45] A daughter though does not inherit her father's property if he has a son.[46] There are only about 15 independent references to women as daughter, and according to Roy (1988), 'the relative paucity of references would suggest that as daughters or sons, women and men had relatively less of an independent access to resources necessary for making a gift'.

Some eight (3.2 per cent) references to daughters-in-law are also met with in the inscriptions. In the *Vinaya literature*,[47] the female members of the family are classified in descending order, as (i) women of the family (*kula itthi*); (ii) daughter of the family (*kula dhitāyo*); (iii) young girl of the family (*kula kumāriyo*); (iv) daughters-in-law of the family (*kula sunhāyo*) and (v) women slaves (*kula dāsiyo*). 'It is important to note that the daughter-in-law appears at the end of the list, just before the slaves who are obviously outsiders' (Wagle 1996). It is quite probable that the list accommodates the members in the order in which these women (according to their age and circumstances) became members of the family.

Sisters also form a donor category by themselves. They have been referred to as '*bhaginī*'. In some 16 (2.4 per cent) cases *upāsikās* identify themselves as '*bhaginī* or the sister of, while only a single instance of a nun (i.e. 0.44 per cent of the total) identifying herself as '*bhagini*' is seen.[48] All these instances save one can be explained as a subconscious attempt to identify themselves through the male members (in this case the brothers) who were the heads of their families. As for the last instance, the brother is mentioned as a monk[49] Mamdāra. Here identification through a brother, who is also an ordained member of the *Samgha*, assumes importance. 'Although the evidence is extremely sparse, it would suggest that as far as affinitive relationships were concerned, brothers were a more important means of identification than sisters, both for men and women'.[50]

In a few other cases women refer to themselves as granddaughter[51] and as sister-in-law.[52] In both these cases there are other modes of identification also that have been employed and they are by themselves not singularly important. They are found to occur in cases where the donor chooses to introduce herself using more than one category of identification, or multiple identities as the inscription mentions woman as a granddaughter, 'daughter' as well as 'the wife of . . .' simultaneously. From the mention of the above-mentioned but rather infrequently used categories, the need to connect with such members who had a certain social standing along with the desire to be associated with power (social as well as economic) is also reflected. On an individual and personal level, as these inscriptions are very few in number,[53] they could also be taken to mean that the individuals they have associated themselves with, in order to identify themselves, exercised a distinctive influence or authority over them.

It will not be wholly incorrect thus to state that the most valued principle for a woman remained that in which she was the dutiful wife and mother, a matriarch who ruled over her vast family consisting of numerous children and grandchildren as exemplified in the person of Viśākha Migāramāta (Chakravarthi 1987:34). *Viśākhā* is referred to as Migara's mother (*Migāramāta*), was one of the chief female lay disciples of the Buddha in the Dhammapada. This is better emphasised from this verse in the *Añguttara Nikāya* (*A*. II.76) where women's existence is described as centring around men, adornment, her son and being without a rival.

Familial attributes

The majority of women have defined their identity in terms of their familial status. However, whereas most women figuring in the Sāñcī and Bhārhūt inscriptions are content with a single familial attribute, those from other regions use more than one such attribute. The centrality of the familial status to the formation of female identity is evident from the fact that it was the most frequently used attribute, at times also in conjunction with other indicators, such as their royal, religious, professional statuses. In some of the examples, the position in the kinship structure as an attribute of identity is more important for women than men, even when they come from the same family. Thus, the emerging picture reflects the influence of patriarchy on women's mind, causing them to define their social self within the parameters of the kinship structure. Nevertheless, a section of women did break out of the conventional parameters and have figured by personal name[54] alone, in a purely non-familial framework. This latter category of donors used different kinds of attributes for the purpose of establishing their identity like personal name, native place and/or their native land and the like.[55]

Caste as category for identification

Caste-based identification is more commonly seen in the case of *upāsikās* than *bhikṣunīs*. Only in one specific case there is mention of a female donor who identifies herself on caste lines.[56] She is mentioned to be a *brahamāni*. This inscription is significant as the *Brāhamanas* formed the largest group of people who subscribed to Buddhism. While many prominent *Brāhamanas* are described as becoming *upāsakas* of the Buddha, they are rarely depicted as being continuously important in the early *Pāli* text. '. . . they do not appear to have contributed any further to the *Samgha*, other than having fed the Buddha and his band of *Bhikṣus.* Although, they were themselves frequently land-based, they never gifted any land to the *Samgha*. Nor is there any reference to them in mentioning construction/donation of the *vihāras* for the *Samgha*. Even the gift of robes was hardly ever made' (Wagle 1965:52).

The *gahapatī*[57], though, features as a continuing lay supporter or *upāsaka* of the *Samgha*, he figures prominently in the Pāli canon as the most important component of the laity and their acceptance of the Buddha's teachings is given considerable importance. This fact is corroborated by the inscriptional records from the Buddhist sites, 'No less than 631 donative inscriptions, representing some thousand individual patrons are to be found at Sāñcī. . . . The remaining three hundred record donations from diverse donors, among whom the largest single group are the ordinary householder (*gahapatī*) and the housewife'[58] (*gharini*).

Summing up the discussion one can say that the dichotomy between the textual provisions and their disregard in practice is quite evident from the analysis of the inscriptional data reviewed.

There is a scriptural injunction against naming a girl with *dattā* or *raksitā*-ending, where such suffixes are preceded by the names of a deity, has been observed more in breach than in compliance. 'It might be argued in this regard that most such names figure in the Buddhist inscriptions and the Buddhists were hardly bound by the Brahmanical injunctions. In answer to this we could cite the classic case of Sakanikā Vishnudattā of the Nāsik cave inscription which is Buddhist in religious affiliation and yet the forepart of her name leaves not even a shadow of doubt that she was considered to be a gift of God Vishnu by her parents, when they selected a name for her.'

The general perception towards women in the classical texts reflects a view that was commonly accepted by most of the commentators. Most law-givers of early India have recommended perpetual subjection of women to men. Vasistha ordains, '*Asvatantra strī purusapradhāna*'. Manu echoes the idea, 'a woman is never fit for independence'. Yajnavalkya, who is considered to be a more liberal law-giver compared to the rest, also said that women are never independent. Central to this provision for perpetual subjection is the divine status of husband in relation to his wife. However, we have no Buddhist counterparts to

Manu and Yajnavakya; references in the canonical literature clearly reflect that the ideal qualities of a wife were servitude and dependence. A slave-like wife is considered ideal among various types of wives. As far as the status of women in the society is concerned, there was hardly any perceptible difference between the Brahmanical and the Buddhist society (Chakravarti 1987). She says '. . .women who led their lives as daughters, wives and mothers were therefore quite clearly subjected to the authority of men and this attitude was projected even into the asocial world of the Samgha'. However, if one is to go by the elements of self-perception in the construction of female identity in the donor records, a section of women was perhaps not so indoctrinated. Normative attributes like *avidhavā* ad *jīvaputa* have been used by only one or two women out of the hundreds figuring in the records. Leave aside the divine status, even the human status of a husband is negated by women like Nāgamulanikā and Samadinikā. For Bāpisirī and Chathisirī, the sole source of identity is her mother rather than her father, who fails to find even a passing mention in her record. In case of northwestern India, there are instances where the sole source of identity for the women is their wifely status, and yet they fail to mention the names of their respective husbands. Most women figuring as *upāsikās* rarely use the familial status as an attribute of identity. Likewise, the few women who figure with the professional attribute of identity also disregard the familial framework in the construction of their identity. Shah explains this phenomenon as 'a section of women was psychologically free from the hold of patriarchal norms enshrined in the legal and canonical literature'.

Moving on from the discussion of the social to the asocial world, that is the world of the renunciants or *Bhikkhūnīs*, is the paradoxical situation of the merging of the two worlds (social and asocial), not only in respect of identity formation but also in that of associating to make a benefaction. A nun was required to take an oath of renunciation, abandoning all family ties. Yet, in ways more than one, the kinship ties continued to have a hold over these renunciants. This explains how a nun, Badhikā, figuring in a Bhārhūt votive inscription, constituted her identity in terms of being a daughter of Mahāmukhī, using familial status as an attribute of identity even after joining the Samgha. Here the articulation of identity appears to be of self-perception, where the merging of the social and the asocial attributes may be understandable. What is less understandable is the predominance of familial attributes in the social construction of the identity of a nun.

As regards the coming together of the laywomen and the nun, there are ample instances of the two interacting in the secular as well as the religious sphere. The latter is attested by the records of joint benefactions made by the two.

The order of the nuns, like that of the monks, was, in theory, a wandering community. But with the concept of permanent residences or *āvasās* gaining ground, the community of nuns also settled into retreats or nunneries. The nuns thus started to take pride in belonging to the towns and cities in which their nunneries were located. This is again attested by the epigraphic records.

The literary texts frequently discuss the subordination of the nuns to monks. However, this insubordination appears to be more theoretical than real. As very few nuns have constituted their identity with reference to their monk teachers, the case of Buddharakṣitā is most distinctive, in which her monk teacher received a separate mention.

> The gift of Dharmadattā and of Samgharaksita . . . of the mendicant (bhikṣunī) Buddharakṣitā with her daughters . . . the pupil of the (antevāsini) venerable thera Buddharakṣitā residing at Rājagiri and Superintendent of the building operations of the caitikas (*Rājgiri-nivāsikasacetika navakamakasa therasa bhayata Buddharakhitasa atevāsi . . . bhikhunina Buddharakhitaya sadhutaka . . .*).

The distance between the normative texts and historical reality is greatest in respect of social stratification. The status of a wife in her husband's home was determined by caste or *varṇa* to which she belonged. 'But it is astonishing to find that *varṇa* and *jāti* have been absolutely ignored by the women of our inscriptions as attributes of identity. The term 'Brāhmana' and its feminine form figure in an isolated case and by and large, the Brahmanic credentials have been constituted by the mention of a *gotra*. The other three *varṇas* find neither explicit nor implicit mention.'

The selection of a native place or place of residence as an attribute of identity may have been governed by regional custom; it offered a mode of constructing identity alternative to that of viewing oneself merely in terms of being a wife or mother. The fact that for many women these were the sole attribute of identity needs to be noted. Some women have figured barely by a name, ignoring both the kinship connection and the place of residence as attributes of identity. At times a subtle conflict of sorts is evident between the choice of kinship connection and the place of residence. Gorakshita of the Bhārhūt Votive

Inscription identified herself exclusively in terms of her place of residence. However when the text of her record was fully incised, she seems to have insisted on adding, as a second thought , the attribute of her wifely status by naming her husband. Her case resembles that of Samādinikā of the Bedsa Cave Inscription, with the difference that she has much more pride in her status as the daughter, than in her wifely status. While power relationships may have been a factor behind the selection and chronology of Samādinikā's attributes, no such factor can be postulated in the case of Gorakhita.

If the wifely status was the most popular among those from familial framework, no less so was the attribute of motherly status. No doubt in purely statistical terms, mothers in relation to sons far outnumber those in relation to daughters and the epigraphic records in this respect confirm the textual preference for sons. However, from a general survey of the epigraphic records, multiple patterns emerge and one cannot discern a single, individual pattern in the choice of attributes. Contrary to our expectations, an *upāsikā*, though a family woman, avoided the familial attributes, whereas some of the nuns have established their identity in terms of the familial framework. A nun was supposed to break free from the fetters of kinship bonds. The one constant struggle for a *bhikṣunī* was 'to seek release and rise above the familial and kinship bonds that limit one's quest for liberation'. It is perhaps for this reason that the urge to include and identify oneself with one's family becomes very pronounced at a subconscious level, and this urge manifests itself in the epigraphic records and other writings composed by the *Bhikkhūnī*, like for example the Thērigāthā.

The general perception towards women in the classical texts reflects a view that was commonly accepted by most of the commentators. Most law-givers of early India have recommended perpetual subjection of women to men. Central to this provision for perpetual subjection is the divine status of husband in relation to his wife. In keeping with the above views, the classical texts reflect that the ideal qualities of a wife are servitude and dependence (*Vin.* iii.139–40).

A slave-like wife is considered ideal among various types of wives.[59] As far as the status of women in the society is concerned, there was hardly any perceptible difference between the Brahmanical and the Buddhist society (Chakravarti 1987). She says '. . . women who led their lives as daughters, wives and mothers were therefore quite clearly subjected to the authority of men and this attitude was projected even into the asocial world of the *Samgha*'. However, if one goes by the elements of self-perception, in the construction of female identity in the donor records, a section of women were perhaps, not so indoctrinated. Normative attributes, like *avidhavā ad jīvaputa*, have been used by only one or two women, out of the hundreds figuring in the records. Save aside the divine status, even their existence does not find mention in such records as those of Nāgamulanikā and Samadinikā. For Bāpisirī and Chathisirī, the sole source of identity is their mother rather than their father, who fails to find even a passing mention in the record. In case of north-western India, there are instances where the sole source of identity for the women is their wifely status, and yet they fail to mention the names of their respective husbands. Most women figuring as *upāsikās* rarely use the familial status as an attribute of identity. Likewise, the few women who figure with the professional characteristic of identity also disregard the familial framework in the construction of their identity. Shah (2001) explains this phenomenon as 'a section of women was psychologically free from the hold of patriarchal norms enshrined in the legal and canonical literature'.

Moving on from the discussion of the social to the asocial world, that is, the world of the renunciants or *bhikṣunīs*, is the paradoxical situation of the merging of the two worlds (social and asocial), not only in respect of identity formation but also in respect of coming together to make a benefaction. A nun was required to take an oath of renunciation, abandoning all family ties. Yet, in ways more than one, the kinship ties continued to have a hold over these renunciants. This explains how a nun, Badhikā, figuring in a Bhārhūt votive inscription, constituted her identity in terms of being a daughter of Mahāmukhī, using familial status as an attribute of identity even after joining the *Samgha*.[60] Here the articulation of identity appears to be in terms of self, where the merging of the social and the asocial attributes may be comprehensible. What is less understandable is the predominance of familial attributes in the social construction of the identity of a nun. As regards the coming together of the laywomen and the nun, there are ample instance of the two interacting in the secular as well as the religious spheres. The latter is attested by the records of joint benefactions made by the two.

The order of the nuns, like that of the monks, was in theory, a wandering community (Horner 1930/2011:240 and 253). But with the concept of permanent residence or *āvasās* gaining ground, the community of nuns also settled into retreats or nunneries. The nuns thus started to take pride in belonging to the towns and cities in which their nunneries were located. This is again attested by the epigraphic records, where nuns most frequently constituted their identity in terms of their place of residence or monastic retreat (see Table 2). The literary texts like the *Mahāparinirvāṇa Sutra* frequently discuss the subordination of the nuns to monks. However, this insubordination appears to be more theoretical than real. As very few nuns have constituted their identity with reference to their monk teachers, the case of Buddharakşitā[61] is most distinctive, in which her monk teacher received a separate mention.

> The gift of Dharmadattā and of Samgharaksita . . . of the mendicant (bhikşunī) Buddharakşitā with her daughters . . . the pupil of the (antevāsini) venerable thera Buddharakşitā residing at Rājagiri and Superintendent of the building operations of the caitikas (*Rājgirinivāsikasacetika navakamakasa therasa bhayata Buddharakhitasa atevāsi . . . bhikhunina Buddharakhitaya sadhutaka . . .*).

The chasm between the normative texts and historical reality is the greatest in respect of social stratification. It is noteworthy that social identity markers like *varṇa* and *jāti* have been absolutely ignored by women of their records as attributes of identity. The term 'Brāhmana' and its feminine form figure in isolated cases and by and large, the Brahmanic credentials have been constituted by the mention of a *gotra*. The other three *varṇas* find neither explicit nor implicit mention. Only 1.6 per cent of the total number of lay female donors have been noticed as constituting their identities on the lines of caste/*gotra*/*kula*.

The selection of a native place or place of residence as an attribute of identity may have been governed by personal choice; it offered a mode for constructing identity alternative to that of viewing oneself merely in terms of being a wife or mother. The fact that for many women these were the sole attribute of identity needs to be noted. Some women have figured barely by a name, ignoring both the kinship connection and the place of residence as attributes of identity.[62] At times a subtle contestation is evident between the choice of attributes. Gorakshita of the Bhārhūt votive inscription[63] identified herself exclusively in terms of her place of residence. However when the text of her record was fully incised, she seems to have insisted on adding, as a second thought, the attribute of her wifely status by naming her husband. Her case resembles that of Samādinikā of the Bedsa Cave inscription,[64] with the difference that she has much more pride in her status as the daughter than in her wifely status. While power relationships may have been a factor behind the selection and chronology of Samādinikā's attributes, no such factor can be postulated in the case of Gorakhita.

However, from a general survey of the epigraphic records, multiple patterns emerge and one cannot discern a single, individual pattern in the choice of attributes. Contrary to our expectations, an *upāsikā*, though woman with a family, avoided the familial itself in the epigraphic records and other writings composed by the *bhikṣunīs*, as in the *Thērigāthā*.

It is mostly seen that the man functions as a source of identity to the woman in a patriarchal society and most attributes of kinship connection have been conceived in relation to men figuring in multiple familial roles. Nevertheless, there are instances in the epigraphic records of men relating to women as a source of identity. Among such attributes of male identity constructions, the most popular is the matronymic used by Gotamīputra Satakarni, which took precedence over his proper name.

Professional category for identification

If women identify themselves through kinship connections, far more often than men (32.57 per cent and 8.16 per cent of laywomen and men, respectively), professional or occupational category appears to have been far more important for men than for women, as approximately 15.5 per cent of the total male donors have preferred this mode of identity construction over all others,[65] though we do come across women workers such as garland-makers, dancers, musicians, rope-walkers, acrobats, domestic help, slave and the like; women on a subconscious level tended to associate more with other forms of identity. For them their profession probably served to fulfil their material needs other than that of providing them with a distinct social identity. The almost complete absence to their nature of occupation can probably be related to the generation and appropriation of economic resources by the male members of the family. They, therefore, probably identified the most by their personal names and also with their place of residence, rather than through any other category.

Religious attributes as an identification category

There are women figuring exclusively with religious attributes[66] (e.g. *upāsikā*, *bhikṣunī*, *vihāraswāminī*, *navakāmika*, etc.), while some have combined the familial with the religious attributes. In rare cases, women have figured with a single religious attribute and yet have built up their full familial identity by listing many family members as associates in the benefaction.[67] The identity of the donor has been constituted in terms of her twin non-familial status, as *vihārasvamini* and *upāsikā*. Sircar believes that the term *vihārasvamini* should be taken to mean 'the owner of a *vihāra*' (1966:371). The unnamed woman should be taken to mean 'the owner of the vihāra' rather than the wife of the owner of the *vihāra*. Had the patron derived her *vihārasvamini* status from that of her husband, the author would have made an explicit mention of its masculine form. Contemporary inscriptions[68] contain references to rich patrons – men as well as women – responsible for financing the construction of *vihāras* and claiming the monastery as 'my own', by the use of the phrase '*svake-vihare*' as seen in the Junnar Buddhist cave inscription;[69]

> Gift of a cave (lena) and a cistern (podhi) by Patibadhaka Giribhuti Sakhuyaru, son of Savagiriyasa of the Apaguriyas and the endowment of these establishments and the nunnery (bhikhuni-upasaya) of the Dhammutariyas (Dharmottariyas) in the town (nakara). The inscription seems to mention also a nunnery of Sivapa[i]tanika (Sivapalitanika), wife of Giribhuti, in the town (nagara).

This record is significant for various reasons other than the one discussed above. It indicates that lay donors made endowments to any number of Buddhist institutions, irrespective of the order or sect, which was probably more of a binding for the monastics. Another aspect worthy of mention is that the records did not necessarily exist only at the place of its actual site; instead the recording of a grant was flexible, depending upon the discretion of the donor and could be recorded anywhere other than the actual site of donation also.

Another reference to the term *vihārasvāminī* occurs in Mathurā Stone Image inscription of the year 135.[70] One might argue that the religious attributes are little more than the feminine forms of male attributes in the contemporary records, and so represent merely a duplication of an established practice with gender differentiation rather than a self-perception of the women concerned. Whichever be the case, it is evident that the use of such terms as *vihārasvāminī* was done by women donors who made a conscious choice of an attribute outside the familial framework, even as lay votaries. On the contrary, a few monastic women conceived their identity in familial framework even after breaking all familial ties and entering the homeless state. Given the decontextualised nature of our records, this merging of the social and asocial identities underlines the dichotomy between theory and practice of Buddhist renunciation.

Regional peculiarities in the content of the donor records

A detailed study of the list of donative inscriptions from the sites mentioned above brought to the fore various issues that need to be discussed in detail. A detailed tabulated chart[71] (Figures 4.1 and 4.2) helps us look at issues like, where did the donors hail from? What were the most favoured pilgrimage sites that the patrons chose to make their donations?[72] Was there any difference in the choice of sites where donations were being made by male and female donors,[73] on the one hand, and between the *upāsikās* and the *bhikṣunīs*, on the other[74]? Did the lay as well as the monastic women donors hail from the same place? Is there any discernible difference in the sites from which the two categories came from?[75]

Thus it is evident from the figure that Sāñci largely scores over the rest of the sites in terms of donations by *upāsikās* (45 per cent). Second

Figure 4.1
Distribution of laywomen donor or *upāsikās* at different sites.

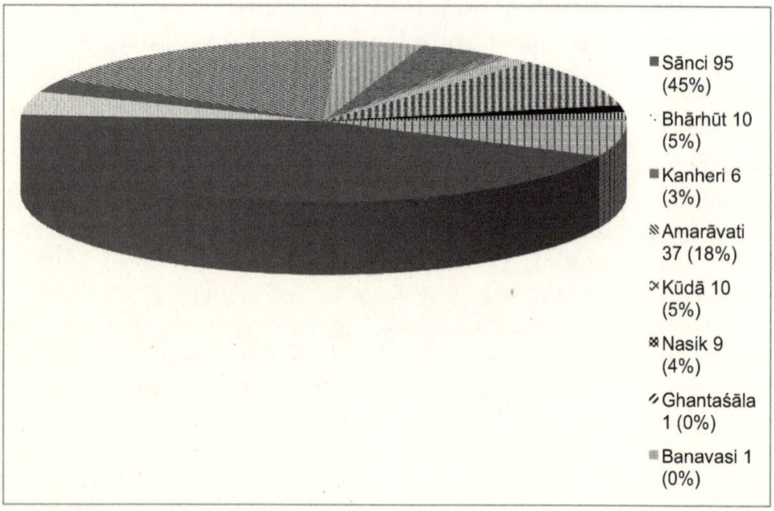

Figure 4.2
Distribution of *bhikṣunīs* as donors at different sites.

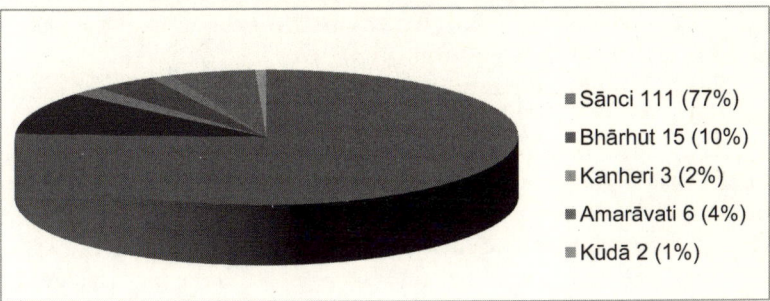

to Sāñci is Amarāvati (18 per cent), followed by Nāgarjunakonda (15 per cent).

In the case of *bhikṣunīs*, however, there is a difference. Even though Sāñci (77 per cent) continues to be the most favoured site for donation for both lay and monastic women, Amarāvati (4 per cent) is displaced by Bhārhūt (10 per cent) for the second most favoured spot. The heavy concentration of inscriptional records of *bhikṣunīs* in and around Bhārhūt and Sāñci points to the existence of most number of *bhikṣuṇī vihāras* around this region. Most of the sites in the inscriptions have been identified as places in Central India in and around Sāñci, which explains Sāñci's position of dominance with respect to the number of female donor records. Most of these like Kurara have been identified as renowned urban centres and this further supports the theory of location of *bhikṣunī vihāras* in nagaras and towns.

The type/nature of donation made affords us a cursory glimpse of the economic status of the donors; what were the different kinds of economic resources at their disposal; to what extent were women controlling these resources?

A Nasik Buddhist cave inscription of the time of Rajan Madhariputra Isvarasena[76] records:

> Endowment of money for the community of monks (bhiksusamgha) of the four quarters residing at the Vihara on Mount Trirasmi by the female lay worshipper (upasika) Vishnudata, the Sakanika, daughter of the Saka Agnivarman, wife of the Ganapaka Rebilla, mother of the ganapaka Visvavarma. The money was invested with the guilds (sreni) of the potters (? Kularika), the workers fabricating hydraulic engines (odayamtrika), the oil pressers (tilapishaka).

This donor record indicates that the lay female donor had the resources and more importantly the wisdom to invest the resources in different enterprises which would ensure the sustenance of the *bhikṣu* order of which she was a patron.

In recent times Kumkum Roy, Upinder Singh and Kirit Shah have used inscriptional data in their efforts to address the women's issue. While the first two have focused exclusively on the records from Sāñci, Shah's macro-analysis works on a much broader canvas with data incorporating Brahmanical as well as Jain donor records. While the first two restrict their analysis to Sāñci, Shah's work though invaluable in its approach does not look at the records in context to the site. This survey on the contrary tries to study the patronage patterns that emerge at the Buddhist sites. A close study of these inscriptions shows that there is a remarkable difference in the structure and contents of the inscriptions from the two groups of sites: those north of the Vindhyas and those south of the Vindhyas. While most of the donors tend to identify themselves in terms of a single category, as coming across from the inscriptions from the north, those south of the Vindhyas are comparatively more detailed; that is, the women (especially the lay donors) tended to identify themselves through more than one category. For example, a woman calls herself 'the mother', 'wife' and in some cases 'the daughter of . . .' making use of multiple categories of identification, all in one inscription.

Another stark differentiation between the inscriptions of the two regions is that in the sites south of the Vindhyas, there are far more instances recording communal patronage, where the donor is a family, a kin group or a loose association of natives of a particular city or monks and/or nuns belonging to a particular place or to a particular sect. Whereas the donor records from the sites north of the Vindhyas rarely mention the kind/nature of donations unlike those from the south. Quantitative differences also persist in the records of the two regions. In the inscriptions of the north, they rarely seem to refer to the kind or the nature of the donations made. The few instances where the exact nature of donations have been recorded, they almost always seem to refer to fragmentary architectural members as objects donated, like rails, pillars, pavement slabs, except for some from Mathurā where images are recorded as donations.

One interesting feature common to the Mathurā records is the fact that apart from recording the names of the donors, the inscriptions also record the kind of merit that the particular donor is desirous of seeking, while making the donations.

The famous Katra Buddha, a masterpiece of Kushana art at Mathurā, is one such example. It was commissioned by Amohāsi, mother of Buddharakhitā and was set up in her own vihāra (svāke), 'to ensure the welfare and happiness of all sentient beings'.[77]

As Mathurā was a major centre of art, the frequency of individual sculpted art pieces produced at Mathurā and gifted for merit is quite high. Mathurā artists were commissioned by men and women donors, both lay and monastic, in large numbers. Many of the donor records from Amarāvati are also found engraved on sculptures. The limitations of studying these epigraphic records with regard to their context is very often seen in the cave sites of the western Deccan. The inscriptions in many of the cases record donations that were made elsewhere (e.g. a Nasik Buddhist cave inscription of the time of Rajan Madhariputra Isvarasena, L.L. no. 1137). Such data do not provide much information on the donor's relation to the site where the donation has been recorded except for the fact that she visited the site and had the resources to record her munificence. Though these are some of the larger differences between the two groups, the convention of recording the name of the donor along with the kind of donation made and the kind of religious merit that the donor was desirous of seeking from the donation made is noticed at most of the sites. But some of the individual sites exhibit their own peculiarities, in style and content, in the rendering and recording of inscriptions. For example, at Bhārhūt, many of the sculpted panels have (instead of the name and other particulars of the donating agency) short inscriptions labelling the sculpted themes.

All the Buddhist sites which have yielded inscriptional records of Buddhist donor women have been compiled in a table. Fifteen such sites from the north and south with donor inscriptions of Buddhist women have been included in the analysis. These sites are Sāñci, Bharhūt, Kanheri, Amarāvati, Kūdā, Nasik, Ghantaśāla, Banavasi, Junnar, Banavasi, Mathurā, Sarnath, Bhattiprolu, Pitalkhora and Nāgarjunakonda. From an analysis of the inscriptional records of the two regions, north and south of the Vindhyas, it emerges that the two most prominent sites, with regard to donatory inscriptions, are Sāñci in the North and Amarāvati in the South. A comparative analysis of the two shows that, of the total number of inscriptions recording the gifts of women donors (361) from the 14 sites of North and South India, almost 70 per cent come from North India, of which 57.06 per cent are exclusively from the site of Sāñci itself.

The examination of the donor records revealed distinct quantitative as well as qualitative differences. The inscriptions from the South almost always mention the nature of donations made. The kind of donations recorded from the South are varied in nature, ranging from fragmentary architectural members to lamps; lion-seat, like the construction of monastic cells (*vihāra*), *chaityas*, cisterns and wells; *stūpas* as also caskets (*manjuśa*) made of semi-precious and precious stones and metals for enshrining of the relics of the Buddha (*Samgha*). One reason that probably explains the fairly large and substantial donations from the South, as opposed to the individual and comparatively smaller donations from the North, is the far greater number of communal donations from the South.[78]

Though we do have a few instances of collective donations from sites like Sāñci and Bhārhūt also, individual donations seem to predominate in the sites north of the Vindhyas. The two regions present stark contrasts with respect to the kind of donations made (as has already been mentioned) as also in the category of women donors. Broadly seen, the number of *bhikṣunīs* donating at various sacred sites of Northern India was far greater than in the South, with *bhikṣunīs* even outnumbering the lay donors/*upāsikās*[79] at a few sites like Sāñci and Bhārhūt, where the percentage of nun donors is 77 and 10 as compared to the 45 per cent and 5 per cent of *upāsikās*, respectively. On the contrary, a southern site like Amarāvati has only 4 per cent nun donors. Another important aspect that needs to be looked into is the spread of women donors vis-à-vis the sites of donation. As is evident from the table,[80] the *bhikṣunīs* hailing from a particular region preferred to make pilgrimages and donate at those sites which were closer to their place of residence but cases of nuns travelling great distances in order to make pilgrimages and donate at those sites is also not unknown, but is certainly rare; for example, a nun from Rajgir, undertaking a pilgrimage all the way to Amarāvati and making a donation is recorded.[81]

> Gift of the nun (bhikhuni) Budharakhita . . . female pupil (antevasini) of the elder (thera) bhayata Budharakhita the overseer of works (navakamaka) of the Chetikas (Chaityakas) who lived at Rajagiri together with her daughter and of Dhamadina and of Samgharakhita.

As is evident from Figures 4.1, 4.2 and 4.3, showing the distribution of lay and monastic patrons at different sites,[82] the lay and

Figure 4.3
Comparative visibility figure, showing *upāsikās* and *bhikşunīs* at various sites of donation.

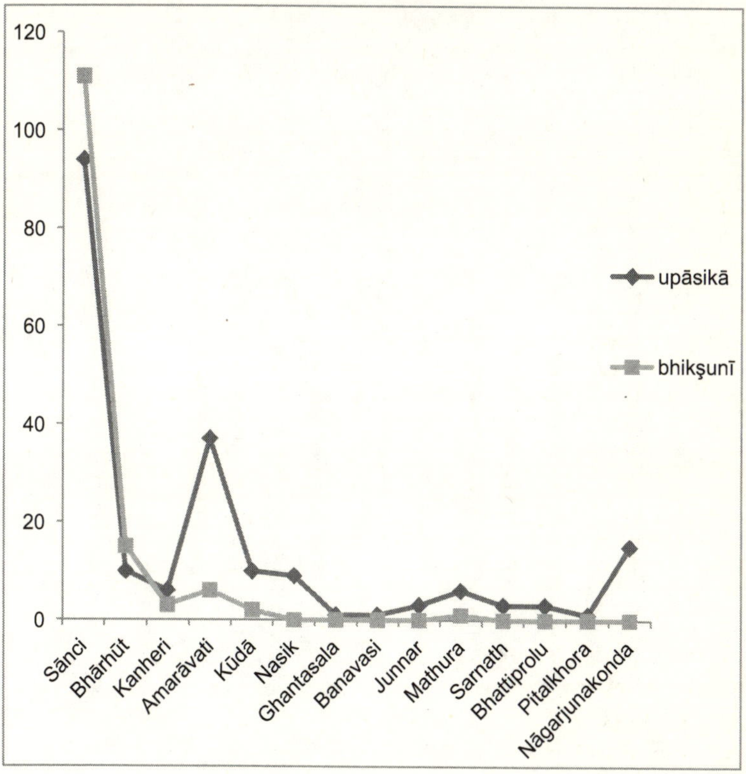

monastic women donors hailed from a number of places. At times both the categories of donors are recorded as having come from the same place. But then a close look at Figure 4.3 shows that the two categories seem to have concentrations at different places also. While the donations of the *bhikşunīs* can be seen to have come from certain clusters, more often from places like Ujjainī, Vidishā, Kurāra and Kurāgāra, the spread of the *upāsikās* can be seen to be more evenly spaced and they came from a myriad of places.[83] This can be explained as the sites mentioned above may have located in themselves convents or nunneries where these nuns resided. These sites were more often urban centres as location of *bhikşunī vihārikās* at such urban centres

Figure 4.4
Comparative figure showing percentage of men donors versus women donors.

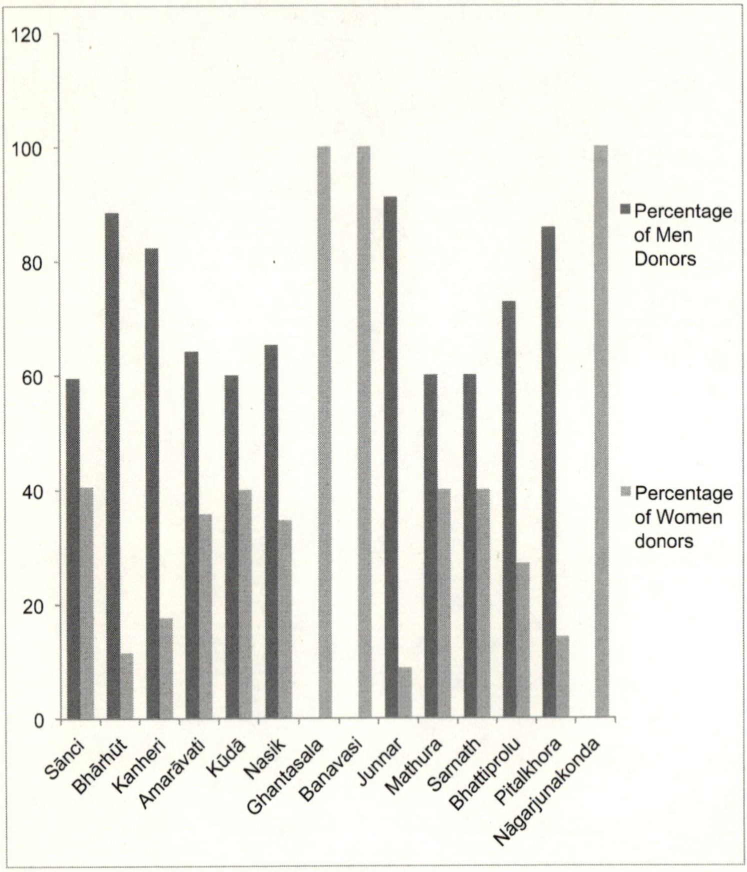

meant easier access to resources, more patrons and better security as compared to far-flung remote areas.

One can discern a difference in the choice of sites where donations were being made by male and female donors.[84] While at certain sites like Bhārhūt, Kanhēri, Junnar and Pitalkhorā we see a predominance of male patrons, at others like Ghantaśāla, Banavāsi and Nāgarjunakonda the female patrons are dominant. A study of Figure 4.4 shows that the male and female patrons largely chose different sites that they preferred to patronise which was to an extent also determined by the relative accessibility of the sacred site too.

Women patrons and pilgrimages

Place names as an identification category: One of the most common modes of identification adopted by both the categories of donors (i.e. the *upāsikās* and the *bhikṣunīs*) is a reference to their place of residence.[85] By doing so, the women attempted to construct an identity for themselves outside the familial framework, though the use of place name (place of residence) as a category for identification is seen to be more frequently used by the *bhikṣunīs*[86] than by the *upāsikās* (85 nuns out of the total tended to identify themselves by the place name as opposed to 70 *upāsikās*). This was probably because for the nuns, on entering the convent, severing of all kinds of social bonds was a prerequisite and therefore the significance of the place names. It is noteworthy that these women were independent and liberated and did not feel the need to identify themselves as part of a particular sect or school, as is seen in the case of some monks. Or maybe the number of sects which might have had a well-developed *bhikṣunī* order was very few and therefore not as many as for the monks which obviated the need to mention the particular sect. An urban centre, for example, may have had only a single *bhikṣunī vihāra* unlike the monasteries for the monks. For example, a sacred site like Nāgarjunakonda has records which refer to various Buddhist sects coexisting within the same sacred landscape. They very often referred only to the place they came from, with/without their names. At other times, they were even content to be known merely as 'the nun', without any reference to their personal name. Laywomen donors at times used other categories of identification also, along with her place of residence.[87]

Another reason in support of the use of place names by *bhikṣunīs* is that monks were associated with formal monastic units while many of the nuns lived with relatives and were not a part of a formalised structures/institutional monastic unit. Therefore, unlike the monks who are seen referring to their particular sect/school, a *bhikṣunī* tended to identify more easily to the place, be it a village or a city.

Sometimes a donor mentions two places simultaneously in a single record. While the donor is stated to be the native of a particular place, she is stated as residing in a second place. Thus, the distinction between the native place and the place of residence is clearly brought out. This was probably done to pinpoint and provide a more accurate address of the donor. While the first could be the native place, the second could refer to the place she was married into. Instead of providing additional details about the husband and so on, she chose to identify herself only by the place she came from.

Out of the total number (56) of place names cited in the inscriptions,[88] to which the donors belonged or identified themselves with, almost 35 (i.e. 53.847 per cent) of the total number of places are exclusive to *upāsikās*, while as many as 12 (21.4 per cent) are exclusive to *bhikşunīs*. The remaining eight sites (14.28 per cent) being common to both the categories. Of these, the maximum number of lay donations comes from Ujjaini, while the largest number of donations of *bhikşunīs* comes from Kurāra and Nandinagara. The greater spread of sites associated with the *upāsikās*, as also the far greater number of lay-women donors, can be explained as the ratio of *upāsikās*, as compared to the nuns, was far greater. While the smaller number of sites that one comes across in connection with the *bhikşunīs* can be explained as the probable location of *bhikşunī vihāras* at these sites only, based on the assumption that instead of being spread out, the *bhikşunīs* chose to reside in clusters and groups, in fixed institutionalised, residential accommodation, and these place names were therefore the location of the convents for the *bhikşunīs*. According to N.G. Majumdar, 'although most of the place names remain obscure at present, it is extremely likely that a large number of these places (*bhikşunī* sites) were in Malwa and its immediate neighbourhood.[89] This can also be taken to explain the relatively few instances of donations made by *bhikşunīs* in the south. Another reason for the almost negligible evidence for donations made by *bhikşunīs* in the sites of the South can also be attributed to the adoption of an alternate mode of identification by these nuns; i.e. for example they choose to record their donations along with other donors (in a group donation) rather than mentioning the place of their residence, or only by their personal names or as the pupil/*antevāsinī* of . . .'.

But then when we look at the data from the various sites under study, it becomes apparent that this statement does not hold true. Roy's explanation of 'motherhood' as a limiting factor, restricting the mobility of women patrons, does not seem to hold true on analysis of inscriptional data. According to Table 2 showing social identification categories used by *bhikşunīs* and *upāsikās* in the donor records, 54 *upāsikās* chose to identify themselves as 'mothers', who hailed from different regions. These lay female donors who identified themselves as 'mothers' form the second-largest category of women patrons – the most popular category being that of women, who identified themselves more readily as 'the wife of . . .'.

If motherhood was indeed a limiting factor, how do we then explain the journeys undertaken between large distances (between the place of residence and the place where the donations were being made) by women patrons, many of whom were mothers? They constitute 17 per cent of the total number of women donors.[90] Interestingly, the nun Budarakhita who travelled all the way from Rajgir to Amarāvati records her grant together with her daughter.

The statement though can be partially accepted as true as the inhospitable and fairly inaccessible tracts could have possibly been a deterrent for the comparatively lesser number of women donors as compared to the number of men donors from various regions, and the women donors (especially the nuns) all hailing from the regions in and around Sāñci. On the contrary, the cave sites of the Deccan have a significantly lesser number of female donors as compared to Sāñci, Amarāvati, Bhārhūt, Nāgarjunakonda and the like. It would mean that instead of embarking on very long and tedious journeys, these devout women generally preferred to undertake pilgrimage to religious centres, which were comparatively closer to their place of residence.[91] But to cite 'motherhood' as a probable reason for lesser participation by women, in undertaking pilgrimages, seems implausible. This is because, unlike the *upāsikās*, the *bhikṣunīs* may or may not have been mothers. And had the former been true, one would always find a greater incidence of nuns at these pilgrimage centres. But on the contrary, the corpus of inscriptional data[92] shows that it is quite the opposite with a greater number of *upāsikās* undertaking these pious journeys than the *bhikṣunīs* on the whole and very often identifying themselves as proud mothers.

Despite the limitations and physical discomfort, women did traverse considerable distances. An inscription records the donation made by an *upāsikā*, a resident of Ujjaini, at the Buddhist site of Nāgarjunakonda.[93] Yet another records a donation by a *bhikṣunī*, who hailed from Rajgir, but travelled all the way to the site of Amarāvati and made her offerings.[94] By not citing these records, we run the danger of discrediting and undermining their contributions. We will be seriously underrating their contributions by basing our conclusions on the clichéd and stereotypical gender-based behavioural norms that are expected of them.

Moreover, one cannot overlook the importance of pilgrimages, as they occupy a significant position within the Buddhist religion. According to the *Mahāparinirvāṇa Sutra*, those visiting the four great pilgrimage sites (Lumbini, Bodh Gaya, Sarnath and Kushinagara) would accrue immense spiritual benefits and after death would be reborn in 'the heavenly world' (Oldenberg 1997). A visit to the sacred places was thus more significant than undertaking journey for other mundane purposes and, therefore, the urge to overcome physical discomfort, so as to gain spiritual merit, even stronger.

The physical limitation imposed on their mobility could not have much affected their contribution to Buddhism. They could have made their endowment, through the monk travellers who travelled collecting subscription or *dāna*, thereby overcoming the physical limitations posed by their restricted mobility. Dehejia (1992:38) suggests monks presumably travelled to numerous township and villages collecting subscriptions (for construction at a sacred site). When the inhabitant of a particular township, for example Nandinagara or Madhuvana, donated money for a series of copingstones or slabs to pave the *pradakṣiṇā-patha*, the construction supervisor[95] ensured that their names were engraved on their gifts. There was, however, no random cutting of stones and donors could not gift finished pieces from their local workshop. Rather it was necessary to adhere to a clean-cut plan of the Sāñci architect.

Thus, we see that with or without the additional and exceptional benefits of being born in heaven, women patrons were contributing their bit to *dēya dhamma*.

It is likely that women found it easier to use major highways linking places emerging as important centres of trade and industry, rather than the roads, which penetrated through what may have been forested terrain. This is better explained/illustrated by the high incidence of donors hailing from Ujjeni.[96] This also logically accounts for the non-monastic followers or *upāsikās* as hailing from urban centres and towns, most of whom identified themselves as wives/mothers of traders and officials who live in cities/towns.[97] V. Nath (1987:72) suggests that the donations made by women should be related to an urban base and the artisanal and commercial activities of the period. Building on this argument. Ollivelle (2006) suggests that the uninscribed copper coins of the post-Mauryan period from the Eastern Malwa region, which include civic issues of Kurara, Vidisha, Nandinagara and so on, attest to the identity of these ancient sites as important trade/urban centres. However, some of the places from where the *bhikṣunīs* came from are specifically referred to as *gāmas* or villages (e.g. Kāmdādigāmā). While these are unfortunately not identifiable archaeologically, they would suggest that women from villages did occasionally make donations as well. The concentration of *bhikṣunīs* especially in the *gāmas* can also be understood in the light of this statement from the *Boudhayāyana Dharmasutra* which states, 'it is impossible for one to obtain salvation, one who lives in a town covered with dust'.[98] The Buddhist *Suttas* stipulate that the monastics should reside away from the town.

The evidence of *bhikṣunīs* coming from certain specific sites only can also be taken as evidence for the existence of nunneries/convents, at these sites, for example, Kurāgāra, Nandinagara, Navagāma and so on. Most of these sites are located in and around Sāñci and Bhārhūt, where we also find the maximum number of donations made by *bhikṣunīs* (Law 1954/1984; Majumdar 1940). Of the many injunctions laid upon nuns, one pertained to mobility. They were confined to live within the confines of a village or town and unlike the monks were forbidden from living alone in the forests[99] and when travelling were supposed to do so either in a group or at least in pairs.[100]

The far greater number of laywomen as also the large number of varied sites they came from can therefore be taken to explain the relatively greater mobility enjoyed by the laywomen, as these women were out of bounds of monastic living, and were free to travel with friends and family. Here it needs to be mentioned that the sites frequented by women were all located in a cluster (most of the sites have been identified as being located in and around the Malwa region). The incidence of women travelling great distances for the purpose of undertaking pilgrimages, though not unheard of, was quite low, as discussed earlier.

The instances of place names as category for identification that we come across show that the women did exercise some autonomy in the epigraphic space offered to them. In spite of their probable indoctrination to view their social self in terms of kinship status, a section of women articulated themselves outside the kinship structure.

Economic resources and its control

While discussing the role of women donors the issue of their economic resource base and inheritance rights cannot be ignored. The fact that these women were frequently donating in individual capacity and also as part of various groups is well attested in archaeological as well as literary records which reinforces the view that they did have economic resources at their disposal, which they put to various uses depending on their will and circumstances; they exercised the right to put the resources to whatever use or gift them away for religious purposes.

This statement gains further credence with the queen's edict of Asoka (Sirkar 1965/1996), which is significant as through it he has given formal recognition to women's freedom to make gifts of both movable and immovable properties belonging to her.

The fact that women had certain access to and control over economic resources (*strīdhana*) is also corroborated by the evidence of donor records as well as by the *Jātakas*, *Vinaya* and the like.

In one instance, a daughter-in-law along with her members of the family makes, in her own capacity, a generous donation of 4,000 coins to the physician Jivaka, on the recuperation of the *setthī gahapati*'s wife, who happens to be her mother-in-law.[101] A wife though did not inherit the property of the husband after his death. In one particular case, the son of a *Brāhamana* after the death of his father goes to his mother's co-wife and asks her to give him back the property of his father (Wagle 1966:120). But this should not be taken to mean that the woman, as wife, had absolutely no control over economic resources. When the wife of a *setthī gahapatī* of Rājagaha was cured by Jivaka, the whole family including the cured wife of the *setthī* as well as her daughter-in-law, that is, her son's wife, each gave 4,000 coins to Jivaka in gratefulness. Moreover, the number of individual donations to the *Samgha* by women who identify themselves as wife also supports the theory that they had certain control over economic resources, which, however limited, were well within their grasp and were used by them at their own discretion.

Most of the previous works on the subject tend to overemphasise the issue of *strīdhana* while at the same time undermining the other sources of generation of economic resources. *Strīdhana* or dowry has been exhaustively dealt with whenever the issue of female inheritance has been discussed. This finds ample textual support in the Buddhist texts as well. Anāthapindika is known to have given splendid presents to his daughter and sent her away in great pomp (Max Müller *et al.* 1881:70).

A wife was also obtained for money, paid to her father's family by the husband. However, she exercised full control over the internal management of the house after her marriage. A particular instance as recorded in the *Therigāthā*[102] shows the prevalence of this custom.

While property in general was conceived of in absolute, universal terms, which was somewhat ahistorical, women's wealth or *strīdhana* was carefully defined in terms of movable goods such as ornaments, utensils and so forth.

What permitted the classification of this assortment of goods under a single term seems to have been their distinctive relation to productive processes. Virtually none of these could have been used for production. But there are instances like the one in which Dhananjara, Viśākhā's father, assessing his future son-in-law's wealth says that 'this is as much his daughter would require of bathing money'. There are also references where the *strīdhana* has been used/disposed as per the wish of its owner.

Viśākhā thought it would be better to sell the ornaments she received at her marriage and erect a *vihāra* with the proceeds; but there was no one in Sevet (Sahēth) who had enough wealth to purchase them. She therefore bought a garden, at the east side of the city, and expended immense treasures in the erection of a *vihāra,* which was called Purwarāma, from the place in which it stood.[103]

Thus, it is evident that the discretion of managing the proceeds of *strīdhana* lay with the woman herself. While discussing the issue of women patrons and the donations made by them, we cannot afford to overlook the issue of generation of economic resources by these women in their own individual capacity.

The economic resources need to be grouped under three subheads. First, which was inherited; second, which was given as *strīdhana,* and third, which included funds that were generated by women. We have evidence (both epigraphical and literary) of women entrepreneurs who were engaged in various enterprises.[104] Furthermore, there is evidence of woman/groups of women investing sums of money with specific guilds for the purpose of investment, and the funds thus generated, being channelised in order to promote religious causes.

Other than these references from the literary records, we have numerous instances of donors, in the inscriptional records, who were donating individually and independently which points to a degree of autonomy from kinship structures (Deo and Gupte 1974:77; Prasad 1977).

Even if we force ourselves to believe that these laywomen were self-centred, enough to leave out the names of their family members (which seem extremely impossible), we cannot explain the same for the nuns. For women who had given up all kinds of social bonds, such donations could not have been possible in the absence of access to such assets. Women could legitimately acquire property (in numerous ways) including gifts, which were to be exchanged between kinsmen and women, as opposed to resources, acquired through direct participation in and control over productive processes. In other words, ideally women's wealth was generated within and restricted to certain domains.

This is also supported by archaeological data from excavated sites. The archaeological excavations at Bhokardan (District of Jaina, Maharashtra) yielded a clay sealing from the Satavāhana layers. It bears the name of Idā (Indra) from Thānenagara (Thane near Mumbai) in the Brāhmī characters of the first century B.C. According to the excavators, she was a trader and her sealing was used for authenticating commercial documents.[105] Bhokārdan is identifiable with Bhogvardhana mentioned in several early inscriptions in the *stūpas* of Sāñci and Bhārhūt (Thosar 1991:77). The excavations have proved beyond doubt that it was a rich industrial and commercial centre during the Satvāhana period and perhaps an emporium. The sealing referred to above clearly indicates that this place had commercial contacts with Thane, which was then an inland port. Considering the brisk trade relations between India and the Roman Empire during this period, the sealing is of special significance. It shows that Thane-based traders purchased products of foreign demand manufactured at Bhogvardhana and exported them to the Roman Empire. What is more significant is that the lady from Thane with her own sealing was involved in this activity of external trade.

An inscription from the Kūdā caves in the Raigarh district of Maharashtra records the gift by Sivadatta, who was the wife of Pushanaka, a Sarthavāha and trader from Nasik. Interestingly the same Pusanaka has recorded a gift in an epigraph in Bedsa caves. This indicates that the Sārthavaha Pusanaka and his wife were engaged in trade separately (Thosar 1991:77). An inscription from Mathurā mentions the name of Dharmasoma, who is described as *Sarthavāhinī*.[106] Sivadatta of the Kūdā inscription also seems to have led her caravan as *Sarthavāhinī*. If this is accepted as true, it will have to be accepted that women in India not only employed themselves in trade individually but were also caravan leaders. Kūdā caves are near Mandad, said to be the Mandagara referred to by Ptolemy, an important port in the Konkan (Gupta and Ramachandran 1991). This is another evidence of the participation of women in foreign trade.

A large number of inscriptions from Mathurā, Sāñcī, Bhārhūt, Amarāvati and the cave sites of the Deccan mention the names of women who are described as the relatives of traders.[107] 'It would not be wrong to presume that they had visited the cave sites and holy places when they were either on their trade missions or accompanying their trader husbands. In both the cases, the involvement of these women in the trading activities cannot be ruled out, though the degree of involvement would have certainly varied. The rock-cut caves in western Maharashtra, lay on trade routes leading to coastal ports. So the ladies from trading families visiting these caves and recording their gifts must be regarded as itinerant merchants/caravan traders'.[108] This also probably explains the relative paucity of records pertaining to *bhikṣunīs* as compared to *upāsikās* in the Buddhist sites in this part of the subcontinent. (Refer to Figure 4.3, comparative visibility graph showing *upāsikās* and *bhikṣunīs* at various sites of donation.)

In the Sanskrit drama *Mrichchakatika* by Śudraka we come across an indirect reference to the involvement of women in shipping activity, which was an essential part of overseas trade. The occasion is of the visit of Chārudatta, the protagonist of the play, to the Palace of Vasantsēna. Highly impressed by the pomp and pageantry of her palace, he asks whether Vasantsēna was the mistress of a shipping company (Gupta and Ramachandran 1991).

Customs or norms governing inheritance are not uniform but reveal variations over space and time and access to property varied across regions/sub-religions/caste/classes/families (Bhattacharya and Mukund 1999).

This would explain to an extent the difference in the quantitative and qualitative nature of the records of the North with that of the South. According to the numerous donative inscriptions found on the ancient monuments of India, a considerable segment of the patrons are women. Over two-thirds of the donations at Bhārhūt are from women, both nuns and laywomen, indicating that women held property in their own names and were free to dispense with their wealth, as they desired. Of the 631 donative inscriptions at Sāñci, close to half record the gifts by women. Similar evidence comes from the richly adorned *stūpa* at Amarāvati (first and second centuries A.D.) where women, including nuns, donated money towards the decoration of the *stūpa*. At the adjoining Buddhist monastic site of Nāgarjunakonda (mostly third century), entire monasteries, chapels and *stūpas* were gifted by highly placed women from the royal circle. The most striking difference in the nature of records from Nāgarjunakonda and other sites under survey is that only at Nāgarjunakonda do we come across women who are associated with the initial development of the sacred landscape, while at most of the other sites the presence of female patrons is seen only in the subsequent phases. They have been seen to be more involved in the subsequent embellishment and maintenance of the sacred sites. While Manu wrote around the year A.D. 200, the monuments at Bhārhūt, Sāñci, Amarāvati and Nāgarjunakonda span the period from 100 B.C. to A.D. 400.

An analysis of the available inscriptional data shows that the female patrons made substantial contributions to faith in economic terms and their donations to the cause, as is seen by their contributions at various Buddhist sites, in terms of additions to Buddhist monastic architecture, in the form of specific donations for the construction of *chaityas*, monastic cells, wells and the like and even smaller contributions like, providing for daily alms for the monks and nuns, providing garments for the members of the *Samgha*, providing butter for the lamps in the *chaityas*, commissioning of Buddha idols and so on, can in no way be undermined.

II

This section deals with historical female characters whose narratives are inextricably woven in the religio-philosophical fabric of Buddhism. This other category of women has surfaced time and again in the literary records, brought alive by commentators and historians alike. It is an exercise to seek out such historical figures, who seemed to have been favourite characters, of the later authors so as to appear repeatedly in their works, and to assess the reasons behind their glorification. This will be followed by an analysis, interpretation and significance of their representation in the visual arts. It tries to analyse why these women were glorified to such an extent as to render, the other group of less conspicuous, real participants almost invisible and non-existent. These women have been categorised and frequently alluded to in this chapter as 'the visible group'. This is so as the women discussed here have been comparatively more visible in the literary as well as the visual records. The visual records include the plastic arts, sculptures, paintings and the like. This section discusses the representation of these popular, legendary female figures within Buddhism, together with the context of their representation. For the purpose, a broad overview, of most of the depictions, from a cross-section of sites, relevant to this study has been taken up for analysis.

These women come from diverse social backgrounds and represent both categories, that is, *upāsikās* and *bhikṣunīs*. A closer study leads us to conclude that, of the two, the laywomen were more popular with the keepers of the doctrine.

Of the lot, the most popular was *Migāramāta* or *Viśākhā*. The accounts of the Chinese travellers concerning are brief. A lengthier account can be found in the Sinhalese chronicles.

She was the daughter of a wealthy merchant of Sāvatthi (Sravasti), who later became a lay *upāsikā* and one of the earliest and most generous donors and patrons in Buddhism. She is credited for having constructed the Pūrvārāma monastery, for use by the members of the *Samgha*. It is Viśākhā who is credited for making the first liberal preparations, on a massive scale, to provide for Buddha's disciples who came to Sravasti. When the Buddha was once dinning with his disciples at Viśākhā's house, the latter requested that the Buddha grant her eight wishes. These were as follows:

> *To provide cloths for the brotherhood during the rainy season.*
> *To provide food for stranger monks who come to Srāvasti.*
> *To provide monks who are passing through Srāvasti with food.*
> *To provide food to the sick and ailing monks.*
> *To provide medicines for the sick.*
> *To distribute a daily dole of boiled rice.*
> *To give bathing dresses to the sisterhood of the nuns.*
> *These wishes were granted to her by the Buddha.*[109]

She is said to have introduced her father-in-law, Migāra, to *Buddhist practice* and thereafter came to be known as Migāramata. Various versions of this story are to be found in the early texts like the *Nikāyas*, *Dhammapada* and so forth. The promulgation of a number of rules for the *Samgha* is also connected with Viśākhā (Nyanaponika and Hecker 2004:254). For example, there is the incident involving one of her nephews, who decided to join the monk's order. But when he requested his acceptance into the order in Sāvatthi, the monks there told him that they had agreed among themselves not to ordain novices during the three-month retreat and therefore he should wait until the rain retreat was over. But when the rainy season had ended, he had given up the idea of becoming a monk. When Viśākhā came to know of this, she went to the Blessed One and said: 'The Dhamma is timeless, there is no time when the Dhamma cannot be followed'. Following this conversation, the Blessed One prescribed that ordination should not be refused during the rainy season.[110]

Over time, the simple narrative of Viśākhā's life acquired epic proportions. This is clearly demonstrated by a Sinhalese version of the same story, but of a much later period. Her narrative acquired a prologue with past lives anecdotes that legitimised her status as the chief lay disciple in her present lifetime. According to the story, one of the incidents mentions that once in her childhood she met the Buddha, who knew at the time that 'from the merit she possessed, she would become the mother of his lay disciples or his principal female disciple; and he therefore preached the *Dharma*, by which she and her five hundred maidens entered the first of the paths'.

In the texts of the later period, the personality of Viśākhā is found to embody special womanly traits (*itthī ratnam*[111] – the pearl among women). With time, many regional variations developed around the main storyline.[112]

There are considerable numerical exaggerations also in the description of wealth, in the number of children (20) grandchildren (200) and great grandchildren (8,000) that she had. Over time, the character of Viśākhā acquired an almost cultic status which is exemplified by the statement: 'every one invites Viśākhā to sacrificial ceremonies and banquets and the dishes offered first to a guest like her brings luck to the house' (Shastri 1978:204). It is significant and therefore needs to be added that a religion whose attitude towards women was never discouraging but decidedly indifferent, which managed to appease contemporary social sensitivity on most issues concerning women, was quite generous and open to let Viśākhā take the centre stage. As if not content to let her be there, the writers grafted mythical tales around her real persona, thus elevating her status further, to the extent that she almost came to be venerated among the laity. The sole historical reference to Viśākhā comes from the travels of the Faxian (Legge 1986:59) in which he says, 'Six or seven li north-east from the Jetavana, mother Viśākhā built another *vihāra*, to which she invited the Buddha and his monks, and which is still existing'.

The other two *upāsikās* that have warranted the attention of the classical writers, albeit marginally, are the mother and wife of Jassā, who was the son of the richest banker of Banaras. The two women are known to be the first of the lay converts to Buddhism.[113] They are believed to have converted after Jassā himself took the monastic vows. Though they have been mentioned in quite a few texts, they have merited just a passing mention, limited to a few sentences. However, Viśākhā is rarely represented in the visual records (pl. 2).

The other preferred character of the Buddhist writers is *Ambāpāli*, a courtesan. Even Ambāpāli finds ample space in the literary compositions from the earliest times onwards. The historical accounts mention her as a famous courtesan in Pāṭalīputra who later converted to Buddhism and became a devout follower of the Buddha. She once invited the Buddha and his followers for a feast. The Buddha obliged and after the meal was over, she gifted a mango grove that she owned and subsequently erected a *vihāra* in it for the use of the *Samgha*, and hence came to be known as Ambāpāli. According to the biographical verses attributed to her in the *Thērigāthā*, 'seeing her own aging body and studying the visible signs of impermanence in her own person, she discerned impermanence in all phenomenon of these planes, and bearing that in mind and meditating upon it, attained *arhatship*'. She is famously known as 'the guardian of the *Āmra*' tree (Davids 1909:120–5) in the Buddhist annals.

Later commentators working on her biography introduced many new and interesting details in her biography wherein, among other things, stories (in keeping with the Buddhist Philosophy of good and bad *karma*) were added in order to justify her former lay existence as a courtesan.

According to the narrative, in the 31st *kalpa*, previous to the present age, when Sikhī was Buddha, Ambāpāli was one of his female relatives, but she renounced the world and, though a member of the royal family, became a priestess. One day when going to worship a certain *dagobā*, in company with other priestess, in the course of their circumambulation of the relic, one of them happened to sneeze and part of the mucous, without her perceiving it, fell on the ground. The princess, however who was next in the order of the procession, saw the court was defiled, and, she without seeing the delinquent, abused her, calling her a prostitute. In consequence to having thus offered an insult to a sacred person, she was next born in the *Amēdya* Hell. As a *bhikṣunī*, observing the precepts, she felt repugnance for rebirth by parentage and set her mind intently on spontaneous regeneration. So in her last birth she came into being spontaneously at Vesali, in the king's garden, at the foot of a mango tree.[114] But before this birth she suffered immense periods in different hells, enduring great pain, was born a female beggar a hundred thousand times and ten thousand times a prostitute. But in the time of Kasyapa Buddha she remained in perfect continence, and was born a *Dēvi* and after enjoying the pleasures of the *dēva loka* she was finally born in the garden of the *Lichchhavi* princes.[115]

A rare specimen from Gandhara depicts courtesan Āmrapāli presenting the mango grove to the Buddha (pl. 3). In the background, to the left is Vajrapani. This specimen is presently in the City Museum, Chandigarh.

Four courtesans, *Vimala*, Abhayā's mother, called *Padumāvati*, *Addhakāśi* and *Ambāpāli* having been converted to Buddhism, entered the order and attained to *arhatship*. To each of these, two verses are attributed to, in the *Thērigāthā* of Vimala,[116] little other mention is made[117] and none of Abhayā's mother.[118] She was the town-belle of Ujjeni, and her son Abhayā was sired by Bimbisara. On the other hand, Addhakāśi is important as in order to circumvent the difficulties of her ordinations, a relaxation in the discipline was granted.[119] But Ambāpāli became and remained famous as one of the most loyal and generous supporters of the order.

The anecdotal reference of Ambāpāli's munificence is corroborated again by the accounts of Fa-Hien (Legge 1965:79), which mentions:

> . . . [I]nside the city (of Vaishali) the women Ambāpāli built a *vihāra* in honor of Buddha, which is now standing as it was at first. Three li south of the city, on the west of the road, (is the) garden (which) the same Ambāpāli presented to Buddha, in which he might reside.

Besides these above-mentioned women, there are other women who serviced the religion in the capacity of the nuns. But these nuns, who occur in *Thērigāthā*, in spite of their spiritual and intellectual attainments, were not as popular as Viśākhā or even Ambāpāli. This can be said as they seem to come up very frequently in the works of the classical writers unlike those (read real characters) who attest their presence only through their recorded donations. There were two 'chief female disciples of the Buddha'[120] (both lay and monastic). The names of these women differ in the different texts. These were the women who were favoured within Buddhism. These women were accorded significant mythical positions with which came eminence and visibility. These characters were promoted within Buddhism, glorified as 'the most generous patrons' and as 'the ideal lay model' to be emulated. The terms of references for these two chief female disciples are *Agasaw* or *Agra-Srāwaka* from *Agra* (chief) and *Sāwaka* (a disciple literally, one who hears). The disciples who receive this office must have practiced the *pāramitās* during one *aśokya-kalp-lakśa*. They are never born of any caste other than the royalty or the Brāhaman clan. The two *agra-srāwikās* or principal female disciples of the last Buddha, Gotama, were *Khēmā*[121] and *Uppalawanna*. Khēmā, who was the daughter of the king's family at Sagala; in Magadha, the wife of king Bimbisāra of Rājagaha, and foremost of the sisters, who were distinguished for insight.[122] She was ranked by the Buddha as a model sister,[123] while Uppalavanna, daughter of a *setthī* of Sāvatthi, was foremost of the sisters who had *iddhī*.[124] The Buddha ranked her along with Khemā as pre-eminent in the sisterhood.[125]

Two other prominent *bikṣunīs* were *Prajāpati* Gautamī and *Yashodhara*. They were the foster mother and wife, respectively, of the Buddha. Though Prajāpati Gautamī's tireless efforts to enter the *Samgha* are well chronicled, and paved the way for the acceptance of women into the *Samgha*, she does not seem to be half as popular with the classical writers as Viśākhā or Ambāpāli.

During her lifetime Mahāpajāpati Gautamī was the first ordained female member of the *Samgha* and also the head of the nuns' order. The *Sinhalese Pūjāwalia* and *Amāwaturā* (Sinhalese texts) mention that Mahāpajāpatī earned the singular distinction of being the first among all of Gotama's disciples to enter *nirvāṇa*.[126]

One of the earliest depictions of the nativity scene and of Māyā's dream is carved on the medallion of a rail post in Bhārhūt. The scene depicts Māyā sleeping on a couch with her head resting on her right hand. A lamp on a high stand burns near her feet. Two attendants seated on cushions seem half-asleep, while the third has her hands folded in adoration. The divine elephant is seen approaching her from above. There is an inscription on top which reads, '*Bhagvato Ukram'ti*' or the decent of the Lord (Cunningham 1994:23).

Similar depictions are also seen at Sāñci (Marshall and Foucher 1940). There are six scenes depicting Māyā at Sāñci. Middle Panel of inner (south) face of North Jamb shows Māyā reclining on her right hand and the elephant can be seen at the top left, above her feet. According to Foucher (Foucher trans. Hargreves 1934/1999), the Sāñci depictions showing a goddess with the quintessential lotus in hand and the twin elephants in attendance are none other than Māyā, and this motif in an archaic aniconic form of the nativity scene. In its subsequent development at the Gandharan sites, the infant Buddha was also introduced (Zwalf 1996). However the images of the female deity with the attendant elephants were later identified as those of 'Gaja-Lakshmi' (Shaw 2006:459). Similar depictions are also known from Amarāvati[127] and Nāgarjunakonda (Stone 1995).

We have three predominant portraits of Queen Māyā at Ajantā.[128]

1) She describes her dream (cave 2).[129]
2) She leans contemplatively against a pillar (cave 2).[130]
3) She delivers a baby (cave 2).[131]

The portrait of Mahāmāyā, the mother of Buddha, is seen in cave 2 at Ajantā depicting different stages (Behl 1998:122) of her conception and birth of the Buddha. The scenes are painted on the wall of the left corridor. At Ajantā 'Mother and Child' motif is very popular in paintings as well as in sculptures.

On the iconographic representation of Māyā Devi, Young (2004:23) states that Queen Māyā's iconography positively represents female sexuality and celebrates the auspicious powers of fecundity (pl. 1). Of even further interest, although Queen Māyā is only briefly treated in the Buddha's biographies, in part because she died soon after his birth, she is pervasive in Buddhist iconography. This suggests that her image carried additional meanings that went beyond her individuality as a particular historical character. In the same way that images of the Buddha represent both the historical Buddha and the state of enlightenment, so too images of Queen Māyā represent her historical individuality and the auspicious fecundity of human and divine women.

Yashodhara has been mentioned in the texts as the wife of Gotama Buddha. She finds frequent mention in the events of Gautama's life, prior to his *abhinishkramana* (The Great Departure). But little has been written about Yashodhara who subsequently joined the order of nuns under Mahāpajāpatī; after Mahāpajāpatī entered *nirvāṇa*, she subsequently succeeded her as the superior of the Buddhist convents. Before she attained *nirvāṇa* according to the later texts, she is supposed to have performed miracles just as Mahāpajāpatī did, in order to demonstrate her advanced spiritual stage of being an *arhat*. She then delivered a discourse on the seven different kinds of wives (Hardy 1995:480).

The depiction of Yasodhara in the visual arts can primarily be seen in the sculpted panels of Gāndhāra[132] and Amarāvati,[133] and more famously in the Ajantā frescoes (caves 17 and 18). In cave 17, at Ajantā (sixth century C.E.), the scene depicts Buddha's return to Kapilavastu, when Yashodhara and her son Rāhula meet him at the palace gate.[134] She receives her lord, now the lord of the universe – in dual acceptance.

More touching is the theme for a mother and remarkable of course for the wife of the Siddhārtha (now Buddha) helping their only son Rāhula forward to accept the begging bowl while entering the order.

In cave 19, at the same place, to the left of the entrance, the Buddha appears in his mendicant's garb at the palace at Kapilavastu where (the mother) Yasodhara and (the son) Rāhula meet him. Rāhula is depicted accepting the bowl from his father (Ghosh 1987). She is (the queen) wife of prince Siddharth. Her portrait with her son Rāhula is drawn on the wall of the antechamber of the cave 17 at Ajantā (Ghosh 1987). It is a very poignant scene, similar to the one just described. When the Buddha returns after his enlightenment to Kapilavastu and stands before the palace gate, he is greeted by his wife Yashodhara and son Rāhula. Both the characters seem dwarfed before the towering and conflated personality of the Buddha, as both of them are human beings, while the Buddha is a superhuman being. Here Yashodhara is shown gazing at her lord with love and admiration (Ghosh 1987). The spontaneity of her movement in driving their only son Rāhula forward is remarkably depicted. She is shown as a *praudha*. She receives the lord – once of her house, now the Universe – in dual acceptance (Ghosh 1987). 'The rhythmic treatment of the different parts of her body . . . all represent art of a high order and make this fresco one of the finest portrayals of the feminine elegance and of the emotion peculiar to the sex' (Yazdani 1953).

Yashodhara's depiction in the 'mother and child motif' – a sculpted slab in the *maṇḍapa* from the Amaresvara Swami Temple, Amarāvati in Andhra Pradesh[135] – contains a very touching scene depicting an episode from the life of Siddhartha (Deglukar 2004), in which Princess Yasodhara is depicted lying with her right hand resting under her head, a position that suggests her deep slumber. To her right side is shown baby Rāhula, beyond this is Prince Siddhartha tenderly touching Rāhula without disturbing his sleep and casting a last glance before renouncing his princely life (Sitapali and Sastri 1980:8). This scene is representative of the moment just prior to Gotama's *Mahābhiniśkramaṇa*.

The few depictions that we have of Yashodhara also present her as a princess, wife of Prince Gautama and/or as the mother of Rāhula where she is portrayed in regal finery, situated in a palace/harem scene and never as a nun, while Māyā is most frequently depicted in the context of the nativity scene. In one instance Mahāpajāpatī is represented as the queen, seated along with the king, in a palace setting, with nurse holding the baby. In spite of the two being the first among the Buddhist nuns, who also eventually attained *arhatship* they were never depicted as a nun. It was always against the backdrop of royalty and pageantry that the two were always depicted by the artists, in the role of a wife and mother. There was a constant and pervasive attempt to underplay their spiritual and religious attainments, as far as their depictions in the visual arts was concerned.

Sujātā was yet another character closely associated with the life of Buddha. She has been mentioned by quite a few different names by later writers, and this change of name over time may also be related to the various local linguistic influences. She has been depicted at quite a few Buddhist sites like Sāñci (Marshall and Foucher 1940), Amarāvati, Nāgarjunakonda, Gandhara (Jones 2005:4328), Ajantā and Ellora.

At Sāñci Sujātā is depicted on the left of the middle lintel of the Northern Gateway with a pitcher in her lowered right hand and an offertory tray on her raised hand. She can be seen approaching from the entrance *toraṇa* of the *Bodhi Maṇḍapa*. Marshall and Foucher identified twin depictions of Sujātā at Sāñci. A slightly different representation from Amarāvati (Gupte and Mahajan 1962:178; Knox 1992:142) depicts the Bodhisattva on his seat of Enlightenment; in the earliest representation, his presence is indicated symbolically. He is surrounded by a group of female worshippers, one of whom is offering him a vessel with food. The rural setting is indicated in the earliest representation by the huts of a village. In a sculpted panel from Nāgarjunakonda (Rama 1995:86), just as in the painting from Ajantā, there are bullocks and a wagon standing to the right of the Bodhisattva indicating a rural backdrop. A group of maidens with the milk are standing to the left of the Bodhisattva.

Among the Gandharan reliefs, two depict the Bodhisattva as an ascetic, sitting down; on the right hand side, one of a group of women who have come to pay homage to the Bodhisattva, is holding the bowl with the milk. The third relief portrays the Bodhisattva standing, and again the woman who is offering him the bowl with the milk is on the right. While another represents the Bodhisattva as a starving ascetic, seated in Padmasana. On the left he is flanked by Indra and Brahma. On the right is Sujātā with a bowl of food and at her back is Vajrapani.

According to *Mulasarvastivādin Vinaya*, after the Bodhisattva had given up his strict asceticism, his travels brought him in the vicinity of a village, where the two daughters of the village headman served him a gruel made with rice and milk (Schlingloff 1988:33). Schlingloff mentions the event of the offering *pāyasa* as depicted at Ajantā. The scene includes bullocks and the covered wagon standing in the background indicates that the event takes place in a rural area. On the right-hand side of the picture, to the left of the bullocks, one of the two young maidens is depicted sitting on the ground, stirring a pot that is standing on some stones. Before her the Ajīvikā is to be seen asking for the milk. Behind him, on the far left, are the disguised gods, who also do not receive the milk. The Bodhisattva, who is portrayed significantly larger than the other figure holding his food bowl in his right hand and the maiden in front of him, is in the process of pouring milk into it.

A significant difference between the individual versions of this episode, which is handed down in all the biographies,[136] is that it is either one maiden named Sujātā[137] or Nandabāla[138] or two maidens named Nanda and Nandabāla[139] who present the milk to the *Bodhisattva*. The Ajīvikā Upaga, who asks for the milk, and the deities, who decline to accept it, are mentioned only in the tradition of the Mulasrāvastivādin.[140]

Among the sculptural representations,[141] the first shows the seated Bodhisattva (inside view) holding out his cupped hands. A maiden is pouring a liquid, presumably the specially prepared milk into them from a jug, while another female figure is bowing down at the Bodhisattva feet. In the sculptures at Ajantā and Ellora, she is sometimes seen as a devotee. At Ellora in caves 11 and 12, she is seen carrying a vessel of the *pāyasa* for the Buddha (Gupte 1962:172 and 178).

In all the images of Sujātā that has been dealt with earlier in the chapter, she has never been portrayed as the protagonist. She is portrayed as an integral part of a theme, where the character central to the theme is the Buddha, who is more often than not depicted larger in proportion than the other figures, in a conflated mode. The frequent reproduction of the scene can be seen as the only way in which the episode of the imminent *Buddhahood* could be depicted. The *Dharmachakra* was meant to symbolise the process of spread of *dhamma* by the Buddha, and the actual episode of the gaining of enlightenment was depicted by the *Bodhi* tree. Just as much the artists took recourse to depicting the episode of 'the offering of rice gruel by Sujātā', as the penultimate episode, subsequently leading to the all-important episode – that of the Enlightenment.

It is also significant as it shows the Buddha awakening to the fact that practicing of austerities and self-inflicted starvation does not lead one to the 'ultimate truth'. The scene shows Buddha coming to terms with this fact, and taking the path of moderation, as a result of which he accepts the rice gruel offered by Sujātā after a bath, before settling down for meditation and soon enough attains *nirvāṇa*.

It is also worth mentioning that when all the canonical prescriptions enjoin that the monks should keep away from women (as they are depicted as temptresses, who obstruct the quest for Buddhahood), the biographical narrative of the Buddha employs the agency of 'the feminine' as a catalyst in Buddha's ultimate attainment of *nirvāṇa*. Here again the religious and spiritual dimensions of the character Sujātā are downplayed (though the later texts do mention the merits accumulated by her in 'previous births' (Hardy 1995:167) that led her to being the agency through which the Buddha attained his final goal). She is depicted in the all too familiar role of a provider and nourisher. She is represented as a young girl, in a rural backdrop, short of any kind of spiritual accoutrements.

Depiction of lay votaries in the visual arts of the period

Last, we need to review the pictorial and sculptural depiction of the female lay Buddhist patrons. The most significant in this group is the unidentified rectangular panel from Sanghol (pl. 5, now preserved in the Archaeological Museum, Sanghol). The obverse depiction has been discussed elsewhere as probably being a representation of the Great Renunciation or *Mahabhinishkramana* of the Buddha. However, it is the depiction on the reverse that immediately pertains to this survey. Executed in the panoptic or panoramic mode, the narrative depicts multiple scenes and actions. There are four characters in the scene. The protagonist is the slightly stooped woman, who occupies the central position in the scene. The woman on the extreme right appears to be a queen who is being attended to by a female *chowrie* bearer. There is another female figure, which is further in the background and occupies a rather inconspicuous position in the narrative frame. Behind the protagonist is a gate (an architectural device denoting spatial boundaries) most probably denoting the precincts of the harem or queens apartments or the city limits and beyond this gate; on the extreme left is a male figure, in meditation. From the elaborate head-dress he appears to be a person of royal lineage, most probably a king. The anonymous 'central character' with the hunchback, on the reverse of the rectangular panel, can be identified with Khujuttara, the foremost lay disciple of the Buddha (Kaushik 2014). She is also mentioned together with

Citta and Dhammika, as female teachers of the laity in the Dhammapada and other commentaries (Schober 1997:47). The character also held a substantial comic role in the Kusa Jātaka. Karmic retribution is mentioned as being the prime cause for the physical deformity in Khujjuttara. According to the legends, mimicking the stoop of a deformed holy man earned a 'corrective rebirth' for Khujjuttara, who appears in the Jātakas and in later Buddhist literature with a hunchback.

There has been constant debate on the issue of the representation and identification of donors in sculptures and paintings (pl. 4). Some historians like Zwalf have tried to establish the correlation between the figures usually found engraved on the bases or pedestals of Buddha figures, and the inscriptions accompanying them.

Zwalf's analysis on Gandharan sculptures in the British Museum made him conclude that the exact relations between the devotional figures and the donative inscriptions (when such exist together) are not clear. However Skilling believes otherwise (Skilling 2001:260). Donors have been seen to be represented on the sculptures, mostly on the bases and at other times in other less-conspicuous positions. Some such specimens with figures of donors are found in Sanghol.

A specimen of a miniature Votive Chaitya from Bihar has on each of the four sides an ornamental chapel with cross-legged Buddha figures. In the intervening minor niches are also Buddha figures. On the countersunk panel beneath the lotus figure on which the central figure stood, there are three objects in low relief: a conch shell, a vessel on which a dish of flour is placed and a burning lamp. 'Evidently these represent the sacrificial implements such as are commonly found on the base of the statues at Bodh Gayā. On both sides of the central panel, we find a couple of human worshippers. The male figure to the proper right has in his right hand a lotus shaped censer, with his left he seems to place a piece of cloth in an alms bowl which stands in front of him. The woman kneeling behind him presents a pearl string as does the male person on the opposite side of the sculpture. The fourth figure folds her hands in adoration. That these 4 persons are the actual donors of the image is borne out by the inscriptions.[142] Along the rim of the central panel we find: *Õm dēyadhramõ yam Thādukasya*- meaning, the pious gift of Thāduka)'. The four remaining inscriptions are placed each over one of the kneeling figures. They tell us that the man with the censer is Thādu himself. The woman behind him, probably his wife, Vallahu. The man on the opposite side bears the name of Yājju-(ka) and may be Thādu's younger brother or son. The fourth figure named Nunne maybe Yājju's wife. The characters are of the ninth to tenth centuries.

One image of Kapardin Buddha in the National Museum, New Delhi, was dedicated by a monk named Virāna; the base depicts four lay figures, of which at least two are women, paying homage to a Bodhi tree (Czuma and Morris 1985:15). At various places, in the caves, as well as in the structural temples, laywomen have been depicted as votaries, worshiping the Buddha or other deities.

Thus it is evident that the donors as subjects were most often represented on the bases or the pedestals of sculpted pieces, in the act of worshipping and paying homage to the image of the Buddha or the Bodhisattva, which served as the central piece.

The painting in cave 17 at Ajantā shows common women witnessing the subjugation of the Nalagiri elephant that was let loose by Dēvadatta, the jealous cousin of the Buddha.

The depiction of women, though extracted from the *Jātakas*, served only the purpose of ornamentation. Their presence was restricted to cutting the monotony and tedium of the dull, blank walls. Their execution betrayed the artist's fascination with the depiction of the feminine form in art with negligible philosophical content, which is normally the objective of these visual representations at the sacred sites. For the representation of spiritual and religious themes, the artists opted for bolder 'and masculine' subjects. The representation of anonymous women scored over depictions of *bhiksūṇīs*, who are conspicuous by their absence.

Among the votaries seen in the Buddhist monuments, one of the earliest is from Pauni in the Bhandara district. On the *thaba* of the *vedika*, around the (second century B.C.) *stūpa*, is the representation of a donor couple. The male is seen standing with his hands crossed on his chest, while the lady is shown with her right hand raised straight above the head indicating her salute to the master. The smile on her face is of contentment. Both of them wear apparels in the Sunga style.

Another specimen depicting lay votaries is a pedestal of a stone image (of which now only the feet remains) which has an inscription of two lines along with the representation of the *Dharmachakra* on a pillar. It is seen flanked by worshippers on both the sides, with three men and two children on the left and four women and two children on the right side. This sculptural specimen from Mathurā is presently in the Indian Museum, Kolkata.[143]

One comes across the depiction of *upāsikās* again at Sāñci. The Dharmachakra/Wheel of law showing the first sermon at Sāñci also has the depiction of lay votaries. Interestingly though as compared to the 14 men and two *Gandharvas*, only two women worshippers have been depicted. Another panel depicting the same theme from Bhārhūt (showing women worshippers) now lies in the National Museum, while there is another from Nāgarjunakonda, depicting *upāsikās.* In a discussion of the richly carved, magnificent life-sized *Mithuna* couples in the Kārlē *chaitya*, Dehejia negates the view generally put forward by scholars that 'the *mithuna* couples could have represented the donor couples at the site'. She says 'the suggestion that these figurines may be donor couples, is negated by the inscription which not only informs us that they were the donations of a monk, but further describes the figures as *mithuna* or loving couples' (Dehejia 1992:40) – a popular motif which is found to be depicted in the plastic art of the period. Here it needs to be pointed out that the inscription cannot be taken to sum up all the donations at the *chaitya* site. It seems improbable that the entire *chaitya* was an outcome of the generous donations of a particular monk. The fact that the other patrons did not or could not record their donations seems more plausible. And therefore one cannot dismiss the fact that the other donors could have been lay patrons also.

Depiction of male and female monastics at the Buddhist sites

In many instances monks have been identified as depicted in sculptures. The only known representation of a nun is a late bronze specimen from Nalanda, which has an image of nun Soma standing on a pedestal, bedecked with *Vajras* and reclining elephants at the four corners and holding with both hands a long branch of a tree (Chandra 1934–5:39).

Be it the visual arts or the folk literature or the *Jātakas*, the *bhikṣunīs*' absence in these records is loud and conspicuous. Whether the absence of nuns in these art forms can be explained as the artist's preoccupation with characters other than the nuns and/or the extension of the dislike that the canon writers as also the not-so-comfortable equation between the female renunciants and the laity needs to be explored, and will be taken up in the subsequent chapter.

At another level, the absence of nuns in the representations may also be explained as the failure on the part of art historians and archaeologists in identifying these women. After all, the monks and nuns were dressed identically, in the prescribed robes with shaven heads, as they are today in many parts of the world. With identical mode of dressing, which can be said to be unisexual and with shaven heads, it is very difficult to identify or rather distinguish the nuns from the monks. In these depictions, the sexual differences have been underplayed which makes it difficult to judge whether these figures are either male or female. And here in this context it will not be wrong to say that it has been the sexist attitude and the prevailing male bias or as Eichler (1987:12) puts it a form of 'gynopia' or 'the invisibility of females' and/or 'overgeneralization' that has led to all such figures being represented in plastic arts as monks/male.

An assessment of the above data can thus be explained as the classical writers' undivided support and advocacy for the *upāsikā* – the foremost among them being Viśākhā. Projecting Viśākhā as the 'ideal' served a twofold purpose for the fraternity. For one, she was a married woman and mother. The image of the 'married woman' was all important, as marriage for the woman was equated with *upanayāna* or initiation prescribed for men belonging to the three higher *varṇas.*[144] As Falk (1989) puts it, 'Marriage and Motherhood represent the proper and effective means of channeling a woman's generative drive . . . in her proper place, with a living husband and surrounded by her children, a woman may achieve great honor'.

In the case of Viśākhā, the concept of fertility and motherhood is clearly overemphasised. Second and of equal significance is the fact that she is the model donor and supporter of the *Samgha* and in the eight wishes she requests of the Buddha are embodied all the various kinds of *dāna* that Buddhism advocates.

They are *chīra dāna* (gift of robes), *Ahāra dāna* (gift of food), *Gilanapatya dāna* (gift of medicines and sick diet), the *sanghika dāna* and the *kala dāna* (proper gifts) to the needy, in times of crises. Thus, the character of Viśākhā is important, as she is the 'personification of the lay Buddhist ideal'. Through the various legends that were woven around the character of Viśākhā, the monks attempted to drive home the various expectations and duties of a lay Buddhist patron.

What we find in the donor records are the individual contributions, which were to a certain extent the positive expression of the creation of the 'ideal' by the monks. They reflect the accomplishment of the ultimate goal, which the Buddhist *Samgha* sought to achieve by the creation of such a model. This model served its purpose, and the ever-increasing popularity of this model can be gauged from the biographical narrative of Viśākhā, in which additions and interpolations were made to such an extent that the original narrative swelled disproportionately with time.

The *upāsikā* had a distinctly more advantageous and enviable position, as compared to the *bhikṣunīs*. Even the two most favoured disciples of the Buddha, Khema and Uppālavanna, who have been stated to be the 'model' nuns, have not been able to command the same popularity and managed to be as visible as the lay patron Viśākhā. It seems a conscious attempt was made to keep the references to these characters to a bare minimum, as compared to that of Migaramāta, whose character was intended to be emulated and is therefore found in various texts across regions with minor and major variations, with the central theme remaining unchanged.

The portrayal of an 'ideal nun' in contemporary art forms of the period has been deliberately avoided. The only available reference so far is that of an image of nun Somā standing on a pedestal bedecked with *Vajras* and reclining elephants at the four corners and holding with both hands a long branch of a tree (Chandra 1934–35:38–9). In this depiction also the nun is represented in a stylised and deified format and not in the usual garb of a nun.

Though the texts mention Khēma and Uppālavanna as the model nuns (as mentioned by the Buddha), the texts as well as the later commentators and their commentaries have hardly treated them as such, the two meriting only a passing reference in the ancient texts. This is in striking contrast to the portrayal of Khujjuttara, the model *upāsikā* or 'lay nun'. As discussed she finds for herself a conspicuous place on a rectangular narrative panel, which according to the excavator occupied a conspicuous, if not central, position in the architectural scheme at the site of Sanghol. The commissioning of such a theme, on a distinctly conspicuous sightline, at an important site must have been the work of a lay donor, but even so her visibility over others distinguished Buddhist women like Khēma and Uppālavanna cannot be overlooked.

Here one needs to remember Buddha's initial hesitation regarding the formation of an institution for the nuns and the initiation of women as members of this institution. This situation stems from the general distrust and antagonism of female ascetics in the then prevailing society. This society glorified the role of the married woman and mother, while at the same time also being very vocal in its criticism of those women who failed to conform to the ideal role they had conceived of, such as the unmarried, childless and widowed women who so often took refuge in the Buddhist community.

'Buddhism was a path of enlightenment, not a revolutionary vision of renewed social order. It made peace with the Hindu *Dharma*'s precepts wherever it could, often incorporating them into its own prescriptions for ordinary human behaviour and social relationships' (Falk 1989:163–4). Thus, the *Samgha*'s attitudes towards the nuns can be 'traced historically to the early community's efforts to stay at least somewhat in line with the conventional practice of the day. Buddhists like their Hindu counterparts, honoured fecund housewives, especially if they were also pious laywomen' (Gross 1993). Obviously, Prajāpati as the first nun, and the other women of the palace who joined the *Samgha* along with her, succeeded in breaking down Sākyamuni's cultural conditioning and enabled him to see women as equal to men in their ability to grasp and practice the teachings. Sākyamuni's sexist view[145] had to have been completely eliminated by the time of the famous *sutra* stories of his encounters with women like Kisā Gotamī (in the tale of the mustard seed) and Queen Vaidehi (Meditation Sutra). In those stories, he would have failed to relate to them if he had held any prejudices against them as women.

Though the *Thērigāthā* happens to be the only text composed by women, nuns figure throughout the Buddhist cannon, albeit fleetingly, except for the *Sutta Nipata*. The presence of the *Thērigāthā*, seen in this context, is therefore remarkable, though its survival can be credited to a distinct oral tradition kept alive by the dedicated and diligent nuns.[146]

The *Thērigāthā*'s subsequent incorporation within the classical texts has to be attributed and credited to the monks, some of whom felt a genuine need for its incorporation. In spite of the numerically greater number of members who displayed a distinct androcentric bias,[147] which often resulted in selective and biased editing and interpolations in the classical texts, in most cases it was the female members (both monastic and to a certain extent even the non-monastic) who were at the receiving end.

Courtesans and the Buddhist society

'Despite the disturbing effect they may have had on the monks, courtesans are never openly condemned in the literature, being regarded more as piteous and low, than blameworthy' (Horner 1930/1989:90). It is the brothel that is referred to as the 'House of ill-fame', which the monks must desist from visiting, even during their begging rounds for alms (Shastri 1978:200). The *bhikṣu* was forbidden from visiting certain places when seeking alms: among others these include:

(i) House of ill fame
(ii) Palaces of kings
(iii) Houses of noblemen
(iv) Dwellings of unbelievers and so forth.

Now whether it were the courtesans and prostitutes referred above or kings like Prasenjit, Bimbisāra, Asoka, noblemen like Anāthapindika or the dreaded, unbelieving bandit Angulimāla, they all subsequently came to the refuge of the *Samgha*. And when all these individuals, from whom the members of the *Samgha* were instructed to keep away from, came of their own accord, as believers and as donors, their roles were highlighted.

In the case of the courtesans, it was the profession that the *Samgha* was against, as it went against the Buddhist precepts or *silās*. As individuals, the courtesans and others were not discriminated against. Although they come towards the end of a long list of trades and professions given in the *Milindapañho* (*Milindapanho*, v, 4), their spiritual credibility was not underestimated and undermined just because the *Samgha*, as an institution, denounced the profession as 'sinful'.

According to the later commentators, a woman was a prostitute on account of the working out of her *karma*. It was partly because of the notion of karma that the profession was frankly permitted by the social code of the day, and was more openly recognised than it is now. Prostitution was regarded as a karmic retribution for some heinous offence committed in a previous existence. But she need not remain in this condition. By willing to change, by willing to strive against the stream, and to cultivate the 'upward mounting way',[148] a woman could overcome such karmic tribulations.

The factors that led a courtesan to the refuge of the *Samgha* could vary. Women as chattel or commodity could be gifted to a man in return for a favour or as a mark of respect. She could be a part of *dakṣiṇā*, fees to a sacrificial priest. At Yudhisthira's horse sacrifice women were sent to other kings as a donation to make up a necessary part of entertainment. Even at a *śrāddha* ceremony, Brāhamanas received thousands of pretty maidens as gifts. They figure in list of material gifts, sacrificial fees, donations, entertainments, prizes, rewards and dowry.[149]

Buddhism provided them the much-needed opportunity for changing their state of being, of being elevated from being 'a subject of donation' to becoming a donor herself. In the classical Brahmanical texts, there is an evident ambivalence regarding the profession. Though their presence and/or participation were important in some rituals and ceremonies, they essentially remained the 'loose women'. Their vilification in the literary records like *Samayapratipāda, Dharmaśāstrā* and the like is well attested.

Buddhism again provided the opportunity to let them move out from the shadows of the social domain by giving them a new identity, with a distinct spiritual connotation that of a *thēri*. Here they also got the rare chance of satiating their academic and intellectual cravings.

It is said that in the assemblies of Sulasa, the courtesan, and of Sirimā, the courtesan, 84,000 people penetrated to knowledge of the *dhamma*.[150] Their generous donations were well received by the *Samgha*, and the latter while profiting by it was also at the same time offering them an opportunity to expiate for the sins of their professions, in addition to a more well-accepted social address and identity.

Moreover, these women in most cases realised the impermanence of their youth and the fact that for most courtesans and prostitutes, old age is full of misery and economic indigence; the institution also provided a respectable and decent arrangement for their insecure, uncertain future lives. These women have found ample space in the works of the early Buddhist monks. Many of the verses of the *Thērigātha* expound on the 'doctrine of impermanence', all leading to the one conclusion that one must accept impermanence (*anicca*) as the basic fact of life, as well as one of the basic elements of the early Buddhist world view. This insight brings them to liberation and enlightenment. The verses attributed to Ambāpāli typify the ageing process of a prostitute (verses 252–70) (Norman 1971:110). The verses (of the *Therigāthā*) resound with the despair of women who once they have become dependent have been disposed of by their family and their loved ones. It is remarkable also that the stories of prostitutes found in the verse all include this theme of bodily decay which is often sharply set against their former beauty and success (Kloppenborg and Hanegraaff 1995:166). Thus, we see that the relationship between the *Samgha* and this particular category of women patrons was that of mutual support and assistance. While, on the one hand, the *Samgha* was an institution helping these women make spiritual progress and undertake the difficult journey from being despised creatures, existing in the fringes of the society, to that of socially acceptable and spiritually inclined individuals, these women contributed their bit to the *Samgha*, in the form of materials and logistics. Other than being prominent beneficiaries of the *Samgha*, they served as a fitting analogy made use of by the Buddha, in driving home to the association of monks, the vainness and impermanence of physical beauty and bodily desires. She was the necessary foil to his purity. In early Buddhism, a sharp line was drawn between two states of existence, *nirvāṇa* ('freedom from suffering') and *samsāra* ('becoming'), a perpetual wandering from rebirth to rebirth. *Samsāra* was the enemy. It had to be overcome for the desired extinction to occur. 'Woman: was the veritable image of the blind urge towards "becoming" that was tantamount to Samsāra or the mundane world. "She was the enemy- not only on a personal level as an individual source of temptation, but on the cosmic level as representation and summation of the process binding all men' (Falk 1989:110).

Thus, it can be said that though women do occur in the texts, some, more often than others (some depicted as more positive and acceptable than others), they are even more invisible in the contemporary art forms of the period. It is evident that the monks were less than generous in acknowledging and demonstrating the acts of munificence of the female patrons. However, it needs to be noted that of the few and far in between depictions that one comes across of the depiction of the feminine characters associated with the Buddha, some are more favoured over others. The texts present the lay Buddhist votary Viśākhā as the most favoured female model, who seems to score even over the *bhikṣuṇīs*, but in the extant visual records Māyā and even Sujātā seem to be more frequently represented while Viśākhā is conspicuously absent. This difference between the textual and archaeological sources needs to be noted. This disparity could stem from the fact that while the literary canonical texts were largely the preserve of the male monastics, the laity had an upper hand in the depiction of themes that were to be sculpted at the sacred sites. Even so the import and enormity of female presence, as a significant part of the support group, could not be ignored. As their support was crucial for the well-being of the *Samgha*, their continued support was sought by the employing of suitable models, which the women were supposed to emulate and strive to live up to. This led to the construction of legendary and idealised figures, who were the epitome of generosity and piety, like Viśākhā and Ambāpāli.

Notes

1 This has been done noting certain distinct features which certainly need a brief mention. These have been left out as they constitute a separate class of patrons with distinct features of their own and attempting to

encompass the data from this region too will make the work too unwieldy and unmanageable, as they are a subject for research all by themselves. Here the differences as seen in the donor records of the North-West as compared to the records of Central and South India have been briefly discussed. Few women figure in Buddhist records of the North-West vis-à-vis hundreds of women donors in the inscriptions from Central and South India. Another notable difference in the inscriptions from the North-West and the rest of the country is that in the Buddhist sites in Central and South India the benefactions aimed at earning religious merit for oneself or one's dear ones, but are rarely articulated as such in the text of the inscription, which is usually laconic and concise in nature. Quite contrary to this, explicit references to a varied nature of aims are present in the inscriptions of north-western India. A specific purpose in some records is '*pūjā*' or honour directed towards the people belonging to the mundane and the supramundane worlds. To the latter category can be assigned the *Buddhas*, the *Pratyēkabuddhās*, the *Arhats*, the *Dharma* and the *Samgha*, whereas to the former category belong donor's parents, relatives and friends, teachers and some high dignitaries. Even the *pūjā* of one's home country (*sarvasa Sakrastanāsa pujāyae*) is mentioned among the aims in some while that of all the beings figures as aim in general. On a purely practical plane, a wish for increase of life and strength also finds a mention in many of the inscriptions. In rare cases, the intention of the donor is to ensure special protection for his children on sensing some danger to them. In a solitary case, the very object of the gift, a relic, is treated as symbol of the souls of donor's parents and the act of depositing it is intended to ensure Buddhahood for them. Thus, there is a clear distinction in the themes and content of the inscription of the two regions, along with the difference in their scripts, while the inscriptions of the north-west were executed in Kharoshti Script (Konow 1991); those from the rest of the country are in Brāhmī. Thus, in order to maintain a semblance of uniformity, in the contents of the epigraphic records, the data to be analysed in this section will comprise those from Central and Southern India only.

2 Table 3 showing the spread of donors from various sites in relation to the sites of donations. The Buddhist sites which do not have any mention of women donors have not been included.

3 This list is in no way indicative of all the sites and represents only a cross-section of the broad spectrum of Buddhist sites in the subcontinent. These sites will be considered individually as and when the data from these sites are discussed subsequently.

4 L.L. no. 1141, Nasik inscription of Mahahahkusiri.

5 L.L. no. 1146, Nasik inscription of Vasu.

6 V.V. Mirashi, *The History and Inscriptions of the Sātavāhanas and Western Kshatrapas*, Pt II, No. 36. Kanheri cave inscription of Mahārathini Nāgamulanika.

7 *Ibid.*, Pt II. No. 37, Vanavāsi Nāga image inscription of Sivaskandanāgasiri.
8 A.S.W.I., Vol. IV, No. 6 (3), Bedsa cave inscription of Mahādevi Samadinikā.
9 *Ibid.*, No. 4 (I), Kūdā cave inscription of writer Sivabhuti.
10 The 17th sutta of the Pali *Digha Nikāya*, the fourth Sutta of the *Mahavagga*, is known as the *Mahasuddasana Suttanta* or *Sutta*. The narrative centres around the protagonist king Mahasudasana, who lived in the city of Kusavati. The king was a Bodhisattva in a previous birth. The Buddha narrates the story about the king and the city to Ananda, just before his Nirvāṇa. The structure of a sub-narrative within the framework of a main narrative scheme follows the structure of a *Jātaka*. Thus, the whole sutta is a *Jātaka*, which links King Mahasudassana, his city and his death to the Buddha and his death.
11 *Mahāsudassana Sutta*, I. 38, S.B.E., Vol. XI, p. 253.
12 The *Manusmrti* is the most important and earliest metrical work of the Brahmanical *Dharmaśāstra* textual tradition. The normative text presents itself as a discourse given by Manu, the progenitor of mankind, to a group of seers, or rishis, who beseech him to tell them the 'law of all the social classes'. *Manusmriti* is commonly dated to fifth century B.C.E. After the breakdown of the Maurya and Shunga empires, there was a period of uncertainty that led to renewed interest in traditional social norms. Manu became the standard point of reference for all future *Dharmaśāstras* that followed it.
13 The *Manusmriti*, Vol. V. 155.
14 V.V. Mirashi, *The History and Inscriptions of the Satavāhanas and Western Kshatrapas*, Pt II, No. 18, Nasik Cave Eulogy of Queen Gotami Bālāśri.
15 Bodh Gaya Buddhist Pillar inscription, 1871, mentioned by Cunningham, Archaeological Survey Report, Vol. I. p. 10; 1880; Bhagvanlal Indraji, Indian Antiquary, Vol. IX, p. 42. There are six known copies of the inscription. L.L. nos 939–4, List of Brahmi Inscriptions from the Earliest Times, *E.I.*, Vol. X (1909–10).
16 See Table 2 showing social identification categories used by *bhikṣunīs* and *upāsikās* in the donor records.
17 L. L. no. 11, Ichchhawar (Dhanesar Kheda) Buddhist Stattuete Inscription, 1985; Smith-Hoey, *Journal of Bengal Asiatic Society*, Vol. LXIV. Pt I. pp. 161–62., and plates IX and X.
18 Table 2. Table showing social identification categories used by *bhikṣūnīs* and *upāsikās.*
19 L.L. nos 717,799, 854, 882, 933, 1292, 125c, 1205 etc.
20 L.L. nos 679, 838, 860, 907, 1065, 1073 etc.
21 L.L. no. 1141.
22 L.L. nos 1053, 1054 etc.
23 L.L. no. 1021.
24 L.L. nos 1059, 1107, 1224, 1237, 1246.
25 L.L. nos 1043, 1145, 1268, 125.

26 L.L. no. 1050.

27 L.L. nos 1207, 1235, 921c, 921d, 929c.

28 L.L. no. 1250.

29 If this was the case, it is a very ancient, historical precedent for the phenomenon. As nuns even today live in their houses in villages of Kinnaur, Himachal Pradesh.

30 L.L. no. 1252.

31 *Khandhaka* (Pali), the second book of the *Theravadin Vinaya Pitaka*, includes the following two volumes: *Mahavagga* and *Cūllavagga*. The former includes accounts of the Buddha's and his great disciples' awakenings, as well as rules for *uposatha* days and monastic ordination, and the latter includes accounts of the First and Second Buddhist Councils and the establishment of the community of Buddhist nuns, as well as rules for addressing offenses within the community. Scholarly consensus date it to the early centuries of the first millennium B.C.

32 There are almost 75 such references. See Table 2 that shows social identification categories used by *bhikṣūnīs* and *upāsikās.*

33 *E.I.*, Vol. II, p. 94.

34 The *Therigāthā*, often translated as verses of the Elder Nuns (Pāli: *thēri* elder (feminine) + *gātha* verse), is a Buddhist scripture, a collection of short poems supposedly recited by early members of the Buddhist Sangha around 600 B.C.

35 *A.*36–38.

36 *L.L.* no. 1123.

37 'Gift of the upasika Kama, the daughter of the housewife Kanha (gharaniya Kanhaya duhutuya). The daughter of the householder Ida (gahapatisa Idasa duhutuya) with her sons, brothers and sisters and of the nun (bhikhunikaya Nagamita . . .)' *A.S.S.I.*, Vol. I, No. 13.

38 L. L. No. 1152, List of Brahmi Inscriptions from the Earliest Times, *E.I.*, Vol. X (1909–10) A.S.I., rep. 1984.

39 *E.I.*, Vol. II, No. 31 (II–29).

40 L.L. nos 1037 and 1079.

41 K. Roy, 1988, *Women and Men Donors at Sanchi*, Vol. I, p. 216.

42 L.L. nos 994,1021,1052,1053,1054,1076,1111,1134,1137,1186,1192,1298.

43 Table 2 showing social identification categories used by *bhikṣūnīs* and *upāsikās.*

44 Vn.iv.334–5.

45 S.IV.182–3.

46 D.II.331.

47 Vn.111.120.

48 597,1021.

49 L.L. no. 1234.

50 K. Roy, 1988, *Women and Men Donors at Sanchi*, Vol. I, p. 217.

51 L.L. no. 1141.
52 L.L. nos 943, 944.
53 Table 2 showing social identification categories for *upāsikās* and *bhikṣunīs*.
54 'of Sivati'. *E.I.*, Vol. II, No. 31 (1–357), Sanchi Votive Inscription, 'The Gift of Ghosa'. *C.I.I.*, Vol. II, Pt II, A-117, Bharhut Votive Inscription.
55 *'The Gift of Worthy Karmā (Aya-Kamāya), Inhabitant of Sadhuga'* (*A.S.S.I.*, Vol. I, No. 14).
56 L.L. no. 1050.
57 *Gahapatī* was one of the two significant social categories mentioned in Budhist texts, the other being the Setthi. He was associated with land and prosperity. In the Buddhist representation of social order he was ranked with the Brahmana and the Kshatriya, indicating his assured power and high social stature. The *gahapatī* component was the backbone of the lay Buddhist order. This is well attested by epigraphic data.
58 V. Dehejia, 'The Collective and Popular Basis of Early Buddhist Patronage: Sacred Monuments, 100 B.C.– A.D. 250' in *Powers of Art* (ed.) p. 37. It is possible that the economic and social system in which the *gahapatī* was located did not create the conditions for renunciation; we must remember that the period was one in which a primarily agrarian economy had emerged and that this economy supposed a rising urban population. The *gahapatī* was the pivot of this economy and the primary tax-payer. The withdrawal of such a category from the social world would have had a crucial, negative impact on the economic and social systems. The two areas, which the *bhikṣū* rigorously abstained from, were production and reproduction. The *gahapatī*, on the other hand, was especially concerned with both these aspects, which is why even though he was not debarred from the *Samgha*, he tended to remain outside it. Instead the *gahapatī* became the most important component of the laity, particularly in terms of support to the Samgha, which was also a vital part of the new movement.
59 The Buddhist conception of woman treasure (discussed later) or *Itthi Ratnam, Mahasudassana Sutta*, Vol. I, pp. 38–9.
60 *C.I.I.*, Vol. II, Part II, Bharhut Inscriptions (ed. H. Luders, Rev. E. Waldschmidt and M. A. Mehendale), 1963, A 42.
61 *A.S.S.I.*, Vol. I, No. 6.
62 *'of Sivati'*, Sanchi Votive Inscription, *E.I.*, Vol. II, No. 31 (1–357).
63 *Nasikā Gorakhitiyā thabo dānam Vasukasa bhāriyaya* (Translation: The pillar is the gift of Gorakhita from Nasika, the wife of Vasuka). *C.I.I.*, Vol. II, Pt I, No. A-46.
64 *Mahābhoyabālikāya Mahādevīya Mahārathinīya*
Sāmaḍinikāya deyadhamma Āpadevaṇakasa bitiyikāya
(Translation: The meritorious gift of Sāmaḍinikā, the Mahādevī (princess), the Mahārathinī, daughter of Mahābhoya and wife of Āpadevanaka) *A.S.W.I.*, Vol. IV, No. VI (3).

65 These statistics have been compiled by a quantitative analysis of the inscriptional records of donor women from the Buddhist sites discussed in the book.

66 'The gift of a female lay-worshipper (*upasika*) from Ujjain'. Sanchi Votive Inscription, *E.I.*, Vol. II, No. 31 (1–146).

67 'Success! The meritorious gift of the lay (*upasika*) Sivala with her son (*saputikaya*), with her daughter (*saduhutukaya*)'. Amravati Votive Inscription, *A.S.S.I.*, Vol. I, No. 5.

68 Bodhisattva Image Inscription of Princess Pusyadatta, Mathura Museum, *E.I.*, Vol. XXVIII, No. 7.

69 1883 Buhler-Burgess, *A.S.W.I.*, Vol. IV, p. 93, pl. XLVIII, Luder's List of Brahmi Inscriptions from the Earliest Times, Appendix, no. 1152. p. 130, *E.I.*, Vol. X (1909–10).

70 J. F. Fleet, *C.I.I.* III. 263.

71 Table 1 showing sites; native place and the place of residence of *upāsikās* and *bhikṣūnīs.*

72 See Figures 4.1 and 4.2 showing the incidence of *upāsikās* and *bhikṣūnīs* at various sites.

73 See Figure 4.4 showing the total number of men donors versus women donors.

74 See Figure 4.3 showing the comparative graph showing *upāsikās* and *bhikṣūnī* donors at various sites.

75 Table 1 showing sites; native place and the place of residence of *upāsikās* and *bhikṣūnīs.*

76 Luder's List of Brahmi Inscriptions from the Earliest Times, Appendix, no. 1137. p. 130, *E.I.*, Vol. X (1909–10).

77 Second century A.D., Katra mound, Mathura region (Government Museum, Mathura).

78 Even in present-day Sri Lanka, *bhikṣūnīs* make pilgrimages with groups of lay patrons and are known to make donations along with them, which is quite uncommon among the Indian nuns from the north. This fact was corroborated by a Swiss nun, follower of Tibetan Buddhism from Dolma Ling Nunnery, Macleodganj, Dharamsala.

79 See Figure 4.1 showing *upāsikās* at different sites.

80 Table 3 showing spread of donors from various sites in relation to the sites of donations.

81 Luder's List of Brahmi Inscriptions from the Earliest Times, Appendix, no. 1250. p. 130, *E.I.*, Vol. X (1909–10).

82 Table 1 showing (sites) native place and the place of residence of *upāsikās* and *bhikṣūnīs.*

83 *Ibid.*

84 See Figure 4.4 showing the percentage of men donors versus women donors.

85 Kol Buddhist Cave Inscription, 1883 Buhler-Burgess, *A.S.W.I.*, Vol. IV, No. 4, p. 89, and Plate XLVI; L.L. no.1076, *E.I.*, Vol. X.
Bharhut Pillar Inscription, *L.L.* no.,784,878,891,1013 etc.

86 See Table 2 showing social identification categories used by *bhikşūnīs* and *upāsikās*.
87 L.L. nos 1001, 1218, 1239, 1292.
88 Table 1 showing sites; native place and the place of residence of *upāsikās* and *bhikşūnīs*.
89 Inscriptions, in *The Monuments of Sanchi*, Vol. I, Sir John Marshall and Alfred Foucher, London, 1940, p. 299.
90 Table 2 showing social identification categories for women.
91 Table 3 showing spread of donors from various sites in relation to the sites of donations.
92 Table 2 showing social identification categories used by *bhikşūnīs* and *upāsikās*.
93 Table 3 showing spread of donors from various sites in relation to the sites of donations.
94 *Ibid.*
95 Pali equivalent as found in the Buddhist texts is *Navakamika*.
96 An important urban centre, which lay at the intersection of the two most important ancient trade routes, the Uttarāpatha and the Dakshināpatha.
97 Of the total, almost half of the women seem to refer to their marital status with indications of the social standing of the husband or his family. These include references to *setthis*, *gahapati*, kings, *Mahābhojas*, *Mahārathis asavārika* (trooper) etc.
98 B.D. II. 3,6,33 as cited in Ananda K. Coomaraswamy, *Essays in Early Indian Architecture*, Oxford University Press: Delhi, Bombay, Calcutta, Madras, 1992, p. 3.
99 It was considered a *Parājika* offense to dwell in the forest or *araṇya*. Hirakawa, 1999, p. 111.
100 Moving about without a companion amounted to a *Saṃghātiśeṣa* Offense. *Ibid.*, pp. 142–43.
101 Vn.I.273 and D.I. 276.
102 *Therigāthā*, verse 420. 'Then my father gave me for second time as bride, content with half my husband's Sire had paid'. *Poems of Early Buddhist Nuns*, C.A.F. Rhys Davids and K.R. Norman (trans.), Oxford: P.T.S., 1989.
103 *Ibid.*, p. 227.
104 Schopen refers to a portion from the *Mulasarvasthivadin Vinaya* that discusses properties and inheritance issues and states that monks and nuns had access to material resources that is indicated by the number of rules regarding the same. The monks and nuns were expected to pay debts and tolls and transport taxable goods; own their own furniture and have the means to pay for any damage they might do to that of other monks; carry personal seals; pay for their own medicine and healing rituals; leave estates, sometimes huge; borrow money from laymen; inherit property from both other monks and laymen; accept and service permanent

endowments; make loans and charge interest; accept and use negotiable securities; provide care for sick and dying laymen, with the understanding that, when the layman died, his estate would go to the monastery; and receive precious and semiprecious materials, sell books, receive gold in various forms, accept money (*kārshāpanas*), sell the property of deceased monks, hire and oversee labourers and buy food.

105 *Ibid.*, fn. 293.

106 *L.L.* no. 22.

107 *L.L.* no. op. cit.

108 *Ibid.*, p. 77.

109 *Dhammapada*, verse 53, Visakha Vatthu, trans. F. Max Müller, in *Buddhist Parables*, by E. W. Burlinghame, 1869; reprinted in *Sacred Books of the East*, Vol. X, Clarendon/Oxford, 1881.

110 Vn. 1:153.

111 The *Mahā-Sudasana Jātaka* (*Mahāsudassana Sutra*) mentions that the Great King of Glory was gifted with seven precious treasures. These were the treasures of a divine wheel, the treasures of an ideal jewel, the treasures of an ideal elephant, the treasures of an ideal horse, the treasures of an ideal wife, the treasures of an ideal steward and the treasures of an ideal counsellor. *Itthī ratnam* was the ideal among women kind. Graceful in figure, beautiful in appearance, neither very tall nor very short, neither very stout nor very slim, neither very dark nor very fair, surpassing human beauty, she had attained unto the beauty of gods.

'The touch too Ānanda [says the Buddha, while narrating the *Jātaka* to Ānanda. (I.37) *Mahāparinirvāna Sutra*] of the skin of that wondrous woman was as the touch of cotton or of cotton wool, in the cold her limbs were warm, in the heat her limbs were cool; while from her body was wafted the perfumes of sandalwood and from her mouth the perfume of lotus.' 'That pearl among women too, Ānanda [*ibid.* (I, 38)] used to rise up before the great king of glory and after him retire to rest; pleasant was she in speech and ever on the watch to hear what she might do in order so to act as to give him pleasure'. 'That pearl among women too, Ānanda, [*ibid.* (I, 39)], was never even in thought, unfaithful to the great king of glory-how much less then could she be so with the body'. This description confirms to that of the 'ideal' for women in Buddhism and the above-mentioned attributes together known as the *Pancha-Kalyāna* (*Kesa Kalyāna*, *Mansa Kalyāna*, *Ashti Kalyāna*, *Chawi Kalyāna* and *Waya Kalyana* as cited in Spence Hardy, Manual of Buddhism, p. 221).

112 A similar story is referred to by Csoma Korosi; but the heroine of the Tibetan tale is called Sumagadha; and several of the incidents here related are, on another occasion, spoken of in connection with a girl from Champa called Sa-ga-ma, as cited, *ibid.*, p. 225.

113 Mahavagga, *Sacred Books of the East*, Vol. XXX. Davids Vol. 11 ed. Max Muller 1879–1924.

114 Apparitional or *opapatika* birth.
115 *Buddhist Sutras*, R. Davids pp. 33–4 also *Manual of Buddhism*, S. Hardy, pp. 456–58.
116 *Thērigāthā*, XXXIX.
117 She surfaces again in *Thērigāthā* verses 1150–7, again being rebuked by Mahā- Moggallana.
118 *Thērigāthā* Commentary on XXXVI.
119 *Thērigāthā* Commentary on XXII.
120 The *Buddhavamsa*, the last book of the *Khuddaka Nikāya* in the second *Pitaka*, gives the lives of all the previous Buddhas. The Pali commentary on the *Jātakās* also gives certain details of these 24 Buddhas (Fausboll's Jataka pp. 2–44 Sutta Nipata p. 40, Turnei's *Mahāvamsa* (these accounts of the Buddha are from the *Nidāna Katha* (as trans.) Rhys Davids), p. 1 and S. Hardy, *Manual of Buddhism*, p. 49). They mention the past Buddhas, along with other details like the city they were born in, the names of their fathers, mothers, as also the names of his two chief male and female disciples (both monastic and lay) (in the Pali and Chinese versions of the sanskrit *Ekottaragāma Khema* and Uppalavarna are the model nuns, while Khujjuttarā and Velukantaki Nandamāta are the model laywomen. The Gilgit version has Mahāpajāpati Gautamī and Utplavarna in the first instance, and Viśakha Migāramāta of Srāvasti and Kumbjottarā of Kauśāmbi in the second), the name of the chief servitor, the dimensions of the bodies of the Buddhas and the duration of their life. What is noticeable here is the start of a convention that recorded the names of the two chief female disciples along with other individuals who were significantly associated with the Buddhas of the past. As stated by Rhys Davids, 'It is sufficiently evident that nearly all these details are merely imitated from the corresponding details of the legend of Gautami; and it is to say the least very doubtful whether the tradition of these legendary teachers has preserved for us any grains of historical fact. If not, the list is probably later than the time of Gautama, for while it is scarcely likely that he should have deliberately invented these names it may well have seemed to latter Buddhists to exclude in them the names held in the high honor by the Brāhamanas themselves'. Oldenberg states, 'It could scarcely be otherwise than that the historical form of the one actual Buddha multiplied itself under dogmatic treatment to a countless number of past and coming Buddhas'. *Sacred Books of the East Series*, Vol. 21, The Saddharma Pundarika (trans. from Pali by Rhys Davids and Herman Oldenberg).
121 *Therigāthā* Commentary, pp. 126–27.; cf. Manorathapurani, p. 205; cf. Anguttara, n. 1, p. 25, in B.C. Law's Buddhist Women, *Center for Buddhist Studies, National Taiwan University*, retrieved from UrbanDharma.org/udharma3/women.html.

122 *Therigāthā* Commentary pp. 182 ff; Manorathapurani, pp. 207ff.; Anguttara N., I, 25.
123 *Ibid.*; S.ii.236.
124 *Ibid.*; *A*. i.25.
125 *Ibid.*; *S*. ii.236
126 Apadana, *Khuddaka Nikāya*, IV, cited in *Life Histories of Bhikhuni Arahats*, retrieved from web.ukonline.co.uk/buddhism/gcobbkn1.htm.
127 Sivaramamurti, *Amaravati Sculptures in the Madras Government Museum*, Madras, 1956, pl. 24.3, pp. 164–5 also see R. Knox, *Amaravati*, London, 1994, Stone, Elizabeth Rosen, *The Buddhist Art of Nagarjuna Konda*, Delhi, 1995, fig. 84, pp. 159, 161, 189–90.
128 She describes her dream (cave 2). In the upper panel, the Buddha is seen enthroned in Tushitā heaven where from, according to the story, he descends to the earth after selecting his parents. Down below on the left side is seen Mahāmāyā lying on a couch, dreaming that a white elephant strikes her right side while entering her womb. In another panel Mahāmāyā seated beside Suddhodhana narrates her dream to the court astrologer for interpretation. The figure of Mahāmāyā is exquisitely carved. Her head slightly bent suggests her thoughtful and meditative mood. When she realises that she has conceived and her baby is going to be either a *chakravartin* (Emperor) or a Buddha if he renounces the world she stands contemplatively, which is shown in the next apartment. She gets absorbed in her thoughts as to what is to be done in case her child tends to renounce this world. She is depicted between the two pillars reclining against one of them. She is superbly delineated with all her features as ideals of beauty. The way in which she is standing has lent her grace. A. Ghosh (ed.) Ajanta Murals, N. Delhi, 1967, fig. 12, Cave 2 (fifth to sixth centuries C.E.).
129 She leans contemplatively against a pillar (cave 2). pl. XLIV, Cave 2 (fifth to sixth centuries C.E.).
130 A.Ghosh (ed.) Ajanta Murals, New Delhi, 1967, pl. XLIV, Cave 2 (fifth to sixth centuries C.E.).
131 Painted on the left-hand wall of Cave 2, Behl Benoy K., Sangitika Nigam, *The Ajanta Caves: Artistic Wonder of Ancient Buddhist India*, 1998.
132 The panel depicts the scene of Buddha's return to Kapilavastu after his enlightenment. Buddha, Yashodhara and Rahula, Kushan, Gandhara, India, second to third centuries. Indian Sculpture-The Asian Arts Museum of San Francisco, California, ACSAA, retrieved on January 29, 2011 from ignca.nic.in/asp/showbig.asp%3Fprojid.
133 Bas-relief from Amaravati, second century B.C., retrieved on January 29, 2011, from ccrtindia.gov.in/wall%2520paintings.html.
134 *Ibid.*, Ghosh, 1987: LXXVI.

135 According to a legend the Shiva temple was originally Buddhist in origin but was later readapted for Hindu worship. It can be seen that the foundations of the Amreshwara temple are laid with the characteristic Buddhist slabs. However the exact date of the temple is not known. Retrieved on January 28, 2011 from temples.newkerala.com/Temples-of-Indi.

136 *Mahavastu* ed. Vol. II, p. 205, 3-p. 206, 19; trans. Vol. II, pp. 195–97. *Buddhacharita*, XII, V. 109–11; (ed.) p. 42; trans. p. 185. T193; (ed.) Vol. Iv, p. 75b. T190, Chapter 25; ed. Vol. III, p. 770c; trans. pp. 191–92. T191; (ed.) Vol. III, p. 949b–c. *Divyadana* (ed.) p. 392, 9–11. *Lalitvistara*, Chapter 18; ed. p. 267,12–p. 270,4; trans. *Nidanakatha*, ed. p. 68, 5–70,13: trans. pp. 91–4; ubers. pp. 124–27. On this passage see E. Lamote (n.81), p. 227, n.3;E.SIEG+W.SIEGLING, Die spei sung des Bodhisattva von der Erleuchtung, in: *Asia Major*, 2, 2, 1925, pp. 277–83.

137 *Mahavastu; Lalitavistara; Nidanakatha.*

138 *Buddhacharita*; T189.

139 *M.S.V.*;T191; *Divyadana*;T190;T184;T193

140 *M.S.V.*; T191.

141 Goli [1] Madras, Government Museum; reproduced in T.N. Ramachandran, *BuddhistSsculptures from a Stupa near Goli Village, Guntur District*, Government Press, 1929, pl.8.

142 *Annual Report*, A.S.I., 1903–4, p. 221.

143 Indian Museum, Calcutta, listed as NS4965; A.S.I., *Archaeological Review*, 1924–25, p. 255.

144 Manu.

145 From the time he was a boy, he was taught that women were only objects, like domesticated animals trained to breed, nurture and entertain men. From his stepmother to his wife, to all the dancing girls and servants of the palace, Shakamuni as a young prince viewed women only as creatures who lived for the rewards of pleasing men. In the Tibetan American book on Buddha's life, Shakamuni is not blamed for his sexist attitude but is recognised as someone whose cultural conditioning allowed for no other view. (Rev. Patti Nakai, *Women in Buddhism*, Part. 1: Prajāpati, the First Buddhist Nun, retrieved from (website) www.faithnet.org.uk/k54/social%20.)

146 The Buddhist texts *Patimokkha* and *Bhikṣūnī Kammavaca* had to be memorised and recited, therefore must have been transmitted by nuns. In the *Khematheri Sutta* of the *Avyakata Samutta*, Khema *thēri* delivers a profound discourse to King Pasenadi (S. iv, 374–80). The nun Thullananda is described as learned, eloquent to preach sermons (Vn.iv.254.4, 255.4, 256.23, 285.18, 290.4). Many came to hear her preach, including King Pasenadi of Kosala (Vn.iv. 254–6). The same epithets are applied to Bhadda Kapillani (Vn.iv.290.7).

147 In the feminist view of world history, the accomplishments of women have been either ignored or appropriated by male-dominated cultures.

This could very well be true for the early nuns. The only surviving text of *Thēravāda* Buddhism that is positively attributed to nuns is a compilation of songs. It is unlikely that the monks trying to keep Buddhism alive were concerned with the works of women when so many other texts needed to be saved from destruction. Yet it is a testament to the nuns' spiritual insight and expressive power that their book of songs was respected enough to be preserved through all the upheavals in South Asia (Rev. Patti Nakai, *Women in Buddhism*, Pt 1: Prajāpati, the First Buddhist Nun. Retrieved on December 12, 2012 from www.livingdharma.org/Living.Dharma. . ./WomenInBuddhism1.html).

148 *Thērigāthā*, verse 99.

149 *Ibid.*

150 *Milindapanho*, vi, 4.

Conclusion

This work highlights the various, invisible aspects of a female Buddhist practitioner, both lay and monastic, in early Buddhism. Each of the chapters deals with little-explored dimensions of the lives of the Buddhist women. It attempts to undo some of the glaring disparities between different kinds of historical and archaeological records by reinterpreting and reanalysing some of the existing data on the subject. On a wider plane the data from this study further underline the involvement and agency of the laity in Buddhism.

On the basis of the analysis of the issues discussed throughout the book, various larger issues pertaining to the women in Buddhism get highlighted. It has become evident that women were not just passive participants, in a secondary role, as mothers and wives, of the more visible members of the *Samgha*. It brings to the forefront, diverse kinds of data on the presence of 'the feminine' in different contexts, which leads us to infer that women participated actively in the activities of the *Samgha*, in both capacities – as lay members and also in the capacity of female renunciants. It has been observed that many of the widely accepted notions that were drawn from the reading of the literary sources stand vindicated by a rereading of the historical data from an archaeological perspective.

'Motherhood' in Buddhism is hailed as 'the ideal', a role that justifies the existence of an individual as a woman. But contrary to this widely accepted and acknowledged gender stereotype that seems to justify woman's existence, only in terms of a singular role of a mother, inscriptions reveal that women tended to identify themselves not just as a member of a singular, homogenous group of 'female Buddhist patrons'. The records indicate that these women tended to use a range of options and criteria by which to identify themselves in the epigraphic records, and there are variations visible even in the quality and quantity of their munificence. The largest number of laywomen donors preferred to be addressed as 'the wife of . . . ', while the second most popular category of identification in their records was by their native place. This is major paradox to the generally accepted social notion that a woman was always dependent (on her father, husband

and sons) as mentioned in the *Buddhacharita* of Aśvaghoṣa (Hamilton 1992:67–8). The third most frequently used category is that of 'the mother'. Thus, it is evident that although the canonical Buddhist as well as the Brahmanical perception hailed 'motherhood' as the Buddhist ideal which each woman should strive to achieve, it happened to be only the third most popular category by which women sought to identify themselves.

The data also reveal that Buddhist women donors cannot be seen as one big homogenous group of Buddhist patrons, as the records reveal a disparity in the donor records with respect to regions, types of donations made, the reasons behind them and the capacity in which they made these donations. The lay as well as the monastic Buddhist women seem to have frequented different Buddhist sites for the purpose of pilgrimage; while some Buddhist sites were more favoured by the lay Buddhist population, the *bhikṣuṇīs* seem to have had a distinct preference for another group of Buddhist sacred sites. The number of *bhikṣuṇīs* donating at various sacred sites of north of the Vindhyas was far greater than in those south of the Vindhyas, with *bhikṣuṇīs*[1] even outnumbering the lay donors/*upāsikās*[2] at a few sites like Sānci and Bhārhut (where the percentage of nun donors is 77 and 10 as compared to the 45 per cent and 5 per cent of *upāsikās* respectively). On the contrary, a southern site like Amarāvati with a large lay donor participation records 4 per cent nun donors.

The *bhikṣuṇīs* hailing from a particular region preferred to make pilgrimages and donate at those sites which were closer to their place of residence but cases of nuns travelling great distances in order to make pilgrimages and donate at those sites are also not unknown, but are certainly rare. Greater mobility is seen in the case of *upāsikās* who travelled much greater distances with family and friends to places of pilgrimages and this is supported by epigraphic sources. The two categories of donors, that is, *bhikṣuṇīs* and *upāsikās*, seem to have had their concentrations at different places. While the donations of the *bhikṣuṇīs* can be seen to have come from certain clusters, more often from places like Ujjaini, Vidisha, Kurāra and Kurāgāra, the spread of the *upāsikās* can be seen to be more evenly spaced and they came from a myriad of places.[3] This can be explained as the sites mentioned above must have had nunneries or *bhikṣuṇī vihārikās*, for the accommodation of the Buddhist *bhikṣuṇīs*.

One can also distinguish a difference in the preference for sites, where donations were being made by male and female donors.[4] While at certain sites like Bhārhut, Kanheri, Junnar and Pitalkhora, we see a predominance of male patrons, at others like Ghantasālā, Banavāsī and Nāgarjunakonda, the female patrons are dominant.

There is a variation in the nature of epigraphic records that record the donations made by the donors. For example, at Sāñcī the donor records can mostly be dated from the second century C.E. to the third century C.E. However from the structural evidence it is apparent that the site continued to be well in use till the medieval period. The absence of donor records for the later period can be explained on the basis of a basic change in the form and nature of patronage at such sites. The change in media that is the shift from engraving on stone sculptures to other forms like palm leaf manuscripts explains the relative invisibility (rather than the complete disappearance) of *bhikṣunīs* during the early medieval period. It can also be taken to assume that during the later period the convention of recording the donations was given up. Also their presence can be attested by a number of monastic structures (which have been identified as *bhikṣunī vihārikās*) for the latter period.

It is evident from the analysis of their contents of their donor records that these women were opinionated individuals with strong Buddhist leanings. The manner in which they choose to address themselves in their records shows that they often choose to move beyond the conventional and codified norms, using their discretion and personal preferences, while recording their *dāna* for posterity, and this held alike for the lay *upāsikās* as well as the *bhikṣunīs*. They exercised their discretion in all matters ranging from social, religious to even the economic spheres. They made their presence felt in a range of circumstances. As Walters explicates, the monuments had a unity of conceptualisation and construction, and the structural developments at the sacred Buddhist sites was based on a complex agency that brought into its gender-inclusive fold, monks, nuns, *upāsakas* and *upāsikās* (Walters 2002). While these donors have been rendered to the background and are hardly visible except for in their recorded donations, another class of women has however been more noticeable in Buddhism.

The legendary characters of Viśākhā, Ambapālli and others were in fact representative of the significant class of female Buddhist patrons. These early women Buddhist patrons were over the years transformed into legendary figures, by constant interpolations that were made into their original, biographical narrative scheme. This served a twofold purpose. On the one hand, it served to acknowledge and honour the women who formed a significant chunk of the larger donor group that supported Buddhism and, on the other hand, it was intended to serve as the model that the female Buddhist patron were supposed to emulate. Here though it needs to be noted that though Buddhism was open to the idea of a monastic institution for the nuns, it did not actively promote it. This is evident from the fact that, in the list of women who were endorsed by Buddhism as 'model Buddhist patrons',[5] nuns are accorded a secondary status as compared to the *upāsikas*; Migāramāta Viśākha is often hailed as the ideal Buddhist, all women should emulate. Owing to the popularity and pre-eminent position accorded to this character in Buddhism, in course of time, the simple narrative of Viśākhā's life acquired epic proportions.

These expansions within the main narrative structure were done in order to project Viśākhā as an ideal lay Buddhist and to glorify motherhood. Even those historical female figures who eventually became nuns have been invariably represented in their pre-monastic contexts; for example, the most favoured representation of Mahāpajāpati Gautamī for the ancient artists was in the context of the 'Nativity Scene' pertaining to her pre-renunciation days, followed by that of Māyā as queen and wife in the scene 'interpretation of Maya's dream'. In its official textual position, Buddhism created for the woman an image of a mother, a provider and nourisher, thus projecting even its monastic women, in their previous, lay roles of a mother, to a large extent. This phenomenon was somewhat inverted in the Tamil epic *Manimekalāi*, where even though the nun is likened to a mother, with an inexhaustible bowl of food or a cow nourishing her young calf, it is seen promoting the nun over the *upāsikā*. Thus, a subtle contestation is discernable in the two roles of a *bhikṣunī* and an *upāsikā* in the social realm. However it cannot be debated that Buddhism preferred to see its female patrons in the role of 'generous lay donors' rather than any other.

In the social sphere again, women exercised considerable discretion, to the extent of even opting for alternate lifestyles and vocations. The space that they commanded in the society received the ardent support of Buddhism. This support was demonstrated in the manner in which Buddhism not only zealously took in followers from all walks of life and of varied vocations but also presented them before the society as ideal or model Buddhists patrons, like the lay *upāsikā* Viśākhā, daughter-in-law of a wealthy merchant, on the one hand, and Ambapāli, a famous courtesan, on the other. The *Samgha* also made provisions by way of rules, which were of the nature of checks, on the lay as well as the monk community, which would deter them from infringing and/or violating the space of the female Buddhists.

An assessment of the rules for the conduct of the *bhikṣus* and the *Bhikṣunī Samgha* brings out the essential differences between the two. The *Bhikṣunī Pāṭimokkha* contains 311 rules. Of these, 181 rules have corresponding rules in the *Bhikṣunī Pāṭimokkha*. The *Bhikṣunī Pāṭimokkha* contains 85 rules for which there are no corresponding rules for the *bhikṣus*. The feminist writers have interpreted these added rules as reflecting a biased and oppressive stance of the *bhikṣus* towards the *bhikṣunīs*; however, it should be noted that more than one-third of these extra rules were formulated to protect *bhikṣunīs* from being the direct recipients of the abusive or careless behaviour of other *bhikṣunīs*; while two of the extra rules (*Pācittiyas* 6 and 44) prevent *bhikṣunīs* from putting themselves in a position of servitude to *bhikṣus* or lay people. According to the rules' origin stories, all but three of the extra rules (*Pācittiyas* 59, 94 and 95) were formulated only after *bhikṣunīs* complained to the *bhikṣus* about an errant *bhikṣunī*'s behaviour. Tellingly, these last three exceptions were formulated after complaints initiated by the *bhikṣus*, and they touch directly on the formal subordination of the *Bhikṣunī Samgha* to the *Bhikṣu Samgha*. However, they are counterbalanced by two rules exclusive to the *Bhikṣunī Pāṭimokkha* (*niḥsargika pāyantika dharmas* – 4 and 17) that were formulated at the request of *bhikṣunīs* to prevent *bhikṣus* from abusing their position in the hierarchy, in a way that would interfere with the *bhikṣunīs*' practice of the *Dhamma*.

Buddhism had not entirely distanced itself from the contemporary social norms, which were largely instrumental in shaping the social ideology that Buddhism professed. The contemporary society did impact the way Buddhism shaped itself. The social antagonism and mistrust of the female ascetics or nuns extended even into Buddhism; several rules were formulated to control and regulate the conduct of the nuns; especially those relating to their interactions in the social sphere prove this point. The interaction of the nuns in the social sphere was governed by stringent rules and the punishments meted out to them for the transgressions committed in the social sphere were categorised as *Samghādisesa* rules, which entailed temporary or permanent expulsion from the *Samgha*, depending on the severity of the transgression. The sentence for the nuns was also more severe as compared to those for the monks.

It is no exaggeration to state that the *bhikṣuṇīs* exercised considerable influence on the contemporary society. This is further proven by a survey of the contemporary lay attitudes and the formulation of norms by them, as they could ill afford to remain indifferent to the presence of *bhikṣuṇīs* around them. Buddhism never really encouraged or promoted its female patrons to take to monastic life, but the rules that were made from time to time for the nuns shows the *Samgha* on its part did try to resolve and lessen the conflict between the lay community and the community of *bhikṣuṇīs* by appeasing the laity and giving in to the lay demands to regulate and control the behaviour of the *bhikṣuṇīs*,[6] on the one hand, and providing security to the order of *bhikṣuṇīs* by making such rules (*Pācittiyas* 6 and 44) that would prevent *bhikṣuṇīs* from putting themselves in a position of servitude to *bhikṣus* or lay people, on the other. But the support it accorded in terms of showing the path to spiritual fulfilment, especially to its women members, who were existing in the fringes of the society like the courtesans and the slave girls like Vimalā and Punnā, made Buddhism ideologically distinct from the contemporary social milieu in which it grew. They also made provisions by way of rules (which were of the nature of checks) for the lay as well as the monk community, which would deter them from infringing and/or violating the space of the female Buddhists.

It should be noted that the Buddha's initially hesitant stance on the subject of women's entry into the order did not indicate his reservations on women taking to the spiritual path, as he believed that gender was no limitation in one's quest for ultimate liberation. He, however, believed that the entry of women into the institutionalised religious community of renunciants would lead to the moral degeneration of the *Samgha* and would ultimately lead to its downfall. In spite of his initial reticence, women did get entry into the *Samgha* as *bhikṣuṇīs*, and women Buddhists – both lay as well as monastic – were successful in carving out for themselves an exclusive, individual epistemic space of their own, which is also reflected in the biographical compositions of the early Buddhist women – the *Therigāthā* and the *Ittivuttaka*. The extension of its sphere gets reflected in other works of male authorship as well, like the *Princess Jātaka* that depicts Buddha as a woman in one of his previous births. This literary innovation is dated to the medieval period (16th century C.E.), at a time when the nuns' order was universally going through a period of decline (as is attested by archaeological records and the marginal availability of inscriptional sources) and is significant. The composition of such a text (wherein the princess is not just making her aspirations for Buddhahood but also directing its course), most probably by the community of *bhikṣus* and its insertion (employing the *Jātaka* format) into the biography of the Buddha, espousing the case of female bodhisattvahood (within an otherwise austere doctrine like the *Theravāda*), needs to be noted. This addition of a female lifetime to the Buddha's biography may not reflect a positive evaluation of women in entirety but is certainly a step towards it. Medieval writers – most reasonably assumed to be monastic men – challenged the gendered identity of the *Bodhisattva* as solely male and altered the traditional vision of the biography. The various existing versions of this tale in the didactic literature of the Buddhist communities of South East Asia attest to its popularity among the *Theravāda* writers of the region as *Mahāyāna* traditions offer a variety of interpretive positions on the gendered identity of Buddhas. The significance of incorporating this narrative in the more popular *Jātaka* format for a larger lay Buddhist audience lay in driving home the point that women were as capable as men in attain Buddhahood.

Other texts like the *Vimānavatthu* and the *Ittivuttaka* also support the issue of liberation for women, although indirectly, with their positive narrative representations.

Thus what is evident from a reading of the classical Buddhist texts is that there was an underlying tension within the Buddhist literature, a tension between certain attitudes that seem unusually positive in their assessment of women and the feminine, on the one hand, and attitudes which are much more blatantly negative, on the other. Often contradictions appear within individual texts. The tone of the early Buddhist texts reflects a range of opinions, each expressing a different set of concerns existing among the members of the early community. Thus the texts reflect a rich multivocality, not a simple inconsistent ambivalence, which is suggestive of an ancient, time-enduring gender debate.

The archaeological evidence for female presence (both lay as well as monastic) has also been noticed and documented at different Buddhist sites. These evidences indicate the association or presence of lay female votaries with specific structures like circular structures, three-room structures, *stūpas* with *āyakas* and *bhikṣunī vihārikās*, at Buddhist sites.

The concept of pollution and purity was closely associated with the female and found frequent mention in the canonical works. It stands corrected by archaeological data, which seek to prove that the female element within Buddhism was not just equated with profanity. The structures dedicated to women within the sacred complexes at the numerous Buddhist sites prove this point. This study should not be taken to mean that archaeology with its emphasis on material culture dispels the notion of the ideal/divine but rather widens the scope and range of the notion of divinity. Within its ambit are also the thus far invisible and unfocussed feminine aspect and its sacred associations.

There is also evidence for the association of female monastics/*bhikṣuṇīs* with monastic structures and these structures have been taken to be the remains of *bhikṣuṇīs viharikās* (the equivalent of monasteries for the male monks), the residential accommodation for female Buddhist renunciants.

Quite a few sites have yielded evidence for the association of the female with sacred structures. The same is also true of monastic/residential structures for Buddhist nuns. It is interesting to note that the data for feminine presence, albeit in varied contexts, come from almost the same sites; that is, the sites that have been found to be probable nunnery sites are almost the same as those that also provide evidence for sacred structures associated with women and also those that provide epigraphic evidence for the presence of female Buddhist patrons. Thus the distinctive association of these sites with women is further reiterated by the presence of numerous donor records that are testimony to the fact that women preferred these Buddhist pilgrim sites at which to make their donations. It is a strange coincidence that they reappear in other gender-related contexts, which further reinforces their gendered association.

Hence from the above study it can be inferred that there was a distinct religious identity for both the sexes within Buddhism, and the organisation of female adherents followed a parallel development to the mainstream Buddhist male-dominated *Samgha*, which is clearly brought out in the archaeological records. From an overview of the archaeological data on the presence of the feminine at Buddhist sites, it can be concluded that just as in the literary records several attitudes towards the feminine can be seen in the archaeological contexts as well.

The presence of structures showing feminine presence at the sacred Buddhist sites is indicative of the philosophical Buddhist attitude of 'soteriological inclusiveness', which accorded space to all individuals irrespective of gender differentiation.

The presence of most of the *bhikṣuṇī vihārikās* at the eastern most extremity of the site suggests that these residences for the *bhikṣuṇīs* was constructed as per some predetermined architectural site plan which was followed at most of the Buddhist sites. This could be indicative of 'institutional androcentrism', which necessitated that women could pursue a religious career, if they choose to, but it was to be followed within a carefully regulated institutional structure that preserves and reinforces the conventionally accepted social standards of male authority and female subordination. This would entail strictly adhering to prescribed spatial layout for the nunneries in one particular direction, maybe the east direction. However, looked at from another perspective the presence of most of the *bhikṣuṇīs vihārikās* at the eastern most reaches of the sites can also be taken to mean that the women members of the *Samgha* enjoyed a position where they could negotiate for the most favourable location for their *vihāras*; this can be said as the eastern quarter was considered the most auspicious as most of the temples, *chaityas* and so on at the Buddhist sites face east. The survey of monastic structures also brought to focus a distinct type of structure – the three-room structure. The literary as well as epigraphic records attest to the presence of some 'lay nuns' or laywomen who although unordained retired to spend their remaining lifetime in the sanctuary of the *Samgha*. They were distinguished women of means, who were very few in number. The three-room structures most probably accommodated such women as is brought out by the find of the copper plate grant of Rani Karpurasri.

The criterion of 'ascetic misogyny' does not seem to hold much ground on reviewing the archaeological data. The feminine presence at a number of Buddhist monastic sites (which were largely monk-dominated institutions) does not seem to indicate a hatred for women; on the contrary, in direct opposition to the Buddhist notions of pollution and purity, accommodating such structures within the sacred complex indicate, on the one hand, a recognition of the religious and spiritual advancements of the female members, both lay as well as monastic and, on the other hand, a tacit compromise between the different member groups within the *Samgha*.

Though the influence of the male members of the *Samgha* in the early setting up of the institution of the *bhikṣuṇīs* cannot be debated, to put the blame for the relatively lesser presence of the feminine solely on 'androcentric bias'[7] of the monks community is hardly pragmatic. As has been discussed in the previous chapters, their lack of visibility can be explained to a number of factors.

Low incidence of literary works authored by women can also be traced to the limited avenues for women to pursue formal education, which to a large extent hindered the historical documentation of compositions of women authors. The situation in later-day Buddhism remains much the same, as Hanna Havenik's recent ethnographical work on the nuns of Tibet states that most nuns pursued neither advanced philosophical studies nor the elaborate yoga practices, but mainly spent their time performing rituals and reciting prayers.[8]

There are references to women who were well known as reciters. According to the *Dhammapada* Commentary (attributed to Dharmapāla), the *Ittivuttaka* was transmitted by the *upāsikā* Khujjutarā, first to the ladies of the Royal Harem of King Udēna of Kosāmbi, who learnt it by heart. Later the monks learnt the collection, which was recited by Ānanda at the First Council. This was a unique case of an entire collection being transmitted by a woman.[9] This text is significant not just for the fact that it was first delivered by a woman but also for the fact that the contents of the sermon were definitely encouraging for women (following the Buddha). It advocated that true deliverance could be won by all, irrespective of one's gender, and in saying so, the Buddha addressed both monks and nuns specifically. In spite of the various references to female reciters/*bhanakās* of the *Sutras*, there is no reference to women writers and compilers of Buddhist texts, which explains the relative paucity of literary works attributed to women. The religious training imparted to women was limited to learning and transmission of scriptures orally, and the task of documenting and writing of the *sutras* continued to be a male monastic privilege.

Had it been for the much-stressed 'androcentric bias' of the male monks, texts like the *Ittivuttaka*, and also the *Princess Jātakam* would have never seen the light of day. There is a need to move beyond attempts to locate gender biases by focusing only on partial records.

Pāli tradition believes that each previous Buddha was offered milk rice from some maiden just before his Enlightenment.[10] The Buddha's biography is replete with positive depictions of female characters that occur at significant junctures within the biography, and are known to have been linked inextricably with the narrative, as supporting the Buddha, like Sujātā, Yaśodharā, Mahāpajāpati Gautamī, Viśākhā, Ambāpālī and the like. The works on gender and Buddhism however tend to skim through these characters and overstress the negative portrayal of Māras's daughters, while at the same time underplaying the negative male identity of Māra.

The subject of gender archaeology and Buddhism is still in its incipient stage. This work endeavours to highlight some of its pertinent issues, and initiates an inquiry on the lines of gender, archaeology in Buddhism, hinting at the possibility of further research on the subject.

Thus summing up, from the above study, it is evident that the flouting of gender stereotypes (that is reflected in the literary sources) by these women in their everyday practices, inherent contradictions within the Buddhist canon on the subject of gender and the marked presence of the feminine at a number of Buddhist sites in the subcontinent indicate that the Buddhist society was in no way indifferent to the issues of gender and women, as the subject was part of a larger socio-religious debate within Buddhism. Buddhism was receptive to issues of gender and it was the active participation and agency of the Buddhist women in religious, spiritual and social matters that prevented the society from remaining unresponsive to their presence.

Notes

1 See Figure 4.2, *bhikśūnīs* as donors at different sites.
2 See Figure 4.1, *upāsikās* as donors at different sites.
3 *Ibid.*
4 See Figure 4.4 showing the percentage of men donors versus women donors.
5 The *Buddhavamsa*, the last book of the *Khuddaka Nikāya* in the second *Pitaka*, gives the lives of all the previous Buddhas. The Pāli commentary on the *Jātakās* also gives certain details of these 24 Buddhas (Fausball's Jataka pp. 2–44 Sutta Nipata, p. 40, Turnei's *Mahāvamsa* (these accounts of the Buddha are from the *Nidāna Katha* (as trans.) Rhys Davids), p. 1 and S. Hardy, *Manual of Bhuddhism*, p. 49). They mention the past Buddhas, along with other details like the city they were born in, the names of their fathers, mothers, as also the names of his two chief male and female disciplines (both monastic and lay) (in the Pāli and Chinese versions of the Sanskrit Ekottaragāma Khema and Uppalavarna are the model nuns, while Khujjuttarā and Velukantaki Nandamāta are the model laywomen. The Gilgit version has Mahāprajāpati Gautami and Utplavarna in the first instance, and Viśakha Migāramāta of Srāvasti and Kumbjottarā of Kauśāmbi in the second), the name of the chief servitor, the dimensions of the bodies of the Buddhas and the duration of their life. What is noticeable here is the start of a convention that recorded the names of the two chief female disciples along with other individuals who were significantly associated with the Buddhas of the past.
6 Most of the rules regarding the conduct of the *bhikṣuṇīs* were made after the laity made complaints to the Buddha regarding the behaviour of a *bhikṣuṇī* or a group of *bhikṣuṇīs* to the Buddha and therefore in most cases

the rules pronounced by the Buddha started with the oft-repeated phrase, 'Thus I have heard . . .'.

7 Feminist writers studying early Buddhism believed that women in Buddhism were either not accorded the space they deserved or were misrepresented.

8 Hanna Havnevik, *Nunneries and Nuns in Tibet*, p. 54.

9 Woodward 1948, p.viii.

10 For example, Vipāssi Buddha accepted the milk rice from the daughter of Sudassāna Setthi; Sikhī Buddha accepted it from the daughter of Piyādassi Setthi; Vessabhu Buddha accepted the milk rice from Sirivāddhana; Kakusandha Buddha accepted the milk rice from a Brahmin girl Vajirindha of the village Suchirindha; Konagāmana from a Brahmin woman Aggisoma and Kassapa Buddha from his wife Sunandā. Last in the list is Gotama Buddha, who accepted the milk rice from Sujātā.

Tables, site plans and plates

Table 1
(Sites) native place and the place of residence of *upāsikās* and *bhikṣunīs*.

Sr. No.	*Name of (residence) sites*	*No. of bhikṣunīs*	*No. of upāsikās*
1	Tumbavana	1	2
2	Ujjaini	8	17[Ω]
3	Navagama	0	1
4	Bedakada	0	2
5	Vidisa	8	3
6	Pokhara	0	1
7	Arpana	0	1
8	Sanukagama	0	1
9	Kapasi	2	1
10	Kurara	18[*]	2
11	Achayata	0	1
12	Ejayati	0	1
13	Sagari	0	1
14	Vepa	0	1
15	Kuragara	5	2
16	Kamadadigama	0	3
17	Viharakata	0	1
18	Bhogavardhana	0	1
19	Tiradapada	0	1
20	Nasik	0	1
21	Purika	0	1
22	Moragiri	1	1
23	Parakotika	0	1
24	Karakatiya	0	1
25	Kaliyana	1	3
26	Pusiliyas	0	1

(*Continued*)

Table 1
(Continued)

Sr. No.	*Name of (residence) sites*	*No. of bhikṣunīs*	*No. of upāsikās*
27	Sreshtiyada	0	1
28	Kevurura	0	1
29	Chandaka	0	1
30	Mamdara	0	1
31	Narasala	0	1
32	Jadikayasa	0	1
33	Dhanyakataka	1	1
34	Adhisthana	0	1
35	Vijayapura	0	1
36	Kudura	0	1
37	Chalisilana	0	1
38	Kosika	0	1
39	Apaguriyas	0	1
40	Javenagara/Uchenagara	0	1
41	Namdapura	0	1
42	Gitanakera	0	1
43	Dhanakas	0	1
44	Pukiyas	0	**3**
45	Nandinagara	**18***	0
46	Pemuta	1	0
47	Madhuvana	**3**	0
48	Vadivahana	**5**	0
49	Madalachikada	**5**	0
50	Darbhina/Dabhinika	1	0
51	Chudathilika/ Chudathila	2	0
52	Bhojakataka	1	0
53	Venukagama	1	0
54	Nagara	1	0
55	Kakamdi	1	0
56	Rajgir	1	0

Ω Most number of *upāsikās*.

* Most number of *bhikṣunīs*.

Table 2
Social identification categories used by *bhikṣunīs* and *upāsikās* in the donor records.

Category of identification	*Bhikṣunī*	*Upāsikās*
As mother	2–0.89%	**54**–21.7%
As wife	0	**75–30.2%**
By the native place	**85–38.11%**	**70–28.2%**
As granddaughter	0	5–2%
As daughter-in-law	0	8–3.2%
By personal name	**118–52.9%**	**24**–9.6%
As sister-in-law	0	2–0.8%
As daughter	5–2.24%	**39**–15.7%
As sister	1–0.44%	16–2.4%
By cast/gotra/Kula	0	4–1.6%
As pupil/antevasini	7–3.1%	12–4.88%
As nun/bhikṣunī	2–0.89%	0
As upāsikā	0	2–0.8%
As neice	3–1.34%	1–0.4%
Others	0	6–2.4%

Table 3

Spread of donors from various sites[1] in relation to the sites of donations, as known from the epigraphic records.

→*Sites of donations*	*Sāñci*		*Bhārhūt*		*Kanheri*		*Amarāvati*		*Nasik*		*Junnar*		*Mathura*		*Bhattiprolu*		*Nāgarjunakonda*	
↓*Sites of donors*	*U*	*B*	*U*	*B*	*U*	*B*	*U*	*B*	*U*	*B*	*U*	*B*	*U*	*B*	*U*	*B*	*U*	*B*
Tumbavana	2	1																
Ujjeni	16	7															1	0
Navagama	1	0																
Bedakada	2	0																
Vidisa	1	8	2	0														
Pusakara	1	0																
Arpana	1	0																
Sanukagama	1	0																
Kapasi	1	2																
Kurara	2	17					0	1										
Achavata	1	0																
Ejavati	1	0																
Sagari	1	0																
Vepa	1	0																
Kuraghara	2	5																
Kamadadigama	3	0																
Viharakataka	1	0																
Bhogavardhana	1	0																

→*Sites of donations*	*Sāñci*		*Bhārhūt*		*Kanheri*		*Amarāvati*		*Nasik*		*Junnar*		*Mathura*		*Bhattiprolu*		*Nāgarjunakonda*	
↓*Sites of donors*	*U*	*B*	*U*	*B*	*U*	*B*	*U*	*B*	*U*	*B*	*U*	*B*	*U*	*B*	*U*	*B*	*U*	*B*
Tiridapada	1	0																
Nandinagara	0	18																
Pemuta	0	1																
Madhuvana	0	3																
Vadivahana	0	5																
Madalachikada	0	5																
Nasik			1	0														
Purika			1	0														
Moragiri			1	1														
Parakotika			1	0														
Karakatiya			1	0														
Darbhina			0	1														
Chudathilika			0	2														
Bhojakataka			0	1														
Venugama			0	1														
Nagara			0	1														
Kakamdi			0	1														
Kalyana					3	1												
Dhenukataka					0	1	1	0										
Pusiliyas							1	0									3	0
Sreshtivada							1	0										
Turulura							1	0										

(*Continued*)

Table 3
(Continued)

→*Sites of donations*	*Sāñci*		*Bhārhūt*		*Kanheri*		*Amarāvati*		*Nasik*		*Junnar*		*Mathura*		*Bhattiprolu*		*Nāgarjunakonda*	
↓*Sites of donors*	*U*	*B*	*U*	*B*	*U*	*B*	*U*	*B*	*U*	*B*	*U*	*B*	*U*	*B*	*U*	*B*	*U*	*B*
Kevurura							1	0										
Chandaka							1	0										
Mamdara							1	0										
Jadikayas							1	0										
Adhisthana							1	0										
Vijaypura							1	0										
Kudura							1	0										
Rajgir							0	1										
Chalisilana									1	0								
Kosika									1	0								
Apaguriyas											1	0						
Javenagara/Uchenagara													1	0				
Namdapura															1	0		
Suvanamaha															1	0		
Dhanakas																	1	0

Abbreviations used:

U: *upāsikās*;

B: *bhikṣunī*.

[1] These are sites mentioned in the inscriptions.

Table 4
Buddhist *stūpa* sites in India, with *āyaka* projections.

Sr. No.	*Site*	*Location/geo coordinates*	*Date*
1.	Piprahawa	Lat. 27° 26′ N.; Long. 83° 7′ 50″ E.; District of Basti (U.P)	Third century B.C.
2.	Lauriya Nandangarh	Lat. 26° 59′ N.; Long. 84° 24′E. District of Champaran, Bihar.	First century B.C.
3.	Bakraur	Lat. 24° 45′ N.; Long. 84° 55′E District of Gaya, Bihar	Ninth- Tenth Centuries A.D..
4.	Amarāvati (Dhanyakataka)	Lat. 16° 34′ N.; Long. 80° 21′E. District of Guntur	Third-Second Centuries B.C.
5.	Nāgarjunakonda	Lat. 16° 6′ N.; Long. 80° 47′E District of Guntur	Third to fourth centuries A.D.
6.	Jaggayyapeta	Lat. 16° 54′ N.; Long. 80° 5′E. District of Krishna	Second to first centuries B.C. to sixth century A.D.
7.	Gummadidurru	Lat. 16° 46′ N.; Long. 80° 26′E. District of Krishna	Second to third centuries A.D.
8.	Alluru	Lat. 16° 46′ N.; Long. 80° 26′E. District of Krishna	Second century A.D.
9.	Bhattiprolu	Lat. 16° 6′ N.; Long. 80° 47′E. District of Guntur	Second to first centuries B.C.
10.	Ghantaśāla (Kamtakasola)	Lat. 16° 8′ N.; Long. 80° 5′E. District of Krishna	Second century A.D.
11.	Chandavaram	Lat. 16° 8′ N.; Long. 80° 5′E. District of Prakasam	Second century B.C.E.
12.	Sannathi	Lat. *17.12°N 77.08°E* District of Gulbarga, Karnataka.	First to second centuries C.E.
13.	Dhulikatta	Lat. 18° 25′ N.; Long. 79° 20′E.; Dist. Karimnagar, Andhra Pradesh	Early second century B.C.
14.	Adurru	Lat. 12° 30′ N.; Long. 75° 10′E.; District of East Godavari, Andhra Pradesh.	Second to third centuries A.D.
15.	Calingapatnam	Lat. 16° 10′ N.; Long. 80° 50′E.; District of Srikakulam, Andhra Pradesh	First to fourth centuries A.D.
16.	Gyaraspur	Lat. 23° 40′ N.; Long. 78° 05′E.; Madhya Pradesh	Eighth to ninth centuries A.D.
17.	Panagoria	Lat. 23° 10′ N.; Long. 77° 05′E.; District of Sehore, Madhya Pradesh	Second century B.C.E.

(*Continued*)

Table 4
(Continued)

Sr. No.	Site	Location/geo coordinates	Date
18.	Satdhara	Lat. 23° 20′ N.; Long. 79° 15′E.; Madhya Pradesh	Second century B.C.E.
19.	Singarakonda	Lat. 15° 15′ N.; Long. 80° 00′E.; Andhra Pradesh	Second century A.D.
20.	Hasargundigi (Sannathi)	Lat. 17° 05′ N.; Long. 76° 35′E.; District of Gulbarga, Karnataka,	Second century A.D.
21.	Lalitgiri	(Lat. 20 35″ N and Long. 86 15″ E) Mahanga Tahsil of Cuttack district, Orissa	Second century B.C.E. to sixth to seventh centuries A.D.
22.	Kesanapalli	Lat. 18° 30′ N.; Long. 79° 35′E Taluk: Palnad, District of Guntur, A.P	Second to first centuries B.C. to third century A.D.
23.	Chaneti	Lat. 28° 15′ N.; Long. 79° 25′E District of Yamunanagar, Haryana.	Third century A.D.
24.	Pandrethan	Lat. 34° 03′ N.; Long. 74° 51′E, District of Srinagar, Kashmir	Eighth century A.D.
25.	Ushkura	Lat. 34° 12′ N.; Long. 74° 22′E, District of Baramulla, Kashmir	Eighth century A.D.
26.	Paraspora	Lat. 34° 08′ N.; Long. 74° 38′E, District of Baramulla, Kashmir	Eighth century A.D.
27.	Paharpur (Somapura)	Lat. 25° 02′ N.; Long. 89° 3′E District of Rajshahi, East Pakistan.	Eighth century A.D.
28.	Mainamati	Lat. 23° 25′ N.; Long. 91° 7′E District of Tippera, East Pakistan.	Tenth-Eleventh Century A.D.
29.	Shah-ji-ki-Deri	Lat. 30° 00′ N.; Long. 71° 37′E, Peshawar	First century B.C.
30.	Antichak	Lat. 34° 08′ N.; Long. 74° 38′E District of Bhagalpur, Bihar.	Eighth to ninth centuries A.D.

Table 5

Present-day identifiable geographical location of Buddhist sites mentioned in the epigraphic records.

S. No.	*Name of site*	*Location*	*Remarks*
1.	Bhojakataka	Unidentified	
2.	Chudathilika	Situated near Varanasi in Kāśi Janapad (Uttar Pradesh (U.P.))	Identified with Cundatthiya mentioned in Petavatthu.[1]
3.	Darbhina	Unidentified	
4.	Dhenukataka	Cunningham identified it with Dhanakataka of Hiuen-Tsang and with modern Dharanikot on the river Krishna River (Andhra Pradesh)	
5.	Kakandi	Kakan, P.S. Sekandra, District of Monghyr, Bihar.	In Bhārhūt inscriptions.[2] B. C. Law locates it in Northern India but D. C. Sircar locates it in Eastern India
6.	Kalyana	District of Thana, 33 miles North-East of Bombay.	Kalyana is located in Aparanta in a Kanheri inscription.[3]
7.	Kapasi	Identified with Kapasi, near Nanded, Maharashtra[4]	
8.	Kuraghara	Identified with Kurdwar, Madhya Pradesh (M.P.).[5]	
9.	Kurara	Unidentified.	From Nadner (District of Sehore M.P.) Pd. IV (300 B.C.–200 B.C.) Two coins of Kururaya, assignable to *c.* second century B.C., were found. It is interesting to note that Kururaya Kurara Koras Koraghara with Nandinagara appear in numerous Sāñci votive inscriptions.
10.	Madalachikata	–	Unidentified[6]
11.	Madhuvana	Identified with Madhubani, near Sāñci, District of Bhopal, M.P.[7]	
12.	Moragiri	Not identified.	Gupta identifies it with Mayura Parvata in a quotation of *Caranavyuha-bhasya* given by Apastamba.[8]

(*Continued*)

Table 5
(Continued)

S. No.	*Name of site*	*Location*	*Remarks*
13.	Nagara	On the left bank of the Beas River, 14 miles north of Sultanpur in Himachal Pradesh.[9]	D. C. Sirkar identifies it with Nagarahara (Jalalabad)
14.	Nandinagara	Unidentified	Gupta believes that if it is identified with Nandigrama of the Ramayana, it could probably be Nundgaon in U.P.[10]
15.	Pemuta	Unidentified[11]	
16.	Rajgir	Modern Rajgir, District of Rajgir, Bihar.[12]	
17.	Tumbavana	Modern Tumain, District of Guna, M.P.	The Buddhaghosha places Tumbavana between Vidisha and Kaushambi on the route from Gonaddha to Gonarda towards the Yamuna.[13]
18.	Ujjeni	Modern Ujjain, District of Ujjain, M.P.	
19.	Vadivahana	unidentified	
20.	Venugama	Identified with Ben Purwa, north-east of Kosam, District of Allahabad, U.P.[14]	
21.	Vidisha	Modern Besnagar, District of Vidisha, M.P.	

[1] Gupta Parmanand, *Geography in Ancient Indian Inscriptions*, Calcutta, 1973:146.

[2] Barua and Sinha, *Bharhut Inscriptions*, 1926, p. 18.

[3] L. L. no. 1013.

[4] Gupta: 168.

[5] *Ibid.*, p. 180.

[6] *Ibid.*, p. 183.

[7] *Ibid.*

[8] *Ibid.*, p. 189.

[9] Sarao, K. T. S., *Urban Centers and Urbanisation as Reflected in the Pāli Vinaya and Sutta Pitakas*, Delhi, 1990:76.

[10] Gupta: 88.

[11] *Ibid.*, p. 200.

[12] *Ibid.*, p. 101.

[13] D. C. Sircar, *Geography of Ancient and Medieval India*, 2nd Ed., Delhi, 1971:272.

[14] Gupta: 235.

Table 6
List of probable monastic sites

Sr. No.	*Name of the site*	*Geographical position*	*Its location within the site*	*Period*
1.	*Vihāra* of Rani Karpurasri	Ratnagiri, Orissa	–	Eleventh-Twelfth Centuries A.D.
2.	Itamundia	Kiching, Orissa	–	Eleventh-Twelfth Centuries A.D.
3.	Monasteries 9–12.	Nalanda, Bihar	Eastern side	
4.	Monastery E	Kasia, Uttar Pradesh	Eastern side	First to second centuries A.D.
5.	Monastery F	Sravasti, Uttar Pradesh	Eastern side	First to second centuries A.D.
6.	Purvārāma Monastery	Sravasti, Uttar Pradesh	South-East/ East	First to second centuries A.D.
7.	Kumāradevī Monastery	Sarnath, Uttar Pradesh	Eastern side	Twelfth Century A.D.
8.	–	Kapilavastu, Uttar Pradesh	–	–
9.	*Vihāra* of Devi (Queen of Asoka)	Sāñci, Madhya Pradesh	–	Eighth to ninth centuries
10.	Monastery 44	Sāñci	Eastern area of the complex	
11.	Site no. 6	Nāgarjunakonda, Andhra Pradesh	–	Third to fourth centuries A.D.
12.	SAN 3	Sannathi, Andhra Pradesh	Eastern bank of River Bhima, in the western part of the site	Second century A.D.
13.	Upper terrace	Bairāt, Rajasthan		Second century A.D.
14.	SGL 5	Sanghol	East	First- Second Centuries A.D.
15.	SGL 5	Sanghol	North East	First- Second Centuries A.D.
16.		Udayagiri		Eighth to Twelfth Century A.D.

Table 7

Buddhist sites with different types of structures, compiled on the basis on archaeological, epigraphic and literary sources.

Name of site	*Bhikṣunī vihāra*	*Stūpa with āyaka*	*Circular structure*
1. Ushkura	√	√	x
2. Paraspora	x	√	x
3. Ujjaini	√	x	√
4. Pandrethan	x	√	x
5. Shah-ji-ki-Deri	x	√	√
6. Sanghol	√	x	√
7. Sui Vihāra	√	x	√
8. Chaneti	x	√	x
9. Mathura	x	√	√
10. Bairāt	√	x	√
11. Sravasti	√	x	√
12. Piprahwa	x	√	√
13. Kasiya/Kushinagar	√	x	x
14. Lauriya Nandangarh	x	√	√
15. Vaishali	x	√	√
16. Rajgir	x	x	x
17. Bakraur	x	√	x
18. Sarnath	√	x	√
19. Kausambi	x	x	√
20. Bhārhūt	√	x	x
21. Nalanda	√	x	x
22. Antichak	x	√	√
23. Gyaraspur	x	√	√
24. Sāñci	√	√	√
25. Satdhara	x	√	x
26. Vidisha	√	x	x
27. Khiching	√	x	x
28. Lalitgiri	x	√	x
29. Udayagiri	√	x	x
30. Ratnagiri	√	x	√
31. Paharpur	x	√	√
32. Mainamati	x	√	x
33. Valabhi	√	x	x

Name of site	*Bhikṣunī vihāra*	*Stūpa with āyaka*	*Circular structure*
34. Kanheri	x	x	√
35. Junnar	x	x	√
36. Sannathi	√	√	√
37. Amarāvati	√	√	x
38. Ghantaśāla	x	√	x
39. Chandavaram	x	√	x
40. Bhattiprolu	x	√	x
41. Calingapatnam	x	√	x
42. Gummadidurru	x	√	x
43. Jaggayyapeta	x	√	x
44. Nāgarjunakonda	√	√	√
45. Bhaja	x	x	√
46. Bedsa	x	x	√
47. Salihundam	x	√	√
48. Ghuntupalli	x	√	√
49. Panagoria	x	√	x
50. Kapilavastu	√	x	x

Kasia, site plan showing excavated structures along with monastery E

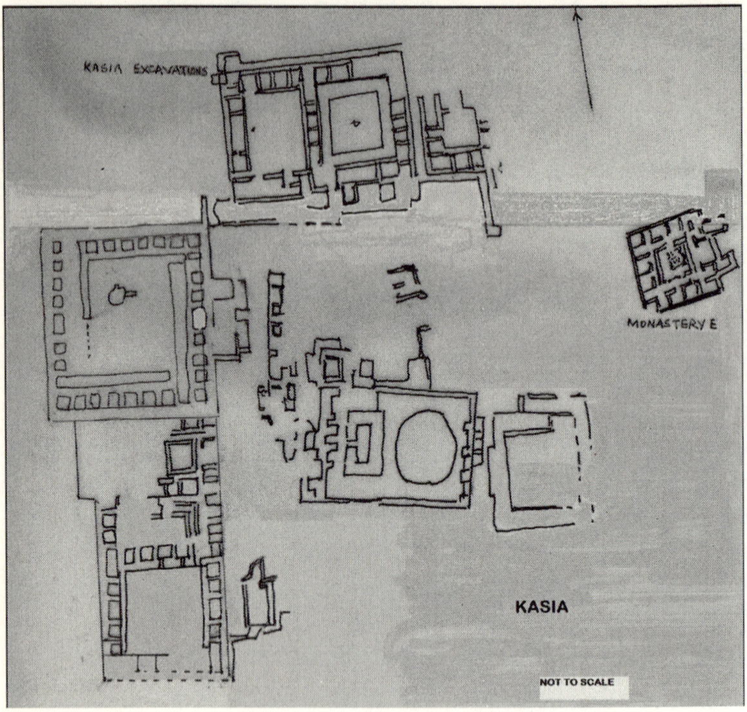

Nāgarjunakonda, site no. 6, plan of *stūpa, chaitya* and *maṇḍapa*

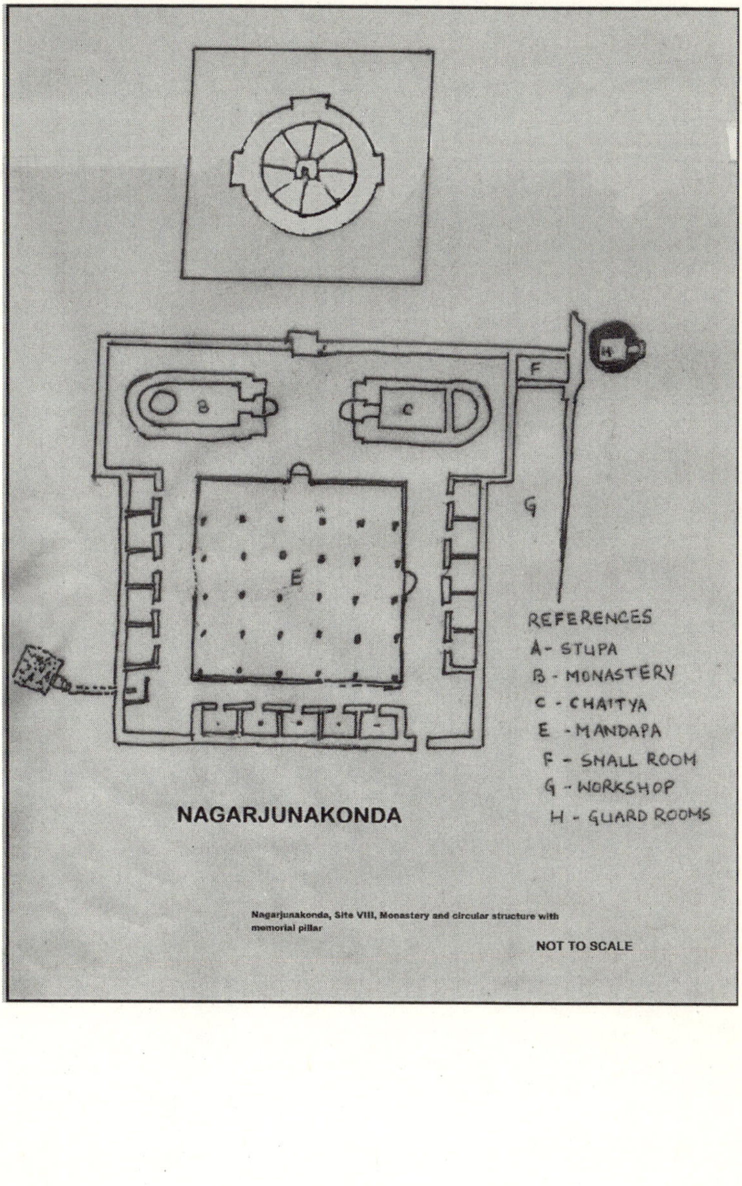

Sravasti

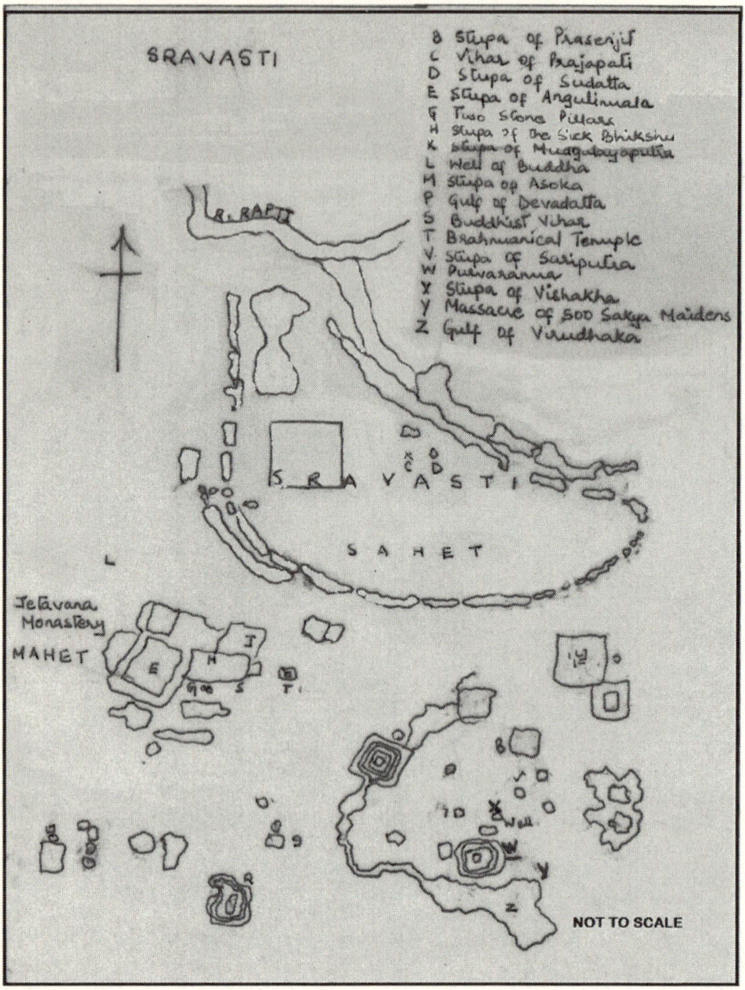
SRAVASTI
B Stupa of Prasenjit
C Vihar of Prajapati
D Stupa of Sudatta
E Stupa of Angulimala
G Two Stone Pillars
H Stupa of the Sick Bhikshu
L Well of Buddha
M Stupa of Asoka
P Gulf of Devadatta
S Buddhist Vihar
T Brahmanical Temple
V Stupa of Sariputra
W Purvarama
X Stupa of Vishakha
Y Massacre of 500 Sakya Maidens
Z Gulf of Virudhaka
R. RAPTI
S R A V A S T I
S A H E T
Jetavana Monastery
MAHET
NOT TO SCALE

Sahēth, Jetavana, ground plan of monasteries F and G

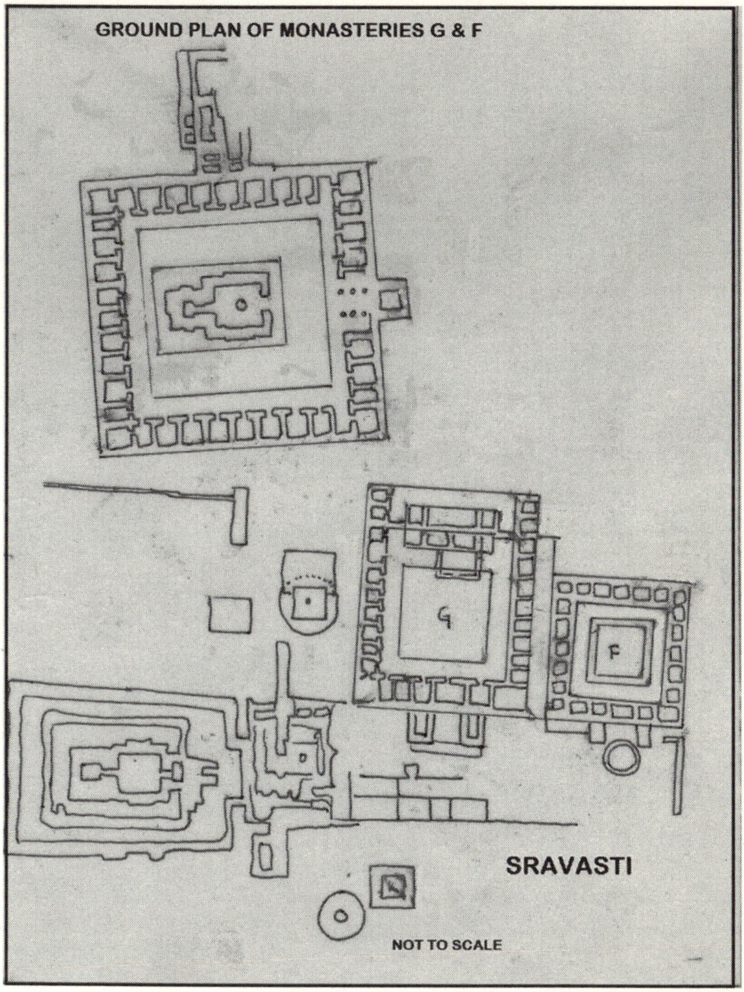

Sannathi, site plan

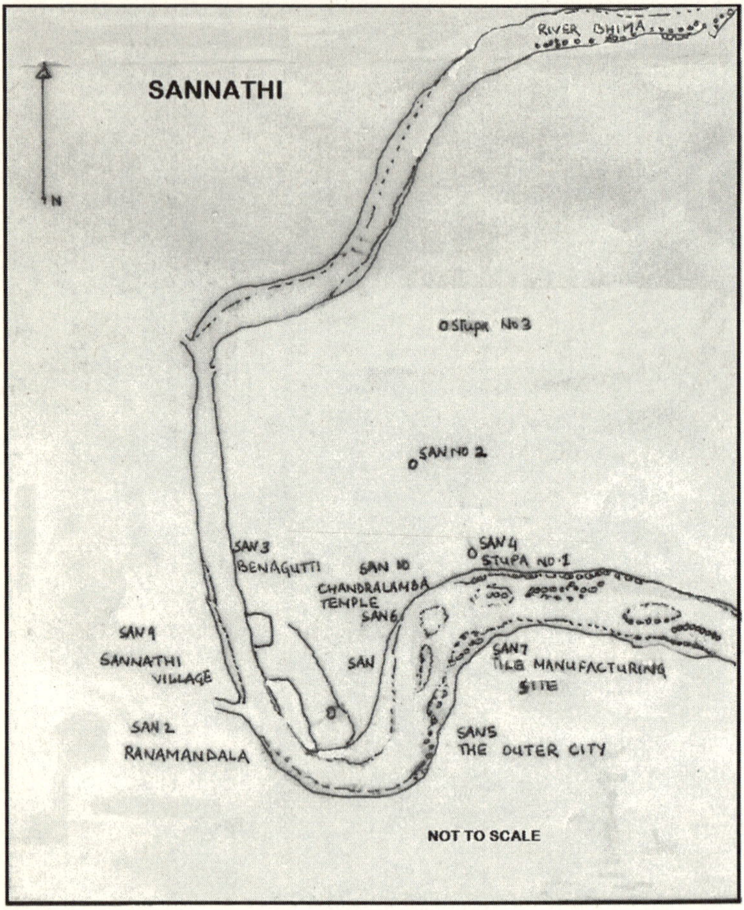

Ratnagiri Hill: contour map, showing excavated sites

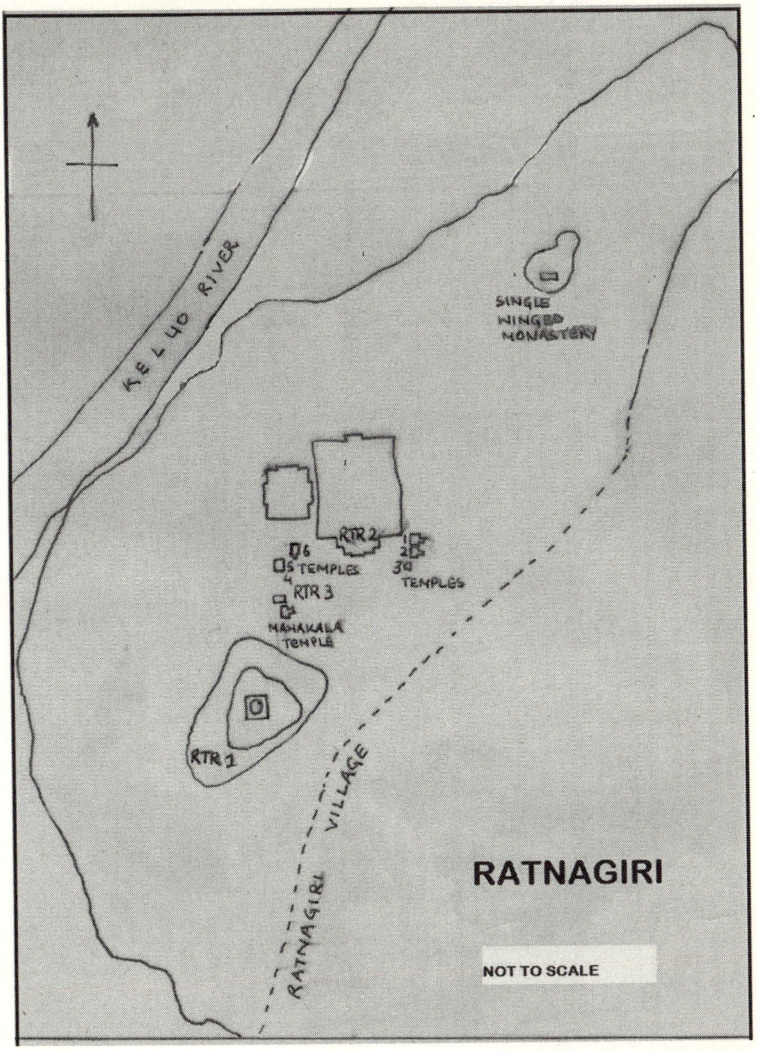

Nalanda, site plan

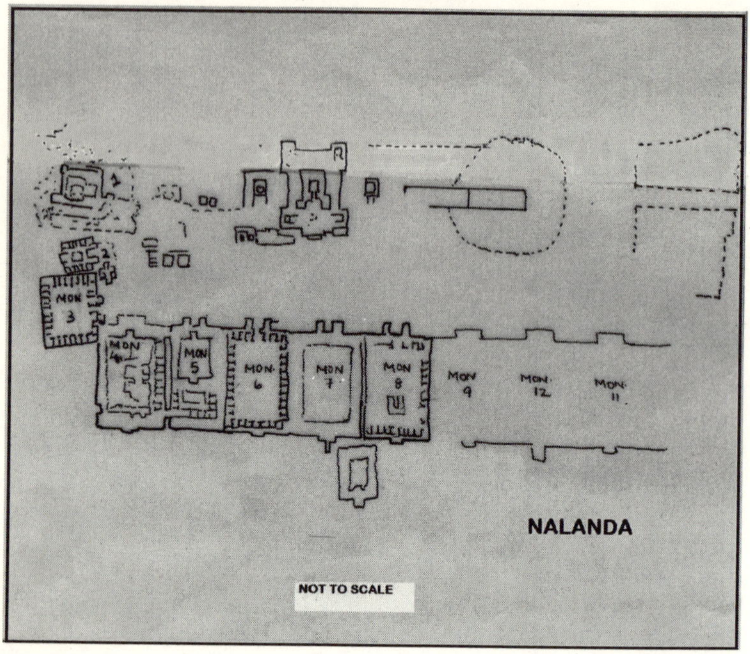

Sanghol site plan showing excavated structures

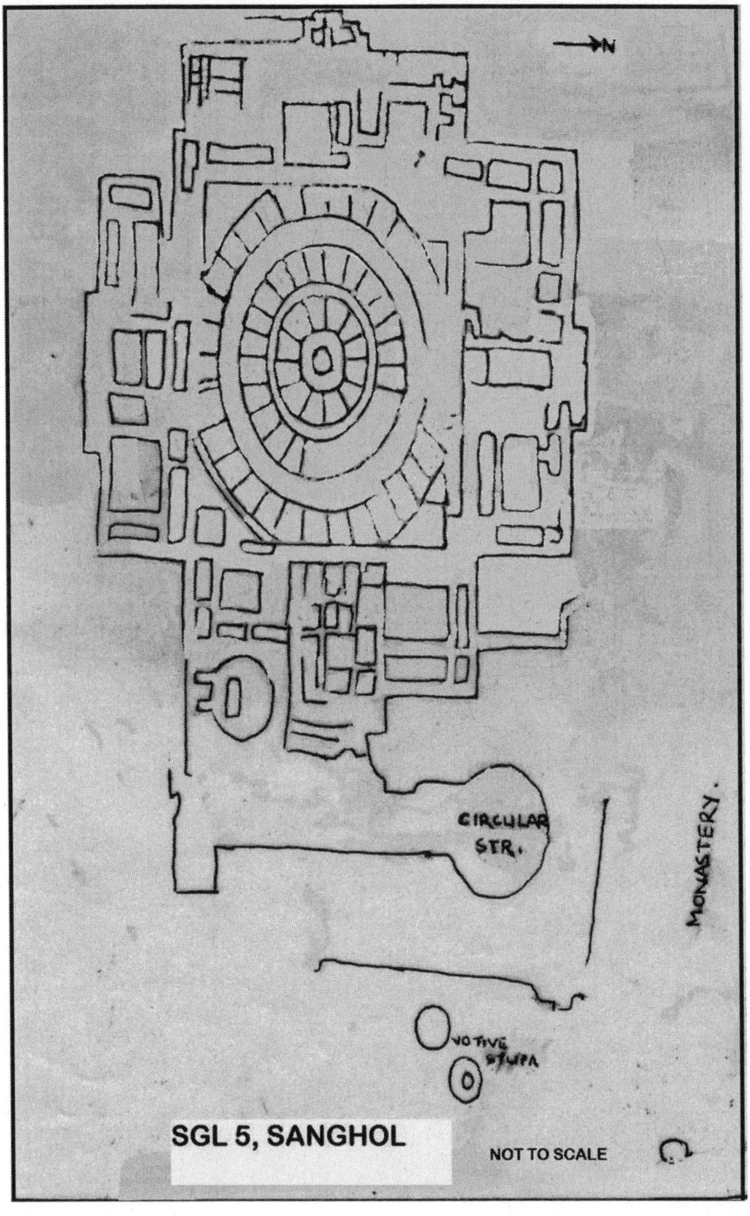

Plan of circular *chaitya* (after Mitra 1980)

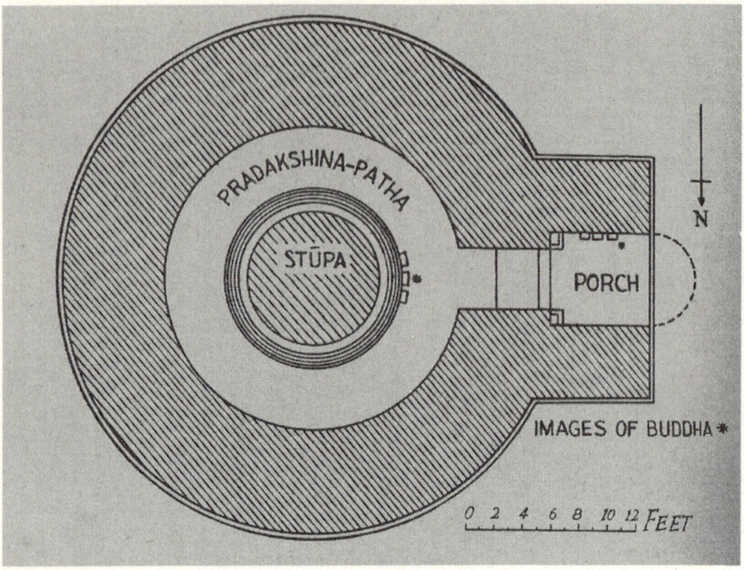

Birth of Siddhartha, c. second century A.D., Chandigarh Museum

Adoration of the Buddha by Viśākhā and her associates, Sikrai, c. second century A.D., Chandigarh Museum

Gift of Āmrapāli, Gandhara, c. third century A.D., Chandigarh Museum

Donor figures on the pedestal, c. second century A.D., from the erstwhile North-West Frontier Province, Chandigarh Museum.

Khujjuttara, Sanghol, c. second century A.D., Archaeological Museum, Sanghol

Stūpa dedicated to Sujātā, Bakraur, Bodh Gaya, c. eighth to tenth centuries A.D.

Circular structure, SGL 5, c. second century A.D., Sanghol

Nāgarjunakonda (site VIII B): circular structure with inscribed pillar lying within it *in situ*. *Indian Archaeology: A Review*, 1955–6, p. 24, pl. XXXVI.

Stūpa with *āyaka* platform, Chaneti, c. third century B.C.

Bibliography

Primary Sources (Excavation Reports, Epigraphic Records, Canonical Texts etc.)

Abeynayake, Oliver. *Khuddaka Nikaya* (1st ed.), Colombo, Sri Lanka, Karunaratne, 1984.

Agarwala, V. S. Sarnath, Delhi, Department of Archaeology, 1956.

Annual Report. Archaeological Survey of India (1903–4; 1910–11; 1913–14; 1924–25.; 1926–27; 1927–28; 1929–30; 1930–34; 1934–35; 1935–36; 1936–37).

Archaeological Survey of Western India, Volume 1–8; Reports. Old Series, Archaeological Survey of India, General Books, 2012.

Bandhopadhyay, Bimal. *Udaygiri-2*, Memoir of the Archaeological Survey of India, No. 100, 2007.

Barua and Sinha. *Bharhut Inscriptions*, Calcutta, India, 1926.

Bays, Gwendolyn. *The Lalitavistara Sutras-the Voice of the Buddha (The Beauty of Compassion)*, Berkeley, Dharma, 1983.

Beal Samuel, Si-yu-ki. *Buddhist Records of the Western World*, Calcutta, Susil Gupta (India) Ltd., 1958.

———. *The Fo-sho-hing-tsan-King, a Life of Buddha*, by Ashvaghosha, Bodhisattva (trans. Sanskrit into Chinese by Dharmaraksha, A.D.420), *Sacred Books of the East*, Vol. 29, Oxford, UK, Oxford University Press, 1883.

Bhandarkar, D.R., B. Chhabra and G.S. Ghai. (eds) *Corpus Inscriptionum Indicarum*, Inscriptions of the Early Gupta Kings, Vol. III, New Delhi, 1981.

Buhler, G. (trans. and ed.) *The Manusmriti, the Laws of Manu*, Vol. XXV, Oxford, UK, Clarendon Press, 1886.

———. "The Bhattiprolu Inscriptions", *Epigraphia Indica*, Vol. 2 (1894), 323.

———. "Further Inscriptions from Sanchi", *Epigraphia Indica*, Vol. 2 (1899), 366–408.

———. "Votive Inscriptions from the Sanchi Stupas", *Epigraphia Indica*, Vol. 2 (1899), 87–116.

Buhler, G. "Preliminary note on a recently discovered Sakya inscription", *Journal of the Royal Asiatic Society of Great Britain and Ireland* (Correspondence: Note 14), 387–9, April 1898.

Bullitt, John T. (ed.) Itivuttaka: This Was Said (by the Buddha). *Access to Insight*, accessed August 23, 2010, http://www.accesstoinsight.org/tipitaka/kn/iti/index.html.

Burgess, J. Report on the Buddhist Cave Temples and Their Inscriptions, Archaeological Survey of Western India, Vol. IV, London, Truber 1883. Reprint, Varanasi, Indological Book House, *Epigraphia Indica*, vol. I to XLII.

———. *Archaeological Survey of South India, Vol. I (The Buddhist Stupas of Amaravati and Jaggayyapeta in the Krishna District, Madras Presidency)*, London, UK, Trubner & Co., 1887.
———. *Archaeological Survey of Western India, Vol. IV (Report on the Buddhist Cave Temples and Their Inscriptions)*. Reprint, Varanasi, India, Indological Book House, 1964.
Chandra, G.C. "Excavation at Nalanda", ARASI, 1934–35, pp. 38–40.
Chattopadhyaya, Debiprasad. (ed.) *Taranath's History of Buddhism in India* (trans. Lama Chimpa), Calcutta, India, Alka Chattopadhyaya, 1980.
Cowell, E.B. *The Jatakas or Stories of the Buddha's Former Births* (trans. Pali by various hands), 6 Vols. London, UK, Pali Text Society, 1885. Reprint, 1973.
———. *The Buddha-Carita by Aśvaghoṣa or Act of Buddha*, New Delhi, New Bharatiya Book Corporation, 2003.
Cowell, Edward Byles, F. Max Müller and Junjiro Takakusu. Buddhist Mahayana texts, *Sacred Books of the East*, Vol. 49, Oxford, UK, Oxford University Press, 1894.
Corpus Inscriptionam Indicarum Vol. II, Pt II, Bharhut Inscriptions. Reprint, 1998.
Cunningham, A. Four Reports Made during the Years 1862–63–64–65. Vol.1, Archaeological Survey of India. 1871. Reprint, Delhi, Indological Bookhouse, 1972.
———. Tour in Boundelkhand and Malwa, 1871–72 and in the Central Provinces, Vol. VII, 1873–74 (1878, reprint 2000).
———. A Tour in the Central Provinces in 1873–74 and 1874–75, Vol. IX (1879, reprint 2000).
———. Tours in Bundelkhand and Malwa 1874–75 and 1876–77, Vol. X (1880, reprint 2000).
———. A Tour in the Punjab in 1878–79, Vol. XIV (1882, reprint 2000).
———. A Tour in Bundelkhand and Rewa in 1883–84 and a Tour in Rewa, Bundelkhand, Malwa and Gwalior in 1884–85, Vol. XXI (1885, reprint 2000).
———. A Tour in the Punjab and Rajputana in 1883–84, Vol. XXIII (1887, reprint 2000).
Davids, C.A.F. Rhys. *Psalms of the Early Buddhists – Psalms of the Sisters*, London, Pali Text Society, 1909.
———. *Psalms of the Sisters* (trans.) C. A. F. Rhys Davids, in *Psalms of the Early Buddhists*, Bristol, Pali Text Society, 1909. Reprint, 1948.
———. *Kindred Sayings on Buddhism*, Calcutta, University of Calcutta, 1930.
Davids, T.W. Rhys. The Mahāsudassana Sutta' (trans.) The Buddhist Suttas, *Sacred Books of the East*, Vol. XI Oxford, Oxford University Press, 1881. Reprint, Motilal Banarsidass, Delhi, 1965.
Davids, T.W. Rhys, and C. A. F. Rhys Davids (trans.) *Dialogues of the Buddha*, 3 vols., Oxford, Pali Text Society, 1889–1921.
Davids, T.W. and Hermann Oldenberg. (trans.) *Vinaya* Texts, *Sacred Books of the East*, Vol. 13, Oxford, UK, Clarendon Press, 1881; Second Khandhaka

(The Uposatha Ceremony, and the Pātimokkha), Volume I, p. 239; Third Khandhaka (Residence during the Rainy Season), Volume I, p. 298; Fourth Khandhaka (The Parāvanā Ceremony), Volume I, p. 325; Fifth Khandaka: Rules for Foot-clothing, seats, Vehicles, etc., Volume II, p. 1; Seventh Khandaka: The Kathina Ceremonies, Volume II, p. 146; Eighth Khandaka: The Dress of the Bhikkhus, Volume II, p. 171.

———. The Kūllavagga/Cullavagga I–II, *Sacred Books of the East*, Vol. 20, Oxford, UK, Oxford University Press, 1885, vol. 3. Tenth Khandhaka, On the Duties of Bhikkhunīs, Volume III, p 320.

Deo, S.B. and R.S. Gupte. *Excavations at Bhokardan*, Marathwada University Press, Nagpur-Aurangabad, India, 1974.

Fleet, J. F. "The Inscription on the Piprahwa Vase", *Journal of the Royal Asiatic Society of Great Britain and Ireland*, 1907, pp. 105–30.

Gupta, P.L. Nanaghat Inscription of an Unknown Queen: A Historical Reappraisal, *Studies in Indian Epigraphy (Bhartiya Purabhilekha Parika) Journal of the Epigraphical Society of India*, Vol. II, Mysore, India, Geetha Book House, 1975.

Gupta, S.P., K.N. Dikshit and K.S. Ramachandran. (eds) Excavation at Sirpur, *PURATATTVA* No. 31. Bulletin of the Indian Archaeological Society, 2000–1.

Gupta, S.P., and K.S. Ramachandran. (eds) Dimensions in Indian History and Archaeology, Indian History and Culture Society, XVth Session, Bhopal, 1991, Indian History and Culture Society, New Delhi, 1993.

Gunaratnam, Edmund Rowland. *The Vimana-Vatthu of the Khuddhaka Nikaya Sutta Pitaka*, Literary Licensing, LLC, Literary Collections, 1886.

Gustav, Roth. (ed.) *Bhikshuni – Vinaya: Manual of Discipline for the Buddhist Nuns*, Patna, India, K. P. Jayaswal Research Institute, 1968.

Foucher, Alfred. (trans.) *Hargreaves, On the Iconography of the Buddha's Nativity*, Manager of Publications, 1934/1999.

Fuhrer, A.A. (ed.) *Shri Vasistha Dharmasastra* (Bombay Sanskrit and Prakrit series, Poona, India, Government Book Depot, 1914.

Hamid, M. Excavation at Sanchi. Annual Report Archaeological Survey of India, 1936–37, Delhi, Director General, Archaeological Survey of India, 1940, pp. 85–7.

Havnevik, Hanna. Combats des nonnes tibétaines, Religieuses bouddhistes du Pays des neiges. St. Michel en l'Herm, Editions Dharma, 1995 (translated, revised and updated edition of Tibetan Buddhist Nuns: History, Cultural Norms and Social Reality). Oslo, Norwegian University Press, 1989.

Hazra, K.L. *Buddhism and Pali Literature of Myanmar*, 1996, Buddhist World Press. Reprint, 2011.

Hirakawa, Akira. *Monastic Discipline for the Buddhist Nuns* (English translation of the Chinese Text of the Mahasamghika Bhiksuni Vinaya), Patna, India, K.P. Jayswal Institute. Reprint, 1999.

The History and Inscriptions of the Satavahanas and the Western Kshatrapas, Bombay, Maharastra State Board for Literature and Culture, 1989.

Horner, I.B. (trans.) *The Book of the Discipline*, 6 Vols. London, UK, Luzac & Company, for P.T.S, 1938–66.

Horner, I.B. and H.S. Gehman. Minor Anthologies [Vol 4] *Vimanavatthu and Petavatthu*, Pali Text Society, The Minor Anthologies of the Pali Canon, Part IV, London, 1974.

Howell, J.R. *Excavations at Sannathi* (1986–89), New Delhi, ASI, 1995.

Indian Antiquary. Vol. XXI. Reprint, Delhi, Swati Publications, 1985.

Indian Archaeology – A Review (1953–54; 1954–55; 1955–56; 1956–57; 1957–58; 1958–59; 1959–60; 1960–61; 1961–62; 1962–63; 1963–64; 1964–65; 1965–66; 1966–67; 1968–69; 1969–70; 1970–71; 1971–72; 1972–73; 1973–74; 1974–75; 1975–76; 1976–77; 1977–78; 1978–79; 1979–80; 1981–82; 1983–84; 1985–86; 1986–87; 1987–88; 1988–89; 1989–90; 1991–92; 1992–93; 1993–94; 1994–95).

Ireland, J.D. (trans.) *Itivuttaka: This Was Said by the Buddha. Itivuttaka: The Buddha's Sayings (Excerpts)*, http://www.accesstoinsight.org/tipitaka/kn/iti.intro.irel.html#intro.

———. Sesavati: Sesavati's mansion (Vv 3.7) (trans. from the Pali) *Access to Insight*, June 7, 2009, http://www.accesstoinsight.org/tipitaka/kn/vv/vv.3.07.irel.html.

———. Sirima: Sirima's Mansion (Vv 1.16) (trans. from the Pali) Vv 137–49; No. 16, *Access to Insight*, accessed June 7, 2009, http://www.accesstoinsight.org/tipitaka/kn/vv/vv.1.16.irel.html.

———. *The Itivuttaka – the Sayings of the Buddha*, Kandy, Sri Lanka, Buddhist Publication Society, 1991.

Kabilsingh, Chatsumarn. *The Bhikkhuni Patimokkha of the Six Schools*, New Delhi, Sri Satguru Publications, 1998.

Kaushik, Garima. Reinterpreting the Sacred Space at Sanghol: A Multidisciplinary Perspective. Paper Presented in the International Conference organised by B.B. Ambedkar University, Lucknow, India, 2014.

Kern, H. The Saddharma-Pundarika or the Lotus of the True Law, *Sacred Books of the East*, Vol. XXI, Oxford, UK, Oxford University Press, 1885.

Konow, Sten. (ed.) *Corpus Inscriptionam Indicarum*, Vol. II, Pt I, Kharoshthi Inscriptions with the Exception of Those of Asoka, Historical Introduction. Reprint, 1991.

Kumar, Dilip. *Archaeology of Vaishali*, New Delhi, Ramanand Vidya Bhawan, 1986.

Kuraishi, M. H., and Chandra, G.C. Excavations at Nâlandâ, Annual Report of Archaeological Survey of India, 1930–34, Delhi, 1936, pp. 38–40.

Lanman, Charles Rockwell. *Buddhist Legends*, Vol. 1, Delhi, Motilal Banarsidas, 2005.

Legge, James. *A Record of Buddhistic Kingdoms: Being an account by the Chinese Monk Fa-Hien of His Travels in India and Ceylon (A.D. 399-414) in search of the Buddhist Books of Discipline*. Oxford, UK, Clarendon Press, 1965. Reprint, New York, Paragon Book, 1886.

———. *Travels of Fa-Hian and Sung Yun* (A.D. 400 and 518), London, UK, 1869.

———. *Travels of Hiouen* Thsang, *Su-Yu-Ki*, Buddhist Records of the Western World, 2 Vols London, UK, Trubner & Co., 1884.

Liuders, H. A List of Brahmi Inscriptions from the Earliest Times to about A.D. 400. (Appendix to Vol. X of the *Epigraphia Indica.*), Calcutta, 1910.

Longhurst, A.H. *Excavations at Nagarjunikonda, in Annual Report of the Archaeological Survey of India, 1929-30*, Delhi, Agam Kala Prakashan, 1933. Reprint, 2002.

———. "The Buddhist Monuments at *Guntupalli* in Krishna District", ARASI, (Southern Circle), 1916–17.

Luders, H. (ed.) *Corpus Inscriptionum Indicarum*, Vol. II, Pt II (Revised by E. Waldschmidt and M.A. Mehedale), Ootacamund, India, Government Epigraphist for India, 1963.

Majumdar, N.G. *The Monuments of Sanchi*, 3 vols, Sir John Marshall and Alfred Foucher, London, UK, 1940.

Mani, B.R. "The Enigmatic Monastery of Kumāradevī at Sarnath: New Identification", *Pragdhara*, Vol. 16, 2005–6, pp. 321–2.

Marshall, Sir John. *A Guide to Sanchi* (Calcutta, 1918) and Annual Report, ASI, 1913–14.

———. Excavations at Saheth Maheth, Archaeological Survey of India, Annual Report 1910–11, Calcutta, 1914, pp. 1–24.

———. *The Monuments of Sanchi*, Delhi, Government of India Press, 1938.

———. "The Monuments of Sanchi: Their explorations and conservation", ARASI 1913–14, Calcutta, 1917.

Marshall, John Hubert, Alfred Foucher and Nani Gopal Majumdar. *The Monuments of Sāñchī*, Vol. 1, London, Probsthain, 1940.

Masih, Farzand. Research Report Sui-Vehar Excavations and Archaeological Reconnaissances of Southern Punjab, Department of Archaeology, Bahāwalpur District, Pakistan, 2014.

Mirashi, V.V. *Corpus Inscriptionum Indicarum*, Vol. IV, *Inscriptions of the Kal Schlingloff achuri – Chedi Era*, Ootacamund, India, Government Epigraphist for India, 1955.

Mitra, Debala. *Ratnagiri*, Memoirs of the Archaeological Survey of India, No. 88, Volumes I–II, New Delhi, 1958–61.

Müller, F. Max. Buddhist Mahāyana Texts, *the Sacred Books of the East*, Vol. 49, 1996.

Müller, F. Max, and Viggo Fausböll. Dhammapada and Sutta-Nipata, *Sacred Books of the East*, Vol. 10, Oxford, UK, Clarendon Press, 1881.

Murcott, Susan. *The First Buddhist Women – Translations and Commentaries on the Therigatha*, California, Parallax Press, 1991.

Nagaraja Rao, M. S. (ed.) *Madhu: Recent Researches in Indian Archaeology and Art History* (Sh. M. N. Deshpande Felicitation Vol.), Delhi, Agam Kala Prakashan, 1987.

Norman, K. R. *Notes on the Gāndhārī Dharmapada*, Delhi, Linguistic Society of India, 1971.

Oldenberg, Hermann, and Kenneth Roy Norman. *Theragatha and Therigatha*, London, Pali Text Society, 1966.

———. *Buddha: His Life, His Doctrine, His Order*, London, Williams, 1882.

Olivelle, Patrick. *Manu's Code of Law – A Critical Edition and Translation of the Manava Dharmashastra*, South Asia Research Series, New York, Oxford University Press, 2005.

Sahni, D.R. *Archaeological Remains and Excavations at Bairat*, Jaipur State, India, Directorate of Archaeology, 1937.

Sahni, Daya Ram. "*Excavations at Bairat*", Annual Report, Archaeological Survey of India, 1935–36, Delhi, 1938, pp. 84–7.

Shastri, Manmatha Nath. *Buddha: His Life, His Teachings, His Order Together with the History of the Buddhism*, Varanasi, Indological Book House, 1978.

Schopen, Gregory. "On Monks, Nuns, and 'Vulgar' Practices: The Introduction of the Image Cult into Indian Buddhism", *Artibus Asiae* XLIX, 1.2, pp. 153–68. Reprint, Schopen 1997, Chap. XI.

Sharma, A.K. *Excavations at Sirpur*, Indian Archaeological Society, Special Report No. 1 (SRP 1–2000), New Delhi, 2007.

Sharma, G.R. *Excavations at Kausambi, Memoirs of the Archaeological Survey of India*, 1949–50.

Sinha, K.K. *Excavations at Sravasti*, Varanasi, India, Banaras Hindu University, 1967.

Sirkar, D.C. *Select Inscriptions Bearing on Indian History and Civilisation*, II vols, Calcutta, India, Calcutta University 1942. Reprint, 1965.

Takakasu, J. *A Record of the Buddhist Religion as Practiced in India and the Malayan Archipelago, by Itsing*, Oxford, UK, Clarendon Press, 1896.

Thanissaro, Bhikkhu. (trans. and intro.) *Itivuttaka: This Was Said by the Buddha*, 2001, http://www.accesstoinsight.org/tipitaka/kn/iti.intro.than.

———. (trans. the Pali) *Muluposatha Sutta: The Roots of the Uposatha* (AN 3.70), *Access to Insight*, July 3, 2010, http://www.accesstoinsight.org/tipitaka/an/an03/an03.070.than.html.

———. (trans. the Pali) *The Buddhist Monastic Code*, Vol. II, Chapter 23. *Bhikkhunī Pāṭimokkha – The Bhikkhunīs' Code of Discipline*, 2007–9.

Theravada Bhikkhuni Vinaya. Vol. 3 of *Vinaya Pitaka*. Pali Text Society.

Venkataramayya, M. *Sravasti*, New Delhi, Archaeological Survey of India, New Delhi, Second Edition, 1981 (First Edition 1956).

Vogel, J. Ph. *Excavation at Kasia*, Annual Report, Archaeological Survey of India, 1905–6.

Watters, Thomas. *On Yuan Chwang's Travels in India, 629–645* A.D. Royal Asiatic Society, London, 1904, http://www.archive.org/stream/cu31924071132769#page/n3/mode/2up.

Williams, Paul. *Buddhism: The Origins and Nature of Mahāyāna Buddhism; Some Mahāyāna Religious Topics*, London, Taylor & Francis, 2005.

Secondary Sources

Abeynayake, O., *Ph.D., Collections, in the Sutta Pitaka, A Textual and Historical Analysis of the Khuddaka Nikaya* (1st ed.), Colombo, Karunaratne, 1984.

Allchin, F. R., George Erdosy. *The Archaeology of Early Historic South Asia: The Emergence of Cities and States*, Cambridge, Cambridge University Press, 1995.

Altekar, A.S. *The Position of Women in Hindu Civilisation* (3rd ed.), Banaras, Motilal Banarsidass, 1956.

Arnold, B. and N. Wicker. (eds) *Gender and the Archaeology of Death*, Walnut Creek, CA, AltaMira Press, 2001.

Asher, F.M. and G.S. Ghai. (eds) *Indian Epigraphy: Its Bearing on the History of Art*, New Delhi, Oxford, 1985.

Bajpai, S.C. *Kinnaur in the Himalayas, Mythology to Modernity*, Concept Publishing Company, New Delhi, 1981.

Bandaranayake, Senake. *Sinhalese Monastic Architecture: The Viharas of Anuradhapura*. Leiden, The Netherlands, E. J. Brill, 1974.

Bartholomeusz, T. *Women under the Bo Tree: Buddhist Nuns in Sri Lanka*, Cambridge, UK, Cambridge University Press, 1994.

Barua, D.K. *Viharas in Ancient India – a Survey of Buddhist Monasteries*, Calcutta, India, Indian Publications, 1969.

Behl Benoy, K. *The Ajanta Caves*, London and New York, Thames & Hudson, 1998/2005.

Bern, S.L. *The Lenses of Gender: Transforming the Debate on Sexual Inequality*, New Haven, CT, Yale University Press, 1993.

Bhattacharyya, B. *The Indian Buddhist Iconography* (2nd ed.), Calcutta, India, Firma K.L. Mukhopadhyay, 1958.

Blackstone, K.R. *Women in the Footsteps of the Buddha: Struggle for Liberation in the Therigatha* (1st ed.), New Delhi, Motilal Banarsidass, 2000.

Buswell, Robert E. *Encyclopedia of Buddhism*, New York, MacMillan, 2004.

Bynum, Caroline Walker. *Fragmentation and Redemption: Essays on Gender and the Human Body in Medieval Religion*, New York, Urzone Publishers, 1991.

———. "Gender and Religion: On the Complexity of Symbols", in *Gender and Religion*, C. Bynum, S. Harrell and P. Richman (eds) *History of Religions*, Boston, Beacon, 1986, pp. 1–20.

Carr, A.E. *Transforming Grace. Christian Tradition and Women's Experience*, New York, Harper & Row, 1990.

Chakladar, H.C. *Social Life in Ancient India, Studies in Vatsyayana's Kamasutra*, Delhi, Indian Ivories, 1976.

Chakrabarti, Dilip K. *Post-Mauryan States of Mainland South Asia*, in F. Raymond Allchin (ed.), *The Archaeology of Early Historic South Asia*, Cambridge, Cambridge University Press, 1995, pp. 274–326.

Chakravarti, Uma. *Everyday Lives, Everyday Histories: Beyond the Kings and Brahmanas of Ancient India*, New Delhi, Tulika Books, 2007.

———. *Gendering Caste through a Feminist Lens*, New Delhi, Popular Prakashan, 2003.

———. *Social Dimensions of Early Buddhism*, New Delhi, Oxford University Press, 1987.

Chauley, G.C. *Monumental Heritage of Orissa*, New Delhi, India Publishing Co., 2004.

Classen, A. *The Power of the Woman's Voice in Medieval and Early Mordern Literatures: New Approaches to German and European Women Writers and to Violence against Women in Premodern Times*, Berlin, Walter de Gruyter, 1994.

Coomaraswamy, A. *Archaic Indian Terracotta*, Cologne, Germany, IPEK, 1928.

———. *The Origin of the Buddha Image*, Delhi, Munshirm Manoharlal Publishers Pvt Ltd, 2001.

Cousins, L. (ed.) *Buddhist Studies in Honor of I.B Honor*, Dordrecht, Holland, 1974.

Cunningham, A. *Mahabodhi or the Great Buddhist Temple under the Bodhi Tree at Bodh Gaya*, London, UK, Allen, 1892.

———. *The Stûpa of Bharhut: A Buddhist Monument Ornamented with Numerous Sculptures Illustrated of Buddhist Legend and History in the Third Century B.C.* London. Reprint, Varanasi, 1962. Cutler, Sally Mellick, 1994.

Czuma, S.J. and R. Morris. *Kushana Sculpture: Images from Early India*, Cleveland, Ohio, Cleveland Museum of Art in Cooperation with Indiana University Press, 1985.

Davidson, R.M. *Indian Esoteric Buddhism; a Social History of the Tantric Movement*, New Delhi, 2003.

Deglukar, G.B. *Portrayal of the Women: In the Art and Literature of the Ancient Deccan*, Jaipur, India, Publication Scheme, 2004.

Dehejia, Vidya. *Discourse in Early Buddhist Art: Visual Narratives of India*, New Delhi, Munshiram Manoharlal, 1997.

———. *Early Buddhist Rock Temples*, London, UK, 1972.

Dhavalikar Madhukar Keshav, Sanchi: A Cultural Study, Deccan College Postgraduate and Research Institute, Poona, 1965.

Donaldson, T.E. *Iconography of the Buddhist Sculpture of Orissa.* Vol.I&II., New Delhi, IGNCA, 2001.

Dutt, N. *Buddhist Sects in India* (2nd ed.), Delhi, Motilal Banarsidass, 1978.

———. *Early Monastic Buddhism*, 2 Vols, Calcutta, India, Calcutta Oriental Book Agency, 1941–45.

Dutt, S. *Buddhist Monks and Monasteries of India*, London, 1962, Motilal Banarsidass, Delhi, India. Reprint, 1988.

———. *Early Buddhist Monachism (600 B.C.–100 B.C.)*, Bombay, Asia Publishing House, 1960.

———. *The Buddha and Five after Centuries*, London, Luzac & Company, Limited, 1957.

Eichler, M. *Nonsexist Research Methods: A Practical Guide*, Boston, Allen & Unwin, 1988.

Falk, Nancy A. and Rita Gross. (eds) *Unspoken Words – Women's Religious Lives in Non-Western Cultures*, San Francisco, CA, Harper and Row, 1980.

Faure, Bernard and Teiser, S.F. *The Power of Denial: Buddhism, Purity, and Gender*, Princeton, NJ, Princeton University Press, 2003.

Fergusson, J. *Tree and Serpent Worship: Or Illustrations of Mythology and Art in India in the First and Fourth Century after Christ (From the Sculptures of the Buddhist Topes at Sanchi and Amaravati)*. Reprint, Delhi, Oriental Publishers, 1971.

Ghosh, A. *Ajanta Murals: An Album of Eighty-Five Reproductions in Colour*, Archaeological Survey of India, 1987.

———. *Encyclopedia of Indian Archaeology*, Vol. 2, New Delhi, I.C.H.R., 1989.

Gilchrist, R. *Gender and Archaeology: Contesting the Past*, London, Routledge, 1999.

———. *Gender and Material Culture, the Archaeology of the Religious Women*, London, Routledge, 2013.

Gombrich, Richard Francis. *Theravāda Buddhism: A Social History from Ancient Benares to Modern Colombo*, Psychology Press, 1988.

Gombrich, R. and G. Obeyesekere. *Buddhism Transformed: Religious Change in Sri Lanka*, New Delhi, Motilal Banarsidass, 1990.

Gross, R. *Buddhism beyond Patriarchy. A Feminist History, Analysis and Reconstruction of Buddhism*, Albany, SUNY Press, 1993.

Gupta, P. *Geography in Ancient Indian Inscriptions*, Delhi, D.K. Pub., 1973.

Gupte, R.S. and B.D. Mahajan. *Ajanta, Ellora and Aurangabad Caves*, B.D Taraporevala, 1962.

Hager, L.D. *Women in Human Evolution*, London, Routledge, 1997.

Hamilton, Edward Johnston. *Asvaghosa's Buddhacharita or Acts of the Buddha*, Delhi, Motilal Banarsidass, 1992.

Handa, O.C. *Buddhist Monasteries in Himachal Pradesh*, New Delhi, Indus Publishing Company, 1987.

Harding, S. *The Science Question in Feminism*, Ithaca, Cornell University Press, June 1986.

Hardy, R.S. *A Manual of Buddhism and Its Modern Development*, New Delhi, Mumshiram Manoharlal, 1995.

———. *Manual of Buddhism*, 1853, Delhi, Kessinger Publishing, 2003.

Havnevik, H. *Tibetan Buddhist Nuns, the Institute for Comparative Research in Human Culture*, Oslo, Norwegian University Press, 1989.

Hodder, I. *Symbolic and Structural Archaeology*, Cambridge, Cambridge University Press, 1982.

———. *The Archaeology of Contextual Meanings*, Cambridge, Cambridge University Press, 1987.

Horner, I.B. *Women under Primitive Buddhism: Laywomen and Almswomen*, London, Routledge & Kegan Paul, 1930. Reprint, Delhi, Motilal Banarsidass, 1975.

Huntington, S.L. *The "Pāla-Sena" Schools of Sculpture*, Brill Archive, Leiden 1984.

Insoll, T. *Archaeology and World Religion*, London, Routledge, 2001.
Jennings, J.G. *The Vedantic Buddhism of the Buddha*, Delhi, Motilal Banarsidas, 1947.
Johnson, P.A. and Janet Kalven. (ed.) *With Both Eyes Open: Seeing beyond Gender*, New York, NY, Pilgrim Press, 1988.
Kane, P.V. *History of Dharmashastras*, Vol. II, Poona, India, Bhandarkar Oriental Research Institute, 1962, 1975.
Kapoor, Subodh. *Encyclopaedia of Ancient Geography*, Vol. I, Cosmo Publication, New Delhi, 2002.
Kaufman, W.O. The *Anthropology of Wisdom Literature*, Westport, Greenwood Publishing Group, 1996.
Kim, Jinah. Unheard Voices: Women's Roles in Medieval Buddhist Artistic Production and Religious Practices in South Asia, *Journal of American Academy of Religion*, Vol. 79, 2012, pp. 200–32.
King, U. *Religion and Gender*, Oxford, Blackwell Publishing, 1995.
Kloppenborg, Ria and Wouter J. Hanegraaff. *Female Stereotypes in Religious Traditions*, Leiden, BRILL, 1995.
Knox, R. *Amaravati: Buddhist Sculptures from the Great Stupa*, London, British Museum Press, 1992.
Kosambi, D.D. *Culture and Civilization of Ancient India*, London, UK, Routledge and Kegan Paul, 1965.
———. *Science Society and Peace*, Bombay, People's Publishing House, 1994.
Kramrisch, Stella and Barbara Stoler Miller. *Exploring India's Sacred Art: Selected Writings of Stella Kramrisch*, Philadelphia, University of Pennsylvania Press, 1983.
Krishnamurthy, K. *Glimpses of Art, Architecture and Buddhist Literature in Ancient India*, New Delhi, Abhinav Publication, 1987.
Kunin, Seth Daniel and Jonathan Miles-Watson. *Theories of Religion: A Reader*, New Jersey, Rutgers University Press, 2006.
Lahiri, N. *The Archaeology of Indian Trade Routes (upto c. 200 BC)*, New Delhi, Oxford University Press, 1992.
Leach, Maria, and Funk Jerome Fried. *Funk & Wagnalls Standard Dictionary of Folklore, Mythology and Legend*, New York, Funk & Wagnalls, 1984.
Malasekera, G.B. *Dictionary of Pali Proper Names Pali-English*, New Delhi, Asian Educational Services. Reprint, 2003.
Mirashi, V.V. *The History and Inscriptions of the Satavahanas and Western Kshatrapas, Part II*, Mumbai, Maharashtra State Board for Literature and Culture, 1981.
Misra, Binayak. *Orissa under the Bhauma Kings*, Calcutta, Vishwamitra Press, 1934.
Mitra, Debala. *Buddhist Monuments*, Calcutta, India. Reprint, New Delhi, Munshiram Manoharlal, 1971.
———. *Ratnagiri* (1958–61), 2 vols., New Delhi, Memoirs of the Archaeological Survey of India, 1981–83.

Mizuno, Kōgen, Gaynor Sekimori. *Essentials of Buddhism: Basic Terminology and Concepts of Buddhist Philosophy and Practice*, Tokyo, Kōsei Publication, 1996.

Mrozik, Susanne. "Materializations of Virtue: Buddhist Discourses on Bodies." In Ellen T. Armour and S.M St. Ville (eds) *Bodily Citations: Religion and Judith Butler*, Chiechester, Columbia University Press, 2006, pp. 15–47.

Nagaraju, S. *Buddhist Architecture of Western India (C.250 B.C.–C. A.D. 300)*, Delhi, Agam Kala Prakashan, 1981.

Nath, V. *Dana and Gift System in Ancient India*, New Delhi, Munshiram Manoharlal, 1987.

Nattier, Jan. *A Guide to the Earliest Chinese Buddhist Translations: Texts from the Eastern Han "Dong Han" and Three Kingdoms "San Guo" Periods*, Tokyo, International Research Institute for Advanced Buddhology, Soka University, 2008.

Nelson, S.M. (ed.) *Women in Antiquity; Theoretical Approaches to Gender and Archaeology*, Lanham, AltaMira Press, 2007.

Nyanaponika, Thera and H. Hecker. (ed.) *Great Disciples of the Buddha*, Boston: Wisdom Publications, 2004.

Oldenberg, H. and William Hoey. *Buddha, His Life, Doctrine and Order*, Delhi, Kessinger Publishing, LLC, 31 March 2003.

Ollivelle, Austin Patrick. *Between The Empires: Society in India 300 BCE to 400 CE*. University of Texas, New York, Oxford University Press, June 2006.

Owen, Lisa B. "Toward a Buddhist Feminism: Mahayana Sutras, Feminist Theory, and the Transformation of Sex", *Asian Journal of Women's Studies*, Vol. 3, No. 4, 1997, p. 8.

Pande, Anupa. *The Nāṭyaśāstrā Tradition and the Ancient Indian Society*, Jodhpur, India, Kusumanjali Prakashan, 1993.

Parimoo Ratan. *Life of Buddha in Indian Sculpture*, New Delhi, Kanak Publications, 1982.

Paul, Diana Y. *Women in Buddhism: Images of the Feminine in the Mahayana Tradition* (2nd ed.) University of California Press, 1985.

Prasad, P.C. *Foreign Trade and Commerce in Ancient India*, New Delhi, Abhinav, 1977.

Rama, K. *Buddhist Art of Nagarjunakonda*, New Delhi, Sundeep Prakashan, 1995.

Ramachandran, T.N. *Buddhist Sculptures from a Stupa Near Goli Village, Guntur District*, Government Press, 1929. Bulletin of the Madras, Government Museum, New series. Volume 1, part 1. Reprint, Chennai, 2000.

Rapson, E.J. *The Cambridge History of India*, Cambridge, Cambridge University Press, 1922.

Ray, H.P. *Monastery and Guild: Commerce under the Satavahanas*, New Delhi, Oxford University Press, 1986.

———. *Winds of Change*, New Delhi, Oxford University Press, 1995.

Rea, A. *South Indian Buddhist Antiquities*, Madras, India, Archaeological Survey of India, 1894.

Renfrew, Colin and Paul G. Bhan. *Archaeology: The Key Concepts*, New York, Routledge, 1996.

Richman, Paula. *Women, Branch Stories, and Religious Rhetoric in a Tamil Buddhist Text*, Syracuse, NY, Maxwell School of Citizenship and Public Affairs, Syracuse University, 1988.

Roerich, G. and A.S. Altekar. *Biography of Dharmaswamin*, KPJRI, Patna, India, 1959.

Roy, Kumkum. *Women in Early Indian Societies*, New Delhi, Manohar Publishers & Distributors, 1999.

Sahni, D.R. *Catalogue of the Museum of Archaeology at Sarnath*, Delhi, India, Indological Book House, 1972.

Salomon, Richard. *Indian Epigraphy: A Guide to the Study of Inscriptions in Sanskrit, Prakrit, and the Other Indo-Aryan Languages*, New York, NY and Oxford, UK, Oxford University Press, 1998.

Sanday, P.R. and R.G. Goodenough. (eds) *Beyond the Second Sex: New Directions in the Anthropology of Gender*, Philadelphia, University of Pennsylvania Press, 1993.

Sarao, K.T.S. *Urban Centers and Urbanisation as Reflected in the Pali Vinaya and Sutta Pitakas*, New Delhi, Vidyanidhi, 1990.

Sastri, K.A.N. *Foreign Notices of South India*, Madras, India, University of Madras, 1939.

Sastri, M.N. *History of Buddhism, Together with the Life and Teachings of Buddha/ Manmatha Nath Shastri*, New Delhi, Aryan, 1996.

Schlingloff, D. *Studies in Ajanta Paintings: Identifications and Interpretations*, New Delhi, Nuova, 1987.

———. *Narrative Wall-Paintings*, Vol. 3, *Wiesbaden*, Harrassowitz, 2000.

Schober, J. *Sacred Biography in the Buddhist Traditions of South and Southeast Asia*, Honolulu, University of Hawaii Press, 1997. Reprint, Motilal Banarsidass, 2002.

Schopen, G. *Bones, Stones, and Buddhist Monks: Collected Papers on the Archaeology, Epigraphy, and Texts of Monastic Buddhism in India*, Honolulu, University of Hawaii Press, 1997.

———. *Buddhist Monks and Business Matters*, Honolulu, University of Hawaii Press, 2004.

Shah, K. *The Problem of Identity: Women in Early Indian Inscription* Delhi, Oxford University Press, 2001.

Shanks, M. and C. Tilley. *Re-Constructing Archaeology: Theory and Practice*, Cambridge, UK, Cambridge University Press, 1987.

Sharma, R.S. *Indian Feudalism*, Calcutta, University of Calcutta, 1965; 2nd ed., New Delhi, Macmillan, 1980.

Sharma, T. *Women in Ancient India*, New Delhi, Ess Ess Publications, 1987.

Sharma, T.R. *Personal and Geographical Names in Gupta Inscriptions*, New Delhi, Concept Publishing Company, 1978.

Shastri, A.M. *An Outline of Early Buddhism*, Varanasi, India, Indological Book House, 1965.

Shaw, Julia. *Buddhist Landscapes in Central India: Sanchi Hill and Archaeologies of Religious and Social Change, C. Third Century BC to Fifth Century AD*, London, British Association for South Asian Studies, The British Academy, 2007.

Shaw, Miranda E. *Buddhist Goddesses of India*, Princeton, Princeton University Press, 2006.

Shwe, Aung Zan (trans.) and C.A.F. Rhys Davids. *Compendium of Philosophy* (*Abhidhammatthasa.ngaha*), P.T.S., 1979.

Sircar, D.C. *Geography of Ancient and Medieval India* (2nd ed.), New Delhi, Motilal Banarsidass, 1971.

———. "*Gotrantara* or Change of a Woman's *Gotra*", *Proceedings (Volume) of Indian History Congress*, Annamalainagar, 1945.

———. *Indian Epigraphy*, Delhi, Motilal Banarsidas, 1966. Sivaramamurti, C. *Amaravati Sculptures in the Madras Government Museum*, Bulletin of the Madras Government Museum, New Series 4, Madras, 1942. Reprint, 1956.

Snellgrove, D. *Indo-Tibetan Buddhism: Indian Buddhists and Their Tibetan Successors*, 2 Vols Boston, Shambhala, 1987.

Stone, Elizabeth Rosen. *The Buddhist Art of Nagarjunakonda*, Delhi, Motilal Banarsidass, 1994.

Suzuki, D.T. *Mulasarvastivada Vinaya Vibhanga*, The Tibetan Tripitaka, Peking Edition, ed. No. 1032, Vol. 42, 43, Tokyo-Kyoto, 1961.

Thakur, U. *Buddhist Cities in Early India*, New Delhi, Sundeep Prakashan, 1995.

Thapar, Romila. *A History of India: Vol. 1*, London, UK, Penguin Books, 1966.

Tharu, S. and K. Lalitha (eds) *Women Writing in India 600 b.c. to the Early 20th Century*, Delhi, Oxford University Press, 1993.

Timm, R.J. *Texts in Context: Traditional Hermeneutics in South Asia*, New York, SUNY Press. Indian print 1997, Delhi: Garib Dass Oriental Series No. 223, 1997.

Trainor, K. *Relics, Ritual, and Representation in Buddhism: Rematerializing the Sri Lankan Theravāda tradition*, Cambridge, Cambridge University Press, 1997.

Varsha, Rani, and Swati Mitra. *Walking with the Buddha; Buddhist Pilgrimages in India*, New Delhi, Eicher Guide, Ministry of Tourism, Government of India, 1999.

Vatsyayana, Kapila. Classical Indian Dance in Literature and the Arts, Sangeet Natak Akademi, New Delhi, 1968.

Virji, K.J. *Ancient History of Saurashtra*, Bombay, India, Konkan Institute of Art and Science, 1952, reprint. Delhi, 1995.

———. *Ancient History of Saurashtra*, Bombay, India, Bombay Archieves, 1955, No. 49.

Wagle, N. *Society at the Time of Buddha*, Bombay, India, Popular Prakashan, 1966. Reprint, 1995.

Walters, Jonathan S. "Stupa, Story and Empire: Constructions of the Buddha Biography in Early Post-Aśokan India", in Juliane Schober (ed.) *Sacred Biography in the Buddhist Traditions of South and Southeast Asia*, Honolulu, University of Hawaii, 2002.

Watters, Thomas, and Vincent Arthur Smith. *Yuan Chwang's Travels in India*, Royal Asiatic Society, 1905.

William, P. *Buddhism: Buddhist Origins and the Early History of Buddhism in South and Southeast Asia*, New York, Routledge, 2005.

Wilson, L. *Charming Cadavers*, Chicago, University of Chicago Press, 1996.

Yazbeck, H.Y. and E.B. Findly. *Women, Religion and Social Change*, Albany, SUNY Press, 1985.

Yazdani, G. and Lawrence Binyon. *Ajanta: With an Explanatory Text, and an Introduction*, London, Oxford University Press, 1930.

Young, S. *Courtesans and Tantric Consorts: Sexualities in Buddhist Narratives*, New York and London, Routledge, 2004.

Zwalf, W. *A Catalogue of the Gandhara Sculpture in the British Museum*, London, British Museum Press, 1996.

Journals and Articles

Agrawal, Ashvini. "The Term *Viharaswamini* in Buddhist Inscriptions of the Kushana and the Gupta Periods", in Ajay Mitra Shastri, Devendra Handa and C.S. Gupta (eds) *Visvambhara, Probings in Orientology* (Prof. V.S. Pathak Festschrift), New Delhi, Harman Publishing House, 1995, pp. 116–19.

Appleton, Naomi. "In the Footsteps of the Buddha? Women and the Bodhisattva Path in TheravādaBuddhism", *Journal of Feminist Studies in Religion*, Vol. 27, No. 1, 2011, pp. 33–51.

Banks, Findly Ellison. "Ther and-Therigatha", Accessed September 3, 2008, www.hundredmountain.com/pages/readingroom_pages/buddhist-women_winter01.html.

Barua, D.K. "Women in Early Buddhist Texts", in Sengupta Sankar (ed.) *Women in Indian Folklore*, Calcutta, India, Indian Publications, 1969, pp. 16–32.

Bhardwaj, Deeksha. "Problematizing the Archaeology of Female Figurines in North West India", in H.P. Ray and Carla M. Sinopoli (eds) *Archaeology As History in Early South Asia*, New Delhi, I.C.H.R., 2004, pp. 481–504.

Bhattacharji, Sukumari. "Prostitution in Ancient India", *Social Scientist*, Vol. 15, No. 2, pp. 32–61.

Bhattacharya, Parnasabari. "Buddhist and Jain Influences on Manu and His Interpretation of the Veda", *The Proceedings of the Indian History Congress*, 53rd Session, 1992, pp. 106–9.

Blackstone, Kate. "Damming the Dhamma: Problems with Bhikkhunis in the Pali Vinaya", *Journal of Victoria University of Wellington*, Vol. 4, 1997, accessed 25.10.2008. Brod, Harry. "The Case for Men's Studies", in Harry Brod (ed.) *The Making of Masculinities: The New Men's Studies*, Boston, Allen & Unwin, 1987, pp. 188–202.

Buhler, G. "Votative Inscriptions from the Stupas at Sanchi", *Epigraphia Indica*, II, 1894, pp. 87–115, 386–407.

Bynum, Caroline Walker. "Gender and Religion: On the Complexity of Symbols", in Harell Stevan Bynum and Paula Richman (eds) *Gender and Religion*, Boston, Beacon, Vol. 28, No. 1, 1987, pp. 1–20.

Chakravarti, Uma. "Beyond the Altekarian Paradigm, Towards a New Understanding of Gender Relations in Early India", *Social Scientist*, Vol. 16, No. 8, 1988, pp. 44–52.

———. "Conceptualising Brahamanical Patriarchy in Early India: Gender, Caste, Class and State", *Economic and Political Weekly*, April 3, 1993, pp. 579–85.

Collett, Alice, "Buddhism and Gender: Reframing and Refocusing the Debate", *Journal of Feminist Studies in Religion*, Vol. 22, No. 2, 2006, pp. 55–84.

Coningham, Robin, "Monks, Caves and Kings: A Reassessment of the Nature of Early Buddhism in Sri Lanka", *World Archaeology*, Vol. 27, 1995, pp. 222–42.

———. Coningham, R.A.E. and B. Edwards. "Space and Society at Sirkap", *Ancient Pakistan*, Vol. 12, 1998, pp. 47–76.

Conkey, Margaret W. and Janet Spector. "Archaeology and the Study of Gender", in Michael B. Schiffer (ed.) *Archaeological Method and Theory*, New York, Academic Press, 1984, Vol. 7, pp. 1–38.

Connor, June O'. "The Epistemological Significance of Feminist Research in Religion", in Ursula King (ed.) *Religion and Gender*, Oxford, Blackwell Publishing, 1995, pp. 45–64.

Crosby, Kate. "Gendered Symbols in Theravada Buddhism: Missed Positives in the Representation of the Female", *Hsuan Chuang Journal of Buddhist Studies*, Vol. 9, 2008, pp. 31–47.

Dehejia, V. "Aniconism and the Multivalence of Emblems", *Ars Orientalis*, Vol. 21, 1991, pp. 45–66.

———. "Collective and Popular Basis of Early Buddhist Patronage: Sacred Monument, 100 B.C.–A.D. 250", in B. Stoler Miller (ed.) *The Powers of Art*, Delhi, Oxford University Press, 1992, pp. 35–45.

———. "Issues of Spectatorship and Representation", in *Representing the Body: Gender Issues in Indian Art*, New Delhi, Kali for Women, 1999, pp. 1–21.

Derris, Karen. "When the Buddha Was a Woman: Reimagining Tradition in the Theravada", *Journal of Feminist Studies in Religion*, September 22, 2008, pp. 29–44.

Dharmasēna (Thera) and Ranjini Obeyesekere. *Portraits of Buddhist Women: Stories from the Saddharmaratnavaliya*, Albany, SUNY Press, 2001.

Falk, Nancy. "An Image of Woman in Old Buddhist Literature: The Daughters of Mara", in Judith Plaskow (ed.) *Women and Religion: Papers of the Working Group on Women and Religion*, Chambersburg, PA, American Academy of Religion, Scholars Press, 1974, pp. 105–12.

———. "The Case of the Vanishing Nuns: The Fruits of Ambivalence in Ancient Buddhism", in Nancy Falk and Rita Gross (eds) *Unspoken Worlds: Women's Religious Lives in Non-Western Cultures*, San Francisco, Harper & Row, 1979, pp. 191–206.

Fogelin, Lars. *Archaeology of Early Buddhism*, University of Virginia, AltaMira Press, 2006, pp. 376–91.

———."Ritual Presentation in Early Buddhist Religious Architecture", *Asian Perspectives: The Journal of Archaeology for Asia and the Pacific*, Vol. 42, 2003, pp. 129–54.

———. "Sacred Architecture, Sacred Landscape: Early Buddhism in North Coastal Andhra Pradesh", in H.P. Ray and Carla M. Sinopoli (eds) *Archaeology as History in Early South Asia*, New Delhi, I.C.H.R. & Aryan Books International, 2004, pp. 376–91.

Ghosh, A. and H. Sarkar. "Beginnings of Sculptural Art in South East India: A Stele from Amaravati", *Ancient India*, Vol. 20–21, 1964, pp. 168–77.

Gibbs, Liv. "Identifying Gender Representation in the Archaeological Record; A Contextual Study", in Ian Hodder (ed.) *The Archaeology of Contextual Meanings – New Directions in Archaeology*, Cambridge, UK, Cambridge University Press, 1987, pp. 79–89.

Gilchrist, R. "Women's Archaeology? Political Feminism, Gender Theory and Historical Revision", *Antiquity*, Vol. 65, No. 248, 1991, pp. 495–501.

Gregory, S. "What's in a Name: The Religious Function of the Early Donative Inscriptions", in *Buddhist Monks and Business Matters*, Honolulu, University of Hawaii Press, 2004, pp. 382–94.

Gurholt, A. "The Androgyny of Enlightenment: Questioning Women's Status in Ancient Indian Religions", *Westminster McNair Journal*, 2004–5, accessed July 5, 2009, www.westminstercollege.edu/mcnair/ind.

Hess, Beth B. "Beyond Dichotomy: Drawing Distinctions and Embracing Differences", *Sociological Forum*, Vol. 5, No. 1, March 1990, pp. 75–93.

Hietzman, J. "Early Buddhism, Trade and Empire", in K.A.R. Kennedy and G.L. Possehl (eds) *Studies in the Archaeology and the Paleoanthropology of South Asia*, New Delhi, Oxford University Press, 1984, pp. 35–61.

Hoek, B.V.D. "Gender and Cast in the Perfect Buddhist Gift: The Samyak Mahadana in Kathmandu, Nepal", in Harald Tambs-Lychre (ed.) *The Feminine Sacred in South Asia*, Manohar Publishers, 2003, pp. 46–62.

Huntington, Susan L. "Early Buddhist Art and the Theory of Aniconism", *Art Journal*, Vol. 49 No. 4, Winter 1990, pp. 401–8.

Jones, L. *Encyclopedia of Religion*, New York, Macmillan Reference, Vol. 7, 2005, p. 4328.

Kabilsingh, C. "Women in Buddhism", *Buddhist Studies*, Buddha Dharma Education Association and Buddhanet, accessed January 16, 2009, www.buddhanet.net/e-learning/history/wbq21.htm.

Kaushik, Garima. *Symphony in Stone: Festivities in Early Buddhism*, Jaipur, 2007.

Klassen, C. "Confronting the Gap: Why Religion Needs to be Given More Attention in Women's Studies", *Thirdspace, Journal of Feminist Theory and Culture*, Vol. 3, No. 1, November 2003, pp. 103–22, accessed April 3, 2010, http://www.thirdspace.ca/journal/article/view/klassen/165Lahiri, Nayanjot. "Cradles of Bygone Cultures", *RIVERS:* Special Issue with the *Sunday Magazine*, from the Publishers of *The Hindu* (July 1, 2001), accessed June 9, 2009, www.hinduonnet.com/folio/fo0107/01070.

Law, B.C. "Bhikshunis in Inscriptions", in *Epigraphia Indica*, Vol. XXV, No. 5, 1939–40. Reprint, 1985, pp. 31–4.

———. *Historical Geography of Ancient India*, Delhi, Ess Ess Publications, 1954.

Magee, P.M. "Disputing the Sacred: Some Theoretical Approaches to Gender and Religion", in Ursula King (ed.) *Religion and Gender*, Oxford, UK, Blackwell, 1995, pp. 101–20.

Malmgreen Gail. *Religion in the Lives of English Women, 1760-1930*, Bloomington and Indianapolis, Indiana University Press, 1986.

Mani, B.R. "A Donative Inscription from Kanheri", in C. Margabandhu, K.S. Ramachandran, A. P. Sagar and D.K. Sinha (eds) *Indian Archaeological Heritage: Shri K.V. Soundara Rajan Festschrif*, New Delhi, Agam Kala Prakashan, 1991, pp. 321–2.

———. "The Enigmatic Monastery of Kumāradevī at Sarnath: New Identification", *Pragdhara*, Vol. 16, 2006, pp. 321–2.

Margabandhu, C., K.S. Ramachandran, A. P. Sagar and D.K. Sinha. (eds) *Indian Archaeological Heritage: Shri K.V. Soundara Rajan Festschrif*, New Delhi, Agam Kala Prakashan, 1991.

Mill, J.S. *Collected Works of John Stuart Mill 21*, Toronto, ON, 1981.

Mukund, K. "Women's Property Rights in South India: A Review", *Economic and Political Weekly*, Vol. 34, No. 22, 1999, pp. 1352–8.

Müller, F. Max. (trans.) Dhammapada Verse 53, Visakha Vatthu, in *Buddhist Parables*, by E.W. Burlinghame, 1869. Reprint, *Sacred Books of the East*, Vol. X, Oxford, UK, Clarendon Press, 1881.

Nakai, Rev. P., *Women in Buddhism*, Part. 1: Prajapati, the First Buddhist Nun, accessed August 6, 2006, www.faithnet.org.uk/k54/social%20.

Neelis, Jason Emmanuel. "Historical and Geographical Contexts for Avadānas in Kharoṣṭhī Manuscripts", in Richard F. Gombrich (ed.) *Buddhist Studies*, New Delhi, Motilal Banarsidas, 2008, pp. 151–72.

Rajapakse, V. *The Therigatha, a Revaluation*, Kandy, Sri Lank, Buddhist Publication Society, 2000, BPS Online Edition © (2007), accessed September 14, 2009, www.bps.lk/olib/wh/wh436.pdf.

Ray, H.P. "The Axial Age in Asia: Archaeology of Buddhism (500 B.C.–A.D. 500)", in Miriam T. Stark (ed.) *The Archaeology of Asia*, Oxford, Blackwell, 2006, pp. 303–23.

———. "The Shrine in Early Hinduism: The Changing Sacred Landscape", *Journal of Hindu Studies*, Vol. 2, No. 1, 2009, pp. 76–96.

Richman, P. "Gender and Persuasion: The Portrayal of Beauty, Anguish, and Nurturance in an Account of a Tamil Nun", in Jose Ignacio Cabezon (ed.) *Buddhism, Sexuality and Gender*, New Delhi, Sri Satguru Publications, 1992, pp. 111–36.

Roy, K. "Women and Men Donors at Sanchi: A Study of the Inscriptional Evidence", in L.K. Tripathi Varanasi (ed.) Position and Status of Women in Ancient India, Seminar Papers, Department of Ancient Indian History, Culture and Archaeology, Banaras Hindu University (Vol. I), 1988, pp. 209–21.

———. "Women, Men and Beasts: The Jatakas as Popular Tradition", *Studies in History*, Vol. 9, No. 1, 1993, pp. 43–69.

Rubertone, Patricia E. "Review of Gender and Archaeology of Death", in Bettina Arnold and Nancy L. Wicker (eds) Walnut Creek, CA, AltaMira Press, 2001, in *American Antiquity*, Vol. 69, No. 1, 2004, pp. 164–5.

Sarkar, H. "The Nagarjunakonda Phase of the Lower Krishna Valley Art: A Study Based on Epigraphic Data", in Frederick M. Asher and G.S. Ghai (eds) *Indian Epigraphy: Its bearing on the History of Indian Art*, New Delhi, Oxford and IBH Publishing House, 1985, pp. 29–34.

Sarma, I.K. "Thematic Labels on Amaravati and Nagarjunakonda Sculptures-a Study", in Ajay Mitra Sastri, Devendra Handa and C.S. Gupta (eds) *Visvambhara, Probings in Orientology*, Vol. 1 (Prof. V.S. Pathak Festschrift), New Delhi, Harman Publishing House, 1995, pp. 112–15.

Sengupta, G. "Donors of Images in Ancient India", *The Proceedings of the Indian History Congress*, 43rd Session, 1982, pp. 158–61.

Sengupta, S. "Buddhism in the Classical Age", in G. Prasad (ed.) *Studies of Buddhism*, New Delhi, Bharatiya Kala Prakashan, 2006, pp. 12–21.

Shah, S. "In the Business of Kama: Prostitution in Classical Sanskrit Literature from the 7th to the 13th Centuries", *Medieval History Journal*, Vol. 5, No. 1, 2002, pp. 141–6.

Shaw, J. "Sanchi and Its Archaeological Landscape: Buddhist Monasteries, Settlements and Irrigation Works in Central India", *Antiquity*, Vol. 74, December 2000, pp. 775–6.

———. "The Archaeological Setting of Buddhist Monasteries in Central India: A Summary of a *Multi*-phase Survey in the Sanchi Area, 1998-2000". In Jarrige C., Lefevre, V. (eds) *South Asian Archaeology 2001: Proceedings of the 16th International Conference of the European Association of South Asian Archaeologists, 2005*, pp. 665–76.

Silva, Lily de. "Nibbaana as Living Experience", *The Sri Lanka Journal of Buddhist Studies*, Vol. I, 1987, accessed July 2009, www.bps.lk/olib/wh/wh407.pdf.

———. "Nibbana as Living Experience/The Buddha and The Arahant: Two Studies from the Pali Canon", *Access to Insight (Legacy Edition)*, 30 November 2013, http://www.accesstoinsight.org/lib/authors/desilva/wheel407.html.

Singh, H. "Women's Patronage to Temple Architecture", in Kumkum Roy (ed.) *Women in Early Indian Societies*, in B.D.Chattopaddhaya (ed.) *Readings in Early Indian History*, Delhi, Mahohar, 1999, pp. 235–86.

Singh, U. "Sanchi: The History of the Patronage of an Ancient Buddhist Establishment", *Indian Economic Social History Review*, Vol. 33, No. 1, March 1996, pp. 1–35.

Sitaramamma, K. "Feminine: Creative and Sacred in Buddhism", in S.P. Gupta and K.S. Ramchandran (eds) *Facets of Indian History, Culture and Archaeology*, New Delhi, IHCS and IAS, 1991, pp. 74–7.

Skilling, P. "Nuns, Laywomen, Donors and Goddesses: Female Roles in Early Indian Buddhism", *Journal of International Association of Buddhist Studies*, Vol. 24, No. 2, 2001, pp. 241–74.

Slocum, S. "Woman the Gatherer: Male Bias in Anthropology", in Ryana Reiter (ed.) *Toward an Anthropology of Women*, New York, Monthly Review Press, 1975, pp. 36–50.

Sponberg, A. "Attitude towards Women and the Feminine in Early Buddhism", in Jose I. Cabezon (ed.) *Buddhism, Sexuality and Gender*, Albany, SUNY Press, 1992, pp. 3–36.

Taehakkyo, I.Y. "Anguttara Nikaya, the Doctrine of Incapability, Pali Nikayas" (trans.) *Asian Journal of Women's Studies*, Vol. 8, No. 2–4, 2002.

Thosar, H.S. "Epigraphical Glimpses of India's Foreign Trade", *JESI*, 1977, Vol. XV, pp. 97–107.

———. "Role of Women in the Commercial Activities in Ancient India", in S.P. Gupta and K.S. Ramachandran (ed.) *Facets of Indian History and Culture*, 1991, pp. 75–8.

Tyagi, A.K. "Courtesans in the Age of the Buddha", *The Proceedings of the Indian History Congress*, Vol. 1, 47th Session, 1986, pp. 220–32.

Vanita, Ruth. "The Self Is Not Gendered: Sulabha's Debate with King Janaka", *N.W.S.A. Journal*, Vol. 15, No. 2, Summer 2003, pp. 76–93.

Wright, R. "Women's Labor and Pottery Production in Prehistory", in Joan M. Gero and Margaret W. Conkey (eds) *Engendering Archaeology: Women and Prehistory*, Oxford, UK, Basil Blackwell, 1991, pp. 194–223.

Wynne, A. "The Oral Transmission of Early Buddhist Literature", *Journal of the International Association of Buddhist Studies*, Vol. 27, No. 1, 2004, pp. 97–127.

Zagarell, A. "Gender and Social Organisation in the Nilgiris", in Kathleen D. Morrison and Laura L. Junker (eds) *Forager Traders in South and South East Asia*, Cambridge, UK, Cambridge University Press, 2002, pp. 77–104.

Zelliot, Eleanor. *From Untouchable to Dalit*, New Delhi, Manohar Publication, 1992.

Index

Abhayantrika Vihāra 56
Abhinishkramana 196
Abhirupā Nandā 113, 114
Achārya 54–6
Acharya Bhadanta Stiramati 56
Addhakāsī 119, 128, 194
Āgamas 142
Agra-Srāwaka 194
Ajantā 152, 196–9, 202, 218
Ajita 55, 56
Amawaturā 195
Amēdya 193
Amohāsi 177
Āmra-Āmradārikā 21
Āmrapāli 21, 194
Amritprabhā 33
Ānanda 1, 36, 40, 98, 111, 123, 131, 141, 211, 215–16, 230
Angulimāla 123, 207
Anguttara Nikāya 90, 94, 98, 101–2, 138, 144, 161, 165, 277
Annā 128
antevasini sardhaviharini 46
antevāsinis 46
Antichak 31, 32, 240, 244
Anuradhapura 23
Apsidal 20, 22, 24, 25, 34, 35, 70
Ārāma 51–2
Arāmika 52
arāmika-pesaka 52
Araṇya 48, 215
Arya-Saraswati Aparajita 79
asāmika (*asvāmika*) 54
Avalokitēsvara 61
Āvāsa 51, 52, 88
Āyakas 15, 22, 31–4, 38, 227
āyaka-stambhas 32
āyaka-type *stūpas* 22
ayyasama 161

Bairāt 22, 23, 35, 74, 243, 244, 264
Bakraur 30, 34, 58, 239, 244
Bala 26
Balanandi 26
Banavāsi 152, 174, 177, 180, 223
Bangle 42
Bappadiya Vihāra 56
Basali 73
bathing platforms 63
bathroom 76
Bēdsa 22, 35, 157, 169, 171, 188, 211, 245
Bhaddā 39, 101, 106, 120, 129, 144, 219
Bhaddā Kaccana 39
Bhaddā Kapilani 39
Bhaginī 112, 164
Bhaginīsama 161
Bhaja 22, 35, 245
Bha-ra ha Monastery 45
Bhattiprolu 32, 152, 177, 236, 238–9, 245, 259
Bhavadeva 55
Bhavapraśiṣya 26
bhikhuni upasaya 162, 173
Bhikṣūṇī khandaka 47
Bhokardan 188, 261
Bijak-kī-Pahādi 22, 35, 74
Bindūmati 119
Bodh Gayā 58, 152, 154, 158, 183, 201, 211, 257
Brahmagiri 22
Brahmanism 17, 39
Brahmi 77, 150, 188, 210–12, 214, 263
Buddha Bhattaraka 55
Buddhadasa Vihāra 56
Buddharakhitā 159, 177

Candā 118
Chamtamula 28
Chamtisri 28
Chaneti 32, 33, 240, 244, 258
Chapala Chaitya 13

Chārudatta 189
Chatiya-grihas 22
Chatusāla 62, 65, 67
Chau-ju-kua 56
Chetiyagiri 91
Chhaya khamba 25, 76
Chopon 86
Chorasama 161
chotrimpa or *geko* 86
choyok 86
circular structures/ circular shrines 22, 24–6, 34,35, 91, 227
courtesan 33, 40, 95, 107, 113, 119–20, 129, 143, 193, 194, 207, 208, 224
cruciform 22, 27, 31, 37, 38, 74
Cūllavagga 1, 16, 40, 60, 91, 96, 115, 116, 123, 124, 145, 212, 265

Dagobā 193
Dākinis 20
Damana Vihāra 26
Damatrata 26
Dāna 53, 54, 82, 108, 119, 122, 125, 134, 152, 162, 184, 204, 223, 269
Dāsisama 161
Devadasis 56
Devapala 30
Devaparvata 55
Dhamadinā 159, 178
Dhamek 70, 72
Dhammā 45, 115, 118, 124, 184, 191, 199, 208, 225, 273
Dhammadinnā 39
Dhamnār 22
Dhananjani 121
Dharamshala 44
Dharmachakrajina Vihāra 70, 71
Dharmaśāstrā 16, 208, 211, 261
Dharmottariyas 162, 173
Dhātugarbha 29
Dhruvasena 55
Dhyani Buddhas 61, 79
Diddā 17, 33
Divirapati Skandabhata 56
Dukkhā 100, 128, 143

Faxian 5, 58, 62, 90

Gahadawala 56, 70
Gahapatis 149, 212
Gandhara 74, 81, 150, 194–6, 198, 201, 218, 256, 272
Gāthās 99, 100, 140, 141
Gautama 21, 30, 44, 117, 134, 196, 197, 217
Ghantaśāla 152, 174, 177, 180, 223, 245
Ghosita 58
Gohaka 55
Gorakshita 168, 171
Govindachandra 56, 70
Gummadiduru 153
Gunamātā' 56
Guntapalli 22
Gurudhammah 47
Gyaraspur 32, 239, 244

Haritī 21, 64
Harwan 14, 22, 35

Idā 112, 160, 188, 212
Ikshavāku 34, 82, 152
Indradevi 33
Isidāsi 103, 104, 120, 128, 161
Itamundia 80, 243
I-Tsing 44, 45, 68
itthī ratnam 157, 213, 216
Ittivuttaka 16, 98, 129, 131, 141, 226, 227, 230

Jagayapetta 153
Jains 17
Jambhala 72, 79
Jātakas 9, 16, 29, 34, 38, 94–6, 98, 99, 109, 117, 119, 120, 131, 140, 143, 161, 186, 201–3, 217, 231, 260, 276
Jayasrama vihāra 55
Jetavana 13, 17, 46, 68, 69, 192, 249
Jēwārgi 26
Jewellery 42
Jhāna 127, 145, 146
Jivaka 186

Junnar 22, 23, 35, 152, 162, 173, 177, 180, 223, 236–8, 245

Kadphises II 65
Kagyupa 83, 85
Kāli 119, 173
Kalpi 49
kalpiya-karika 46
Kamma 45, 47, 126
Kanhēri 22, 35, 152, 154, 174, 175, 177, 180, 210, 223, 236, 238, 241, 244, 275
Kanishka 25, 65
Kannauj 56, 70
Kanum 49
Kapilavastu 44, 48, 61, 72, 90, 114, 115, 196, 197, 218, 243, 245
kappiya-kārika 46
Kāppiya-kuti 52
Karādh 22
Kārlē 144, 152, 203
Karpurasri 56, 79, 82, 229, 243
Kāśi 70, 119, 241
Kasia/Kushinagara 64, 78
Kausambi 44, 67, 217, 231, 244, 264
Khadana 33
Khēmā 39, 106, 116, 195, 205, 217, 219, 231
Khenpo 86
Khuddaka Nikāya 94, 98, 140, 141, 217, 218, 231, 259, 265
Kinnaur 61, 79, 243
Kisā Gotami 40, 128, 206
Kondivte 35
Kosam 58, 242
Kūdā 22, 152, 154, 174, 175, 177, 188, 211
Kularika 175
Kumāradevī 56, 70, 71, 82, 243, 263, 275
Kundalakēsi 39, 106
Kuramgi 158
Kurara 175, 179, 182, 184, 222, 233, 236, 241

*Lalitavistāra Sutra*29, 259
Lalitgiri 33, 62, 240, 244
Lauriya Nandangarh 24, 31–4, 239, 244
Lokesvar 79
Lotus Sutra/Saddharmapundārikā Sutrai 16, 94, 104, 142
Lumbini 21, 64, 90, 183

Madanapāla 57
Mādhavapura Mahāvihāra 61
Madhuvana 184, 234, 237, 241
Madnāvati 33
Mahād 22, 158, 211, 213, 274
Mahādevī 158, 211, 213
Mahakassapa 142
Mahāparinirvāṇa 16, 21, 64, 171, 183, 216
Māhāprajāpati 21, 231
Mahasaṁghika Bhikṣūṇī Vinaya 48, 50, 261
Mahasamghika Vinaya 43
Mahāśrībhadrā 57
Mahāsudassana Sutra 16, 216
Mainamati 31, 33, 55, 240, 244
Maitrakas 55
Maitreya 79
Mallika 57, 87, 90, 103, 121
Mallikādevī' 57
Mallikarama 57, 87
Mamdāra 164, 234, 238
Manatta 47
Mandagara 188
Maṇḍala 55, 56, 70, 71, 90
maṇḍapa 32, 33, 41, 74, 76, 197, 198, 247
Mānikchandra 33
Manimekalāi 94, 106, 107, 108, 113, 137, 143, 224
Manjuśa 178
Manjusri 36, 61, 79, 143
Mara 101, 103, 230, 274
Marīchi 36
Mathurā 54, 56, 150, 152–4, 173, 176–7, 188, 202, 214, 236, 238, 244
*Mātughara*163
Mātusama 161
Māyā Devi 21, 38, 64, 196

Meghavana 41
memorial pillar 26
Migāramāta 165, 191, 205, 217, 224, 231
Mimma 56
Mithuna 34, 38, 203
Moggalana 142
Mohen-jo-Daro 60
Motherhood 2, 27, 115, 162, 182, 183, 204, 221, 222, 224
Mrichchakatika 189
Mrigdāva 70, 90
Mūlagandhkuti 70
Mūlasaravastivādin 16
Muluposattha Sutta 102

Nadner 61, 241
Nāgadatta 25, 26
Nāgamitā 112, 160, 212
Nagarjuna 91, 218
Nāgarjunakonda 14, 22, 25, 27, 28, 31–5, 41, 60, 61, 75, 76, 81, 87, 91, 152, 153, 156–9,175, 177, 180, 181, 183, 189, 190, 195, 198, 203, 218, 223, 236–7, 243, 245, 247, 258, 269, 271, 276
Nalanda 61, 62, 82, 203, 243, 244, 252, 260, 262
Nana-samvasaka 51
Nandā 39, 113–5, 119
Nandanavana 85
Nandinagara 182, 184, 185, 234, 237, 241, 242
Nanduttarā 126
Nasik 152, 154, 157, 158, 166, 174, 175, 177, 188, 210–11, 233, 236–8
Navagāma 185, 233, 236
Navakāmikā 159, 172, 215
Nāyaka 54
Nibbānna 101
Niranjana 30
Samgha (nun) 109
Nyaggrodha 48
Nyerpa 86
Nyingmapa 83–4, 87, 92

Odayamtrika 175
Onpo 85

Pacattika 49, 50
Paharpur 14, 31–3, 35, 240, 244
Pajāvati 261
Panagoria 32, 239, 245
Pandrethan 31, 240, 244
Paraspora 31, 33, 240, 244
Pariveṇā 52, 89
Pasenādi 103, 219
Patacāra 39, 120, 129
Pāṭalīputra 193
Patriarchy 5, 96, 103, 165, 267, 273
Piparhawa 27
Pitalkhorā 152, 177, 180, 223
Prajanapāramita Sutras 16
Pratihara 38
Pratimokśa 46
Punnā 128, 129, 226
Puranabhatta 56
Purvārāma 69, 87, 191, 243
Puśkkalāvati 21

Rajagaha 44, 101, 113, 116, 119, 140, 141, 186, 195
Rajgir 35, 62, 159, 168, 171, 178, 183, 234, 238, 242, 244
Ranaka Sri Vinitatunga 55
Ranjuvula 56
Ratnagiri 35, 60, 61, 62, 78, 79, 243, 244, 251, 263, 268
Reliquary 27, 29, 31
Rishipattana 70, 90
Rsidāsi 163
Rudrapurushadatta 25
Rupādēi/Rupādēvi/Rummindēi/ Rummindēvi 21

Sahēth 24, 68, 127, 249, 263
Sakhīsama 161
Śakra 21, 210
Sakula 39
Sākya 21, 28, 33, 37, 48, 56, 57, 69, 83, 90, 112, 115, 206, 259
Salāvati 119
Salihundam 22, 34, 35, 245

Sāmā 120
Samagga 45
Samana-samvasaka 45, 51
Samatata 44
Samāvati 121, 141
Saṁghadisesa 47, 225
Saṁghamahāttari 46
Saṁgharāma 48, 52
Saṁgha-thavirina 46
Saṁghatisesa 49, 215
Samhasthavira 46
sāmika (*svāmika*) 54
Sāmmā 33
*Sangha*rakhitā 159
Sanghatisesa 89
Sanghol 24, 78, 79, 80, 200, 201, 205, 243, 244, 253, 257, 262
Saniyāsa 114
Sannathi 26–7, 61, 77–8, 239, 240, 243, 245, 250, 262
Sapatna 161
Śāriputra 62, 101, 104, 105, 142
Sarthavāhinī 188
Sāvatthi 46, 90, 101, 115, 191, 195
Serkhyim gonpas 85
Shah-ji-ki-Deri 31, 33, 240, 244
Shaivas 17
Sheng-chi 44
Shiksamana 46
Siddhās 20
Sigalamātā 40
Siitibhūta 127, 129
Silās 53, 117, 207
Silawādi 22
Simā 45, 48, 49–53, 65, 87–9
Simhala Sutra 16
Sirimā 119, 129, 146, 208, 262
Sirpur 42, 60, 261, 264
Sivakaradeva 55, 56, 82, 152
Soma 64, 103, 113, 203, 205
Somapura 31, 240
Somavanshi 56
Sonā 39
Sramanerikās 46
Sreni 175
Srimala Sutra 139
Śriparvata 75, 91
Sthiramatī 55, 56
Strīdhana 186–7
Śubhā 99, 100, 117
Suddhodana 72
Sui Vihāra 25–7, 35, 54, 244
Sujāta 30, 34, 58, 59, 149, 198–200, 209, 230, 232, 257
Sujata Quilā 30
Sukiti 28
Sulasa 119, 208
Sumana 115
Sumedha 128, 133, 135
Sutta Pitaka 44, 98, 142, 261, 265
svake-vihare 173

Tara 36, 56, 61, 79
Taxila 22, 81
Thānenagara 188
Therigāthā 2, 3, 9, 16, 43,44, 94, 98–106, 109, 111, 113–15, 118, 119, 121, 126, 128–9, 138, 140–1, 143–6,161, 162, 169, 172, 193, 194, 206, 208, 212, 215, 217, 218, 220, 226, 263–5, 272, 275
Tilapishaka 175
Tosala 55
trayo nisrayah 89

ubhatosaṁgha 47
Udāna121
Udayagiri 33, 61, 62, 243, 244
Ujjeni 34, 185, 194, 236, 242
Umtse Umtse 86
Upadhyāyini 49
Upalavanna 39
Upasampada 47, 49, 125
Upasanta 129
upatthana-śāla 52
uposatha 47, 48, 52, 53, 66, 78, 89, 102, 144, 212, 261, 264
Uppalāvanna 115, 195, 205
Ushkura 31, 240, 244

Vaishali 13, 17, 33, 44, 194, 244, 262
Vaishnavas 17
Vajrasattva 36

Vajrayana 62, 138, 152
Vallabhi 43, 55, 82
Vammabhata 25
Varṇa 168, 171
Vasantsēna 189
vassa-vāsa 50–2, 136, 160
Vasudhara 70, 72, 79
Vidisagiri 91
Vidudabha 28, 29
Vihārasvamin 54, 55
Vihāraswāminī 26, 172, 272
Vihārikāi 15, 16, 56, 61, 152, 159
Vijayaśrībhadrā 57
Vikramshila Mahavihara 31
Vimalā 119, 127, 194, 226
Vimalagupta 55
Vimalakirti Sutra 104, 142
Vimāna 129, 141, 142, 261
Vimānavatthu 16, 94, 129, 132, 133, 141, 227, 262
Virudhaka 69
Viśākhā 2, 33, 69,102, 149,165, 187, 191, 192, 194, 195, 204, 205, 209, 216, 217, 223, 224, 230, 231, 255, 275

Wadhaka 161

Xuanzang 22

Yaksasri 55
Yakṣhasura 56
Yamari 79
Yashodhara 117, 161, 195, 196, 218
Yasthi 26
Yodhavaka 56
Yukādevi 85